Penguin Education

Thought and Personality

Edited by Peter B. Warr

Penguin Modern Psychology Readings

General Editor

B. M. Foss

Thought and Personality

Selected Readings

Edited by Peter B. Warr

Penguin Books

Penguin Books Ltd, Harmondsworth,
Middlesex, England
Penguin Books Inc., 7110 Ambassador Road,
Baltimore, Md 21207, U.S.A.
Penguin Books Australia Ltd,
Ringwood, Victoria, Australia

First published 1970
This selection copyright © Peter B. Warr, 1970
Introduction and notes copyright © Peter B. Warr, 1970

Made and printed in Great Britain by
Richard Clay (The Chaucer Press) Ltd,
Bungay, Suffolk
Set in Monotype Times New Roman

Contents

FEB 26 1973

Introduction

This is a book about individual differences. We are concerned with differences in the way people think which can be related to their more general personality differences. Such a topic is a large one, and we shall need to leave aside some parts of it. These parts will have to be specified, but before identifying the work we shall focus upon, a brief look at its historical antecedents may be helpful.

Psychologists in the nineteenth century had little doubt that their task was to study what went on in people's minds. They were interested in thoughts and images, sensations and perceptions, instincts and mental energies as well as other 'internal' phenomena. But the advance of positivist philosophy and behaviourist methodology in the twentieth century led to a marked shift in emphasis – away from 'the mind' over to 'behaviour'. For nearly half a century psychologists' confrontation with human and animal behaviour was largely a struggle for experimental rigour and statistical refinement.

Now, however, the behaviourist ice-cap is receding, and psychologists are turning more and more to examine what it had enveloped. In a sense they have rediscovered 'the mind' and are as intent on understanding it as were the psychologists of earlier days. The enormous difference lies in the vastly improved tools now at their disposal. With its analyses of variance, latin-square designs, reliability coefficients, scaling techniques and laboratory procedures, contemporary 'introspectionism' (for that is what it is) is a much more sophisticated affair than those studies of mental processes with which the last century closed.

Psychology's new tools are increasingly being employed to examine cognitive activities, and the last twenty years have seen a variety of new approaches to thinking and judging. We are now quite accustomed to enquiring about dissonance between cognitive elements (e.g. Festinger, 1957, 1964) or about their congruity (Osgood and Tannenbaum, 1955) and balance (Cartwright and Harary, 1956; Heider, 1946). Components of thought

9

and attitude are now frequently studied (e.g. Feldman, 1966; Insko, 1967) and, more importantly, the professional propriety of such studies is at last beyond question.

This book illustrates one facet of the new concern with mental events. The reader should expect papers of an empirical, rigorous kind addressed to questions about thought, belief and judgement. It is helpful to reconstrue these activities in terms of information processing – taking 'information' in a broad, non-technical sense. Studies of thought and judgement are in effect studies of how people process information about their environment. Work in this field might deal with efforts towards consistency (as we have just seen), or it might embrace communications-theory definitions (e.g. Attneave, 1959; Garner, 1962), the role of language in our commerce with the environment (e.g. Osgood and Sebeok, 1965; Neisser, 1967), the nature of reasoning strategies and tendencies (e.g. Wason and Johnson-Laird, 1968), aspects of mental imagery (e.g. Holt, 1964) or even studies of particular aspects of the environment such as other people, social situations and logical problems.

This book deals with one particular question about information processing. It concentrates upon *differences between people* in their ways of handling the information at their disposal. We shall examine some major characteristics of thinking which form part of larger systems of personality. An important distinction at this point must be drawn between the *content* of a thought, belief or attitude and its non-content characteristics. Much work on personality, thought and attitude has dealt with *what* a person thinks or wants (that is, with content variables), but it is also possible to enquire about *the way* in which he thinks or wants (that is, about variables of style). A convenient example of this difference is provided by work on the authoritarian personality (Adorno *et al.*, 1950) and dogmatism (see Reading 2). Authoritarianism is measured in terms of *what* a person thinks and wants, whereas dogmatism is more a question of *how* he thinks and wants.

It is clear that the interdependence in personality of content and style (or of 'what' and 'how') is a close one. But the conceptual distinction may be used to delimit the kind of papers selected for this book of readings. We shall examine work on personality-related differences in thinking only in so far as this work stresses individual variations in style of thought at the expense of content differences. Our focus will thus be on recent research into what have come to be called 'cognitive styles' – habitual ways or modes of dealing with information about oneself and one's environment which are to a large degree independent of the content of the information being handled.

The styles which we shall discuss are assumed to be trans-situational, in that they are operative in a variety of tasks and domains. The limits of this generality have in practice often yet to be identified, but the trans-situational assumption is an important one for us to be able to distinguish a cognitive style from a *response* style. The latter is usually viewed as a characteristic way of responding to a particular kind of situation, for example a specific test-taking situation, and is in a sense a very particularized cognitive style. These particularized styles (e.g. McGee, 1962; Rorer, 1965; Warr and Coffman, 1970) will not be covered in the present book.

It has also been necessary to omit other stylistic consistencies. It is apparent for instance that some styles of *behaviour* are relatively trans-situational. Amongst these are risk-taking style (e.g. Kogan and Wallach, 1964), tendency to conform (e.g. Janis *et al.*, 1959), accident proneness (e.g. Mintz and Blum, 1949), and so on. These are clearly related to the more cognitive styles but for the present may be left aside. Another associated concept is that of cognitive *ability*. (We should here include intelligence, reasoning ability, creativity, and so on.) The line of distinction is again a fluctuating and a dubious one, but in a general way we can say that a measure of cognitive ability is an index of how *well* a person *can* think, whereas a measure of cognitive style is an indication of how he habitually *does* think. It is the latter with which we shall here be primarily concerned.

One other fundamental concept has still to be introduced. This is the notion of 'cognitive structure'. The notions of style and structure are closely intertwined and in one sense a 'structure' may be regarded as a hypothetical construct to account for the stylistic consistencies in thinking which we have been discussing. A statement about cognitive structure is a statement about some kind of enduring entity, whereas a statement about cognitive style is more a statement about regularly observed consistencies in thinking. The 'enduring entity' which seems to be assumed by the notion of structure is usually thought of as a personality system or subsystem. However we conceptualize this system, it must be assumed to have certain parts which are organized in stable and specifiable ways. It is these parts and their inter-relationships which constitute the system's structure.

In this way what is common to all discussions of 'structure' is an emphasis upon parts and inter-relationships. This is perhaps more obvious when we talk of the structure of groups – here we are referring to members and their inter-relationships – or the structure of an organization – its departments and their inter-relationships (see Katz and Kahn, 1966). But in practice structural notions have been used in personality theories for quite some time. Freud's psychoanalytic formulation was for example basically a structural account of mental organization, dealing with the mind's major components (ego, super-ego and id) and their inter-relationships (Freud, reprinted 1965, p. 64). In a somewhat different field Bartlett's (1932) discussion of memory schemata was in effect an examination of structural characteristics, as was Zajonc's (1960) concern with complexity, unity and differentiation in judgement.

Structural statements are thus statements of 'how' more than of 'what'. And, as we have seen, this is also the case with statements about style. 'Cognitive style' and 'cognitive structure' are thus overlapping terms; the difference lies in the fact that 'cognitive style' refers to certain aspects of thought processes and 'cognitive structure' refers to the system which mediates these processes.

The selections in this book are intended to clarify these points by providing detailed examples of psychologists' work on stylistic and structural features of thought. The first five Parts of the book (Readings 1 to 14) describe those stylistic and structural features of individual cognitive differences which are of major importance at the present time. Interest in these selections centres upon the nature and measurement of each variable. In this way papers have been included which summarize work on rigidity and dogmatism, category usage, conceptual complexity, psychological differentiation, levelling–sharpening and other fairly content-free aspects of thinking. As has already been indicated, the selections concentrate upon *differences between* people, so that several important papers about the general characteristics of cognitive systems have regretfully been excluded.

The later Readings of the book are rather different. The stylistic and structural formulations introduced in the first fourteen Readings ought by their trans-situational nature to be relevant to work in a wide variety of psychological fields. That this is so is demonstrated in the latter part of the book. Readings 15 to 25 have been put together to illustrate the value of a cognitive style and structure approach in many areas of psychological activity. Studies of interpersonal behaviour, for instance, are partly concerned with how people process information about each other. Quite naturally then differences in cognitive style should account for some differences in interpersonal interaction. A structural approach to attitude systems or to psychopathology should also prove valuable, and our understanding of perception and memory might be increased by the same orientation. The importance of cognitive style and structure research in each of these fields is illustrated in the last three Parts.

These selections leave little doubt that stylistic and structural differences between people in their thinking are of considerable significance to psychologists of many inclinations. It should however be recognized that work on these differences is of fairly recent origin. The maturation of new scientific concepts seems typically to involve two separate but interdependent stages. During the first stage the concept is created and developed through empirical work so that its semantic and operational definitions become acceptable within the original perspective of its creators. The second stage encompasses attempts to extend the concept outside this original perspective and to see how it must be modified by contacts with quite different ideas and research approaches.

The concepts examined in this book are at present only growing out of the first of these stages. Definitions and measurement procedures are still not finalized, and firm decisions about which formulations are fruitful ones and which may be discarded have yet to be made. Research is however turning to the second maturation stage. This is observable in a contemporary concern with the introduction of a quite different universe of variables – the parameters of the environment rather than of the person. We need to know how the situation in which a person finds himself interacts with cognitive style and structure variables to determine his experience and behaviour. It is becoming apparent that cognitive styles extend only over a limited range of situations, so that a measure of style or structure (and indeed of more content-loaded personality dimensions) is of restricted predictive value. But the extent of these ranges of situations is at present far from clear. This leads to the paradox that psychology (which is usually seen as a study of people) must turn more to study environments and situations if its developmental momentum is not to be lost.

Most of the authors whose work appears in this book are clearly aware of the need to study persons-in-environments, and their work (reflected in the selections to follow) is now moving into this second developmental stage. Progress to date has been exciting and rapid, and future studies in this field are also likely to be of a fundamental and broad-ranging significance.

References
ADORNO, T. W., FRENKEL-BRUNSWIK, E., LEVINSON, D. J., and SANFORD, R. N. (1950), *The Authoritarian Personality*, Harper.
ATTNEAVE, F. (1959), *Applications of Information Theory to Psychology*, Holt, Rinehart & Winston.
BARTLETT, F. C. (1932), *Remembering: A Study in Experimental and Social Psychology*, Cambridge University Press.
CARTWRIGHT, D., and HARARY, F. (1956), 'Structural balance: a generalization of Heider's theory', *Psychol. Rev.*, vol. 63, pp. 277–93.
FELDMAN, S. (ed.) (1966), *Cognitive Consistency*, Academic Press.
FESTINGER, L. (1957), *A Theory of Cognitive Dissonance*, Row, Peterson.
FESTINGER, L. (1964), *Conflict, Decision and Dissonance*, Stanford University Press.
FREUD, S. (1965), *New Introductory Lectures on Psychoanalysis*, Norton, rev. edn.
GARNER, W. R. (1962), *Uncertainty and Structure as Psychological Concepts*, Wiley.
HEIDER, F. (1946), 'Attitudes and cognitive organization', *J. Psychol.*, vol. 21, pp. 107–12.
HOLT, R. R. (1964), 'Imagery: the return of the ostracized', *Amer. Psychol.*, vol. 19, pp. 254–64.
INSKO, C. A. (1967), *Theories of Attitude Change*, Appleton-Century-Crofts.

Janis, I. L., Hovland, C. I., Field, P. B., Linton, H., Graham, E., Cohen, A. R., Abelson, R. P., Lesser, G. S., and King, B. T. (1959), *Personality and Persuasibility*, Yale University Press.

Katz, D., and Kahn, R. L. (1966), *The Social Psychology of Organizations*, Wiley.

Kogan, N., and Wallach, M. (1964), *Risk-Taking: A Study in Cognition and Personality*, Holt, Rinehart & Winston.

McGee, R. K. (1962), 'Response style as a personality variable: by what criterion?', *Psychol. Bull.*, vol. 59, pp. 284–95.

Mintz, A., and Blum, M. L. (1949), 'A re-examination of the accident-proneness concept', *J. appl. Psychol.*, vol. 33, pp. 195–211.

Neisser, U. (1967), *Cognitive Psychology*, Appleton-Century-Crofts.

Osgood, C. E., and Sebeok, T. A. (1965), *Psycholinguistics: A Survey of Theory and Research Problems*, Indiana University Press.

Osgood, C. E., and Tannenbaum, P. H. (1955), 'The principle of congruity in the prediction of attitude change', *Psychol. Rev.*, vol. 62, pp. 42–55.

Rorer, L. G. (1965), 'The great response-style myth', *Psychol. Bull.*, vol. 63, pp. 129–56.

Warr, P. B., and Coffman, T. L. (in press), 'Personality, involvement and extremity of judgment', *Brit. J. soc. clin. Psychol.*

Wason, P. C., and Johnson-Laird, P. N. (1968), *Thinking and Reasoning*, Penguin Books.

Zajonc, R. B. (1960), 'The process of cognitive tuning in communication', *J. abnorm. soc. Psychol.*, vol. 61, pp. 159–65.

Part One **Rigidity and Dogmatism**

The concept of rigidity has been employed by psychologists for more than thirty years. During this time it has assumed a variety of meanings and has been associated with a broad range of research activities. The first of the two Readings in Part One traces the development of these meanings and research approaches from the work of R. B. Cattell through to the present time. Rigidity, as some form of limitation on information processing, is observed in perception and in problem solving as well as in judgements of a more social kind.

A related notion – that of dogmatism – is introduced in the second Reading. This paper contains an incisive discussion of structural features of thought and illustrates the main characteristics of dogmatic functioning. Dogmatism is distinguished from rigidity on two main counts – that it is a less specific concept and that it is primarily manifested in person-to-person situations.

1 Penelope Jane Leach

A Critical Study of the Literature Concerning Rigidity

Penelope Jane Leach, 'A critical study of the literature concerning rigidity',
British Journal of Social and Clinical Psychology, vol. 6, 1967, pp. 11–22.

Introduction

A large amount of effort has been devoted to the study of rigidity
during the last forty years. Yet there is still little agreement as to
its identity or its components. Rigidity has been studied as a
neurologically determined peculiarity of perception, as a type of
perceptual defence and as a manifestation of basic personality
variables. It has been studied in the laboratory and in the social
field, among selected groups of subjects and among general
populations. And throughout, the concept has given rise to
heated controversy between eminent psychologists.

Perhaps because the definitions of rigidity remained general and
various for so long, the actual research carried out has varied with
the swings in psychological thinking over the years. As the
increasing sophistication of statistical techniques led to their
increasing use in psychology, so rigidity was subjected to factor
analyses. As this statistical trend led to the breaking up of every
concept into its component parts for study, so rigidity was
fractionalized. When the trend was towards putting concepts
together again, so rigidity was reshaped into a totality. Even today, when one main trend in psychology can be described as the
tendency to study individuals in their environments, utilizing
sociological concepts, rigidity can be seen to share in the trend.

*Rigidity as a perceptual phenomenon: perseveration and
co-satiation*

The label 'rigidity' was first attached, by R. B. Cattell (1935), to a
kind of perceptual behaviour observed in the laboratory by
Spearman (1927) and consisting of perseveration from one simple,
repetitive motor task to another. Following Spearman, Pinard

(1932) and Cattell later designed batteries of tests to elicit this behaviour. They found that it arose not only in motor behaviour, but whenever subjects were required to shift from one task to another. Cattell noted extensive individual differences in degree of perseveration, and found that its extremes were related to certain crude measures of personality, such as passivity. He described extremely perseverative individuals as having a 'rigidity disposition'.

Further work demonstrated individual variations in degree of perseveration. Shakow and Rosenzweig (1937), for example, found that paranoid schizophrenics were more rigid, in this sense, than hebephrenic schizophrenics. They related this to the greater caution and suspicion of the paranoids in dealing with other people, and thought that both these phenomena might arise from the greater defensiveness of the paranoid group.

Spearman had originally ascribed perseveration to a 'mental inertia'; Cattell had talked of a 'rigidity disposition'. Both these terms imply that the observed rigid phenomena arose out of some inherent characteristic of the subjects' mental make-up. This idea was taken further by Lewin. Lewin (1935) saw personality as being made up of many different 'psychical systems' differing from each other in their degree of energy or tension, their differentiation and their rigidity, in the sense of fixity. He believed that rigidity arose through a lack of differentiation between psychical systems in the individual. He demonstrated this by a series of experiments on co-satiation carried out with feeble-minded and normal children. Using a structured task involving drawing stereotyped 'moon-faces', Lewin (1938) found that although feeble-minded children took longer than normals to reach satiation, having reached satiation they were unwilling to embark on a new task. The normal children, though rapidly satiated with moon-faces, were not co-satiated: they willingly went on to the second task. Lewin thought that the greater flexibility of the normal subjects enabled them to differentiate completely between the first and second tasks, so that satiation with the first did not affect the second.

This work, which has been well reviewed by Sheila Chown (1959), started one of the major controversies in rigidity research. Kounin (1941), a follower of Lewin, repeated his work and achieved opposite results. His feeble-minded subjects were far less liable to co-satiation than his normal group. Kounin's explanation was that rather than differing in the degree of differentiation of their psychical systems, the groups differed in the degree of segregation of these systems. The subparts of the personalities of the feeble-minded children were so completely segregated that the subparts dealing with the first task had no communication with the subparts dealing with the second. Co-satiation could not therefore occur.

The Lewin–Kounin controversy threw rigidity research into a linguistic chaos. It was no longer clear whether 'communication' between subparts of the personality, or between psychical systems, was to be seen as rigid or flexible. The difference between segregation and differentiation of these regions was unclear, and the question of whether rigidity or flexibility should be expected to arise from each was hopelessly confused. It was left to Hans Werner (1946) to postulate a reconciling explanation of the opposing results, and to try to reshape the theoretical background.

Werner's explanation of the results was a very simple one which was nevertheless a vital pointer for subsequent work on rigidity. He suggested that since Lewin's second task had been a free-drawing one, quite different from his first task, while Kounin's second task had been a structured one, very similar to his first, it was likely that co-satiation was irrelevant. Rather, it seemed that feeble-minded subjects were less easily satiated than normals on a repetitive and structured task, but less willing to embark on a free, imaginative one.

Werner followed up this work by re-analysing a series of experiments on word list repetition (Werner and Strauss, 1942). The results showed that brain-damaged subjects perseverated far more than normals. Werner was therefore able to destroy Kounin's concept of segregation between personality subregions, since the application of this concept would have meant classifying the brain-damaged subjects as flexible, since their perseveration would have indicated lack of segregation. Perseveration was therefore restored to its former place as a indicator of rigidity in the sense of 'sluggishness in the variation of a response'.

Werner further clarified the theoretical background to rigidity study by pointing out that rigidity was not to be confused with stability. In a constantly changing environment, if behaviour is to be stable, response must be flexible. Differentiation of response is therefore essential to stability. It must not be confused with Kounin's segregation, which implies difficulty in shifting across figurative personality boundaries, and is therefore a concomitant of rigidity.

Personality and rigidity

Although attempts to relate rigidity to some neurophysiological peculiarity of the individual continued, the 1930s and 1940s saw many demonstrations of the effects of experimentally induced emotions on perception. Murray (1933), Sherif (1936), and later Bruner and Goodman (1947) had all shown that social or visual perception could be affected by such emotion. This work led to an increasing interest in the relationship between personality and perception as a whole. Research into rigidity shared in this development.

In 1944, L. L. Thurstone introduced his formidable study of perceptual rigidity, saying: 'The individual differences which we find in these effects are probably not of the peripheral kind involved in mere sensory acuity . . . [they] depend upon attitudes which the individual adopts spontaneously . . . [they] reflect in some way the parameters which characterize him as a person.' This study of Thurstone's is of interest partly because it was designed with such an explicit intention of demonstrating the personality variables affecting perception, but also because the data were analysed by factor analysis. The three main factors produced have remained central to rigidity study. Firstly, speed of various perceptual functions, such as speed of closure, has been shown to be related to such variables as tolerance of ambiguity. Secondly, flexibility in the manipulation of several Gestalten at once has been related to abstract thinking and symbolic performance. The third factor, that of primary mental abilities, remains a bugbear in rigidity research to this day.

Thurstone's attempt to relate his findings to individual personality, by means of the Rorschach test, failed. But his intention was taken up by Kurt Goldstein who, finding that the degree and site of damage to the brain in his neurological patients was insufficient explanation of their perceptual differences, turned to their personalities for this explanation.

Goldstein's test battery (Goldstein and Scheerer, 1941) included sorting, matching and classification tests, many of which have been adapted for the measurement of rigidity in normal individuals. Goldstein (1943) found that far from being a perceptual peculiarity of certain individuals – as much former work had implied – some degree of rigidity, or slowness of response adaptation, is a natural human phenomenon. Among those patients who exhibited it to an extreme degree he observed two distinct types of rigid response. The first arose when the subject was faced with a problem which was too difficult for him. An extreme anxious blocking took place; the subject categorically refused to acknowledge any change in proffered stimuli, and clung rigidly to any previous response, however inappropriate, which had formerly led to success. The second type arose when some offered stimulus aroused such strong responses that subjects were unable to break off their reactions when the stimulation changed. Such subjects would continue, for example, to sort by colour, when the experimenter had requested a classification by shape. This description was vitally important. A distinction was at last being made between the kind of perseverative behaviour originally observed by Spearman and his followers, and the defensive reaction which had so confused Lewin in his feeble-minded subjects.

Goldstein's assumption that variations in degree of rigidity arose from personality variables, received support from many leading theorists who were increasingly concerned with the intimate entanglement between personality and perception. As Bruner (1948) put it: 'What emerges in the individual's perceptual field is a compromise reflecting his adjustive needs.' Klein and Krech (1951) took a similar standpoint with the assertion that 'an organism is always responsible for its behaviour' and therefore every piece of behaviour must be seen as adaptive for that organism.

But this approach to the study of rigidity did not go unchallenged. From that time, until the present day, there has been a comparatively clear division of interest between workers who, like Goldstein, felt that personality effects were the most interesting and important part of perceptual research, and those who, while accepting the existence of these effects, were anxious to exclude them in order to study perceptual responses in isolation.

Ironically, since he was among the first to note the relationship between rigidity and personality variables, the latter group included R. B. Cattell (Cattell and Tiner, 1949). He wanted to isolate further the 'rigidity disposition' he had postulated in 1935; he believed it to arise from 'resistance to change of neural discharge paths'; and he thought that it could only be isolated if tests were devised which excluded all 'spurious causes of rigid behaviour'. Cattell's spurious causes included all personality variables: emotions, conflicts and defences. He accepted that an individual might fail to adapt his behaviour to new stimuli because the new behaviour 'might conflict with satisfaction of some other trait, or of the total dynamic economy of the organism . . . because of, say, a fear drive', but he relegated this kind of rigidity to the province of the psychiatrist.

Although Cattell listed the ways in which personality variables might produce rigid behaviour only in order to dismiss them, his list served subsequent research workers as the clearest statement of these effects which had yet been made. The factor analytic study of 'disposition rigidity' which followed was far less useful. Three factors were isolated, whose content was rather similar to those described by Thurstone. They were an intelligence factor, a perseverative factor and a factor of inability to learn from gradually changing stimuli.

An even stronger stand against the inclusion of personality variables in perceptual research was taken by Luchins. He had administered his own water-jar test of the Einstellung effect to some 10,000 subjects, and had listed the reasons he had observed for subjects failing to change set at the appropriate point in the test. It had occurred to Rokeach (1948) and others that all these reasons could be explained in terms of an underlying rigidity in the individual subjects. Luchins' test had accordingly been incorporated in a rigidity test battery. Luchins' (1948) first objections were made on the legitimate grounds that the test had been designed to measure readiness to change set, while this use of it assumed that it measured ability to do so. A later study by Levitt and Zelen (1953) suggests that this objection was a valid one. They showed that if the efficiency with which the water-jar problems were solved was measured in terms of speed, it was often more efficient to maintain the established set throughout.

But this was not Luchins' only objection. He was categorically opposed to any attempt to assess personality effects in perception. He bitterly criticized Bruner's 'organism centred' approach saying: 'Experiments are conducted and interpreted as if needs, values, etc. were essences of the organism, operating rather independently of field conditions' (Luchins, 1951). He reiterated the vital importance of field conditions but was also convinced that they could not be assessed. Field conditions therefore became the vital enigma which permitted him to explain individual differences in perceptual responses without resorting to personality considerations.

Just as Cattell's dismissive list of the personality causes of rigid behaviour was used by subsequent personality-oriented workers, so Luchins' list of reasons for failure to change set became a vital statement of the distorting effects of rigidity on problem-solving behaviour. Some Einstellung tests have been included in almost every subsequent rigidity test battery.

Rigidity as a defence mechanism: the link between perceptual and social rigidity

Among those workers who did accept the importance of personality considerations in rigidity research, attention began to be turned towards the purpose which rigid defences served for the individual. Fisher (1950) designed an extensive battery of sorting, matching, aesthetic and problem-solving tests which he administered to matched groups of conversion hysterics, paranoid schizophrenics and normal controls. While the battery did hang together, so that individuals scoring rigidly on one test area tended also to score rigidly on others, there was considerable variance both within and between groups. Fisher believed that this variance could be accounted for by means of the variable, hinted at by Lewin, Werner and Goldstein, of ego-involvement. He thought that rigidity served a primarily defensive purpose and that it would therefore show itself most strongly when the individual felt challenged or threatened by the test material. His belief in the defensive nature of rigid responses was strengthened by finding a greater degree of rigidity among mental hospital patients than among the population at large (Fisher and Fisher, 1951). Without their rigid defences, he postulated, many of the patients might have suffered complete ego-breakdown.

If rigid responses serve a primarily defensive purpose for the individual, what kind of threat is this defence erected against? The answer was to be pioneered by a group of workers who, led by Else Frenkel-Brunswik, entered the field of rigidity study through the work which was eventually to be reported in *The Authoritarian Personality* (Adorno *et al.*, 1950).

Whereas most of the workers discussed so far had their primary interest in perception and had come, gradually, to realize the importance of personality variables in this field, Frenkel-Brunswik had started from research in psychoanalysis. Gradually she had found that the personality variables with which she was concerned also had perceptual manifestations. Her interest in rigidity – or, as she descriptively termed it, intolerance of ambiguity – started from findings concerned with individual variations in tolerance of emotional ambivalence in the self (Frenkel-Brunswik, 1948a). Finding that this dislike of internal conflict was related to a dislike of conflicting situations in other social areas, she went on to find it mirrored also in the cognitive and perceptual areas. This work was vitally important to the development of rigidity research. It was the first time that variables such as perseveration, premature closure, reluctance to change set or inability to learn from changing stimuli had been demonstrated in social relationships and social attitudes. It now began to seem that not only was rigid perceptual behaviour correlated with certain personality traits, but that it was, in itself, a manifestation of total personality structure. Frenkel-Brunswik reached this conclusion when she found that extremely ethnically prejudiced children tended to display marked perceptual rigidity (Frenkel-Brunswik, 1948b) and that they also shared the personality characteristics which she and her colleagues had found to be typical of high authoritarians. This relationship was later summed up as follows (Frenkel-Brunswik, 1954): 'They tend to display authoritarian aggression, cruelty, superstition, externalization and projectivity, denial of weakness, power orientation and tend towards dichotomous conceptions of sex roles, of kinds of people and of values.' Both ethnic prejudice and rigidity were therefore seen as manifestations of the latent drives making up the authoritarian personality.

A large body of research linking social and perceptual rigidity followed. Rokeach (1948) demonstrated that the rigid social thinking which characterized prejudiced subjects was mirrored in rigid problem-solving behaviour. Kutner (1951) showed that highly prejudiced children found difficulty in concept formation, and failed on syllogism-deductive problems. J. Fisher (1951) showed that prejudiced subjects even displayed, to an abnormal degree, the law of Pragnanz, by which memory traces became simpler and more symmetrical with time: he thought that this might be related to their tendency to over-simplify in conscious thought. Jack and Jeanne Block (1951) used the autokinetic effect as a measure of intolerance of ambiguity. Highly prejudiced subjects made premature closure on this test, stabilizing their norms for movement of the light far more rapidly than unprejudiced subjects. E. E. Levitt (1953) found positive correlations between intolerance of ambiguity in visual perception and acceptance of popular misconceptions. He related both these to ethnic prejudice. Similar inter-relationships were found by T. T. Coulter (unpublished).

Rigidity as a limitation on originality

During the 1950s yet another aspect of the individual's life was found to be effected by rigidity. This was the area of aesthetic preference and originality and creativity of thought. Eysenck (1940) who had pioneered factor analytic studies of aesthetic judgements had found one clear factor, named the K-factor, which divided subjects up according to their preference for the simple or the complex in a variety of aesthetic experiences ranging from pictures, through poetry, to scents. Further investigations showed this factor to be related to various measures of personality. Barron and Welsh (1952) found a similar dimension of preference for simplicity–complexity in artistic choice. Preference for the simple went with many of the personality traits defined by Frenkel-Brunswik in her work on intolerance of social ambiguity. In a later paper, Barron (1953) specifically linked these findings with the rigidity–flexibility dimension. A rigidity scale, together with various ratings of rigidity derived from self-description, was found to be positively correlated with preference for the simple on the Barron–Welsh art scale, and also with ethnocentrism and social conformity.

The relationship between flexibility and preference for the artistically complex can be explained via the intervening variable of originality. Originality is positively associated with preference for the aesthetically complex; originality demands the fullest possible utilization of stimuli from the environment. This full utilization of stimuli is impossible for the rigid individual who selects out and filters stimuli in accordance with his defensive needs. Such an explanation is further supported by two other papers which, while they are not directly concerned with rigidity, do throw further light on this aspect of it. Myden (1957) found that highly creative subjects were more inner-directed, and less dependent either on the judgements of other people or on conventional role definitions, than were less creative subjects. Munsterburg and Mussen (1953) found a markedly greater need for self-expression among individuals judged creative, together with an outright rejection of social stereotypes and prejudices, on the grounds that these were limiting to the intellect.

Golann (1962) has recently taken this work even further. He has shown that the Barron–Welsh art scale not only discriminates between individuals judged creative and non-creative, but also between occupation groups which differ along this dimension, and even between art students and others. High and low scorers also show marked differences on measures of conventionality and the desire to conform. Even among fourteen-year-old children, the art scale discriminated between those who preferred free play activities and those who preferred organized and supervised games. One is reminded of Lewin's feeble-minded children who infinitely preferred drawing moon-faces to embarking on a free-drawing task.

Much of the recent work on creativity has concerned itself with the total 'cognitive style' of individuals. Despite the wide differences in terminology used to delineate these styles, it is clear that the 'high creative' of Getzels and Jackson (1962), the field independent of Witkin et al. (1962), the allocentric of Schachtel (1959), or the 'growth' individuals of Maslow (1956), all share in one characteristic: they are flexible in their approach to life, receptive to environmental stimuli. As a recent review of this field puts it (Gallagher, 1964a): 'Two distinctly different patterns or strategies . . . begin in childhood and extend to all aspects of life. One of these patterns is characterized by freedom and striving for expression, the other by caution, and concern for the opinions of others.'

The personality variables underlying rigidity

Implicit in much of the work so far described, particularly that dealing with rigidity in relation to creativity and originality, was a conception of rigidity as a fundamental restriction on the individual's perception of his environment, and therefore of the use which he could make of that environment. Earlier workers had thought that individuals needed this kind of restriction on their perceptual intake, as a defence against ego-involving situations which they found threatening. But while this may be a satisfactory explanation of the way in which rigid defences serve the individual personality, it does nothing to explain why certain personalities need such defences, nor why rigidity should be the chosen mode of defence.

Again, it was Frenkel-Brunswik who pioneered the answers to these questions. She had found a marked similarity between the retrospective descriptions of their parents and childhoods given to her by her authoritarian adult subjects (Adorno *et al.*, 1950), and descriptions in the here-and-now given to her by highly prejudiced child subjects (1948a and b). The accuracy of the latter accounts was confirmed by interviews with the parents. Out of this large body of work Frenkel-Brunswik found that she was able to describe the kind of parent who seemed to produce rigid children (1949). 'The requested submission and obedience to parental authority is only one of the many external, rigid and superficial rules which such a child learns . . . dominance–submission, cleanliness–dirtyness, badness–goodness, virtue–vice, masculinity–femininity are some of the dichotomies customarily upheld in the homes of such children.'

Frenkel-Brunswik came to believe that this kind of upbringing could strongly affect the process of early socialization, as described in the psychoanalytic literature. She believed that these parents made demands on their children for behaviour which could neither be understood nor achieved. Faced with these unreachable and incomprehensible standards, the child found himself able to retain his parents' approval only by learning, by rote and piecemeal, the specific kinds of behaviour which they required. The child therefore learned to subdue libidinal impulses rather than to control and channel them. And he learnt to subdue them without comprehension: in obedience to external demands rather than to internalized standards. This perilous structure of social learning, with no foundations in internalized values, could only be supported by a rigid system of defences within the self, with black and white as recognizable and manageable dichotomies, and grey the colour of threat: the threat of ambiguity where the piecemeal learning gave no cues and the lack of internalized values left the child threatened with the complete disintegration of his defensive structure.

With this theoretical formulation Frenkel-Brunswik indicated the reasons for individuals requiring the particular kind of defence given by rigidity. A large body of research followed, demonstrating the correctness of different parts of the theory. Gough, Harris and Martin (1950) found that the mothers of highly prejudiced children were far more authoritarian, rigid and fussy in their child-rearing practices than were the mothers of a control group. Willis (1956), in a three-generation study, found positive relationships between Swedish subjects' acceptance of external, rule-bound discipline when they were children, their tendency to impose a similar régime on their own children and authoritarian political beliefs. Kates and Diab (1955), in a study of undergraduates none of whom were parents, found that authoritarian ideology was closely related to intolerance of ambiguity and to attitudes of dominance and possessiveness towards children. It seems likely that the subjects in this study were responding with a mixture of remembered attitudes towards their own parents and 'intended' attitudes towards any children they might have in the future. A clinical study (Rosenthal, Finkelstein and Robertson, 1959) showed that mothers who were rigid and over-controlling in their child-handling produced children who were over-conforming, submissive to authority and extremely conventional and rule-bound both in their attitudes and in their behaviour. Similar findings were described by Baldwin (1948), who found that democratic handling produced children with all the qualities associated with a fearless exploration of the environment, while autocratic and authoritarian handling produced quiet, non-resistive, passive and over-conventional children. Radke (1946) further showed, in a three-generation study, that rigid disciplinary policies experienced by parents when they were children led to a tendency to use similar methods with their own children, and that those children showed a lack of internalization and of comprehension of those disciplinary methods, tending to obey by rote rather than by intention. A study of matched groups of highly rigid and highly flexible children (Leach, unpublished) showed that the rigid group tended to have mothers who were highly authoritarian both in their general attitudes to life, their attitudes to child-rearing and their reported child-rearing practices.

Future trends: towards combating rigidity

This kind of research continues to show in ever-greater detail the relationship between certain kinds of child-rearing and a variety of manifestations of rigidity. Meanwhile the reality of these formulations has been so widely accepted that attention is already being turned to what can be done about it. Although some of the aspects of rigid thinking which have been discussed are unfortunately likely to be of some value in present-day society, with its plethora of repetitive routine jobs and its comparatively low rewards for creative work, it is widely accepted that rigidity, restricting as it does the individual's full utilization of his own potentialities, is undesirable. A considerable amount of effort is therefore being devoted to finding out whether actual teaching can effectively help individuals to overcome the social and intellectual concomitants of rigidity, even though it cannot alter the defensive mechanisms which lie beneath them.

In the field of social rigidity, most of this work is concerned with combating ethnic prejudice and teaching people to consider social issues for themselves, rather than accepting current stereotypes. Specific suggestions for this have been made by Bibby (1959), and assessed by Banton (1962). The whole field has been reviewed by Leach (1964).

In the field of intellectual and perceptual rigidity much attention has been focused on teaching in schools. Pringle and

McKenzie (1965) have shown that different approaches to the teaching of school subjects can result in differing degrees of rigidity in the pupils, at least at the lowest ability levels. Gallagher (1964b) and Ferris (1962) have both shown that teaching methods which guide the child into making his own discoveries, rather than supplying him with facts, upset the results of established aptitude tests to a considerable extent; often putting the formerly unsuccessful pupil ahead of his previously excelling peers. Ausubel and Fitzgerald (1961), Ervin (1960) and Gagné and Smith (1962) have all demonstrated the importance of teaching children by general principles rather than by rote facts, if the learning is to be effectively transferred and generalized. Myers and Torrance (1961) have even suggested specific exercises for the improvement of mental flexibility.

While all these attempts are valuable if they improve, even for a few individuals, the possibility of utilizing their own powers to the full, they are probably irrelevant to the main problem in rigidity. If the causes for the establishment of rigid defences lie in the individual's early socialization experiences, then specific teaching at a later date can be, at the best, only a way of palliating some of the effects of those defences. Furthermore, the truly rigid individual is likely to be the one who is least helped by such measures. For a rigid child, an attempt to abandon for example conventional arithmetical teaching, in favour of a self-discovery approach, is likely to be a threat in itself. Feeling threatened by the ambiguity of this situation, with its removal of safe black and white arithmetical rules in favour of threatening exploration, such a child's rigid defences are likely to be further mobilized. In this way a vicious circle is likely to be formed, such that the more one attempts to break through the rigid patterns of thought, the more rigid they become. Such a programme might well backfire: helping those children who needed it least and by-passing those at whom it was aimed.

If rigidity is a manifestation of basic personality variables, as recent work suggests, then any attempts to combat it must be directed at that level. It is of little real use to try to combat it by methods more suitable to reversing the perceptual peculiarity which rigidity was thought to be in the 1930s.

References

ADORNO, T. W., FRENKEL-BRUNSWIK, E., LEVINSON, D. J., and SANFORD, R. N. (1950), *The Authoritarian Personality*, Harper.

AUSUBEL, D. P., and FITZGERALD, D. (1961), 'Meaningful learning and retention: intrapersonal cognitive variables', *Rev. educ. Res.*, vol. 31, pp. 500–510.

BALDWIN, A. L. (1948), 'Socialization and parent–child relationships', *Child Devel.*, vol. 19, pp. 127–36.

BANTON, H. (1962), 'Teaching race questions in British schools', *Int. soc. Sci. J.*, vol. 14, pp. 732–42.

BARRON, F. (1953), 'Complexity–simplicity as a personality dimension', *J. abnorm. soc. Psychol.*, vol. 48, pp. 163–72.

BARRON, F., and WELSH, G. S. (1952), 'Artistic perception as a possible factor in personality style: its measurement by a figure preference test', *J. Psychol.*, vol. 33, pp. 199–203.

BIBBY, C. (1959), *Race, Prejudice and Education*, Heinemann.

BLOCK, J., and BLOCK, J. (1951), 'An investigation of the relationship between intolerance of ambiguity and ethnocentrism', *J. Personal.*, vol. 19, pp. 303–11.

BRUNER, J. (1948), 'Perceptual theory and the Rorschach test', *J. Personal.*, vol. 17, pp. 157–68.

BRUNER, J., and GOODMAN, C. C. (1947), 'Value and need as organizing factors in perception', *J. abnorm. soc. Psychol.*, vol. 42, pp. 33–44.

CATTELL, R. B. (1935), 'On the measurement of perseveration', *Brit. J. educ. Psychol.*, vol. 5, pp. 76–92.

CATTELL, R. B., and TINER, L. G. (1949), 'The varieties of structural rigidity', *J. Personal.*, vol. 17, pp. 321–41.

CHOWN, S. M. (1959), 'Rigidity – a flexible concept', *Psychol. Bull.*, vol. 56, pp. 195–223.

ERVIN, S. (1960), 'Transfer effects of learning a verbal generalization', *Child Devel.*, vol. 31, pp. 537–63.

EYSENCK, H. J. (1940), 'The general factor in aesthetic judgements', *Brit. J. Psychol.*, vol. 41, pp. 94–102.

FERRIS, F. L., JR (1962), 'Testing in the new curriculum: numerological tyranny or common sense', *School Rev.*, vol. 70, pp. 112–31.

FISHER, J. (1951), 'The memory process and certain psycho-social attitudes with special reference to the law of Pragnanz', *J. Personal.*, vol. 19, pp. 406–12.

FISHER, S. (1950), 'Patterns of personality rigidity and some of their determinants', *Psychol. Monogr.*, vol. 64, pp. 1–48.

FISHER, S., and FISHER, R. (1951), 'Value of isolation rigidity in maintaining integration in seriously disturbed personalities', *J. Personal.*, vol. 19, pp. 41–7.

FRENKEL-BRUNSWIK, E. (1948a), 'A study of prejudice in children', *Hum. Rel.*, vol. 1, pp. 295–306.

FRENKEL-BRUNSWIK, E. (1948b), 'Tolerance towards ambiguity as a personality variable', *Amer. Psychol.*, vol. 3, p. 268.

FRENKEL-BRUNSWIK, E. (1949), 'Intolerance of ambiguity as an emotional and perceptual personality variable', in J. S. Bruner and D. Krech (eds.), *Perception and Personality*, Duke University Press.

FRENKEL-BRUNSWIK, E. (1954), 'Further explorations by a contributor to *The Authoritarian Personality*', in R. Christie and M. Jahoda (eds.), *Studies in the Scope and Method of 'The Authoritarian Personality'*, Free Press of Glencoe.

GAGNÉ, R. M., and SMITH, E. C. (1962), 'A study of the effects of verbalization on problem-solving', *J. exp. Psychol.*, vol. 63, pp. 12–18.

GALLAGHER, J. J. (1964a), 'Productive thinking', in M. L. Hoffman and L. W. Hoffman (eds.), *Child Development Research*, Russell Sage Foundation.

GALLAGHER, J. J. (1964b), *Teaching of the Gifted Child*, Allyn & Bacon.

GETZELS, J. W., and JACKSON, P. W. (1962), *Creativity and Intelligence*, Wiley.

GOLANN, S. E. (1962), 'The creativity motive', *J. Personal.*, vol. 30, pp. 588–600.

GOLDSTEIN, K. (1943), 'Concerning rigidity', *Char. Personal*, vol. 11, pp. 209–26.

GOLDSTEIN, K., and SCHEERER, M. (1941), 'Abstract and concrete behavior: an experimental study with special tests', *Psychol. Monogr.*, vol. 53, no. 2, pp. 1–151.

GOUGH, H. G., HARRIS, D., and MARTIN, W. (1950), 'Children's ethnic attitudes. II: relation to parental beliefs concerning child training', *Child Devel.*, vol. 21, pp. 169–81.

KATES, S. L., and DIAB, L. N. (1955), 'Authoritarian ideology and attitudes on parent–child relationships', *J. abnorm. soc. Psychol.*, vol. 51, pp. 13–6.

KLEIN, G., and KRECH, D. (1951), 'The problem of personality and its theory', *J. Personal.*, vol. 20, pp. 2–23.

KOUNIN, J. S. (1941), 'Experimental studies in rigidity', *Char. Personal.*, vol. 9, pp. 251–82.

KOUNIN, J. S. (1948), 'The meaning of rigidity: a reply to Hans Werner', *Psychol. Rev.*, vol. 55, pp. 157–66.

KUTNER, B. (1951), 'Patterns of mental functioning associated with prejudice in children', *Amer. Psychol.*, vol. 6, pp. 328–9.

LEACH, P. J. (1964), 'Teaching tolerance', *Int. Rev. Educ.*, vol. 10, pp. 190–204.

LEVITT, E. E. (1953), 'Studies in intolerance of ambiguity. I. The decision-location test with grade-school children', *Child Devel.*, vol. 24, pp. 263–8.

LEVITT, E. E., and ZELEN, S. L. (1953), 'The validity of the Einstellung test as a measure of rigidity', *J. abnorm. soc. Psychol.*, vol. 48, pp. 573–80.

LEWIN, K. (1935), *A Dynamic Theory of Personality*, McGraw-Hill.

LEWIN, K. (1938), 'Conceptual representation and the measurement of psychological forces', *Contr. psychol. Theory*, vol. I, pt 4, pp. 1–247.

LUCHINS, A. (1948), 'Rigidity and ethnocentrism. A critique', *J. Personal.*, vol. 17, pp. 449–66.

LUCHINS, A. (1951), 'On an approach to social perception', *J. Personal.*, vol. 19, pp. 64–84.

MASLOW, A. H. (1956), 'Defense and growth', *Merrill–Palmer Quart.*, vol. 3.

MUNSTERBURG, E., and MUSSEN, P. H. (1953), 'The personality structure of art students', *J. Personal.*, vol. 21, pp. 457–66.

MURRAY, H. A. (1933), 'The effect of fear on estimates of the maliciousness of other personalities', *J. soc. Psychol.*, vol. 4, pp. 310–29.

MYDEN, W. D. (1957), 'An investigation and evaluation of personality structure and characteristics of creative individuals in the context of psycho-analytic theory and ego-psychology', *Dissert. Abstr.*, vol. 17, pp. 897–8.

MYERS, R. E., and TORRANCE, E. P. (1961), *Invitation to Thinking and Doing*, Perceptive Publishing Co.

PINARD, J. W. (1932), 'Tests of perseveration. I. Their relation to character', *Brit. J. Psychol.*, vol. 23, pp. 5–19.

PRINGLE, K. M. L., and McKENZIE, I. R. (1965), 'Teaching method and rigidity in problem-solving', *Brit. J. educ. Psychol.*, vol. 35, pp. 50–59.

RADKE, M. (1946), 'The relation of parental authority to children's behaviour and attitudes', *Inst. child Welf. Monogr.*, vol. 22, University of Minnesota Press.

ROKEACH, M. (1948), 'Generalised mental rigidity as a factor in ethnocentrism', *J. abnorm. soc. Psychol.*, vol. 43, pp. 259–78.

ROSENTHAL, M. J., FINKELSTEIN, M., and ROBERTSON, R. E. (1959), 'A study of mother–child relationships in the emotional disorders of children', *Genet. Psychol. Monogr.*, vol. 60, no. 1, pp. 65–116.

SCHACHTEL, E. G. (1959), *Metamorphosis*, Basic Books.

SHAKOW, D., and ROSENWEIG, S. (1937), 'Play techniques in schizophrenia and other psychoses. II. An experimental study of schizophrenic constructions with play material', *Amer. J. Orthopsychiat.*, vol. 7, pp. 36–47.

SHERIF, M. (1936), *The Psychology of Social Norms*, Harper.

SPEARMAN, C. (1927), *The Abilities of Man, Their Nature and Measurement*, Macmillan.

THURSTONE, L. L. (1944), *A Factorial Study of Perception*, University of Chicago Press.

WERNER, H., and STRAUSS, A. A. (1942), 'Experimental analysis of the clinical symptom "perseveration" in mentally retarded children', *Amer. J. ment. Def.*, vol. 47, pp. 185–8.

WERNER, H. (1946), 'The concept of rigidity', *Psychol. Rev.*, vol 53, pp. 43–52.

WILLIS, R. H. (1956), 'Political and child-rearing attitudes in Sweden', *J. abnorm. soc. Psychol.*, vol. 53, pp. 74–7.

WITKIN, H. A., DYK, R. B., FATERSON H. F., GOODENOUGH, D. R., and KARP, S. A. (1962), *Psychological Differentiation*, Wiley.

2 Milton Rokeach

The Nature and Meaning of Dogmatism

Excerpt from Milton Rokeach, 'The nature and meaning of dogmatism', *Psychological Review*, vol. 61, 1954, pp. 194–204.

In this paper we will attempt to provide the theoretical ground-work for a research project on the phenomenon of dogmatism in various spheres of human activity – political, religious and scienti-fic. Our main purpose is to present a detailed theoretical state-ment of the construct of dogmatism which is guiding the research. More specifically, we will define the phenomenon of dogmatism by representing it as a hypothetical cognitive state which mediates objective reality within the person, describe the properties of its organization, and present a number of postulates regarding the rela-tion between dogmatism and other variables. On the basis of part of such a formulation we have thus far developed a preliminary scale for measuring individual differences in dogmatism and several testable hypotheses relevant to our conceptual definition.[1]

A second purpose stems from the fact that our construct of dogmatism involves the convergence of three highly interrelated sets of variables: closed cognitive systems, authoritarianism and intolerance. By virtue of this convergence it will be possible to examine certain assumptions underlying previous research on authoritarianism and intolerance (Adorno *et al.*, 1950) with the aim of achieving a possibly broader conceptualization of these phenomena.

It is not within the scope of this paper to inquire into the social or personal conditions which give rise to dogmatism. This is con-sidered to be an independent theoretical problem. Having defined the problem of dogmatism and its representation at the cognitive level – the main purpose of this paper – one can then seek explana-tions according to one's theoretical orientation.

1. A later publication which develops these 1954 ideas is M. Rokeach, *The Open and Closed Mind*, Basic Books, 1960 [*Ed.*].

A basic assumption guiding the present formulation is that despite differences in ideological content, analysis will reveal certain uniformities in the structure, the function and, to some extent, even the content of dogmatism. Accordingly, attention will be directed to both political and religious dogmatism and, within each area, to diverse and even opposed dogmatic orientations. In the religious sphere, for example, one can observe expressions of dogmatic Catholicism and dogmatic anti-Catholicism, dogmatic orthodox Judaism and dogmatic anti-orthodox Judaism, dogmatic theism and dogmatic atheism. In the political sphere one can observe expressions of dogmatic conservatism and dogmatic liberalism, dogmatic Marxism and dogmatic anti-Marxism.

The problem of dogmatism, however, is not necessarily restricted to the political and religious spheres. It can be observed in other realms of intellectual and cultural activity – in philosophy, the humanities, and the social sciences. To take some examples from psychology, it is possible to observe expressions of dogmatic Freudianism and dogmatic anti-Freudianism, dogmatic learning theory and dogmatic anti-learning theory, dogmatic Gestalt theory and dogmatic anti-Gestalt theory, and so forth.

Dogmatism, furthermore, need not necessarily involve adherence to this or that group-shared, institutionalized system of beliefs. It is conceivable that a person, especially one in academic circles, can be dogmatic in his own idiosyncratic way, evolving a unique rather than institutionalized integration of ideas and beliefs about reality. The present formulation will attempt to address itself to noninstitutional as well as institutional aspects of dogmatism.

General Setting for a Cognitive Representation of Dogmatism

To conceptualize dogmatism adequately at the cognitive level it is first necessary to employ a set of conceptual tools in terms of which all cognitive systems, varying in degree of dogmatism, may be represented.

Organization into belief and disbelief systems

Objective reality can be assumed as being represented within a person by certain beliefs or expectations which to one degree or

37

another are accepted as true, and other beliefs or expectations accepted as false. For the sake of analysis this can be formalized by conceiving of all cognitive systems as being organized into two interdependent parts: a belief system and a disbelief system. This belief–disbelief system can further be conceived as varying in terms of its structure and content as follows:

Structure. The total structure of a belief–disbelief system can be described as varying along a continuum from open to closed. This continuum, in turn, may be conceived as a joint function of: (a) the degree of interdependence among the parts within the belief system, within the disbelief system, and between belief and disbelief systems (Kounin, 1948; Krech, 1949; Lewin, 1942; Rokeach, 1951a); (b) the degree of interdependence between central and peripheral regions of the belief–disbelief system (Lewin, 1951); and (c) the organization of the belief–disbelief system along the time perspective dimension (Crossman, 1949; Frank, 1939; Hoffer, 1951; Lewin, 1942).

Content. One can further describe all belief–disbelief systems in terms of the formal content of centrally located beliefs, especially those having to do with beliefs about authority and people in general.

A Cognitive Representation of Dogmatism

In line with the above considerations we will now define dogmatism as (a) a relatively closed cognitive organization of beliefs and disbeliefs about reality, (b) organized around a central set of beliefs about absolute authority which, in turn, (c) provides a framework for patterns of intolerance and qualified tolerance toward others. A cognitive organization is considered to be closed to the extent that there is (a) isolation of parts within the belief system and between belief and disbelief systems, (b) a discrepancy in the degree of differentiation between belief and disbelief systems, (c) dedifferentiation within the disbelief system, (d) a high degree of interdependence between central and peripheral beliefs, (e) a low degree of interdependence among peripheral beliefs and (f) a narrowing of the time perspective.

More specifically, in the relatively closed belief–disbelief system there is assumed to be a relation of relative isolation among the various parts of the belief system and between belief and disbelief systems. The latter, in turn, is composed of a series of disbelief subsystems, each arranged along a gradient of similarity to the belief system, the most similar disbelief subsystems being represented as regions most adjacent to the belief system. Each of these disbelief subsystems is conceived, to the extent that it is part of a closed system, as being relatively less differentiated than the belief system and, the farther away their positions from the belief system, as increasingly dedifferentiated with respect to each other.

Belief–disbelief systems can also be represented along a central–peripheral dimension. The more closed the system the more the central part corresponds to absolute beliefs in or about authority, and the more the peripheral part corresponds to beliefs and disbeliefs perceived to emanate from such authority.

With respect to the time perspective dimension, increasingly closed systems can be conceived as being organized in a relatively future-oriented or past-oriented direction rather than in terms of a more balanced orientation of past, present and future.

With regard to the content of dogmatism, while the specific content of both central and peripheral parts may vary from one particular ideological system to another, it is possible to specify that in general the formal content of the central part of the system, to the extent it is closed, has to do with absolute beliefs in and about positive and negative authority, either external or internal, and related beliefs representing attempts on the part of such authority to perpetuate itself. Furthermore, the central part can be conceived to provide a framework for the organization of other beliefs representing patterns of rejection and qualified acceptance of people in general according to their patterns of agreement and disagreement with the belief–disbelief system.

Dogmatism Distinguished from Rigidity

Before going on to elaborate further on our conceptual definition of dogmatism, it may be illuminating first to distinguish the construct of dogmatism in a general way from that of rigidity. Both dogmatism and rigidity refer to forms of resistance to change, but dogmatism is conceived to represent a relatively more intellectualized and abstract form than rigidity. Whereas dogmatism refers to total cognitive *organizations* of ideas and beliefs into relatively closed ideological systems, rigidity, when genotypically conceived, refers solely to the degree of isolation between regions (Krech, 1949; Rokeach, 1951a) or to a 'property of a functional boundary which prevents communication between neighboring regions' (Kounin, 1948, p. 157); when phenotypically conceived, rigidity is defined in terms of the way a person or animal attacks, solves, or learns *specific* tasks and problems (Rokeach, 1948). Thus, dogmatism is seen as a higher-order and more complexly organized form of resistance to change. While dogmatism may well be hypothesized to lead to rigidity in solving specific problems, the converse is not necessarily the case. Rats, the feeble-minded and the brain-injured, for example, can be characterized as rigid (also compulsive, fixated, perseverative, inflexible) but hardly as dogmatic.

Furthermore, whereas rigidity refers to person-to-thing or animal-to-thing relationships, dogmatism is manifested almost necessarily in situations involving person-to-person communication. Thus, we speak of a person as tying his shoelaces or solving an arithmetic problem rigidly, but of a professor, a politician, an orator, a theoretician or an art critic as expressing himself to others dogmatically.

A final differentiation, closely related to the preceding, is that dogmatism has a further reference to the authoritarian and intolerant manner in which ideas and beliefs are communicated to others. Thus, the range of behavior considered under the rubric of dogmatism is considerably broader than rigidity and at the same time of possibly more intrinsic interest to the sociologist, the political scientist, and the historian, as well as the psychologist.

Postulates Involving the Cognitive Structure of Dogmatism

To the extent that the belief–disbelief system is closed, it is subjected to continual stresses and strains from objective and social reality. Reality can be coerced into congruence with the belief–disbelief system by virtue of the arrangement of parts within the belief–disbelief systems, within and between the central and peripheral regions thereof, and by virtue of its organization along the time perspective dimension.

Isolation within and between belief and disbelief systems

The greater the dogmatism the greater are the assumed degree of isolation or independence between the belief and disbelief systems and the assumed degree of isolation among the various parts of the belief system. On the basis of these considerations we introduce the following postulates.

Accentuation of differences between belief and disbelief systems. The greater the dogmatism the more will the belief system be perceived as different in content or aim from the disbelief system (e.g. Catholicism and Protestantism; the United States and the U.S.S.R.; Fascism and Communism; psychoanalysis and behaviorism).[2]

The perception of irrelevance. The greater the dogmatism the more will ideological arguments pointing to similarities between belief and disbelief systems be perceived as irrelevant.

Denial. The greater the dogmatism the greater the denial of events contradicting or threatening one's belief system (e.g. on grounds of 'face absurdity', that the true facts are not accessible, that the only available sources of information are biased because they are seen to emanate from the disbelief system, etc.).

Coexistence of contradictions within the belief system. In line with the assumption that in increasingly closed cognitive organizations there is relatively more isolation among subparts of the belief system, as well as between belief and disbelief systems, it is postulated that the degree of adherence to contradictory beliefs will vary directly with the degree of dogmatism. Some examples of contradictory beliefs are an abhorrence of violence together with the belief that it is justifiable under certain conditions; expressions

2. The parallel between this suggestion and latitudes of acceptance and rejection (e.g. M. Sherif and C. I. Hovland, *Social Judgment*, Yale University Press, 1961) is worthy of note. See also the discussions of structural concepts in Part Three of this book [*Ed.*].

of faith in the intelligence of the common man and at the same time the belief that the masses are stupid; a belief in democracy and along with this the belief that our country can best be run by an intellectual élite; a belief in freedom for all but at the same time the belief that freedom for certain groups should be restricted; a belief that science makes no value judgements about 'good' and 'bad' but also that scientific criteria are available for distinguishing 'good' theory from 'bad' theory, and 'good' experiment from 'bad' experiment (Rokeach, 1951b).

The disbelief gradient

We have already indicated that in relatively closed systems there is relative isolation between belief and disbelief systems. However, the various disbelief subsystems cannot all be assumed to be equally isolated from the belief system. Rather, degree of isolation can further be conceived as varying with the degree of perceived similarity of the various disbelief subsystems to the belief system. Those disbelief subsystems most similar to the belief system can be represented as regions most adjacent to the belief region and, hence, in relatively greater communication or interaction with the belief system than less similar disbelief subsystems.

Strength of rejection of various disbelief subsystems. The greater the dogmatism the more will the disbelief subsystem most similar to the belief system (factional or 'renegade' subsystems) be perceived as threatening the validity of the belief system and hence the greater the tendency to exert effort designed to reject this subsystem and the adherents thereof. For example, with an increase in dogmatism there will be an increasingly militant rejection of Protestantism by the Catholic, of reformed Judaism by the more conservative Jew, of Trotskyism and Titoism by the Communist, and vice versa. In the academic realm, too, the greater the dogmatism the more antagonism there will be among representatives of divergent views within a single discipline as compared with related disciplines.

Willingness to compromise. Even though a person or group may reject a disbelief system it is often necessary, for the sake of achieving political or religious aims, to form working alliances with other individuals or groups. It is here postulated that such compromising varies inversely with dogmatism: the greater the dogmatism the less compromise there will be with adherents to the disbelief subsystem closest to the belief system.

Relative degrees of differentiation of belief and disbelief systems

In our cognitive representation of dogmatism we have assumed that the greater the dogmatism the more differentiated the belief system will be as compared with the disbelief system. Moreover, various disbelief subsystems have been assumed to become relatively more dedifferentiated with respect to each other the farther away their positions from the belief system. The following postulates are based upon these considerations:

Relative amount of knowledge possessed. The greater the dogmatism the greater the discrepancy between degree of knowledge of facts, events, ideas and interpretations stemming from the belief system and any one of the disbelief subsystems. Thus, for example, with an increase in dogmatism there will be an increasing discrepancy in the Freudian's knowledge of classical psychoanalysis as compared with Adlerian psychology or learning theory.

Juxtaposition of beliefs and disbeliefs. Under special conditions, however, e.g. social or personal conditions which lead to disillusionment with the belief system and thence to conversion wherein beliefs and disbeliefs become juxtaposed, it is conceivable that one of the disbelief subsystems will be more differentiated than the belief system. It is therefore postulated that as a function of the reversal of belief and disbelief systems, the greater the dogmatism the greater the discrepancy between degrees of differentiation of belief and disbelief systems in favor of the latter.

Dedifferentiation within the disbelief system. The greater the dogmatism the more will two or more disbelief subsystems represented as positions relatively far away from the belief system along the disbelief gradient be perceived as 'the same' (e.g. that communism and socialism are the same, that the Democrats and Republicans are both run by Wall Street, etc.).

Relation between central and peripheral parts

We have assumed further that, to the extent we are dealing with closed systems, the central part corresponds to beliefs in and about absolute authority and the peripheral part to beliefs and disbeliefs perceived to emanate from such authority. Thus, the more closed the system the greater the assumed degree of communication between central and peripheral beliefs and, at the same time, the less the assumed degree of communication among the various peripheral beliefs. From these considerations it follows also that any given change in the peripheral part represents an isolated change in cognitive content without concomitant changes either in cognitive structure or in *over-all* ideological content.

It is this interrelation between central and peripheral parts which gives the relatively closed system its integrated and systematic character.[3] Specific peripheral beliefs and disbeliefs are organized together not so much by intrinsic logical connexions as by virtue of their perceived origination with positive and negative authority, respectively. Whatever characterizes the authority's ideology, as represented by the central part, will be mirrored 'gratuitously' in the closed system. If the authority is logical, the closed system will appear logical; if the authority is illogical, the closed system will appear illogical. The more closed the system the more will it reflect *in toto* the authority's own system with its logic or illogic, its *manifest* intellectualism or anti-intellectualism, and so forth.

'*Party-line*' *changes*. It is commonly observed that relatively dogmatic views on specific issues are stubbornly resistant to change by logical argument or objective evidence. One possible reason for this becomes apparent in the light of the preceding considerations. The greater the dogmatism the more will there be a

---

3. This is illustrated very nicely by the following, which we believe is from Sholom Aleichem: 'I did not borrow your pot; besides it was broken when you lent it to me; besides I have already returned it to you.' Despite its illogical character, the statement is nevertheless systematic. While each of the beliefs expressed is contradictory to the others, they all reinforce each other to serve the end of protecting the central authority (in this case, the person speaking) against threat.

change in a given peripheral belief (e.g. about birth control) if it is preceded by a perceived corresponding change by the authority (e.g. the Catholic Church). Moreover, the greater the dogmatism the less will any given change in a peripheral belief effect changes in other peripheral beliefs (e.g. about divorce, federal aid to education, etc.).

Assimilation. Further considerations regarding the relation between central and peripheral parts lead also to the following postulate: the greater the dogmatism the greater the assimilation of facts or events at variance with either the belief or disbelief system by altering or reinterpreting them such that they will no longer be perceived as contradictory.

Narrowing. Assuming, as we have, that the central region is crucial in determining what aspects of reality will be represented within the peripheral region, it follows that it will also be crucial in determining what aspects of reality will *not* be represented (Rokeach, 1951a). The greater the dogmatism the more the avoidance of contact with stimuli – people, events, books, etc. – which threaten the validity of the belief system or which proselyte for competing disbelief systems.

Cognitive narrowing may be manifested at both institutional and noninstitutional levels. At the institutional level, narrowing may be manifested by the publication of lists of taboo books, the removal and burning of dangerous books, the elimination of those regarded as ideological enemies, the omission of news reports in the mass media unfavorable to the belief system or favorable to the disbelief system and the conscious and unconscious rewriting of history (Orwell, 1951).

At the noninstitutional level, narrowing may become apparent from the systematic restriction of one's activities in order to avoid contact with people, books, ideas, social and political events, and other social stimuli which would weaken one's belief system or strengthen part of one's disbelief system. Relevant here are such things as exposing oneself only to one point of view in the press, selectively choosing one's friends and associates solely or primarily on the basis of compatibility of belief systems, selectively avoiding social contact with those adhering to different belief systems and avoiding those who formerly believed as one does.

In academic circles cognitive narrowing over and above that demanded by present day specialization may be manifested by a selective association with one's colleagues and selective subscription, purchase, and reading of journals and books such that one's belief system becomes increasingly differentiated while one's disbelief system becomes increasingly dedifferentiated or 'narrowed out'.

Time perspective

Attitude toward the present. The greater the dogmatism the more will the present be perceived as relatively unimportant in its own right – as but a passageway to some future Utopia. Furthermore, with an increase in dogmatism there will be a concomitant increase in the perception of the present as unjust and as full of human suffering.

Belief in force. Such a disaffected conception of the present can readily lead to the belief that a drastic revision of the present is necessary. Thus, we are also led to the following postulate: the greater the dogmatism the greater the condonement of force.

Knowing the future. Another aspect of time perspective has to do with one's understanding of the future. With an increase in dogmatism there will be the following variations: an increasing confidence in the accuracy of one's understanding of the future, a generally greater readiness to make predictions, and a decreasing confidence in the predictions of the future made by those adhering to disbelief systems.

Postulates Involving the Cognitive Content of Dogmatism

We have already pointed out that while the specific content of beliefs and disbeliefs varies from one system to another, it is nevertheless possible to point to certain uniformities in the formal content of centrally located beliefs which, to the extent that they are part of a closed system, form the cognitive bases for authoritarianism and intolerance.

Authoritarianism

At the center of the belief–disbelief system, to the extent it is closed, is assumed a set of absolute beliefs about positive and negative authority and other closely related beliefs representing attempts by such authority to reinforce and perpetuate itself.

Positive and negative authority. With an increase in dogmatism there will be not only increasing admiration or glorification of those perceived in positions of positive authority but also increasing fear, hatred and vilification of those perceived in positions of authority opposed to positive authority.

The cause. With an increase in dogmatism there will be an increasing strength of belief in a single cause and concomitantly a decreasing tendency to admit the legitimacy of other causes. Manifestations of strength of belief in a single cause might be making verbal references to 'the cause', expressing oneself as 'feeling sorry' for those who do not believe as one does, believing that one should not compromise with one's ideological enemies, perceiving compromise as synonymous with appeasement, believing that one must be constantly on guard against subversion from within or without and believing that it is better to die fighting than to submit.

The élite. With an increase in dogmatism there will be an increase in strength of belief in an élite (political, hereditary, religious or intellectual).

Intolerance

Beliefs in positive and negative authority, the élite and the cause all have to do with authority as such. Coordinated with such beliefs are others representing organizations of people in general according to the authorities they line up with. In this connexion there may be conceived to emerge, with increasing dogmatism, increasingly polarized cognitive distinctions between the faithful and unfaithful, orthodoxy and heresy, loyalty and subversion, Americanism and un-Americanism, and friend and enemy. Those who disagree are to be rejected since they are enemies of God, country, man, the working class, science or art. Those who agree are to be accepted but only as long as and on condition that they continue to do so. This sort of qualified tolerance is, to our mind, only another form of intolerance. That it can turn quickly into a frank intolerance is often seen in the especially harsh attitude taken toward the renegade from the cause.[4]

It is in this way that the problem of acceptance and rejection of people can become linked not only with authoritarianism but also with the acceptance and rejection of ideas. Perhaps the most clear-cut single behavioral manifestation of this linkage is the employment of opinionated language in communicating beliefs and disbeliefs to others. Opinionation is a double-barrelled sort of variable which refers to verbal communications involving acceptance or rejection of beliefs in an absolute manner and, at the same time, acceptance or rejection of others according to whether they agree or disagree with one's beliefs.

Opinionated rejection. This refers to verbal statements which imply absolute rejection of a belief and at the same time rejection of persons who accept it. The following examples illustrate this: 'Only a simple-minded fool would think that . . .,' 'A person must be pretty stupid to think . . .,' 'The idea that . . . is pure hogwash (or poppycock, nonsense, silly, preposterous, absurd, crazy, insane, ridiculous, piddling, etc.).'

The preceding considerations lead us to postulate that opinionated rejection will vary directly with dogmatism.

Opinionated acceptance. This refers to an absolute acceptance of a belief and along with this a qualified acceptance of those who agree with it. Some examples are: 'Any intelligent person knows that. . . .' 'Plain common sense tells you that. . . .'

Opinionated acceptance will also vary directly with dogmatism.

4. We have already discussed the concept of a gradient of disbelief systems. In the present connexion, we might also point to parallel gradients of intolerance and authority.

Some Implications for Further Theory and Research on Authoritarianism and Intolerance

Through the pioneering research of Adorno *et al.* (1950) significant theoretical and empirical advances have been made recently in understanding the phenomena of authoritarianism and intolerance. Since our construct of dogmatism also involves a representation of these phenomena, it is proper to ask: to what extent is the present formulation of the problem of dogmatism consonant with the work on the authoritarian personality?

To be noted first is a historical fact. The research on the authoritarian personality was launched at a time when the problem of Fascism and its attendant anti-Semitism and ethnocentrism was of overriding concern to both social scientist and layman. Given this social setting as a point of departure, it was almost inevitable that the general problem of authoritarianism would become more or less equated with the problems of adherence to fascist ideology and ethnic intolerance. Thus, the personality scale designed to tap underlying predispositions toward authoritarianism was called the F (for Fascism) Scale and was found to correlate substantially with measures of ethnic intolerance.

It is widely recognized, however, that authoritarianism is also manifest among radicals, liberals and middle-of-the-roaders as well as among conservatives and reactionaries. Furthermore, authoritarianism can be recognized as a problem in such areas as science, art, literature, and philosophy, where fascism and ethnocentrism are not necessarily the main issues or may even be totally absent as issues. As pointed out in this paper, dogmatism, which is assumed to involve both authoritarianism and intolerance, need not necessarily take the form of Fascist authoritarianism or ethnic intolerance.

It is thus seen that the total range of phenomena which may properly be regarded as indicative of authoritarianism is considerably broader than that facet of authoritarianism studied so intensively by the authors of *The Authoritarian Personality*. On theoretical grounds, we are in accord with the view that authoritarianism has a greater affinity to leanings to ideologies which are anti-democratic in content. But it need not be conceived as *uniquely* connected with such ideologies. If a theory of authoritarianism is to be a general one, it should also be capable of addressing itself to the fact that to a great extent authoritarianism cuts across specific ideological orientations. As we have tried to suggest, dogmatic authoritarianism may well be observed within the context of any ideological orientation, and in areas of human endeavor relatively removed from the political or religious arena.

One way to test the validity of the above considerations is to demonstrate that scores on the F-Scale are related substantially to measures of dogmatism independently of liberalism–conservatism, or of the kinds of attitudes held toward such groups as Jews and Negroes. The results of one study, already reported (Rokeach, 1952), show that dogmatism and authoritarianism correlate over 0·60 when ethnocentrism or political-economic conservatism is held constant. Corroborative findings from several studies will be presented in a more detailed future report.[5]

Consider further the way the problem of intolerance has been conceived in social-psychological research (Adorno *et al.*, 1950; Jahoda *et al.*, 1951). Parallel to the more or less rough equating of authoritarianism with Fascism, and perhaps for similar reasons, intolerance too can be said to have become more or less equated with one aspect of intolerance, namely, ethnic intolerance. Examination reveals that such concepts as intolerance, discrimination, bigotry, social distance, prejudice, race attitudes and ethnocentrism are all defined operationally in much the same way – by determining how subjects feel or act toward Jews, Negroes, foreigners, and the like.

It is reasonable to assume that there are persons who, although they would validly score low on measures of ethnocentrism or similar scales presently in use, would nevertheless be characteristically intolerant of those whose belief–disbelief systems are at odds with their own.

It has already been suggested that while dogmatic authoritarianism may 'attach' itself to any ideology, it is probably more closely related to those having anti-democratic content. A similar point may well be made in connexion with dogmatic intolerance. Preliminary data already available suggest that measures of dogmatic intolerance (opinionation) and ethnic intolerance are, as

5. See footnote 1 on page 36 [*Ed.*].

expected, related to each other to a significant degree. At the same time they are also found to cut across each other in a relatively independent fashion.

The preceding considerations point to other aspects of man's intolerance to man, in addition to ethnic intolerance, which deserve scientific attention. And, as we have tried to point out in discussing the problem of authoritarianism, here too we think there is a need for a more comprehensive conceptualization of the problem of intolerance.

References

ADORNO, T. W., FRENKEL-BRUNSWIK, E., LEVINSON, D. J., and SANFORD, R. N. (1950), *The Authoritarian Personality*, Harper.

CROSSMAN, R. (1949), *The God That Failed*, Harper.

FRANK, L. K. (1939), 'Time perspectives', *J. soc. Philosoph.*, vol. 4, pp. 293–312.

HOFFER, E. (1951), *The True Believer*, Harper.

JAHODA, M., DEUTSCH, M., and COOK, S. W. (1951), *Research Methods in Social Relations*, Dryden.

KOUNIN, J. (1948), 'The meaning of rigidity: a reply to Hans Werner', *Psychol. Rev.*, vol. 55, pp. 157–66.

KRECH, D. (1949), 'Notes towards a psychological theory', *J. Personal.*, vol. 18, pp. 66–87.

LEWIN, K. (1942), 'Time perspective and morale', in G. Watson (ed.), *Civilian Morale*, Houghton Mifflin.

ORWELL, G. (1951), *Nineteen Eighty-Four*, New American Library. [Penguin edn 1954.]

ROKEACH, M. (1948), 'Generalized mental rigidity as a factor in ethnocentrism', *J. abnorm. soc. Psychol.*, vol. 43, pp. 259–78.

ROKEACH, M. (1951a), 'A method for studying individual differences in "narrow-mindedness" ', *J. Personal.*, vol. 20, pp. 219–33.

ROKEACH, M. (1951b), 'Toward the scientific evaluation of social attitudes and ideologies', *J. Psychol.*, vol. 31, pp. 97–104.

ROKEACH, M. (1952), 'Dogmatism and opinionation on the left and on the right', *Amer. Psychol.*, vol. 7, p. 310 (abstract).

Part Two **Category Usage**

Results of an early investigation into categorizing behaviour led Gardner to conclude that 'persons are characterized by consistent differences in what they will accept as similar or identical in a variety of adaptive tasks' (Gardner, 1953, p. 229). He had been primarily concerned with the way people sort objects into groups, classes or categories, and he suggested that 'equivalence range' was a convenient term to describe the breadth of variety of objects which a person treated as 'the same'.

The first two Readings in Part Two deal with this aspect of judgemental style. Gardner and Schoen's paper develops the notion of equivalence range and suggests as an improved label 'conceptual differentiation'. Conceptual differentiation is mainly studied in free-sorting tasks, and is seen to be consistent across such tasks. This consistency is further delineated by Glixman in Reading 4. One of his conclusions is that the absolute number of categories used to conceptualize a domain varies with the personal relevance of that domain.

The other Readings in Part Two are by Tajfel, Richardson and Everstine and by Pettigrew. These articles also examine category usage, but it is important to recognize a difference in focus from that of the previous two studies. The second focus is upon the limits of categories *along a single dimension* – a dimension which is provided by the investigator. This contrasts with studies of conceptual differentiation, where dimensions-of-judgement are not specified and where the subject imposes his own organization upon the stimulus array. In a sense the object-sorting tasks used by Gardner and Schoen and by Glixman yield measures of how many dimensions a subject uses, whereas the procedures of Tajfel and of Pettigrew indicate instead how he uses a single dimension. Category usage of this second type – along a single dimension – is usually referred to in terms of 'band width' or 'category width'.

Just as we need to be alert to differences of definition in this field, so also must the measurement procedures be scrutinized for comparability. Even within studies of conceptual differentiation, responses to object-sorting tasks may be scored in different ways. Gardner and Schoen derive scores from the *reasons* given by subjects for their grouping, whilst Glixman uses as his index the actual number of groups generated. It has been suggested by Messick and Kogan (1963) that there may be occasions in research into free sorting when the total number of elicited groups should be divided into two separate scores – the number of categories of two or more objects and the number of miscellaneous objects left ungrouped. (Note however that many studies in practice involve only the former class.) In a similar fashion, studies which are more concerned with band width than with conceptual differentiation can generate different types of score. Tajfel, Richardson and Everstine are largely interested in whether or not a stimulus is judged as a member of the stipulated category, whereas Pettigrew's index is a more direct estimate of the over-all breadth of the several categories being studied.

References

GARDNER, R. W. (1953), 'Cognitive styles in categorizing behavior', *J. Personal.*, vol. 22, pp. 214–33.

MESSICK, S., and KOGAN, N. (1963), 'Differentiation and compartmentalization in object-sorting measures of categorizing style', *Percept. mot. Skills*, vol. 16, pp. 47–51.

3 Riley W. Gardner and Robert A. Schoen

Differentiation and Abstraction in Concept Formation

Excerpts from Riley W. Gardner and Robert A. Schoen, 'Differentiation and abstraction in concept formation', *Psychological Monographs*, vol. 76, 1962, no. 41 (whole no. 560).

The studies described in this report were performed to explore relations between a dimensional principle of cognitive control called conceptual differentiation and a number of other aspects of concept formation in which individuals are known to differ widely. Gardner *et al*. (1959, p. 145) have suggested that the enduring strategies or 'programs' of cognitive functioning that emerge during development represent ever-increasing control over action. The individual's position on the dimension of control called conceptual differentiation is presumably but one of the enduring characteristics of his concept formation that together comprise an over-all style of regulation of motive expression through concept formation. The fact that concept formation can be conceived of as a basic attribute of thought which finds expression in a great range of behavior (Rapaport, Gill and Schafer, 1945) in itself points to the complexity of the behavioral structures relevant to it. In view of this complexity, the present studies were in part designed to integrate findings concerning conceptual differentiation and abstraction with findings concerning individual differences in concept formation reported by a number of investigators, including Kelly (1955) and Rokeach (1951a and b). The general assumption underlying these studies was that human concept formation will be adequately understood only when effective laws are formulated for both the general phenomena of concept formation and the organization of relevant cognitive structures in the individual.

Earlier Studies of Conceptual Differentiation

Studies of the degree of differentiation spontaneously imposed upon heterogeneous arrays of objects and events under the requirement to categorize them (Clayton and Jackson, 1961; Dickman, 1954; Gardner, 1953; Gardner and Long, 1961; Gardner, Jackson and Messick, 1960; Gardner *et al.*, 1959; Marrs, 1955; Sloane, 1959) have suggested that individuals differ consistently in this aspect of concept formation; that these individual consistencies persist over time; that the consistencies are most apparent when categorizing occurs under relatively 'free' conditions; and that the consistencies are largely independent of the level of abstraction at which the person chooses to function.

Gardner (1953) originally described individual consistencies in conceptual differentiation as a dimension of 'equivalence range' dispositions. At the extremes of the dimension, people divided a heterogeneous array of objects into as many as thirty groups, each including a limited realm of items, or as few as four groups, each including a much larger realm of items. In this first study, persons high in conceptual differentiation (i.e. persons of 'narrow equivalence range') seemed to show their realm-limiting tendency in more accurate retinal and object matches in size-constancy tests following preparatory explanation and demonstration of retinal matching.[1] It appeared that these subjects (*S*s) were accurate by virtue of imposing severe limitations on the categories 'retinal' and 'actual', following the demonstration period. This result was confirmed only for women, however, in a further study (Gardner *et al.*, 1959) in which the equivalence range dimension was conceived as one of a larger group of cognitive control principles. A subsequent study (Gardner, Jackson and Messick, 1960) provided evidence that another independent principle of cognitive control, relevant to the selectiveness of attention deployment (in this case, to either of the two simultaneous aspects of size experience), is also a determinant of response to such constancy tests. Using a score for the Concealed Figures Test (which Gardner, Jackson and Messick, 1960, have shown to be correlated with, and factorially similar to, scores for Witkin's Embedded-Figures and Rod-and-Frame Tests), Baggaley (1955) provided evidence that this second principle of cognitive control (originally called field dependence–independence by Witkin *et al.*, 1954) is a significant determinant of concept attainment when

1. Sloane (1959) included constancy tests in his study but did not replicate key aspects of the preliminary demonstration.

attainment requires selective attention to relevant features of stimuli in the face of compelling irrelevant features. Thus, at least two independent cognitive control principles are relevant to independent aspects of concept formation. These results are in close agreement with the description of control principles by Gardner *et al.* (1959) as dimensions of individual difference in cognitive structures that mediate the expression of particular intentions when the person is confronted with particular classes of stimulus conditions.

Studies by Marrs (1955) and Sloane (1959), both of whom employed Gardner's original Object Sorting Test (OST), have made it clear that the dimensional principle of cognitive control referred to here as conceptual differentiation is demonstrable in a wide variety of categorizing procedures (e.g. procedures in which *S* is required to sort objects, pictures of people, Chinese characters, etc.). A study by Clayton and Jackson (1961) suggests that low conceptual differentiation (broad equivalence range) may be associated with overgeneralization. Clayton and Jackson devised paper-and-pencil, object-sorting tests that appear to provide criterion scores comparable to those for Gardner's OST. In Sloane's (1959) study, both correlations and relative factor loadings for the number of groups formed in Gardner's OST and in these paper-and-pencil tests seemed to support this interpretation. The present authors contend, however, following Gardner (1953), that accepting *S*'s groupings without requiring definitions of them (as did Clayton and Jackson and Sloane) leads to gross errors in scoring the number of groups *S* conceptualized. In addition to providing valuable information concerning the level of abstraction at which *S* is functioning, the formation of groups with distinct subdivisions, etc., the requirement to define each group not infrequently reveals that *S* has formed a 'wastebasket group' of 'things that don't belong with anything else'. Following the logic of the original scoring scheme, each item in such a collection is appropriately scored as a separate 'group'.

In a study by Gardner, Jackson and Messick (1960), responses to the original OST were scored not only in terms of the conceptual differentiation indicated by the numbers of groups into which *S*s divided the seventy-three objects, but also in terms of the level of abstraction represented by their definitions. Interestingly enough, spontaneous differentiation and abstraction were not significantly associated in this test, nor was either significantly associated with the various intellectual ability scores included in the study, even though two scores represented each of the abilities called 'induction' and 'deduction'. The obvious conclusion to be drawn from the study is that concept formation and the cognitive control principles involved in the individual's style of concept formation are more complex than has ordinarily been assumed.

In a recent study of the stability of cognitive controls over a three-year period, Gardner and Long (1961) found an r of 0.75 for the number of groups formed in Gardner's OST.

Purposes of the Present Studies

After considering all the earlier findings concerning equivalence range and after examining the recent concept formation literature for closely related approaches, the present authors undertook the series of further studies of differentiation and abstraction in concept formation described in the present report. These studies were designed to serve the following specific purposes: (a) exploration of the situational generality of individual consistencies in conceptual differentiation; (b) exploration of the relations of conceptual differentiation to effective level of abstraction (i.e. the level of abstraction on which S *chooses* to function when allowed to decide for himself) and capacity for abstraction; and (c) exploration of the relations of spontaneous conceptual differentiation and abstraction to individual differences in concept formation reported by a number of other investigators. The second of these major purposes may have the most important implications for our understanding of the essential nature of concept formation and the organizing principles involved in individual styles of concept formation. The theoretical considerations summarized in the sections immediately below served as a basis for the design of the three studies reported here.

Conceptual Differentiation in Free-Sorting Tests

For several reasons, the term equivalence range used earlier seems inadequate to describe the number of groups Ss form in the free-sorting tests that have provided criterion scores. Much more than conceptual *span* (i.e. realm size) is involved in grouping items 'in the way that seems most logical, most natural and most comfortable' (from the instructions for the original OST). In contrast to category-width tests,[2] in which each item assesses the limits of one conceptual realm, free-sorting tests require the spontaneous differentiation of heterogeneous items into a *complex* of more or less related groups. The size of the realm of items *S* includes in any group may be as much a product as a source of the more complex level of conceptual behavior referred to here as 'conceptual differentiation'. Although it was anticipated that the number of groups formed in free-sorting tests would be significantly associated with category width in tests in which each item is a separate subtest assessing the size of a single conceptual realm, the overlap between the two types of responses is obviously only partial.

Conceptualization of responses to free-sorting tests primarily in terms of spontaneous conceptual differentiation, and only secondarily in terms of equivalence range or category width, also raises intriguing questions concerning the rationale of disparate performances. Observation and inquiry in the original study (Gardner, 1953) suggested that *S*s who formed many groups were not different from *S*s who formed few groups in ability to recognize differences, but were more difference oriented, i.e. were more impelled to group in terms of differences. Is this all the formation of many groups implies? Is the person who shows a high degree of conceptual differentiation simply more difference oriented or is he, in a much more general sense, unusually responsive to questions concerning similarity–difference? In one set of operational terms, would he also show evidence of greater conceptual differentiation if asked to state the *similarity* between disparate items, as in Rokeach's (1951a) Narrow-Mindedness Test (N-MT)? Rokeach required *S*s to define ten terms, then state the relationship among these. Rokeach's scores for these statements – 'comprehensive', 'narrow' and 'isolated' – represent three degrees of conformance to the second test requirement. The test seems obviously to involve *S*'s capacity for abstraction. But conceptual differentiation – here assumed to be logically independent of

2. See Reading 6 [*Ed.*].

abstraction – could also be a determinant of response. Under the instruction to define the *relationship* among all the items, an *S* high in conceptual differentiation may offer a 'comprehensive' definition, indicating that his tendency to emphasize differences in free-sorting tests is but one aspect of a cognitive control principle combining analysis and synthesis of similarity–difference relationships. Whether or not individual consistencies in conceptual differentiation primarily reflect degrees of emphasis upon differences, the term adopted here seems clearly more adequate to represent the relational quality of complex categorizing and its correlates than does the earlier term, equivalence range.

This discussion above is predicated on the assumption that spontaneous conceptual differentiation, preferred level of abstraction, and capacity for abstraction are distinguishable dimensions of concept formation. It is obvious, of course, that this hypothetical distinction may be obliterated under special conditions, e.g. when grouping *requires* true abstraction.

Conceptual Differentiation and Level of Abstraction

A vast literature on human 'concept attainment' (capacity to abstract) is capped by two recent reports: the delineation of strategies of concept attainment by Bruner, Goodnow and Austin (1956) and the discussion by Piaget and Inhelder (1959) of two essential, interacting components in the development of effective concept formation – comprehension and extension (comparable to abstraction and realm delineation). Relatively little attention has been paid to certain other aspects of concept formation that seem to demand formulation (see Gardner, Jackson and Messick, 1960) and that may not be subsumed under the general rubric, 'abstraction'. The studies of conceptual differentiation originally described in terms of equivalence range lead us to differ sharply, for example, with Harvey, Hunt and Schroder (1961), who seem to assume that capacity to abstract is a *unitary* phenomenon of vast generality in the determination of cognitive behaviors.[3] The series of studies described in this report was, in

3. These authors would probably disagree with such a statement of their current position. Abstract functioning is considered to be general across domains only in so far as these are linked by similar degrees of perceived

fact, stimulated principally by prior evidence suggesting that capacity to abstract, although of undoubted importance to the individual's concept formation, is in many situations not the primary determinant of concept formation, nor even of the level of abstraction at which the person actually functions. The apparent independence of conceptual differentiation from preferred level of abstraction (as distinguished from capacity to abstract) in earlier studies in itself points to a critical and hitherto largely unexplored area of concept formation.

Conceptual Differentiation and Category Width

Wallach and Caron (1959) and Bruner and Tajfel (1961) suggest that category width, equivalence range, etc., are basically matters of attitudes toward risk taking, to which Bruner and Tajfel add 'sensitivity to change'. Their recent study purportedly shows that *S*s of narrow category width are more responsive to change in sequentially presented patterns of stimuli, whether the change leads to broadening or narrowing of the category in question.

The present authors neither believe that these arguments capture the essence of category width nor that Bruner and Tajfel's study provides clear evidence that category width is associated with sensitivity to change or risk-taking attitudes. In contrast to Pettigrew (1958) and Fillenbaum (1959), whose category-width tests explicitly elicit responses indicating *S*s' category widths, Bruner and Tajfel (1961) used a criterion score 'defined as the proportion of stimuli assigned by a subject to the inclusion category 20 in Phases I, II and III' (p. 233) of a test in which clusters of twenty to thirty dots were projected for 0·5 second per cluster. The *S* said Yes, if he thought there were twenty dots in each cluster, and No, if he did not. This procedure does not control the well-known tendency of response sets toward agreement to contaminate (if not dominate) scores for such tests. In addition, a number of the tests of sensitivity to change reported by Bruner and Tajfel are based on relationships between scores that bear *artifactual* relations to each other, e.g. a rho of −0·433 is reported

---

importance or involvement. This point is discussed by Harvey in Reading 17. Scott's comments (in the final part of Reading 7) are also of interest in this respect [*Ed.*].

between 'breadth of category in Phase I and the shift from Phase I to Phase II in the per cent of calls of 20' (p. 233)![4] Bruner and Tajfel also report a highly significant relationship between initial breadth of category and I.Q. The correlations they found may actually, however, indicate a negative relationship between response set for agreement and I.Q. Their attempts to partial out I.Q. involve combinations of the artifacts referred to above. The ambiguity of these results does not necessarily mean, of course, that there is no association between category width and sensitivity to change or risk taking. The hypothesis has simply not been tested effectively.[5]

A further distinction can be drawn between conceptual differentiation in free-sorting tests and more appropriate tests of category width. In the latter case, assessment is performed by asking *S* to define, directly or indirectly, the limits of a category along a single dimension. Here again, we would point to the only partial overlap with the more complex process of dividing disparate objects and events into groups, each of which represents a *different* 'basis of pertinence' (Bolles, 1937). In the latter procedure, *S* is free to select reasons for grouping from an all but infinite variety of possible reasons. And the division of heterogeneous items into groups involves not only definition of boundaries for a variety of categories but a pattern of relationship among the categories.

Pettigrew (1958) has pointed out that some of the items in his category-width test seem to bring out skill and personal orientation in respect to quantitative concepts. Although it is more true of some items than others, it seems to us that all such category-width items require *S* to respond in terms of quantitative conceptions. In our view, the specific demand for quantitative thinking, rather than '*conceptual* [italics added] conservatism', could account for the 'sex' difference Wallach and Caron (1959) have observed in response to category-width tests. Girls may only

4. See Lacey (1956) on the indefensibility of this type of 'change' score.
5. Further discussion of these criticisms can be found in *Journal of Personality and Social Psychology*, vol. 2 (1965), pp. 261–8. Bruner and Tajfel's comments on the opinions presented here are followed by a reply from Gardner and Schoen, which is succeeded in turn by Bruner and Tajfel's rejoinder [*Ed.*].

appear to have narrower (i.e. more 'conservative') category widths than boys. In actuality, they may simply be showing their well-known, apparently socially conditioned, inhibitions in respect to quantitative thinking.

Pettigrew (1958) has reported that category width in his test is associated with the number of adjectives checked as true of oneself in Gough's Adjective Check List (ACL). His result suggests a link between specific categories of limited realm size and extremely broad categories with very heterogeneous contents. Like other tests in which S responds by agreeing or disagreeing, however, the effects of response sets must be evaluated before the meaning of such scores as the number of items checked in an adjective check list can be stated unequivocally. The present study provided an opportunity to assess relations between conceptual differentiation, category width, and response set in performance on Gough's ACL and a variety of other check lists.

Consideration of relations between conceptual differentiation and category width raises the question of links to studies of overinclusiveness in categorizing by persons diagnosed as 'schizophrenic', and underinclusiveness in categorizing by brain-damaged persons (see, e.g. Cameron, 1938a and b, 1939a and b; Chapman, 1961; Chapman and Taylor, 1957; Epstein, 1953; Friedman, 1961; Goldstein and Scheerer, 1941; Lovibond, 1954; Zaslow, 1961).[6] Scoring of OST sortings and definitions by large groups of normal Ss makes it clear, however, that inappropriate overinclusiveness does not account for the groupings of Ss low in conceptual differentiation, nor can inappropriate underexclusiveness of the kind observed in brain-damaged persons account for the groupings of Ss high in conceptual differentiation. The nature of groups and definitions and the relationship of conceptual differentiation and category width to abstraction appear to be different in normal, schizophrenic and brain-damaged populations. Tests of conceptual differentiation have proved useful, however, in the study of these broad classes of disorder (see, e.g. Goldstein and Scheerer, 1941; Halstead, 1947; Lovibond, 1954; McGaughran and Moran, 1956; Rapaport, Gill and Schafer, 1945).

6. See also Reading 24 [Ed.].

Conceptual Differentiation and 'Cognitive Complexity'

Conceptual differentiation in categorizing can be conceived of as an aspect of cognitive complexity. It is therefore necessary to consider relations between this dimension of individual consistencies and that inferred from responses to the role construct repertory tests developed on the basis of Kelly's (1955) work and used by a number of investigators to assess cognitive 'complexity–simplicity' (see, e.g. Bieri, 1955; Bieri and Blacker, 1956a and b; Bieri and Messerley, 1957; Dopp, 1960; Leventhal, McGaughran and Moran, 1959; Lundy and Berkowitz, 1957).[7] Kelly (1955) emphasizes the importance of contrast in concept formation. Persons of great 'cognitive complexity' presumably make more, and more complex, distinctions between persons and events. The items of the Role Construct Repertory Tests, which are said to measure cognitive complexity, consist of triads of persons. The S is required to state the likeness between any two persons and how the third differs from them. If S responds to twenty such items, the number of different constructs he employs is said to indicate his cognitive complexity. Granting that this may be true in a limited sense, the present authors are impressed with the fact that such tests measure complexity indirectly, as compared to a free-sorting test in which S is required to group all items simultaneously and may actually measure some form of ideational fluency, rather than the assumed inherent complexity of cognition. In these tests, S is not required to deal with all the person elements at one time, and nothing in the instruction impels him to use different constructs as he progresses through the triads. A person with highly differentiated conceptions of similarities and differences could, therefore, select a few key attributes as the most essential ones and use these repeatedly, thereby limiting the number of distinct constructs and revealing nothing of his true conceptual complexity. An S of equal complexity who adopted a different set could use many constructs. The ineffectiveness with which such tests sample 'complexity' could lead to description of these two hypothetical Ss as opposite, rather than identical, in cognitive complexity. In addition, the term cognitive complexity seems grossly overgeneral. There is ample evidence (see, e.g.

7. See also Reading 8 [*Ed.*].

Gardner *et al.*, 1959, on the variety of cognitive controls and intellectual abilities) that most persons are relatively 'complex' in some areas of cognition, relatively 'simple' in others.[8] No single principle can be expected to account for cognitive complexity–simplicity.

Grid forms of repertory tests (in which S is required to check all members of an array of persons who could fit the category S defines by selecting two members of a triad as similar) may, by tapping the breadth of the conceptual realm to some degree, provide scores that are related to conceptual differentiation as defined in the present report (see Dopp, 1960). The meaning of the number of distinct constructs S uses in such tests remains ambiguous, however, and may not be related to conceptual differentiation.

Study I

The initial study was performed primarily to test the hypotheses that *conceptual differentiation*, as defined by the number of groups formed in the criterion OST, is a determinant of the number of groups formed in a Behavior Sorting Test (BST) and a Photo Sorting Test (PST), and of category width in tests developed by Pettigrew (1958) and Higgins (1961). It was also hypothesized that Ss show consistent differences in the level of abstraction at which they function in the three sorting tests, and that this level of abstraction is correlated with number-of-groups scores for these tests as a function of their difficulty, i.e. that level of abstraction is uncorrelated with the number of groups formed in the easy OST, correlated somewhat more with the number in the more difficult BST, and correlated still more with the number in the difficult PST.

Rokeach's (1951a and b) N-MT, two variations of Kelly's (1955) Role Construct Repertory Test, and check lists developed by Tresselt and Mayzner (1958) and Gough (1960) were included for exploratory purposes. As discussed earlier, it seemed possible that both conceptual differentiation and level of abstraction are determinants of the 'cognitive organization' score for N-MT and the number of distinct constructs produced in role construct repertory tests, and that Ss high in conceptual differentiation

8. See footnote 3 on page 60 [*Ed.*].

check few items in adjective check lists as characteristic of a person or a concept. Pettigrew's (1958) finding of a relationship between category width in his test, number of adjectives checked in the Gough ACL, and the comprehensiveness of definitions in Rokeach's N-MT led to the tentative prediction of similar findings in the present study.

Method

Subjects. The total sample consisted of seventy women aged sixteen to forty-four, with a mean age of 24·2. Twenty-eight were members of Protestant church clubs and forty-two were business college students. All *S*s were paid $1 per hour. Twelve procedures were administered in the same order to groups of twenty-eight and forty-two *S*s in two 2·5-hour sessions separated by a three-day interval.

Sorting tests: 1. Object Sorting Test (OST). A criterion measure of conceptual differentiation was obtained from one of the fifty-item paper-and-pencil forms of Gardner's (1953) OST developed by Clayton and Jackson (1961). In contrast to Clayton and Jackson (1961) and Sloane (1959), who did not require *S*s to give their reasons for including objects in each group, the present authors required *S*s, following their grouping, to define each group. As in the original study by Gardner (1953), these definitions served as the basis for determining the number of groups conceptualized. Some examples may elucidate the use of definitions in determining the number of groups. If *S* gave two reasons, such as 'sporting goods and entertainment', for example, the decision to score one or two groups depended on the scorer's evaluation of the degree of overlap of the two realms. If all the items grouped could be conceptualized under both rubrics, one group was scored. If there was a clear line of demarcation between 'sporting goods' and objects relevant to 'entertainment', two groups were scored. A more typical example is 'tools – some for children and some for adults', clearly indicating subcategorization and scored as two groups. When *S* formed pseudo groups, e.g. 'things left over', each object was scored as a separate group.

Each definition (i.e. the reason *S* gave for any grouping of two or more objects) was scored concrete (C), functional (FD) or conceptual (CD), according to the scoring scheme provided by Rapaport, Gill and Schafer (1945). The abstraction score used was

$$\frac{CD}{CD+FD+C}.$$

The CD score was reserved for true abstraction, i.e. a definition based on a common attribute of objects with disparate other properties. The FD score was given to two types of definitions, exemplified by 'they are all used to make things' and 'they can all be played with'. The C score was given most frequently to definitions of location (e.g. 'all in a kitchen'); of belongingness (e.g. 'all belong to a child'); and of simple association (e.g. 'all have to do with smoking').

2. Behavior Sorting Test (BST). The Ss were required to categorize fifty phrases describing behavior (e.g. graduating from high school, chewing gum, running for president) by assigning the same number to the phrases forming each group. Subsequently, they were required to define each group. The instructions and scoring procedures were as identical as possible to those for OST.

3. Photo Sorting Test (PST). The Ss were required to categorize fifty-three numbered pictures of people (black and white or colored magazine cutouts representing varied age, race, dress, activity, etc.) affixed to a large white cardboard background. The Ss indicated their groupings by writing down the numbers of the pictures forming groups. Subsequently, they were required to define each group. The instructions were as identical as possible to those for OST and BST. Since this test all but forces grouping on the basis of abstract definitions, only the number of groups, defined in the same manner as for OST and BST, was used in the correlational and factor analytic portions of these studies.

'Narrow-Mindedness' Test (N-MT). In this test (Rokeach, 1951a and b), Ss are required to define each of ten terms (Buddhism, Capitalism, Catholicism, Christianity, Communism, Democracy, Fascism, Judaism, Protestantism and Socialism), then to write a paragraph stating how all the terms are interrelated. Following Rokeach (1951a, pp. 222–6), these cognitive organization scores

were obtained: *narrow*, if 'one or more of the objectively present parts' was 'clearly missing from the S's organization'; *isolated*, if S's response indicated 'something less than a complete integration of all ten concepts', so that 'all the parts . . . are phenomenologically present but . . . broken down into two or more substructures which are relatively isolated from each other'; *comprehensive*, if the written paragraph indicated that S's interrelating of the items was 'broad and integrated'; that is, if all ten concepts were included and the relationship between all of them was specified. Scores of 1, 2 and 3 were assigned to these types of response to provide a quantitative score for each S. A score of 3 indicated an effective integration of the ten terms; i.e. an adequate 'comprehensive' definition.

Category-width tests: 1. Category-Width Scale (C-WS). Pettigrew's (1958) test consists of twenty multiple-choice items in each of which an average value is stated (e.g. the average width of windows). The Ss are required to indicate their choice of one of the four upper and one of the four lower extremes listed. Pettigrew assigned the values 0, 1, 2, 3, to the four degrees of discrepancy from the mean. The total score is the sum of the forty values for the twenty items. Pettigrew also factor analysed item scores. Factor 2, with high loadings on items requiring direct, rather than indirect judgements seemed most relevant to conceptual differentiation. Factor 2 scores were computed in the present study by multiplying S's score for each item by its loading on Factor 2 in Pettigrew's study and summing these values.

2. Social Comprehension Questionnaire (SCQ). Higgins (1961) employed thirty-two probability statements about everyday events to sample an aspect of category width apparently related to that sampled by Pettigrew's C-WS. Items were of the following form: 'The chances that an adult American will earn at least $4000 a year are about — in 100.' The S's score for each item was the absolute difference between his estimate and the closer extreme, 0 or 100. The mean of the thirty-two values was S's mean probability estimate. The S was also required to indicate confidence in each judgement on a five-point scale. The S's 'mean confidence rating' was used to obtain the second score suggested by Higgins: mean probability preference. To obtain this score,

Higgins multiplied each S's mean probability estimate by his mean confidence rating for each item, then summed and averaged the products. Higgins interpreted high probability-estimate or probability-preference values as indicating moderate probability judgements (in Pettigrew's terms, narrow category width).

Role Construct Repertory Tests: 1. Person Perception, Form A (PP-A). Higgins (1961) also developed a modification of Kelly's (1955) Role Construct Repertory Test, Group Form, in which Ss are presented with all twenty possible triads of six concepts (Science, Business, Religion, Politics, the Arts, Social Service). Our modification of Higgins' procedure, administered to the twenty-eight church club members, involved triads of persons (Self, Your Mother, Your Father, Friend, Admired Person, Disliked Person). In each item, S was first required to state how any two persons were similar but different from the third and then to state the opposite of this characteristic. Following Higgins, each S's protocol was scored for the number of distinct constructs in his twenty triadic judgements. A stringent criterion was used in scoring the number of distinct constructs: both poles of a construct had to be unlike any other similarity or opposite in the protocol.

2. Person Perception, Form B (PP-B). Preliminary analysis indicated essentially no relationship between the criterion measure of conceptual differentiation and the number of distinct concepts produced with Form A. Form B was constructed to explore the possibility that a relationship would be apparent if relatively 'neutral' concepts (Sculptor, Aviator, Professor, Surgeon, Inventor, Lawyer) were employed. In other respects, this test was identical with Form A. It was administered to the forty-two business college students. The number of distinct constructs was scored by the same stringent criterion.

Check lists: 1. Word-Concept Check List (W-CCL). In a recent study, Tresselt and Mayzner (1958) listed seventy-eight words infrequently checked as belonging to any of the six concepts sampled by the Allport–Vernon–Lindzey Study of Values. Our Ss were asked to check the concepts to which each of the seventy-eight words applied. Pearson rs among the numbers of words checked for the six concepts ranged from 0·13 to 0·82. The score used was the total number of words checked.

2. Adjective Check List, Self (ACL, Self). Gough's 300-word check list was employed for these self-evaluations. The score used was the number of adjectives checked.

3. Adjective Check List, Heroine (ACL, Heroine). The Ss were required to check the adjectives in Gough's list which they felt applied to the young mother in an eight-minute portion of a sound film entitled *Angry Boy*. The score used was the number of adjectives checked.

4. Adjective Check List, Others (ACL, Others). The Ss were required to check the adjectives in a 110-word list (104 from Gough's list, plus dishonest, discourteous, hardworking, impractical, neat, and sad) applicable to (a) Your Mother, (b) Your Father, (c) Diplomat and (d) Bullfighter. Pearson rs between the numbers of adjectives checked in these four subtests ranged from 0·61 to 0·87. The score used was the total number of adjectives checked.

Results

In view of the theoretical importance of relations between conceptual differentiation and level of abstraction in the three sorting tests, a preliminary analysis was done of the percentages of definitions in OST, BST and PST at the three levels of abstraction – concrete, functional and conceptual. The results clearly showed the anticipated progression in the level of abstraction required for grouping in the three tests.[9] In OST, S can form groups at any level of abstraction; concrete responses predominate. In BST, functional definitions are all but impossible; the percentage of conceptual definitions increases notably over that for the OST. In PST, grouping all but requires some form of abstraction; both concrete and functional definitions are rare. Inspection of PST definitions indicated that many were abstractions of a relatively low order. The rare concrete definitions were predominantly definitions of location implying a concrete visual image or definitions implying that the objects of a group all 'have to do with' such activities as sports, entertainment, etc.

9. Data are presented in the original article to support this assertion [*Ed.*].

Table 1 contains the intercorrelations among the sixteen scores of Study I. These results tend to confirm the hypothesis that OST, BST and PST sample conceptual differentiation, that Ss tend to be consistent in level of abstraction in the first two of these tests, and that this level of abstraction affects grouping in OST and BST in the predicted order. Correlations between the number-of-groups scores (0·46 to 0·67) remain significant, however, in spite of the variations in level of abstraction required by the three tests.

The rs between the organization score for the N-MT and the number of groups in OST, BST and PST are not significant, although consistent in direction. Level of abstraction in the OST and BST seems unrelated to the organization score.

All rs between the number of groups scores for OST, BST and PST and scores for Pettigrew's C-WS are in the predicted direction, but only one is significant. Similar consistent relationships are not present, however, between the number-of-groups scores and category width in Higgins' Social Comprehension Questionnaire.

The anticipated relationship of Pettigrew's category-width scores to the mean probability estimate from Higgins' category-width test (SCQ) clearly does not obtain. In addition, Pettigrew's (1958) findings that Ss with broad categories in his test check more adjectives in Gough's ACL and give comprehensive definitions in Rokeach's N-MT are not confirmed. In the latter case, the rs suggest that broad categories in Pettigrew's procedure are associated with narrow and isolated, rather than comprehensive definitions.

The number of distinct constructs used in PP tests is not systematically related to conceptual differentiation, abstraction, or any of the other variables included in Study I, with the possible exception of the organization score for N-MT. The r of -0.45, $p < 0.05$, between the number of constructs for PP-A and the organization score is based on only 28 Ss, however, and the r for PP-B, $N = 42$, is only -0.15.

A largely independent cluster of highly significant relationships is evident among the number of items checked in the different adjective check lists. The W-CCL score seems to involve independent determinants.

Table 1

Intercorrelations of Major Scores from Study I*

Score	1	2	3	4	5	6	7	8	9	10	11	12	13	14	15
1. OST, Number of groups															
2. OST, Abstraction	−02														
3. BST, Number of groups	67	−15													
4. BST, Abstraction	−13	43	−36												
5. PST, Number of groups	46	−29	55	−30											
6. N-MT, Organization	18	06	10	−02	08										
7. C-WS, Total	−19	14	−18	03	−12	−19									
8. C-WS, Factor 2	−22	12	−23	07	−17	−23	90								
9. SCQ, Estimate	21	21	15	01	−11	−11	05	07							
10. SCQ, Preference	10	23	06	16	−22	−12	02	07	68						
11. PP-A, Number of constructs	13	26	09	09	−05	−45	17	02	23	−09					
12. PP-B, Number of constructs	−05	−10	−09	−14	16	−15	06	−03	−26	−09	—				
13. W-CCL, Number checked	−20	−01	−23	04	−09	05	14	19	−22	−16	13	23			
14. ACL, Self, Number checked	05	07	18	−02	11	−01	01	−01	06	−12	−02	09	09		
15. ACL, Heroine, Number checked	−06	07	07	00	−02	−01	−05	−09	02	−11	13	25	24	69	
16. ACL, Others, Number checked	03	−07	20	−21	12	02	−09	−15	01	−24	22	04	22	71	75

* $N = 70$ except for PP-A for which $N = 28$, and PP-B for which $N = 42$. For $N = 70$: $0·23 = p < 0·05$; $0·30 =$

Discussion of Study I results

Individual consistencies in the spontaneous conceptual differentiation imposed upon heterogeneous stimuli are evident in response to OST, BST and PST. The variations in content characterizing these three tests is notable. Conceptual differentiation and preferred level of abstraction appear to be distinctly different variables, even though both are determinants of response in difficult sorting tests. Knowledge of conceptual differentiation does not allow prediction, however, of the number of adjectives checked in the check lists, which Pettigrew (1958) considered concept-span or realm-width tests assessing the range of attributes S will attribute to a single person-category.

The fact that an independent syndrome of high correlations links three of the check list performances has important implications for the usefulness of such procedures for evaluations of personality. The diversity of the concepts involved (Self, Heroine of Movie, Mother, Father, Bullfighter, Diplomat) suggests that response sets present a severe impediment to interpretation of check list performances whether the person using the check list evaluates himself or another person (cf. Gough, 1960). Response sets in respect to agreement (see e.g., Couch and Keniston, 1960), the social desirability of certain items (see e.g., Edwards, 1957), or degrees of awareness that any trait may characterize any individual in some way or at some time are among the possible interpretations of these striking individual consistencies.

The lack of a systematic relationship between 'cognitive complexity' (Bieri, 1955) in PP tests and either conceptual differentiation or effective level of abstraction is worthy of special attention. The spontaneous differentiation Ss imposed in categorizing the items of OST, BST and PST can also be thought of as representing cognitive complexity. As noted earlier, whether or not S offers the same or different constructs in progressing through the triads may depend as much on a form of ideational fluency as on 'cognitive complexity'. An unpublished study by Dopp (1960) may point to a relationship between conceptual differentiation and the number of checks in *grid* forms of such tests, in which S is asked how many of the additional roles or persons his triad concepts could be applied to. But the number of checks is quite different from the number of distinct constructs.

Harvey, Hunt and Schroder (1961, pp. 257–8) have suggested that the number of distinct constructs produced in Role Construct Repertory Tests based on Kelly's (1955) work may reflect a general syndrome of behaviors they have defined as 'abstraction'. The present results cast doubt both upon their specific hypothesis and upon their core assumption that the wide variety of behaviors they describe as abstraction are referable to a single, generic aspect of cognitive functioning.

Study II

The results of Study I served as a basis for more refined predictions concerning the effects of conceptual differentiation on performance in a wider variety of situations. The general hypothesis, based on Study I results, was that three distinct factors – conceptual differentiation, effective level of abstraction, and number checked in adjective check lists – would be demonstrable in responses to selected Study I scores, plus a representative sample of new scores obtained from additional procedures. It was hypothesized that the number of groups Ss form in the sorting tests *is* related to the number of groups formed in categorizing the adjectives of a check list and to the number of different rating values used when Ss are required to rate the *degree* of relevance of each adjective to a person or concept, rather than simply to check relevant items. Fillenbaum's (1959) Self Sorting Test (SST), plus appropriate modifications of Study I Adjective Check Lists, were used to test the latter hypothesis. A Free Association Test (FAT) was included in an attempt to confirm the earlier finding (Gardner *et al.*, 1959) that associations of Ss high in conceptual differentiation remain 'close' to the meaning of the stimulus words. The Ss were also required to write a story to Card 18BM of TAT. These stories were ranked in terms of the degree to which S 'moved away' from the concrete physical properties of the picture. The hypothesis was that the stories of Ss high in conceptual differentiation would show relatively little departure from the 'category' defined by the picture. A new procedure was designed to test the hypothesis that conceptual differentiation is apparent in the difference between S's drawings of a square and a rectangle.

Study II also provided an opportunity to include, for exploratory purposes, other categorizing and category-width procedures developed by Fillenbaum (1959) and the Evaluation of Revisions test of Frederiksen and Messick (1959).

Method

Subjects. Eight months after Study I, the 40 available Ss returned for Study II. Their ages again ranged from sixteen to forty-four; mean age was 24·9. All Ss were paid $1.00 per hour. Fifteen procedures were administered in the same order to two groups of twenty-five and fifteen Ss in two-hour sessions separated by a three-day interval.

Additional tests: 1. Object Sorting Test (OST, Repeat). The criterion measure of conceptual differentiation was readministered. The instructions and scoring procedures were exactly the same as in Study I.

2. Adjective Sorting Test (AST). In this procedure, Ss sorted the 110 adjectives of ACL, Others, Study I, into groups according to OST instructions. The number of groups was scored according to OST scoring procedure.

3. Self Sorting Test (SST). In Fillenbaum's test (1959), Ss were required to rate the degree to which each of seventy adjectives (covering a wide range of personality traits) described them. In addition to zero, S could use as many positive or negative numbers as she chose, beginning with $+1$ and -1. Following Fillenbaum, the score used was the number of categories, including only those used more than once.

4. Self Rating Test (SRT). The Ss were presented with a list of eighty adjectives: seventy-eight from ACL, Others, plus 'happy' and 'mean'. The Ss were instructed to assign a number from 0 (completely unlike me) to 100 (exactly like me) to each adjective according to the degree to which it described them. The score used was the number of different ratings.

5. Free Association Test (FAT). This procedure is based on one originally used by Klein (1954) and later by Gardner *et al.* (1959). The Ss were asked to write their associations to the word

'dry' for three minutes. The score used was the percentage of response units classified as most distant from the stimulus word, i.e. the percentage of units in the 'most distant' of the seven categories described by Gardner *et al.* (1959). A response unit was defined as the least number of words that could represent a single thought.

6. Thematic Apperception Test (TAT). One card (18BM) of TAT (Morgan and Murray, 1935) was presented to Ss, who were instructed to write a dramatic story about it. Three independent judges ranked the stories in terms of the degree of 'distance' from the physical properties of the stimulus card represented by the story. Stories consisting of concrete descriptions of the physical details of the card were ranked as least distant. Highly imaginative stories, some of which did not even involve the figure shown in the picture, were ranked as most distant. Kendall's co-efficient of concordance for the three rankings was 0·79. The rank of the average rank was used as the distance score.

7. Square-Rectangle Test (S-RT). The Ss were asked to draw a square and a rectangle, in that order, on separate sheets of blank paper. The ratio of the vertical to horizontal axes of each S's square and rectangle was computed. The score used was the difference between these ratios.

8. Range Width Task (RWT). This procedure of Fillenbaum (1959) consists of ten items in each of which S is required to estimate the largest, most nearly average and smallest instances of a class (e.g. the number of pages in a very long novel, an average novel, and a very short novel). His brief instructions were modified so that they were almost identical with those for Pettigrew's C-WS. Following Fillenbaum, the range was computed for each item and these values ranked for the forty Ss. The score was the sum of nine ranks (one item was eliminated because eight of the forty Ss wrote in words instead of numbers, making quantitative scoring impossible).

9. Synonymity Task (Syn. T). In this procedure (Fillenbaum, 1959), Ss are presented with thirteen sentences and a list of ten additional words for each sentence. In our slight modification of Fillenbaum's procedure, the task is to check (rather than to underline) each of the ten words that could be substituted for the capitalized word in each sentence without substantially changing

the meaning. The score was the total number of adjectives checked.

10. Evaluation of Revisions Test (ERT). In this test (Frederiksen and Messick, 1959), each of forty items consists of a short passage from a dispatch and a revision of the dispatch. The Ss were asked to judge each revision as the same as (could safely be substituted for) or different from the original passage. Both set and content scores were obtained, as suggested by Frederiksen and Messick. The total number of revisions checked as different was also scored.

Results

The value of Study II depends, in part, on the degree to which the forty Ss tested were a representative subsample of the seventy used in Study I. Study I and II Ss were closely matched in age range (sixteen to forty-four in both studies) and mean age (24·2 and 24·9). There were fewer significant differences between the correlations among Study I scores for the 70 Ss and the comparable correlations for the subgroup of 40 Ss who participated in Study II than would be expected by chance. [. . .]

The second consideration important to evaluation of Study II results is the stability of various scores over the eight-month interval between the two studies. Test–retest rs were obtained only for the paper-and-pencil OST. For the number-of-groups score, this r was 0·62, $p < 0·001$, apparently lower than the r of 0·75 over three years for the number of groups formed in Gardner's original OST (Gardner and Long, 1961). The r for effective level of abstraction over the eight-month period was only 0·30, $p = 0·05$. Correlations between at least these Study I scores and Study II scores (Scores 17–32) were undoubtedly reduced by the unreliability of test measures, with a consequent decrease in the likelihood of confirming predictions.

As noted earlier, the remarkable individual consistencies in number of responses to the three adjective check lists precludes effective analysis of the specific items checked by individual Ss. However, the mean numbers checked in the 300-item Gough ACL, Self, were nearly identical (86·3 and 90·6) for the nineteen Ss below the median and the twenty-one above the median in number of groups formed in OST. Comparisons of the items checked by these groups were therefore performed, in the hope of identifying differences in the conscious self-conceptions of Ss high and low in conceptual differentiation. The two groups differed, however, on only *three* of the 135 items (far less than chance). Either the groups are astonishingly similar in the aspects of conscious self-conception assessed by ACL, the ACL does not assess their differences effectively, or the factors contributing to the *number* of items checked so predominate in determining response that effective evaluation of 'content' is impossible.

Factor analysis. Eighteen scores were selected for inclusion in a principal axis factor analysis. Of these scores, only one (Number 21, TAT, Distance) was significantly correlated with age (0·42, $p < 0.01$). This correlation could have been an artifact of sampling. The older Ss were the generally more sophisticated church group members. Scores largely uncorrelated with other scores were eliminated from the factor analysis. In the case of ERT scores, the content score, rather than the set score, shows a low, consistent relationship to sorting test measures. Since it seems questionable, however, that such content and set scores are logically independent of each other, both were eliminated. Five centroid iterations were performed in advance of the principal axis analysis to obtain stable estimates of the communality of the eighteen scores. [. . .]

Factor rotation. Rotation of the four factors accounting for the largest percentages of variance by the normal varimax method (Kaiser, 1958) produced factors that, when plotted, obviously required minor adjustments. These were made by orthogonal hand rotation. Since results of these adjustments indicated that the factor structure might be represented still better if slight correlations were allowed between certain factors, the four unrotated factors were also rotated by the oblique analytical (oblimax) method of Pinzka and Saunders (1954). This analytical procedure also provided a check on the hand adjustments of the normal varimax rotation. The three sets of rotated loadings appear in Table 2. [. . .]

From an interpretive standpoint, the loadings obtained by the normal varimax and oblimax procedures are essentially similar

Rotated Factor Loadings

Score	Normal varimax factor				Adjusted normal varimax factor				Oblimax reference factor			
	1	2	3	4	1	2	3	4	1	2	3	4
1. OST, Number of groups	−77	08	−25	22	−84	08	00	−04	82	−05	19	−04
2. OST, Abstraction	−10	10	60	−07	13	10	60	−03	01	−18	06	57
3. BST, Number of groups	−60	15	−52	26	−79	15	−31	02	72	−09	09	−30
4. BST, Abstraction	02	−10	66	10	20	−10	62	17	−06	00	−14	64
5. PST, Number of groups	−22	05	−74	25	−50	05	−64	10	38	05	−06	−59
6. N-MT, Organization	−52	−19	18	03	−42	−19	33	−10	44	16	21	25
8. C-WS, Factor 2	64	−02	07	−02	61	−02	−13	17	−59	01	−29	−04
13. W-CCL, Number checked	28	−01	05	−26	35	−01	−04	−16	−37	02	09	−08
14. ACL, Self, Number checked	05	82	−04	21	−03	82	−05	21	12	−82	−23	10
15. ACL, Heroine, Number checked	01	82	14	−18	10	82	14	−15	−03	−82	12	16
16. ACL, Others, Number checked	00	85	−18	−07	−03	85	−12	−09	05	−80	05	−11
17. AST, Number of groups	−23	00	00	53	−37	00	07	44	42	−04	−36	19
18. SST, Number of categories	−08	−16	−14	54	−28	−16	−11	48	30	14	−42	02
19. SRT, Number of ratings	03	19	−35	47	−22	19	−34	42	22	−17	−41	−18
20. FAT, Distance	30	−16	19	45	19	−16	09	54	−11	11	−55	24
21. TAT, Distance	50	04	−01	00	45	04	−17	14	−45	−04	−23	−08
22. S-RT, Difference	−36	00	−37	38	−56	00	−24	22	52	03	−14	−19
23. RWT, Σ ranks	60	03	−10	54	35	03	−28	68	−30	−05	−75	−03
Percentage of variance	15	13	12	10	18	12	10	9	—	—	—	—

(note that Factors 3 and 4 are reversed in the two rotations). Intercorrelations among the oblique reference factors are low, in spite of the fact that all the tests were originally selected or designed to assess aspects of concept formation. In view of the smallness of the sample, the adjusted orthogonal loadings are used in the detailed factor interpretations offered below.

Factor 1 is the anticipated conceptual differentiation factor. Of the thirteen scores on which defining loadings were anticipated, the factor loaded less than 0·30 on only three: number of different ratings in S R T, number of categories in Fillenbaum's SST, and

Factor 1

Score	Loading
1. OST, Number of groups	−84
3. BST, Number of groups	−79
8. C-WS, Factor 2	61
22. S-RT, Difference	−56
5. PST, Number of groups	−50
21. TAT, Distance	45
6. N-MT, Organization	−42
17. AST, Number of groups	−37
13. W-CCL, Number checked	35
23. RWT, Σ ranks	35

percentage of conceptually distant responses in FAT. All three are, however, loaded in the predicted directions. The loading for the organization score of N-MT is particularly intriguing. Instead of giving narrow subcategorizations in defining the similarity between the ten concepts, when specifically asked to do so in this test, Ss high in conceptual differentiation tend to give comprehensive definitions. The result suggests that the categorizing of Ss high in conceptual differentiation may be an organized structuring of experience that also leads to synthesis of heterogeneous items into meaningful units when this is required. It is particularly interesting, therefore, that this conceptual differentiation factor appears to be independent of the level of abstraction (Factor 3) at which these Ss function in free-sorting tests.

The conceptual differentiation control principle is also apparent in the degree of differentiation Ss impose in categorizing items of four sorting tests (OST, BST, PST and AST), in category width in two tests (C-WT and RWT), in the difference between drawings of a square and a rectangle, in the number checked in W-CCL, and in the degree of distance from the literal givens of the picture of responses to Card 18BM of TAT. This loading for TAT ratings may not, however, indicate that *S*s high in conceptual differentiation use the stimulus card as a category, thereby imposing restrictions on their story productions. This loading could mean that these *S*s are simply more literal, less original, or less creative in constructing stories. This 'distance' rating appears similar, for example, to Barron's (1955) ratings of the originality of TAT productions. Further studies are needed to clarify the meaning of this loading, since the factor is loaded only 0·19 on the superficially similar 'distance' score applied to FAT productions.

Factor 2

Score	Loading
16. ACL, Others, Number checked	85
15. ACL, Heroine, Number checked	82
14. ACL, Self, Number checked	82

As noted in the discussion of Study I results, this factor could indicate response sets toward agreement or toward the social desirability of items, awareness of the complexity of individual personalities, or unknown variables.

Factor 3

Score	Loading
5. PST, Number of groups	−64
4. BST, Abstraction	62
2. OST, Abstraction	60
19. SRT, Number of ratings	−34
6. N-MT, Organization	33
3. BST, Number of groups	−31

Factor 3 is the anticipated factor representing effective level of abstraction. As expected, the factor has no loading (00) on the number-of-groups score for OST (see Table 2), a higher loading (−31) on the number of groups score for BST, and a still higher loading (−64) on the number of groups score for the difficult PST, in which grouping nearly always requires abstraction. Apparently, a tendency to function on a relatively abstract level also leads to the use of few different ratings in SRT. Perhaps abstraction is necessary for categorizing the ratings. The loading on the organization score for N-MT, although not anticipated from the Study I results and therefore somewhat questionable, is not surprising; achievement of a comprehensive definition including all ten items obviously involves abstraction.

Factor 4

Score	Loading
23. RWT, Σ ranks	68
20. FAT, Distance	54
18. SST, Number of categories	48
17. AST, Number of groups	44
19. SRT, Number of ratings	42

This factor apparently shows a relationship between broad conceptual spans in RWT and FAT and narrow spans in two sorting tests and a rating test. This paradoxical result stands in sharp distinction to Factor 1, in which high conceptual differentiation is associated with narrow conceptual spans in both Pettigrew's C-WS and Fillenbaum's RWT. Perhaps SST, SRT and AST loadings actually indicate breadth of conceptional span for the self and other persons, with a concomitant high number of subdivisions within the span. This is but a guess, however, at the meaning of an unanticipated factor.

Discussion of Study II results

The factor analytic results indicate that consistent individual differences in spontaneous conceptual differentiation in the process of categorizing occur in situations that vary widely in the content of the material categorized, in the directness with which categorizing is assessed, and in the nature of the response operations from which conceptual differentiation is inferred. There is also an apparent link between conceptual differentiation in active categorizing of heterogeneous items and category width, although some category-width tests (e.g. Fillenbaum's RWT) involve other factors of equal or greater importance. The results also indicate that conceptual differentiation is independent of the less stable preferred level of abstraction, i.e. the level on which S chooses to function when concept-attainment is not specifically demanded and when various levels of abstraction are possible. A question remains, however, concerning the relationship between the level of abstraction at which an individual chooses to operate and his *capacity* to abstract. As noted at the beginning, many studies of concept formation have dealt with the capacity to abstract. Few, if any, have been focused on the level of abstraction at which the person chooses to function when given a choice. Because of the potential importance of this distinction, relationships between spontaneous conceptual differentiation, preferred level of abstraction, and one form of capacity for abstraction were explored in Study III.

Two of the factor analytic results obviously require further exploration and verification: the relationship of conceptual differentiation to the 'distance' from the concrete characteristics of a TAT card represented by Ss' stories (with Ss low in conceptual differentiation showing greater distance); and the apparent relationship of conceptual differentiation to comprehensiveness of definitions in N-MT. The former result may or may not indicate use of the stimulus to define a category of greater or lesser breadth within which the story is constructed. Several other interpretations are possible. The very tentative finding that conceptual differentiation is linked to superior comprehensiveness of definitions of the relationship between the ten items of N-MT could, if verified, suggest that not only conceptual separation by emphasis on differences, but also sensitivity to similarity, independent of abstraction, may be involved. This possibility is of theoretical importance: consistent individual differences in responsiveness to difference alone have fewer implications for the organization of concept formation than responsiveness to similarity–difference.

Study III

The third study provided information concerning the relationship of conceptual differentiation and preferred level of abstraction in Gardner's (1953) original OST to Wechsler–Bellevue I.Q. and subtest scores, particularly that for the Similarities subtest (Wechsler, 1944), which provides a commonly used score for capacity to abstract.

Method

Subjects. The sample consisted of thirty-three secretaries and housewives. Their age range was twenty-four to forty-six; mean age was 34·7.

Tests. Gardner's (1953) original OST was given as one of a battery of cognitive control tests included in a larger study to be reported elsewhere. The Wechsler–Bellevue was given by members of another research group.

Results

The *r* between the number of groups and the abstraction score,

$$\frac{CD}{CD+FD+C}$$

for OST was 0·21. In order to test the possibility that the percentage CD score does not adequately represent preferred level of abstraction, a mean level of abstraction score was computed by assigning values of 1, 2 and 3, to C, FD and CD definitions, respectively, and dividing the sum for each *S* by the number of her groups to which abstraction scores could be assigned (i.e. the groups of two or more objects). The *r* between the two abstraction scores was 0·97. Like percentage CD, mean level of abstraction was correlated 0·21 with the total number of groups.

Pearson correlations between the number of groups score for OST and both the Wechsler–Bellevue I.Q. scores and the Similarities subtest score were nonsignificant. Similarly, none of the comparable correlations for the percentage CD score was significant.

Discussion of Study III results

The results of Study III offer no support to the assumption that the number of groups formed in OST is determined by 'intelligence', by the level of abstraction at which *S chooses* to function in OST, or by her capacity to abstract in a test heavily dependent on verbal skills, as indicated by performance in the Similarities subtest of the Wechsler–Bellevue. These findings concerning conceptual differentiation and preferred level of abstraction are directly in line with the results of Study II.

Conclusions

In addition to providing new evidence of individual consistencies in the degree of conceptual differentiation spontaneously imposed in a variety of categorizing and related tests, these three studies point to the independence of conceptual differentiation both from the level of abstraction at which S chooses to function and S's capacity to abstract. The level of abstraction at which S chooses to function in free sorting-tests and her capacity to abstract in a test heavily dependent on verbal skills also appear to be independent of each other. The intriguing finding about the preferred level of abstraction at which S operates is that the individual seems to be consistent with himself in various test situations over a relatively brief period of time, but quite variable over longer periods. The obvious implications are (a) that tests of capacity to abstract tell us little or nothing about the level of abstraction at which the person actually functions in many situations and (b) that the preferred level of abstraction fluctuates greatly over time as a result of unknown variables. The latter interpretation may be qualified somewhat by the very great dependence of the level of abstraction scores for the present studies on the wording of Ss' definitions of groups.

It is important to note here that Gardner, Jackson and Messick (1960) found no relationship between either preferred level of abstraction or conceptual differentiation in the Gardner's OST and performance on the Wide Range Vocabulary test, which is often used to represent the intellectual ability, Verbal Knowledge. The scoring scheme for abstraction used in these studies thus seems to indicate the nature of the conceptual links the subject attributes to the objects grouped, rather than the acquisition of words, *per se*. In fact, the use of unusual words as a means of achieving abstract, superordinate definitions (cf. Brown, 1958) in OST is extremely rare among normal persons.

Reichard, Schneider and Rapaport (1944) found 'a rather steady increase with age in ability to group objects which belong together and in ability to give abstract conceptual explanations of the groupings' (p. 160). These authors applied the abstraction scoring scheme elaborated upon later by Rapaport, Gill and Schafer (1945) and used in the present studies. The present studies point to enduring adult consistencies in spontaneous conceptual differentiation which, in normal adults, are apparently independent of the capacity to abstract and of the preferred level at which S actually performs in relevant tests. As yet, nothing is known of the development of these consistencies in conceptual differentiation and their relationship to the development of the capacities for discrimination and abstraction. Familiar objects were used in Gardner's original sorting test to reduce the effects of discrimination capacity and word acquisition on performance. With younger children and brain-damaged persons, these variables may, however, have much greater effects on performance. Developmental studies of conceptual differentiation therefore require effective experimental or statistical control of these variables.

Taken together, results of these studies point to the complexity of concept formation and the dimensions of cognitive control that may ultimately account for individual differences. And, as noted in the introductory matter, an independent principle of cognitive control, relevant to the selectiveness of attention, is a determinant of capacity to abstract under one special set of conditions. In addition, Gardner, Jackson and Messick (1960) found that neither conceptual differentiation nor selectiveness of attention was related to the abilities earlier defined as Induction and Deduction, although laboratory scores of selectiveness of attention were predictably related to performance in a test of Induction that incidentally requires selective attention. Any attempt to employ the capacity to abstract as a comprehensive variable accounting for disparate facets of concept formation is, therefore, doomed to failure. The present studies, which demonstrate the complexity of concept formation, in themselves represent only a very limited segment of the total realm of behaviors involving concept formation.

Results of the three studies reported here suggest several lines of further research. One of the most obvious of these is a further test of the possibility that high conceptual differentiation implies emphasis on differences in some situations and facility in integration in others. The link between spontaneous conceptual differentiation and category width suggests studies of relations between conceptual differentiation and true stimulus generalization (i.e. generalization accompanied by effective discrimination). The possibility that conceptual differentiation is a determinant of individual differences in recall under certain conditions should also be explored. Goss (1961) has recently summarized some of the impressive earlier findings indicating that categorization improves recall. When the material to be learned is amenable to spontaneous categorization, persons high in spontaneous conceptual differentiation may show superior recall. In fact, the effects of categorizing on recall might be studied with the sorting tests of the present study.

Individual consistencies in spontaneous conceptual differentiation may also have determining effects on other forms of cognitive behavior. It is known, for example, that the degree of assimilation among new percepts and memories of related earlier percepts is a function of the perceived similarity of the new and prior stimuli. Persons high in conceptual differentiation may experience a relatively small realm of new stimuli as similar to any prior stimulus or group of stimuli and hence show less assimilation under certain conditions. Given a range of variation in similarity among sequential stimuli, the control principle defined here as conceptual differentiation and the independent control principle of leveling–sharpening (see Gardner, Jackson and Messick, 1960), which seems specifically relevant to the process of assimilation *per se*, may interact with predictable effects on experience and memory. Under such conditions, high conceptual differentiation and extreme sharpening in combination could lead to minimal assimilation, low conceptual differentiation and leveling to maximal assimilation.

With the possible exception of its implications for literalness versus creative imaginativeness, more general correlates of conceptual differentiation are as yet unknown. Since this dimension of cognitive control presumably implies individual differences in cognitive structures relevant to concept formation, one obvious method of exploring this question is to investigate relationships to the cognitive structures called defense mechanisms, several of which have specific implications for concept formation. Two of these – repression and isolation – seemed unrelated to conceptual differentiation in Gardner's OST and associated procedures in the study by Gardner, Jackson and Messick (1960). Projection, however, was not assessed in that study and can lead to extreme emphasis on the distinctions between persons and events. Results of earlier investigations of relations between cognitive control principles and defenses (e.g. Gardner and Long, 1962; Gardner, Jackson and Messick, 1960; Holzman and Gardner, 1959) have suggested that persons extreme in the employment of a particular defense may be at one extreme of a particular control dimension, but that the reverse is not true. That is, many other persons at the same extreme of the control dimension do not employ the defense to an unusual degree. It may be that similar relationships will hold for protection and conceptual differentiation. If so, conceptual differentiation may be optimally viewed as a basic characteristic of cognitive organization serving as a precondition for the extreme employment of a particular defense by certain individuals.

In addition to the above studies, one further major area of exploration is clearly indicated by the present studies. The fact that some persons consistently show high conceptual differentiation independent of preferred level of abstraction, I.Q. scores, capacity to abstract as represented by the Wechsler–Bellevue Similarities subtest, etc., suggests that in certain situations they are particularly impressed by or impelled to act upon awareness of *distinctions* between objects, persons, and events. Persons low in conceptual differentiation seem more 'relaxed' about ordering their experience in terms of highly refined conceptual schemes. One implication may be that persons high in conceptual differentiation are more rigid and intolerant of change in conceptual schemes once formed. They may, for example, be less 'open-minded', in the sense described by Rokeach (1960). The narrow categories implied by high conceptual differentiation may be 'closed' to discrepant information (or objects, etc.) as compared to the broader categories of persons low in conceptual differentiation. If this is true, persons high in conceptual differentiation may also be given to a greater degree of 'black–white thinking' and the associated 'need for definiteness', described by Guilford *et al.* (1957) and related by Guilford (1959) to intolerance of ambiguity. Since individual differences in conceptual differentiation are quite stable in adults, confirmation of such hypotheses would have important implications for individual differences in the organization of beliefs and attitudes.

References

BAGGALEY, A. R. (1955), 'Concept formation and its relation to cognitive variables', *J. gen. Psychol.*, vol. 52, pp. 297–306.

BARRON, F. (1955), 'The disposition toward originality', *J. abnorm. soc. Psychol.*, vol. 51, pp. 478–85.

BIERI, J. (1955), 'Cognitive complexity–simplicity and predictive behavior', *J. abnorm. soc. Psychol.*, vol. 51, pp. 263–8.

BIERI, J., and BLACKER, E. (1956a), 'External and internal stimulus factors in Rorschach performance', *J. consult. Psychol.*, vol. 20, pp. 1–7.

BIERI, J., and BLACKER, E. (1956b), 'The generality of cognitive complexity in the perception of people and inkblots', *J. abnorm. soc. Psychol.*, vol. 53, pp. 112–17.

BIERI, J., and MESSERLEY, S. (1957), 'Differences in perceptual and cognitive behavior as a function of experience type', *J. consult. Psychol.*, vol. 21, pp. 217–21.

BOLLES, M. (1937), 'The basis of pertinence: a study of the test performance of aments, dements and normal children of the same mental age', *Arch. Psychol.*, vol. 30, whole no. 212.

BROWN, R. (1958), *Words and Things*, Free Press.

BRUNER, J. S., GOODNOW, J., and AUSTIN, G. A. (1956), *A Study of Thinking*, Wiley.

BRUNER, J. S., and TAJFEL, H. (1961), 'Cognitive risk and environmental change', *J. abnorm. soc. Psychol.*, vol. 62, pp. 231–41.

CAMERON, N. (1938a), 'Reasoning, regression, and communication in schizophrenics', *Psychol. Monogr.*, vol. 50, no. 1, whole no. 221.

CAMERON, N. (1938b), 'A study of thinking in senile deterioration and schizophrenic disorganization', *Amer. J. Psychol.*, vol. 51, pp. 650–64.

CAMERON, N. (1939a), 'Deterioration and regression in schizophrenic thinking', *J. abnorm. soc. Psychol.*, vol. 34, pp. 265–70.

CAMERON, N. (1939b), 'Schizophrenic thinking in a problem-solving situation', *J. ment. Sci.*, vol. 85, pp. 1012–35.

CHAPMAN, L. J. (1961), 'A reinterpretation of some pathological disturbances in conceptual breadth', *J. abnorm. soc. Psychol.*, vol. 62, pp. 514–19.

CHAPMAN, L. J., and TAYLOR, J. (1957), 'Breadth of deviate concepts used by schizophrenics', *J. abnorm. soc. Psychol.*, vol. 54, pp. 118–23.

CLAYTON, M. B., and JACKSON, D. N. (1961), 'Equivalence range, acquiescence, and overgeneralization', *Educ. psychol. Measmt*, vol. 21, pp. 371–82.

COUCH, A., and KENISTON, K. (1960), 'Yeasayers and naysayers: agreeing response set as a personality variable', *J. abnorm. soc. Psychol.*, vol. 60, pp. 151–74.

DICKMAN, H. R. (1954), An investigation of the relationship between the cognitive organization of objective and behavioral stimuli, *Unpublished Master's Thesis, University of Kansas*.

DOPP, R. (1960), The relation of cognitive complexity–simplicity and the PPS personality variables to equivalence range, *Unpublished Master's Thesis, University of Kansas*.

EDWARDS, A. L. (1957), *The Social Desirability Variable in Personality Assessment and Research*, Dryden.

EPSTEIN, S. (1953), 'Overinclusive thinking in a schizophrenic and a control group', *J. consult. Psychol.*, vol. 17, pp. 384–8.

FILLENBAUM, S. (1959), 'Some stylistic aspects of categorizing behavior', *J. Personal.*, vol. 27, pp. 187–95.

FREDERIKSEN, N., and MESSICK, S. (1959), 'Response set as a measure of personality', *Educ. psychol. Measmt*, vol. 19, pp. 137–57.

FRIEDMAN, G. (1961), 'Conceptual thinking in schizophrenic children', *Genet. Psychol. Monogr.*, vol. 63, pp. 149–96.

GARDNER, R. W. (1953), 'Cognitive styles in categorizing behavior', *J. Personal.*, vol. 22, pp. 214–33.

GARDNER, R. W., and LONG, R. I. (1961), 'The stability of cognitive controls', *J. abnorm. soc. Psychol.*, vol. 11, pp. 120–27.

GARDNER, R. W., and LONG, R. I. (1962), 'Control, defense, and centration effect: a study of scanning behaviour', *Brit. J. Psychol.*, vol. 53, pp. 129–40.

GARDNER, R. W., JACKSON, D. N., and MESSICK, S. J. (1960), 'Personality organization in cognitive controls and intellectual abilities', *Psychol. Issues*, vol. 2, no. 4, whole no. 8.

GARDNER, R. W., HOLZMAN, P. S., KLEIN, G. S., LINTON, H. B., and SPENCE, D. P. (1959), 'Cognitive control: a study of individual consistencies in cognitive behavior', *Psychol. Issues*, vol. 1, no. 4, whole no. 8.

GOLDSTEIN, K., and SCHEERER, M. (1941), 'Abstract and concrete behavior: an experimental study with special tests', *Psychol. Monogr.*, vol. 53, no. 2, whole no. 239.

GOSS, A. E. (1961), 'Acquisition and rise of conceptual schemes', in C. N. Cofer (ed.), *Verbal Learning and Verbal Behavior*, McGraw-Hill, pp. 42–69.

GOUGH, H. G. (1960), 'The Adjective Check List as a personality assessment research technique', *Psychol. Rep.*, vol. 6, monogr. suppl. no. 2, pp. 107–22.

GUILFORD, J. P. (1959), *Personality*, McGraw-Hill.

GUILFORD, J. P., CHRISTENSEN, P. R., FRICK, J. W., and MERRIFIELD, P. R. (1957), 'The relations of creative-thinking aptitudes to non-aptitude personality traits', *Univ. S. Calif. Psychol. Lab. Rep.*, no. 20.

HALSTEAD, W. C. (1947), *Brain and Intelligence: A Quantitative Study of the Frontal Lobes*, University of Chicago Press.

HARVEY, O. J., HUNT, D. E., and SCHRODER, H. M. (1961), *Conceptual Systems and Personality Organization*, Wiley.

HIGGINS, J. C. (1961), 'Cognitive complexity and probability preferences', *Student Res. Psychol. Univ. Chicago*, vol. 2, no. 2, pp. 1–28.

HOLZMAN, P. S., and GARDNER, R. W. (1959), 'Leveling and repression', *J. abnorm. soc. Psychol.*, vol. 59, pp. 151–5.

KAISER, H. F. (1958), 'The varimax criterion for analytic rotation in factor analysis', *Psychometrika*, vol. 23, pp. 187–200.

KELLY, G. A. (1955), *The Psychology of Personal Constructs*, vol. 1, *A Theory of Personality*, Norton.

KLEIN, G. S. (1954), 'Need and regulation', in M. R. Jones (ed.), *Nebraska Symposium on Motivation: 1954*, University of Nebraska Press, pp. 224–74.

LACEY, J. I. (1956), 'The evaluation of autonomic responses: Toward a general solution', *Ann. N.Y. Acad. Sci.*, vol. 67, pp. 123–64.

LEVENTHAL, D. B., MCGAUGHRAN, L. S., and MORAN, L. J. (1959), 'Multivariable analysis of the conceptual behavior of schizophrenic and brain-damaged patients', *J. abnorm. soc. Psychol.*, vol. 58, pp. 84–90.

LOVIBOND, S. H. (1954), 'The Object-Sorting Test and conceptual thinking in schizophrenia', *Austr. J. Psychol.*, vol. 6, pp. 52–70.

LUNDY, R. M., and BERKOWITZ, L. (1957), 'Cognitive complexity and assimilative projection in attitude change', *J. abnorm. soc. Psychol.*, vol. 55, pp. 34–7.

MARRS, C. L. (1955), Categorizing behavior as elicited by a variety of stimuli, *Unpublished Master's Thesis, University of Kansas*.

MCGAUGHRAN, L. S., and MORAN, L. J. (1956), ' "Conceptual level" vs. "conceptual area" analysis of object-sorting of schizophrenic and nonpsychiatric groups', *J. abnorm. soc. Psychol.*, vol. 52, pp. 43–50.

MORGAN, C. D., and MURRAY, H. A. (1935), 'A method for investigating phantasies: the Thematic Apperception Test', *Arch. neurol. Psychiat.*, vol. 34, pp. 289–306.

PETTIGREW, T. F. (1958), 'The measurement and correlates of category width as a cognitive variable', *J. Personal.*, vol. 26, pp. 532–44. [See Reading 6.]

PIAGET, J., and INHELDER, B. (1959), *La Genèse des Structures logiques Elémentaires: Classifications et Serations*, Delachaux & Niestlé, Neuchâtel.

PINZKA, C., and SAUNDERS, D. R. (1954), 'Analytic rotation to simple structure: II. Extension to oblique solution', *Research Bulletin, Educational Testing Service*, RB-54-31, Princeton, New Jersey.

RAPAPORT, D., GILL, M., and SCHAFER, R. (1945), *Diagnostic Psychological Testing*, vol. 1, Year Book Medical Publishers.

REICHARD, S., SCHNEIDER, M., and RAPAPORT, D. (1944), 'The development of concept formation in children', *Amer. J. Orthopsychiat.*, vol. 14, pp. 156–61.

ROKEACH, M. (1951a), 'A method for studying individual differences in "narrow-mindedness" ', *J. Personal.*, vol. 20, pp. 219–33.

ROKEACH, M. (1951b), 'Prejudice, concreteness of thinking and reification of thinking', *J. abnorm. soc. Psychol.*, vol. 46, pp. 85–91.

ROKEACH, M. (1960), *The Open and Closed Mind*, Basic Books.

SLOANE, H. N. (1959), The generality and construct validity of equivalence range, *Unpublished Doctoral Dissertation, Pennsylvania State University*.

TRESSELT, M. E., and MAYZNER, M. S. (1958), 'Consistency of judgments in categorizing verbal material', *Psychol. Rep.*, vol. 4, pp. 415–21.

WALLACH, M. A., and CARON, A. J. (1959), 'Attribute criteriality and sex-linked conservatism as determinants of psychological similarity', *J. abnorm. soc. Psychol.*, vol. 59, pp. 43–50.

WECHSLER, D. (1944), *The Measurement of Adult Intelligence*, Williams & Wilkins.

WITKIN, H. A., LEWIS, H. B., HERTZMAN, M., MACHOVER, K., MEISSNER, P. B., and WAPNER, S. (1954), *Personality through Perception*, Harper.

ZASLOW, R. W. (1961), 'A study of concept formation in normals, mental defectives, and brain-damaged adults', *Genet. Psychol. Monogr.*, vol. 63, pp. 279–338.

4 Alfred F. Glixman

Categorizing Behaviour as a Function of Meaning
Domain

Excerpts from Alfred F. Glixman, 'Categorizing behavior as a function
of meaning domain', *Journal of Personality and Social Psychology*, vol. 2,
1965, pp. 370–77.

In recent years the concept 'cognitive structure', the organization
of meanings, has received ever increasing attention. Chein (1962)
and Scheerer (1954), for example, have been concerned with the
general role of cognitive concepts in the development of psychological theories. Brehm and Cohen (1962), Festinger (1957), Heider
(1958), Kelly (1955), Peak (1958) and Witkin *et al.* (1962) have
concerned themselves directly with formal properties of cognitive
structures, with the relationships among different sets of meanings, and with the behavioral correlates of cognitive structures.
Bruner, Goodnow and Austin (1956) and Hunt (1962) have
studied the ways in which meaning categories (concepts) are
formed, and Gardner (1953), Gardner and Schoen (1962) and
Sherif and Hovland (1961) have brought into focus the process of
dividing a meaning domain into a set of categories. The present
study is concerned with the last-mentioned process.

Hovland and Sherif (1952) and Sherif and Hovland (1953)
demonstrated that there is a relationship between an individual's
stand on an issue and the way in which he categorizes items
related to the issue. The more extreme the position is, the more
likely is the person to use a small number of categories, to use the
extreme categories and to place the greatest number of items into
the category furthest from his position. (For a discussion of the
significance of differential concentration of items for scaling procedures in general, see Sherif and Hovland, 1961.) Independently
of the work by Sherif and Hovland, and following the reasoning
which led Klein (1949) and Holzman and Klein (1950) to posit the
existence of perceptual attitudes, Gardner (Gardner, 1953;
Gardner, Jackson and Messick, 1960; Gardner *et al.*, 1959) studied categorizing behavior as a cognitive control. 'Cognitive

control' refers to a relatively transsituational mode of dealing with stimulus events. This mode is seen as a process which serves as one of the mediators between drive states and perceptual and judgemental functions. Over time, they become quasiautonomous and function relatively independently of momentary drive states.

As Gardner and his colleagues dealt with categorizing behavior, the major emphasis was placed upon equivalence range (a revision of their position appears in Gardner and Schoen, 1962). 'Equivalence range' refers to the range of stimuli placed into a category; for a fixed number of stimuli, equivalence range is inversely proportional to the number of categories. Individual differences in number of categories used for a particular realm of stimulus events are taken as a reflection of differences in 'inclusiveness of conceptual realms' (Gardner, Jackson and Messick, 1960). A number of studies have been conducted which attempt to discover the degree to which the control equivalence range is related to other functions (Gardner, 1953; Gardner and Schoen, 1962; Gardner, Jackson and Messick, 1960; Gardner et al., 1959; Pettigrew, 1958; Sloane, 1959; Wallach and Caron, 1959).

In the sets of studies by Sherif and by Gardner, the subject's task is to categorize a set of items (statements, objects, photographs, and so on). Sherif and Hovland (1961) refer to this activity as an 'own category' technique; Gardner refers to it as a 'sorting test' to determine equivalence range. One of Sherif's concerns has been with 'latitudes of acceptance and rejection' (Sherif and Hovland, 1961). These latitudes are equivalence ranges in the parts of a scale that include the subject's position (latitude of acceptance) and the position furthest from the subject's (latitude of rejection). Gardner, on the other hand, has not dealt with intrasubject, intradomain differences in equivalence range across a set of categories. One reason for the difference in approach may be that, typically, Sherif has used items that are ordered along a clear-cut dimension – favorableness of an item to Negroes, for example – while Gardner's items are subject to a greater degree of idiosyncratic ordering. Sherif's items may be referred to an outside criterion, and the term 'extreme position' takes on immediate meaning, but this is not true for Gardner's items. The studies of these investigators are embedded in markedly different conceptual systems, and there is a difference in emphasis which they would place upon the generality of categorizing behavior. This difference is not sharp (since both of them would agree that categorizing performance is a function of the person and of the specific items), but one would expect somewhat more generality from Gardner's position than from Sherif's. A question which is relevant to both positions is: what is the relationship between categorizing behavior with respect to a set of relatively neutral objects and such behavior with respect to a set of statements dealing with a social issue?

In considering the relationship between the organizing (categorizing behavior) in two different meaning domains, one is led back to the nature of cognitive structures. Categorizing behavior involves the relatively basic function of dividing a meaning domain into subsections. This division becomes an integral part of (and probably also is affected by) any hierarchical ordering which exists within the domain. Across domains, too, one would expect to find a hierarchical ordering, so that some domains would affect others more than they would be affected by them. Some domains would be more personally significant than would others. Witkin *et al.* (1962), for instance, present the point of view that the degree to which an individual differentiates his behavioral world is dependent upon (or is related to) the way in which he differentiates himself. Given this point of view, another question becomes pertinent: to what degree is categorizing of a set of items which refer to the self related to categorizing behavior in other meaning domains?

In addition, in almost a self-evident manner, it is expected that the more peripheral the domain the weaker is the structure within the domain; therefore there should be a larger number of categories used in more peripheral domains.

Given items which sample each of three meaning domains – relatively neutral objects, reactions to nuclear war, and self-statements – two questions are raised:

1. Is there consistency of categorizing behavior across domains; that is, are there significant interdomain correlations?
2. Does categorizing behavior change as a function of the

domain? If the domains considered above are ordered objects, war, self (from least to most personally significant), subjects should use the largest number of categories for objects.

Method

The thirty-six subjects were juniors, seniors and nonpsychology graduate students at the University of Oklahoma who volunteered to participate in the study; nineteen of them were men. None of them was familiar with the techniques used or with the purpose of the study. Each subject spent about an hour working on three sorting tasks. The order of presentation was counterbalanced so that each of the six permutations of order of task was used, six subjects being assigned randomly to each permutation.

The material for each of the tasks consisted of a number of statements, each one typed on a four-by-six inch card. Three sets of cards were used: a set of seventy-three verbal descriptions of the objects used by Gardner (1953), a set of ninety-two self-referring statements developed by Butler and Haigh for a Q-sort (Rogers and Dymond, 1954, pp. 79, 275–7, 388–9) and a set of thirty-six statements used to determine attitudes toward nuclear war. These sets of statements and the categorizing tasks associated with them will be referred to as 'object', 'self' and 'war', respectively.

Before presenting the tasks to the subject, the experimenter attempted to establish a warm, permissive atmosphere and to remove any kind of time pressure. The same set of instructions, modified appropriately for nature of the material and for order of presentation, was used for each of the tasks. The instructions (Gardner, 1953) were:

You will be given a number of tasks to perform. There are neither right nor wrong ways to do them, so you do them in ways that are comfortable for you. Although some of them may seem similar to each other, you regard each task as though it were the only one you are to perform. There is no timing of the tasks, so you can take as much as you need.

First of all [again], I want you to know that there is no answer to this task. Everyone does it in his own way. I want you to do it in the way that seems most natural, most logical, and most comfortable to you.

The instructions are simply to put together into groups the statements which seem to you to belong together. You may have as many or as few statements in a group as you like, so long as the statements in each group belong together for one particular reason. If, after you have thought about all the statements, a few do not seem to belong with *any* of the others, you may put those statements into groups by themselves. Please sort all the statements.

Results

The interdomain correlation coefficients reported below are measures of the relationship between the number of categories used in a domain and the number of categories used in some other one. Sex differences with respect to correlations have not been found consistently (Gardner *et al.*, 1959), but consistent sex differences with respect to equivalence range have been reported (Pettigrew, 1958; Wallach and Caron, 1959). These differences will be preserved in the analysis of the data.

Question 1. Is there consistency of categorizing behavior across domains?

Table 1

Interdomain Correlation Coefficients for Men, Women and Total

Domain	Men (n = 19)		Women (n = 17)		Total (n = 36)	
	war	self	war	self	war	self
Objects	0·44	0·20	0·40	0·59*	0·47**	0·47**
War		0·80**		0·45		0·66**

* $p = 0.05$.
** $p = 0.01$.

The answer to this question may be found in Table 1. For men, only the correlation between self and war differs significantly from zero. It is significantly greater than the correlations between self and objects ($p < 0.01$), but it is not greater than the objects–war correlations. For women, only the correlation between self and objects differs from zero. No significant differences exist among

97

the three correlation coefficients for women. All of these rs are too unstable (men, $df = 17$; women, $df = 15$) to warrant further consideration.

Since there are no significant men–women differences between corresponding correlation coefficients, total correlation coefficients are presented. For total, all three are significantly different from zero, and there are no significant differences among them (the difference between $r = 0.66$ and $r = 0.47$ yields $t = 1.45$, $df = 33$, $p = 0.15$). Using these results, the answer to the first question is that (for the meaning domains sampled here) categorizing behavior is consistent across domains.

Question 2. Does categorizing behavior change as a function of the meaning domain?

Consider a situation in which one tries to predict the category into which the subject will place an item chosen at random. If the subject uses only one category into which to place such items in a domain, his behavior is completely predictable – there is minimum uncertainty, maximum structure. If he uses a very large number of categories, and distributes the items equally over all categories, there is a high degree of uncertainty and a low degree of structure. Suppose, now, that the number of categories which the subject uses is fixed. Then the degree of uncertainty (and inversely, the degree of structure) changes as a function of the distribution of items over categories; that is, uncertainty is maximal when the distribution is rectangular, and the degree of uncertainty decreases as the distribution departs from rectangularity. Therefore, the degree of structure in the subject's categorial system is a function of the number of categories he uses and of the rectangularity of the distribution of items over categories (Attneave, 1959; Garner, 1962).

H (the measure of uncertainty in bits) and its components, number of categories and H/H_{max}, will be used to indicate the degree of structure in a domain. Degree of structure varies inversely with all three measures. H/H_{max} indicates the amount of uncertainty in the subject's response set relative to the amount of uncertainty which would exist if the subject used all of his categories equally often; therefore, it may be used to indicate degree of rectangularity of the distribution of items over categories. (See Garner, 1962.)

Table 2 contains the Sex × Domain distribution of mean H.
Table 3 contains the Sex × Domain distribution of mean number
of categories. For both measures, sex and domain effects are
significant.[1] There are higher H values and a greater number of

Table 2

Distribution of Means over Sex and Meaning Domain H
(in bits)

Sex	Meaning domain			Total
	objects	war	self	
Men	2·97	2·03	1·82	2·28
Women	3·59	3·02	2·87	3·16
Total	3·26	2·50	2·32	2·69

categories for women than for men, indicating a lower degree of
structure which is attributable to a larger number of categories
for women than for men. Application of the Duncan multiple
range test (Edwards, 1960) to the domain means reveals that for
both measures there is a higher mean for objects than for war or

Table 3

Distribution of Means over Sex and Meaning Domain
Number of Categories

Sex	Meaning domain			Total
	objects	war	self	
Men	13·00	5·42	5·53	7·98
Women	17·82	10·18	11·71	13·24
Total	15·28	7·67	8·44	10·46

self ($a = 0.01$), but there is no difference between the means for
war and self ($a = 0.05$). That the number-of-categories differences
cannot be accounted for by the numbers of items used (objects =
73, war = 36, self = 92) is indicated by the fact that objects has
the highest mean but an intermediate number of items.

1. This assertion (and a similar one in the next paragraph) is supported
in the original article by tabular details of three-way analyses of variance.
These tables have here been omitted [Ed.].

Table 4 contains the Sex $\times$ Domain distribution of mean H/H_{max}. There is no significant sex effect but, again, there is a significant domain effect. The Duncan multiple range test reveals that self has a lower relative-uncertainty mean than does either of the other domains ($a = 0.01$), but that war and objects do not differ from each other ($a = 0.05$).

Table 4

Distribution of Means over Sex and Meaning Domain H/H_{max}

Sex	Meaning domain			Total
	objects	war	self	
Men	0·90	0·90	0·84	0·88
Women	0·89	0·93	0·85	0·89
Total	0·90	0·91	0·84	0·89

The answer to Question 2 now may be stated as: categorizing behavior does change as function of meaning domain. If the domains are ordered objects, war, self as from least to most personally relevant, the least relevant domain (objects) has the greatest uncertainty (lowest degree of structure) associated with it. Since the measure of uncertainty is a function of the number of categories used and of the concentration of items in the categories, two substatements may be made: the largest number of categories is associated with the least significant domain (objects) and the most unequal distribution of items over the categories used is associated with the most significant domain (self).[2]

2. The data presented above may be accounted for by showing that different degrees of item homogeneity characterize different domains. If there were increasing homogeneity (independent of 'significance') from objects to war to self, then one would expect the lowest degree of structure in objects and the highest degree in self. No attempt was made to control this variable because I do not believe that such control is appropriate. One of the consequences which follows from acceptance of a conceptual system which is based on the proposition that an individual develops his own view of the world is that, for many regions of activity, 'reality' takes on an idiosyncratic cast. The further one goes from simple events and from achievement criteria, the more difficult it is to say how many categories there 'really' are unless one also specifies the categorizer. Sherif and Hovland (1961) have shown that categories differ with respect to relatively

Discussion

Sex differences

Although minor differences appear with respect to cross-domain correlation coefficients, an $r \times r$ comparison across sexes yields no significant differences. No consistent body of information exists with which to compare these results.

Women exhibit a lower degree of structure (have higher H values) than do men, and this difference may be accounted for specifically by the fact that women use a greater number of categories than do men; they do not concentrate the items over categories more than do men. The finding that women use more categories than do men apparently is consistent with the results of studies by Pettigrew (1958) and by Wallach and Caron (1959). These authors found that females used smaller category widths on the Pettigrew Category-Width Scale than did males, and that girls tolerated less deviation from a standard on a similarity-judgement task (Wallach and Caron, 1959). Wallach and Caron account for these results by referring them to differential sex training which results in greater independence of external standards for males than for females. Pettigrew also suggests that women may have less tolerance for errors of overinclusiveness than do men. A question may be raised as to the compatibility of underlying factors related to category-width performance and to sorting performance. Further study is needed to answer such a question and to determine whether the same child-rearing practices affect both kinds of behavior.

Interdomain consistency

The total rs reported in Table 1 show clearly that such consistency exists; however, a strong note of caution is required. Sloane (1959) offers evidence that there may be a factor which is specific to sorting operations. In order to make a definitive statement about interdomain consistency, it is necessary to use other sets of

clear-cut issues. As more and more uniquely determined categorial systems are studied, one can specify the properties of events in different meaning domains only by sampling categorizers, procedures, and items (Brunswik, 1956).

operations to measure the categorizing process (Campbell and Fiske, 1959).

The magnitude of the correlation coefficients among objects, war and self lends support to the positions of both Sherif and Gardner. Since variation in any one domain accounts for only 0·22 to 0·46 of the variance of some other domain, a large proportion of the variance in a domain is specific to that domain (or to factors other than the ones considered here). Since all of the correlations are reliably different from zero, it is equally clear that a general form of behavior is involved. Hovland and Sherif (1952) and Sherif and Hovland (1953) have shown that categorizing may be used to ascertain an individual's organization of a particular domain. The data presented here indicate that the individual's organization of events in a specific domain is also a function of his general mode of organizing events.

The finding that self correlates with objects and with war is consistent with the idea that the degree to which an individual differentiates his behavioral world is dependent upon the way in which he differentiates himself (Witkin *et al.*, 1962). In view of the apparent importance of self to the subject, it is tempting to think of self as a core domain around which the others are organized. There is no direct evidence in this study to support this view, and it will not be developed further.

Organization of domains as a function of domain

The findings with regard to changes in categorizing behavior as a function of meaning domain may be seen, in part, as an extension of the work of Sherif and his associates. They have demonstrated that a decrease in the number of categories used and an increase in differential concentration of items across categories (heavier concentration in the extreme categories) are the result of the extremeness of the subject's position (as an indication of the intensity of significance of the issue for the subject). This demonstration depends upon a comparison of the subjects who hold different positions on a single issue. In a similar manner, it has been demonstrated here that as a meaning domain increases in personal relevance *within* individuals, there is a decrease in number of categories used and an increase in differential concentration of items across categories.

The particular fashion in which subjects respond to unrestricted conditions of categorizing suggests that the organization of meanings involves a two-stage process. In the first stage, the subject controls the amount of information with which he has to deal by setting the number of categories to be used for a meaning domain. In the second stage, he makes another adjustment by using some categories more frequently than others. This two-stage process may be understood by considering the fact that controlling the amount of information brings into play the risks inherent in overinclusiveness and in overexclusiveness, risks of accepting negative instances and of rejecting positive ones.[3] If the subject uses a small number of categories there are fewer events to deal with, there is a higher degree of organization, but the risk of misplacing items has increased. Since the subject must deal with all of the items presented to him, overinclusiveness in some categories implies overexclusiveness in others. For a highly significant category within an important domain, if the subject considers an error of overinclusiveness as being more serious than an error of overexclusiveness, then he can protect himself against accepting too many negative instances by placing relatively few items in the category of concern and relatively many items in other categories. (This is exactly what subjects in the Sherif and Hovland, 1953, study seem to have done.)

Subjects in the current study behave as though there is an optimum degree of organization for a particular subject dealing with a particular domain. Suppose this optimum degree to be high; that is, the optimum level of H is low. If the subject achieves the optimum level of H only by using a small number of categories, he must accept the consequences of having too many misplaced items in categories of high significance. Since he can control these consequences by manipulating the frequency of items in a category, the optimum level of organization (optimum level of H) may be achieved by choosing a number of categories that results in a higher-than-optimum level of H and then bringing the level

---

3. Generally, investigators of equivalence range (Gardner, 1953; Gardner, Jackson and Messick, 1960; Gardner *et al.*, 1959; Pettigrew, 1958; Wallach and Caron, 1959) have treated inclusiveness–exclusiveness as though it were uniform over the entire set of categories. Evidence reported in Sherif and Hovland (1961) and in this study indicate that this is not so.

down to optimum by means of concentrating items (reducing H/H_{max}). The first stage of organization apparently is used to differentiate between a relatively inconsequential domain (objects) and domains of moderate to high relevance (war and self). The second level of organization differentiates between a highly relevant domain (self) and domains of moderate to low relevance (war and objects).

If this interpretation is correct, then it may be said that individuals control the information in a domain by using fewer or more categories according to whether the domain is more or less significant to them. Within significant domains they differentiate among more or less significant categories, and they further control information by placing items unequally into the categories. They seem willing to tolerate the risk of misplacing items into other categories in order to preserve the homogeneity of items in highly significant ones.

References

ATTNEAVE, F. (1959), *Applications of Information Theory to Psychology*, Holt, Rinehart & Winston.

BREHM, J. W., and COHEN, A. R. (1962), *Explorations in Cognitive Dissonance*, Wiley.

BRUNER, J. S., GOODNOW, J. J. and AUSTIN, G. A. (1956), *A Study of Thinking*, Wiley.

BRUNSWIK, E. (1956), *Perception and the Representative Design of Psychological Experiments*, University of California Press.

CAMPBELL, D. T., and FISKE, D. W. (1959), 'Convergent and discriminant validation by the multitrait-multimethod matrix', *Psychol. Bull.*, vol. 56, pp. 81–105.

CHEIN, I. (1962), 'The image of man', *J. soc. Issues*, vol. 18, pp. 1–35.

EDWARDS, A. L. (1960), *Experimental Design in Psychological Research*, 2nd edn, Rinehart.

FESTINGER, L. (1957), *A Theory of Cognitive Dissonance*, Stanford University Press.

GARDNER, R. W. (1953), 'Cognitive styles in categorizing behavior', *J. Personal.*, vol. 22, pp. 214–33.

GARDNER, R. W., HOLZMAN, P. S., KLEIN, G. S., LINTON, H. B., and SPENCE, D. P. (1959), 'Cognitive control: a study of individual consistencies in cognitive behavior', *Psychol. Issues*, vol. 1, no. 4, monogr. no. 4.

GARDNER, R. W., JACKSON, D. N., and MESSICK, S. J. (1960), 'Personality organization in cognitive controls and intellectual abilities', *Psychol. Issues*, vol. 2, no. 4, monogr. no. 8.

GARDNER, R. W., and SCHOEN, R. A. (1962), 'Differentiation and abstraction in concept formation', *Psychol. Monogr.*, vol. 76, no. 41, whole no. 287. [See Reading 3.]

GARNER, W. R. (1962), *Uncertainty and Structure as Psychological Concepts*, Wiley.

HEIDER, F. (1958), *The Psychology of Interpersonal Relations*, Wiley.

HOLZMAN, P. S., and KLEIN, G. S. (1950), 'The "schematizing process": Perceptual attitudes and personal qualities in sensitivity to change', *Amer. Psychol.*, vol. 5, p. 312 (abstract).

HOVLAND, C. I., and SHERIF, M. (1952), 'Judgmental phenomena and scales of attitude measurement: item displacement in Thurstone scales', *J. abnorm. soc. Psychol.*, vol. 47, pp. 822–32.

HUNT, E. B. (1962), *Concept Learning: An Information Processing Problem*, Wiley.

KELLY, G. A. (1955), *The Psychology of Personal Constructs*, Norton.

KLEIN, G. S. (1949), 'Adaptive properties of sensory functioning: some postulates and hypotheses', *Bull. Menninger Clinic*, vol. 13, pp. 16–23.

PEAK, H. (1958), 'Psychological structure and psychological activity', *Psychol. Rev.*, vol. 65, pp. 325–47.

PETTIGREW, T. F. (1958), 'The measurement and correlates of category width as a cognitive variable', *J. Personal.*, vol. 26, pp. 532–44. [See Reading 6.]

ROGERS, C. R., and DYMOND, R. F. (eds.) (1954), *Psychotherapy and Personality Change*, University of Chicago Press.

SCHEERER, M. (1954), 'Cognitive theory', in G. Lindzey (ed.), *Handbook of Social Psychology*, vol. 1, *Theory and Method*, Addison-Wesley.

SHERIF, M., and HOVLAND, C. I. (1953), 'Judgmental phenomena and scales of attitude measurement: placement of items with individual choice of number of categories', *J. abnorm. soc. Psychol.*, vol. 48, pp. 135–41.

SHERIF, M., and HOVLAND, C. I. (1961), *Social Judgment*, Yale University Press.

SLOANE, H. N., JR (1959), *The Generality and Construct Validity of Equivalence Range*, University Microfilms, Ann Arbor, Michigan, pp. 59–1863.

WALLACH, M. A., and CARON, A. J. (1959), 'Attribute criteriality and sex-linked conservatism as determinants of psychological similarity', *J. abnorm. soc. Psychol.*, vol. 59, pp. 43–50.

WITKIN, H. A., DYK, R. B., FATERSON, H. F., GOODENOUGH, D. R., and KARP, S. A. (1962), *Psychological Differentiation: Studies of Development*, Wiley.

5 Henri Tajfel, Alan Richardson and Louis Everstine

Individual Consistencies in Categorizing

Henri Tajfel, Alan Richardson and Louis Everstine, 'Individual
consistencies in categorizing: a study in judgmental behavior',
Journal of Personality, vol. 32, 1964, pp. 90-108.

In the past few years, a considerable amount of research effort
has been devoted to the study of individual differences in cognitive styles. Some of this work was critically reviewed by Wallach
(1962) in a recent symposium. He notes inconsistent or uncon-
vincing results and points to theoretical rationales which are so
general that they allow, for example, two different research teams
to 'accept the outcome that verbal subtests of the Wechsler *did
not* or *did* correlate with their other measures, as consistent with
their analytical-global interpretation' (p. 205).

Wallach suggests the need for a closer specification of the
analytical-global dichotomy which underlies much of this research. The effect of the present generality of the construct
'could be to generate an interpretational common denominator
whose necessary vagueness and scantiness of properties at the
theoretical level renders it of little explanatory significance'
(p. 209). In his view, attempts should be made to separate more
distinctly sets of specific variables in the areas of motivation and
personality, as these variables are likely to affect the consistency
of cognitive styles and thus to reduce the predictive value of the
findings.

It is likely that a similar task of specification should be under-
taken with regard to the cognitive variables. A further analysis is
needed of the cognitive operations involved in the tasks, of their
common features and differences; some of these differences may
well be responsible for the inconsistencies and the low predictive
value of the reported results.

The investigation into the generality of a cognitive style can
proceed in a number of directions. One research strategy – risky
but holding the promise of the more interesting results – is to

extend this generality as far as it will reach through demonstrating it in a large variety of apparently unrelated aspects of cognitive functioning. The other possibility is to work one's way from the particular to the general – the method suggested by Wallach (1962) with regard to the personality 'moderator' variables – discarding on the way those generalizations which crack under the strain of over-extension. A good example of such narrowing was recently provided by Messick and Kogan (1963) who found two distinct components in object-sorting measures of categorizing style. These two components – referred to as 'differentiation' and 'compartmentalization' by Messick and Kogan – were hitherto lumped together in the various measures of object sorting. The essential difference between them is in the nature of cognitive operations involved in each.

Two steps in this type of analysis of a cognitive style seem essential. The first is a specification of the task confronting the Ss. The second step is really a series of steps: once a task is defined it should be possible to play a number of variations on the theme, to introduce changes in the task and in the conditions under which it is performed. The limits of the possible stylistic generalizations can thus be determined empirically and pursued as far as they will go.

The present paper is concerned with such an exploration of one cognitive variable. This variable has been referred to in a number of ways by various authors: equivalence range, category width or breadth of category, coarseness and fineness of category, etc. The differences between the studies are not, however, confined to terminology. Various types of tasks were studied: in some experiments the Ss were requested to determine whether a stimulus did or did not belong to a previously defined inclusion class (e.g. Bruner and Tajfel, 1961; Wallach and Caron, 1959); in others, the task was to sort a number of objects into a number of groups (e.g. Gardner, 1953; Gardner et al., 1959; Messick and Kogan, 1963); in others, this sorting task was of a more psychophysical nature (e.g. Fillenbaum, 1959); in others still, the subjective limits of an individual's categories were determined either in purely verbal tasks (e.g. Fillenbaum, 1959; Pettigrew, 1958) or on continuous dimensions in manipulative form (e.g. Bruner and Rodrigues, as reported in Bruner, Goodnow and Austin, 1956).

It is not the purpose of this paper to review these studies or to decide which is the 'proper' way to measure individual consistencies in categorizing – this is, at any rate, likely to remain a sterile question. This brief enumeration points, however, to one of the possible reasons for the inconsistencies of the findings and for the low relationships often obtained between performances on the various tasks. The tendency to overgeneralize without articulate and specific rationale to which Wallach (1962) pointed at the general level of inquiry into stylistic consistencies seems to exist as well at the more specific level of one particular aspect of these consistencies. Some of the studies mentioned above were concerned with conceptual behavior, some with judgemental, some with perceptual. Deciding whether a stimulus is sufficiently large or sufficiently small to fall within certain limits on a psychophysical continuum *need not* be a manifestation of the same cognitive process as, e.g. formulating rules for dividing a heterogeneous collection of objects into a small or a large number of conceptual groupings.

The aspect of categorizing behavior investigated in the present experiment is a judgemental one. In a general way, it may be described as the flexibility of subjective judgement categories once they are established. The problem is that of the limits of acceptance into, and rejection from, a class defined as a specific segment of a quantitative continuum. Can it be said that individual consistencies exist in this mode of functioning which span time intervals, judgement modalities and different probability distributions of events in the environment?

The choice of this particular aspect of categorizing was not dictated by a view that it is in some ways more 'fundamental' than others. Several more specific reasons determined the lines of the study.

A specific *judgemental* process can be postulated to determine the hypothetical individual consistencies in this behavior, independently of possible links and correlates with personality variables. In a previous paper (Bruner and Tajfel, 1961) this process was described in the context of anchoring phenomena:

When a subject has been judging a range of stimuli in terms of categories of absolute magnitude, the introduction of new stimuli larger than the range has either a 'contrast' or an 'assimilation' effect. A contrast effect is responding strongly to the newly introduced stimulus – say a stimulus larger than any previously encountered – by judging previous stimuli as contrastingly smaller. Assimilation, both in common-sense terms and technically, is 'not heeding' the new anchoring stimulus, i.e. judging it as no larger than the stimuli previously encountered. We might well predict that narrow subjects, sensitive to differences, will be subject to contrast effects. Broad subjects, on the other hand, should by virtue of their less acute reactiveness to change, show less of the contrast effect and may indeed assimilate the stimuli of the extended range to the psychophysical scale established with the smaller range of stimuli (p. 232).

It is possible to extend this formulation beyond judgement situations in which anchoring stimuli are employed. Sensitivity to change is essentially an aspect of general sensitivity to differences. When an S has determined for himself the upper and lower limits of an inclusion class on a quantitative continuum, each new incoming stimulus is evaluated in relation to these limits. This evaluation can proceed in terms of a search for similarity to stimuli which form the implicit basis for comparison or in terms of differences from such stimuli. No doubt, efficient and flexible functioning would involve an evaluation of both similarities and differences. It remains, however, that in any population of Ss one finds those who fall into the extremes of 'broad' and 'narrow' categorizing. The question is whether these extremes are just the inescapable randomly determined ends of any distribution of responses or rather a consistent phenomenon for those 'extreme' individuals who display a strong *relative* preference either for search for similarities or for search for differences.

There is some evidence that changes in this type of sensitivity are not only a matter of individual differences. They can be produced situationally (Tajfel and Wilkes, 1963; Wallach, 1959); they can be shown to vary when one varies the relevance to the subject of the dimensions that he is judging (Tajfel, 1959; Tajfel and Cawasjee, 1959). In the field of individual differences, the most striking specifications of extremes has perhaps been provided by Zaslow (1950) who found that in judgements of triangularity and circularity 'the range of similarity that the schizophrenic treats as

109

functionally equivalent tends to be either constricted to an abnormal degree or diffusely expanded due to over-inclusion of essentially dissimilar objects' (p. 337).[1]

It is highly suggestive that schizophrenics should be found at both ends of the continuum. It is as if there was here a breakdown of the check mechanism. A patient who, for whatever reasons, searches for an over-extended range of similarities does not temper this search by taking into account the differential aspects of the situation. The converse is true at the other end of the continuum.

This postulated search for similarities to, or differences from, dimensional typical instances of an inclusion class is not *necessarily* a determinant of performance in some of the tasks employed in the various studies. The obvious examples are the more conceptual measures of categorizing, such as object grouping, verbal measures of category width or determination of similarity in the meaning of words. Decisions which the Ss take in these situations are not based on the judged extent of dimensional similarity or differences or, at least as Messick and Kogan (1963) found in the case of object grouping, other factors are also likely to intervene. The main point is that definitions of inclusion classes, explicitly or implicitly used by the Ss, can vary along a number of unspecified dimensions: the more abstract those definitions the less will performance depend on the judged dimensional *extent* of similarities and differences. The only way in which such definitions can vary in a task employing a segment of a dimensional continuum is in the width or range of that segment.

This is not necessarily true of judgemental tasks employing as their measure of equivalence range the extent to which the S segments a dimensional continuum (e.g. Fillenbaum, 1959). The number of categories used by Ss is not based here on 'in' and 'out' decisions; nor is it in a task employing several target categories univocally related to width of categorizing. We have some evidence concerning differences in tendencies towards the use of more extreme categories (Sherif and Hovland, 1961; Tajfel and Wilkes, 1964); these tendencies are often totally unrelated to the problem of individual consistencies in equivalence range.

1. This point is further examined in Reading 24 [*Ed.*].

In this context it is also interesting to note the inconsistent results reported by Perloe (1961) who correlated the amount of assimilation found in a task employing two target categories with performance on the Schematizing Test. Perloe's attempt was based on '. . . the hypothesis that the predispositional variable of "levelling" as measured by the Schematizing Test is a determinant of assimilation toward the typical instances of categories' (p. 157). In discussing the discrepancy between his results and those of a similar study conducted earlier by Harvey and Caldwell (1959) who used one category only, Perloe writes:

The discrimination task may have led Ss to exaggerate the differences between the two classes of stimuli. That is, Ss in the present study may have displaced the discrepant dim stimuli away from the boundary between the two categories in order to make their task of separating the stimuli easier. Ss in Harvey and Caldwell's experiment would not have been subject to this pressure (p. 161).

It is important to stress at this point that it is not the aim of this discussion to contest the general validity of the studies concerned with category width. Rather, we wish to emphasize the need for a closer analysis of the nature of cognitive behavior displayed in these studies. From this point of view, judgement tasks which involve assignment of incoming stimuli into a category previously defined as a segment of a dimensional continuum seem relatively unaffected by irrelevant variables. Therefore, they should be given some measure of priority in the establishment of categorizing consistencies.

Wallach and Caron (1959) used this type of task in their study of the relationship between the criteriality of an attribute and the range of assignment of stimuli into a category. They reported the following results: (a) when the dimensional attribute was criterial the range of assignment into the target category was narrower than when that attribute was not criterial; (b) the range of assignment was significantly broader for boys than for girls; (c) it was significantly correlated with Pettigrew's (1958) measure of category width for the total sample, though this correlation did not reach significance when the groups of boys and girls were considered separately. As the Pettigrew measure also correlated with sex, Wallach and Caron write,

'. . . category width does not reflect any factor critical for similarity other than the sex difference, since, as Table 3 indicates, correlations *within* sex between category width and similarity measures are all non-significant' (p. 49). In a study using tasks of a similar character, Bruner and Tajfel (1961) found that the extreme broad and narrow groups of categorizers tended to maintain their relative positions when (a) the modality of judgement was varied from numerosity to length; (b) the frequency of stimuli which actually belonged to the target class varied from one-third to two-thirds of the total; (c) the range of stimuli presented was shortened or lengthened.

The present study is an attempt at a further exploration of this type of consistency. It had several aims:

1. Both studies just referred to used children as subjects. There would be many reasons to suspect that categorizing consistencies found in children between the ages of ten to twelve could well evaporate in an adult population. The first aim of the present study was to ascertain whether the results reported by Bruner and Tajfel could be extended to adults.

2. In the study by Bruner and Tajfel, the range of stimuli presented to the Ss was altered after some presentations in order to investigate the reaction to change of the two extreme groups of categorizers. Therefore, data about direct effects of practice on individual consistencies in categorizing were not obtained. In the present study the Ss dealt with the same range of stimuli throughout each experimental session. It was assumed that any categorizing consistencies found to exist should stabilize and become more marked as a function of more prolonged exposure to the judgement situations.

3. The effects of practice just mentioned are closely related to another possible manifestation of consistency behavior when a 'second chance' is given to the subject for specifying the relative proportions of stimuli falling inside and outside the inclusion class. In order to provide this, in one of the tasks we required the Ss to estimate these total proportions as soon as they had finished judging the individual stimuli. Our hypothesis was that the extreme groups of categorizers should differ in their handling of this task; they should both correct in a manner consistent with

their preferred mode of judgement; the broad group in the direction of even wider acceptance, and the narrow group in the opposite direction.

4. A further extension of the limits of consistency was attempted in the study. In the dimensional tasks, categorizing decisions are made on the basis of unambiguous criteria about the *nature* of the inclusion class, though its subjective limits may vary from individual to individual. Would the consistency hold in a situation in which the *S* would have to decide not only about the limits of the inclusion class but also about its defining criteria?

5. The relationship between performance on these various judgemental tasks and on the more conceptual ones was also investigated.

Method

Subjects

Seventy graduate and undergraduate students from Oxford University (thirty-four women and thirty-six men) volunteered to take part in the study. However, the analysis of results was based on slightly varying numbers of *S*s as not all of them completed all the tasks.

Description of the tasks

The psychophysical tasks: 1. The 'dots' task: the procedure for administering this task was similar to that employed by Bruner and Tajfel (1961).[2] Seven series of slides were used. Each series consisted of nine slides and on each slide was a different random arrangement of black dots on a white background, from twenty to twenty-eight dots per slide. The series were presented in seven successive random orders. Each slide was projected onto a screen for a period of 1·5 seconds, and the *S* was required to judge whether each slide contained twenty, twenty-one or twenty-two dots or whether it contained a greater number than these. If an *S* judged a slide to contain a cluster of dots within this target range he was required to place a tick in his answer booklet in which a numbered page was reserved for each judgement. If

2. This task is discussed by Gardner and Schoen on page 61 and also in articles referred to at the foot of page 62 [*Ed.*].

the S judged that the slide contained any other number of dots he was to make a cross. An S's score on this task was the percentage of ticks given out of the total number of sixty-three responses: the higher the percentage obtained by an S the greater his width of categorizing. Ss were tested in groups of from two to seven persons, and before the task was begun the group was told that no slides containing less than twenty dots would be presented. Ss were also shown sample slides containing clusters of twenty, twenty-one and twenty-two dots.

Immediately after the completion of the task just described, all Ss were asked to make an estimate as to the actual percentage of the slides shown that had contained twenty, twenty-one or twenty-two dots. The Ss were told to write their estimate as a percentage on the last page of their answer booklets.

2. The 'lines' task: this was administered about a month after the task described above. Small groups of Ss were required to make judgements as to whether a straight black line flashed onto the screen for 1·5 seconds was inside or outside a target range of from 7 inches to 9·5 inches. Prior to the administration of the task proper Ss were told that no slide would contain lines of less than 7 inches. To familiarize them with the target range, slides were shown in random order, of lines varying in length from 7 to 9·5 inches in steps of half an inch. It should be noted that whereas in the 'dots' task one-third of all stimuli to be judged were within the target range, in the 'lines' task two-thirds of all stimuli fell within this range. In the task proper, seven series of nine slides were used containing lines of 7, 7·5, 8, 8·5, 9, 9·5, 10, 10·5 and 11 inches. The position and inclination of lines were randomly varied from slide to slide. The series of nine slides were presented in successive random orders, providing a total of sixty-three stimuli in all. If an S judged a line to be within the target range he was required to place a tick in his answer booklet. If the line was judged to be longer than any within the target range then the S was required to make a cross. An S's score consisted of the number of ticks expressed as a percentage of the sixty-three judgements recorded.

The unstructured task ('*figures*'). This task was administered during the month separating the two previously described tasks.

Fifty cards containing each six to seven figures, a total of 352 different abstract figures, were shown one card at a time to each *S* individually. The instructions required each *S* to look at each card in turn (there was no time limit) and to judge which of the figures on each card was considered by him to be 'regular'. The term 'regular' (whose connotations are slightly different in Britain and in America) was left undefined and consequently there was no objective target category. The score obtained was the number of figures judged to be regular out of 352. This score was then converted to a percentage.

The conceptual tasks. Four such tasks were used. They were all performed in a group session which took place nearly a month after the completion of the judgement tasks previously described.

1. Grouping of objects: a list of fifty heterogeneous objects was presented (e.g. lamp-post, sweater, spoon, etc.) and the *S*s were asked to 'put together into groups [those] which seem to you to belong together'. The scores here were: the number of groups, and the mean number of words assigned to the first two groups.

2. Substitution of words: in a list of sixty-seven sentences, the *S*s were asked to decide 'whether the [additional] expression in parenthesis could safely be substituted for the underlined expression'. The score consisted of the percentage of expressions considered equivalent to the original ones.

3. Synonymity task: in a list of thirty words each 'key' word was followed by a number of additional words. The *S*'s task was 'to underline all the words in the list which have the same meaning as the key word, i.e. all the words that could be substituted for the key word in most usages'. The score consisted of the mean percentage of words chosen as equivalent to the key words.

4. Prediction of probabilities: in twelve fictitious situations with uncertain outcomes, the *S*s were asked to choose the 'lowest [quantitative] probability that you would consider acceptable' for undertaking a successful course of action or for a successful outcome. This was scored as the mean level of acceptable probabilities over the twelve situations.

115

The hypotheses of the study can now be presented in the context of the methods used:

There should be a positive relationship between proportions of the stimuli assigned to the inclusion class in the two psychophysical tasks, despite the different judgement modalities and the different proportions of stimuli actually belonging to that class.

This relationship should be more marked for the second than for the first half of the judgements in these two tasks.

The extreme groups of broad and narrow categorizers in these two tasks should differ in the directions of discrepancy shown by them between frequency of the stimuli that they assign to the target category during the judgement task and their subsequent estimates of proportions of stimuli belonging to this category. For 'broad' categorizers these estimates should show a relative increase over the frequency of initial 'in' judgements: for 'narrow' categorizers a relative decrease.

If the performance on the 'figures' task is based on the same type of categorizing activity as the two psychophysical tasks, there should be a positive relationship between scores on that task and on each of the two previous ones.

The same applies to the relationship between the scores on the judgement tasks and the conceptual tasks.

Results

A computer analysis of all the relevant scores was made. This analysis provided information about the following aspects of the results:

1. Product-moment correlations of each set of scores with each other set.

2. The performance of the two groups which were extreme at each one of the tasks on each of the other tasks. For example, the groups of *S*s who were broad and narrow categorizers on the 'dots' task (at a cut-off point of 27 per cent at both ends of the distribution) were selected in the program and the means of their performance on the 'lines' task were obtained; the converse operation used extreme performance on the 'lines' task as the criterion for division into groups, and scores on the 'dots' task as

the dependent variable. In this way, all the possible relationships were obtained and no arbitrary assumptions made about which tasks should or should not be used as a criterion for predicting performance on other tasks. In addition, the program provided statements of the significance of the differences between each two groups using the Mann–Whitney U-statistic.

The general pattern of results

No useful purpose would be served by presenting here a complete table of the correlations. Most of them are slightly positive. The list of all the correlations which are better than, at or near 5 per cent significance level (two-tailed) is presented in Table 2. Table 1 contains the code names of the various sets of scores.

Table 1

Scores and Their Codes

Description of score	Code
Dots – percentage of 'yes' responses in first half of session	A
Dots – percentage of 'yes' responses in second half of session	B
Dots – total percentage of 'yes' responses	C
Dots – percentage estimates subsequent to judgement session	D
Dots – percentage discrepancy between judgements and estimates (+ if estimates larger; – if estimates smaller)	E
Lines – percentage of 'yes' responses in first half of session	F
Lines – percentage of 'yes' responses in second half of session	G
Lines – total percentage of 'yes' responses	H
Figures – total percentage of 'regular' responses	I
Grouping – mean number of words grouped in first two categories	J
Substitution – percentage of sentences in which substitution was made	K
Synonymity – mean percentage of words found equivalent	L
Estimation of probability – mean percentage of 'likelihood'	M

As can be seen from Table 2, the correlations do not present a consistent pattern. For example, there are no significant correlations between any of the four conceptual tasks. On the other hand, performance on the grouping task (J) relates positively to one of the measures on the 'dots' task (A) and two of the

117

measures on the 'lines' task (F and G); the same is true of performance on the estimation of probability (M). Within the judgement tasks the discrepancy between judgements and estimates in the 'dots' task (E) seems to have the most general relationship to other aspects of the judgemental behavior. The general pattern is consistent with the results previously reported in this field; weak to moderate positive relationships with some curious exceptions which are not easily explained.

Table 2

Correlations between Sets of Scores

Correlations between judgement tasks (A to I)		Correlation between judgement tasks (A to I) and conceptual tasks (J to M)	
A–E	0·27	A–J	0·28
A–I	0·21	B–L	0·36
B–G	0·24	B–M	0·29
D–F	0·24	F–J	0·25
D–G	0·21	G–J	0·25
D–H	0·24	G–M	0·25
E–F	0·27	H–M	0·32
E–G	0·21	I–K	0·25
E–H	0·29		

With regard to the specific problems of the present inquiry, it seemed that the most informative analysis of results would consist of a detailed inspection of the degree of predictability that could be achieved by seeing how *S*s who belong to extreme groups on any of the tasks performed on other tasks. These results are presented below.

Extension to an adult population of categorizing consistency found in children

There is no doubt that the level of consistency reported by Bruner and Tajfel (1961) for children is not reached for the adult *S*s employed in the present study. The correlation reported in the previous study was 0·57. In the present one it only reaches 0·12. The finding of differences in breadth of category for boys and girls reported by Wallach and Caron (1959) is also not replicated;

there are no significant differences between the scores of men and women.

It remains, however, that the performance of the Ss who were broad and narrow categorizers on the 'dots' and on the 'lines' tasks differs in the direction which supports consistency on *all* the other tasks. Table 3 sets out the relevant mean scores.

Table 3

| | 'Dots' task as criterion: performance on other tasks | | | 'Lines' task as criterion: performance on other tasks | |
	broad categorizers	narrow categorizers		broad categorizers	narrow categorizers
E	−2·8	−4·8	C	56·4	51·2
H	68·1	63·7	D**	57·4	42·8
I	33·6	26·8	E**	+0·9	−8·4
J	6·7	5·6	I	30·1	26·4
K	58·8	52·5	J***	6·8	5·0
L	39·0	36·5	K	56·9	51·4
M	46·1	44·2	L	37·6	36·3
			M	44·6	38·7

** $p < 0.025$. *** $p < 0.01$.

Effects of practice on the judgement consistencies

Tables 4 and 5 set out data relevant to the effects of practice – the relationships to other tasks when the first and the second halves of performance on the 'dots' and on the 'lines' tasks are taken as criteria. A comparison of these relationships leaves little doubt that as the task becomes longer the efficiency in the prediction of performance of extreme groups, between the 'dots' and the 'lines' tasks, improves considerably.

Relationship between estimates and judgement tasks

The criteria for the relationships set out in Table 6 are total estimates of the proportion of stimuli falling into the target category in the 'dots' task and discrepancy between these estimates and the judgements of individual stimuli in the 'dots' task. Total estimates provide a supplementary measure of consistency. The discrepancy scores reflect the direction of the 'second chance'

Table 4

| | First half of 'dots' task as criterion: performance on other tasks | | | Second half of 'dots' task as criterion: performance on other tasks | | |
	broad categorizers	narrow categorizers			broad categorizers	narrow categorizers
E*	−0·7	−8·8	E		−3·6	−4·9
F	71·4	62·5	G**		69·5	62·3
I	32·1	25·4	I		30·9	26·4
J*	9·2	5·6	J		6·6	6·2
K	56·0	53·9	K*		63·6	52·1
L	35·3	32·5	L*		39·7	33·8
M	47·6	44·6	M		48·0	41·1

* $p < 0.05$. ** $p < 0.025$.

behavior: Ss who showed the highest positive discrepancies between their estimates and judgements were assigned to one extreme group; those showing the highest negative discrepancies to the other.

As can be seen from Table 6 estimates in the 'dots' task do relate significantly to judgements on the 'lines' task. This relationship is, therefore, more consistent than that between

Table 5

| | First half of 'lines' task as criterion: performance on other tasks | | | Second half of 'lines' task as criterion: performance on other tasks | | |
	broad categorizers	narrow categorizers			broad categorizers	narrow categorizers
A	54·6	51·6	B***		59·6	49·3
D**	53·8	42·8	D**		58·2	46·4
E	−0·7	−7·8	E		+1·1	−5·5
I	29·1	24·9	I		30·2	29·7
J*	6·6	4·8	J		8·4	5·2
K	53·0	52·1	K		58·2	49·9
L	37·9	36·0	L		37·0	31·9
M	44·4	39·5	M		45·0	42·0

* $p < 0.05$. ** $p < 0.025$. *** $p < 0.01$.

judgements on the 'dots' and on the 'lines' tasks. (See Table 3.)

Table 6

	Estimates in 'dots' task as criterion: performance on other tasks			Discrepancy between estimates and judgement in 'dots' task as criterion: performance on other tasks	
	broad categorizers	narrow categorizers		broad categorizers	narrow categorizers
H*	73·8	65·0	C*	58·6	52·2
I	32·7	30·8	H**	73·4	64·6
J**	7·6	5·3	I*	32·6	28·4
K	58·3	58·0	J	6·9	6·1
L	36·6	35·1	K	57·9	50·6
M	45·4	43·2	L	34·1	33·5
			M	45·3	44·6

$* \ p < 0.05. \ ** \ p < 0.025.$

The evidence of relationship between direction of discrepancy in the 'dots' task and the judgement tasks is quite clear. Those Ss who place their estimates upwards of their original assignments of stimuli into the target category in the 'dots' task tend to have wider ranges of acceptance in all three judgement tasks than those who tend to place them downwards. With regard to the 'dots' task, this finding is quite striking as one would expect Ss who started with higher proportions to change to lower ones and the converse to happen to Ss who started with lower proportions.

Relationship between the psychophysical and the unstructured judgement tasks

These are in the expected direction but do not reach significance. The only relationship with the 'figures' task which does reach significance is that with the substitution task (K) (broad categorizers on 'figures' have a mean score of 63·0 on substitution task, the narrow categorizers a mean score of 55·7; $p < 0.025$).

121

Relationships between the conceptual and the judgement tasks

Table 7 sets out all the significant relationships with the judgement tasks when performance on the various conceptual tasks was taken as the criterion. Most of the other relationships are also in the direction of consistency.

Table 7

Conceptual tasks as criterion: performance on judgement tasks

Criterion task	Performance on judgement tasks		
	broad	task	narrow
J	70·9	H**	59·7
K	35·9	I**	27·8
L	57·1	C*	50·7
M	55·9	C*	51·4

* $p < 0.05$. ** $p < 0.025$.

Relationship between the various conceptual tasks

Here again, the relationships are in the direction of consistency but only one of them reaches significance; with the synonymity task (L) as criterion the mean score of the broad group in the substitution task (K) is 62·1; of the narrow group – 49·1; $p < 0.05$.

Conclusions

The over-all results of the study are by no means startling: there is general evidence of moderate categorizing consistencies supporting previous results in this area. But many of these relationships are sufficiently low to underscore the arguments put forward by Wallach (1962) and in the first section of this paper: that these consistencies are bound to be powerfully affected by 'moderator' variables of motivational or cognitive nature, and that therefore a more detailed analysis of such variables is necessary before wide generalizations are made. In relation to the specific problems of the study, the following conclusions seem to emerge.

1. There is no doubt that judgemental consistencies in our adult population do not reach the level of these consistencies found in children. Therefore, a developmental study of such consistencies seems one of the most urgent research requirements in this area. If the present findings are validated by further studies, their implications may be important in a number of ways.

2. In the same way, the finding of sex differences in width of categorizing in a judgement task reported by Wallach and Caron (1959) was not replicated in the present study. Clear conclusions from this lack of replication cannot be reached as the two studies differ not only with regard to the age of the *S*s but also in their cultural context. This second variable may be quite important in view of the argument put forward by Wallach and Caron that the differences they found are culturally determined.

3. There is clear evidence in the results that individual judgement consistencies become more marked as function of prolonged practice in a repetitive task.

4. Estimates of the proportion of stimuli falling into a target category subsequent to one judgement task relate to judgements of these proportions in another task. This is not an independent finding since there is a high correlation, as one would expect, between the estimates and the judgements on the same task. The finding provides, however, a subsidiary confirmation of judgement consistencies.

5. The findings concerning the discrepancy between judgements and subsequent estimates are fairly convincing. It was found that (a) there was some evidence of broad categorizers on the 'dots' task decreasing their subsequent estimates *less* than the narrow categorizers; (b) there was evidence of broad categorizers and narrow categorizers on the 'lines' task differing clearly in the same direction on the scores expressing discrepancies between judgements and estimates in the 'dots' task. In addition, when these scores are taken as a criterion for division of *S*s into two extreme groups it is found that the group of *S*s with the most positive discrepancies tends towards significantly wider categorization scores on both judgement tasks than the group with the most negative discrepancies. This finding seems important because it provides additional and independent evidence of a preferred and consistent mode of categorizing in ambiguous judgement situations.

6. There is no evidence of a significant relationship between performance on dimensional and unstructured judgement tasks – though the results are in the direction of consistency of functioning. It is very likely that the task of labelling abstract figures as 'regular' or 'not regular' is confounded by some variable or variables other than category width.

If the judgement of 'regular', as applied to a particular abstract figure, is assumed to be associated with an S's readiness to place many or few stimuli within an inclusion class it must also be assumed that the relationship between the label 'regular' and properties of the figure stimuli are the same for all judges. Not all judges, of course, will be equally prepared to admit that any particular figure is within the defined inclusion class. However, there are, in fact, many criteria and combinations of criteria which might lead different judges to apply the label 'regular' to a particular figure, e.g. symmetry, simplicity, familiarity, balanced asymmetry, curved continuity of outline. If, for example, symmetry is the underlying criterion used by a particular 'narrow' categorizer, and many of the abstract figures provided some objective support for the judgement of symmetrical, then the verbal label of 'regular' will be applied relatively often. On the other hand, a different 'narrow' categorizer might restrict his use of the label 'regular' to those figures which were judged to present a balanced asymmetric appearance. If there were relatively few such figures in the stimulus series, then the label of 'regular' would be applied less often – yet this outcome would not indicate any necessary inconsistency in width of categorizing between the two judges.

The 'figures' task was originally included in the study because it appeared to provide a relatively simple though unstructured judging situation. The results reveal once more the dangers referred to in the introduction. To include inadequately analysed though apparently analogous tasks may or may not lead to the confirmation of a prediction. Either way, it is impossible to provide an unequivocal interpretation.

7. Nearly all the relationships between the judgemental and the conceptual tasks are in the direction of categorizing consistency though relatively few of them are statistically convincing. This

lack of statistical consistency lends further support to the argument that a more detailed analysis of the nature of cognitive tasks employed is needed in this type of study.

8. The same applies to the relationships between the various conceptual tasks. Only one such relationship was sufficiently marked to reach the level of statistical significance.

References

BRUNER, J. S., GOODNOW, J. J., and AUSTIN, G. A. (1956), *A Study of Thinking*, Wiley, pp. 28–30.

BRUNER, J. S., and TAJFEL, H. (1961), 'Cognitive risk and environmental change', *J. abnorm. soc. Psychol.*, vol. 62, pp. 231–41.

FILLENBAUM, S. (1959), 'Some stylistic aspects of categorizing behavior', *J. Personal.*, vol. 27, pp. 187–95.

GARDNER, R. (1953), 'Cognitive styles in categorizing behavior', *J. Personal.*, vol. 22, pp. 214–33.

GARDNER, R., HOLZMAN, P. S., KLEIN, G. S., LINTON, H., and SPENCE, D. P. (1959), 'Cognitive control: a study of individual consistencies in cognitive behavior', *Psychol. Issues*, vol. 1, no. 4.

HARVEY, O. J., and CALDWELL, D. F. (1959), 'Assimilation and contrast phenomena in response to environmental variation', *J. Personal.*, vol. 27, pp. 125–35.

MESSICK, S., and KOGAN, N. (1963), 'Differentiation and compartmentalization in object-sorting measures of categorizing style', *Percept. mot. Skills*, vol. 16, pp. 47–51.

PERLOE, S. I. (1961), 'Assimilation as a consequence of categorization', *J. Personal.*, vol. 29, pp. 148–66.

PETTIGREW, T. F. (1958), 'The measurement and correlates of category width as a cognitive variable', *J. Personal.*, vol. 26, pp. 532–44. [See Reading 6.]

SHERIF, M., and HOVLAND, C. I. (1961), *Social Judgment. Assimilation and Contrast Effects in Communication and Attitude Change*, Yale University Press.

TAJFEL, H. (1959), 'The anchoring effects of value in a scale of judgments', *Brit. J. Psychol.*, vol. 50, pp. 294–304.

TAJFEL, H., and CAWASJEE, S. D. (1959), 'Value and the accentuation of judged differences: a confirmation', *J. abnorm. soc. Psychol.*, vol. 59, pp. 436–9.

TAJFEL, H., and WILKES, A. L. (1963), 'Classification and quantitative judgment', *Brit. J. Psychol.*, vol. 54, pp. 101–14.

TAJFEL, H., and WILKES, A. L. (1964), 'Salience of attributes and commitment to extreme judgments in the perception of people', *Brit. J. soc. clin. Psychol.*, vol. 3, pp. 40–49.

WALLACH, M. A. (1959), 'The influence of classification requirements on gradients of response', *Psychol. Monogr.*, vol. 73, no. 8, whole no. 478.

WALLACH, M. A. (1962), 'Commentary: active-analytical vs. passive-global cognitive functioning', in S. Messick and J. Ross (eds.), *Measurement in Personality and Cognition*, Wiley, pp. 199–218.

WALLACH, M. A., and CARON, A. J. (1959), 'Attribute criteriality and sex-linked conservatism as determinants of psychological similarity', *J. abnorm. soc. Psychol.*, vol. 59, pp. 43–50.

ZASLOW, R. W. (1950), 'A new approach to the problem of conceptual thinking in schizophrenia', *J. consult. Psychol.*, vol. 14, pp. 335–9.

6 Thomas F. Pettigrew

The Measurement and Correlates of Category Width as a
Cognitive Variable

Excerpt from Thomas F. Pettigrew, 'The measurement and correlates of
category width as a cognitive variable', *Journal of Personality*, vol. 26,
1958, pp. 532–44.

Bruner and Rodrigues have demonstrated that Ss reveal marked
individual consistency in the range or width of their cognitive
categories (see Bruner, Goodnow and Austin, 1956). Using
standard laboratory equipment, such as color mixing wheels and
audio-oscillators, these investigators asked their Ss to select the
extremes, e.g. the darkest and lightest or highest and lowest, of a
wide variety of categories. For such diverse categories as the
brightness of an overcast sky and the pitch of a female singing
voice, Ss in this situation tended to be consistently broad, medium,
or narrow in their category widths relative to the total sample.

Such consistency suggests that category width may be fruitfully
thought of as an *Anschauung* (Klein, 1951), complementing Klein's
dimensions of leveling–sharpening and tolerance–resistance to
the unstable (Holzman and Klein, 1954; Klein, 1951). Several
interpretations can be made as to precisely what this category
width *Anschauung* is tapping. It can be thought of as measuring
S's typical equivalence range for classifying objects. This would
make category width an important factor in similarity problems.
Wallach (1958), for instance, has recently suggested that psychological similarity can be effectively studied in terms of factors
influencing equivalence ranges. Another not incompatible possibility is that category width is tapping a 'risk-taking' dimension.
Broad categorizers seem to have a tolerance for type I errors:
they risk negative instances in an effort to include a maximum of
positive instances. By contrast, narrow categorizers are willing
to make type II errors. They exclude many positive instances by
restricting their category ranges in order to minimize the number
of negative instances. It will require further research before these
two possible interpretations can be properly evaluated.

The extensive cognitive and personality implications of this consistency of range phenomenon have led first to the development of an objectively scored, paper and pencil measure of category width. The present paper introduces the scale ($C\text{-}W$ scale), lists its properties and correlates, and suggests its future research possibilities.

Scale Development

The first form of the $C\text{-}W$ scale consisted of fourteen items which supplied each category's average and required open-ended estimates of each category's extremes. Thus, one item stated that an average of fifty-eight ships enter New York harbor daily, and S was asked to write down his guesses as to what were the largest number and the smallest number of ships to enter New York harbor in a single day. Two later forms replaced items with low item-test correlations and enlarged the scale. On all of these forms Ss revealed significant consistency from one item to another in the breadth of their estimates. That is, when Ss were ranked as to their category widths on each item, Kendall's W statistic repeatedly indicated for five college and high school samples significant concordance in rankings. Ss proved to be reliably broad, medium, or narrow in their estimated ranges of such varied categories as speeds of birds in flight, length of whales and annual rainfall in Washington, D.C.

Following these paper and pencil replications of the Bruner and Rodrigues phenomenon, a final and more easily scored twenty-item form of the scale was devised with fixed alternatives. This is reproduced in Table 1. The alternatives offered were empirically derived by choosing the 10th, 35th, 65th and 90th percentile choices of the 750 college students who took the earlier, open-ended forms of the $C\text{-}W$ scale.[1] Scoring of the items is based on how far from the given mean of the category is the particular alternative: $+3$ is assigned the alternative farthest from the mean, $+2$ for the next farthest, etc. Table 1 provides in parentheses the points assigned each alternative. The orders of

1. When the correct alternatives were available – as in items 15 and 19 – they were supplied in place of the nearest alternative that would otherwise have been used.

these alternatives are varied to minimize response sets. Scores for questions (a) and (b) of each item are added together to obtain the total item score. Hence, the higher the score, the broader is the category width.

Properties of the scale

Chief correlates and tentative college distributions. C-W relates significantly to both sex and quantitative (Q) scores on the ACE with University of North Carolina student samples. Table 2 shows that C-W has a significant, though low, correlation of +0·17 with total ACE scores which is chiefly due to a higher +0·26 coefficient between C-W and the ACE Q-score.

The sharp difference between the sexes on C-W is indicated in Table 3. Since these male and female populations do not differ on ACE Q-scores, the males' typically broader category estimates cannot be accounted for in terms of the quantitative variable. Both sex distributions do not significantly deviate from normality. Separate limits for the thirds of these distributions are provided in Table 3 for each sex. Using a children's form of the C-W scale, Wallach and Caron report equally striking sex differences among sixth graders (1958).[2]

Over-time reliability. Odd and even item split-half forms of the C-W were given to ninety-seven University of North Carolina undergraduates at intervals of at least six weeks (the even and odd item forms were reversed as to order of presentation to two groups of Ss). The Spearman–Brown corrected coefficient proved to be +0·72.

Internal consistency. Five college samples varying in size from forty-two to sixty-six yield Spearman–Brown corrected even–odd reliabilities ranging from +0·86 to +0·93. When the total 281 Ss are combined, the Spearman–Brown corrected even–odd coefficient is +0·90.

The 190 inter-item tetrachoric correlations calculated on 270 Ss for factor analytic purposes also give some indication of the

2. It is not yet clear how far this finding can be generalized to other measures of category usage. Glixman finds a significant sex difference with his object-sorting task (see Reading 4, page 93), but Tajfel *et al.* fail to observe this in their situation (see Reading 5, page 106) [*Ed.*].

Table 1

The Category-Width Scale Items[1]

---

1. It has been estimated that the average width of windows is *34 inches*. What do you think

  (a) is the width of the widest window . . .

  | 1. | 1363 inches | (3)[2] | 3. | 48 inches | (0) |
  | 2. | 341 inches | (2) | 4. | 81 inches | (1) |

  (b) is the width of the narrowest window . . .

  | 1. | 3 inches | (2) | 3. | 11 inches | (1) |
  | 2. | 18 inches | (0) | 4. | 1 inch | (3) |

2. Ornithologists tell us that the best guess of the average speed of birds in flight would be about *17 m.p.h.* What do you think

  (a) is the speed in flight of the fastest bird . . .

  | 1. | 25 m.p.h. | (0) | 3. | 73 m.p.h. | (2) |
  | 2. | 105 m.p.h. | (3) | 4. | 34 m.p.h. | (1) |

  (b) is the speed in flight of the slowest bird . . .

  | 1. | 10 m.p.h. | (1) | 3. | 12 m.p.h. | (0) |
  | 2. | 2 m.p.h. | (3) | 4. | 5 m.p.h. | (2) |

3. The average length of whales in the Atlantic Ocean has been estimated by zoologists to be roughly *65 feet*. What do you think

  (a) is the length of the longest whale in the Atlantic Ocean . . .

  | 1. | 120 feet | (2) | 3. | 86 feet | (1) |
  | 2. | 190 feet | (3) | 4. | 75 feet | (0) |

  (b) is the length of the shortest whale in the Atlantic Ocean . . .

  | 1. | 6 feet | (3) | 3. | 52 feet | (0) |
  | 2. | 43 feet | (1) | 4. | 21 feet | (2) |

4. Shipping authorities have calculated that the average weight of merchant ships registered with the U.S. Maritime Commission in 1946 was *5705 tons*. What do you think

  (a) is the weight of the heaviest ship registered with the commission . . .

  | 1. | 10,500 tons | (1) | 3. | 23,000 tons | (2) |
  | 2. | 62,000 tons | (3) | 4. | 7500 tons | (0) |

  (b) is the weight of the lightest ship registered with the commission . . .

  | 1. | 3900 tons | (0) | 3. | 2700 tons | (1) |
  | 2. | 1100 tons | (2) | 4. | 2 tons | (3) |

---

1. Presented to all *S*s with the title 'Estimation Questionnaire', instructions stressing accuracy, and a simple example.

2. Indicates the weights assigned to each item alternative.

Table 1 – *continued*

5. Weather officials report that during this century Washington, D.C. has received an average rainfall of *41·1 inches* annually. What do you think

 (a) is the largest amount of rain that Washington has received in a single year during this century . . .

1.	82·4 inches	(3)	3.	63·7 inches	(2)
2.	45·8 inches	(0)	4.	51·2 inches	(1)

 (b) is the smallest amount of rain that Washington has received in a single year during this century . . .

1.	20·2 inches	(2)	3.	9·9 inches	(3)
2.	36·3 inches	(0)	4.	29·7 inches	(1)

6. An average of *58 ships* entered or left New York harbor daily during the period from 1950 through 1955. What do you think

 (a) was the largest number of ships to enter or leave New York in a single day during this period . . .

1.	69 ships	(0)	3.	76 ships	(1)
2.	153 ships	(3)	4.	102 ships	(2)

 (b) was the smallest number of ships to enter or leave New York in a single day during this period . . .

1.	34 ships	(1)	3.	16 ships	(2)
2.	3 ships	(3)	4.	43 ships	(0)

7. For the past twenty years, Alaska's population has increased an average *3210 people* per year. What do you think

 (a) was the greatest increase in Alaska's population in a single year during these twenty years . . .

1.	6300	(2)	3.	3900	(0)
2.	21,500	(3)	4.	4800	(1)

 (b) was the smallest increase in Alaska's population in a single year during these twenty years . . .

1.	470	(3)	3.	980	(2)
2.	1960	(1)	4.	2520	(0)

8. Boating experts estimate that the average speed of all sailing craft in America is around *4·1 knots*. What do you think

 (a) is the speed of the fastest sailing boat in America . . .

1.	8·2 knots	(1)	3.	5·9 knots	(0)
2.	30·7 knots	(3)	4.	21·3 knots	(2)

Table 1 – *continued*

(b) is the speed of the slowest sailing boat in America . . .

1.	3·3 knots	(0)	3.	2·2 knots	(1)
2.	0·6 knots	(3)	4.	1·2 knots	(2)

9. Book review editors guess that around *300 new American novels* have appeared annually since the Second World War. What do you think

(a) is the largest number of novels to be published in America in a single year during this period . . .

1.	380 novels	(0)	3.	870 novels	(3)
2.	495 novels	(1)	4.	620 novels	(2)

(b) is the smallest number of novels to be published in America in a single year during this period . . .

1.	145 novels	(2)	3.	90 novels	(3)
2.	205 novels	(1)	4.	260 novels	(0)

10. Between 1900 and 1940 there was an average of *48 lynchings* per year in the United States. What do you think

(a) was the largest number of lynchings in any one year during this period in the United States . . .

1.	79	(2)	3.	53	(0)
2.	63	(1)	4.	135	(3)

(b) was the smallest number of lynchings in any one year during this period in the United States . . .

1.	1	(3)	3.	33	(0)
2.	11	(2)	4.	19	(1)

11. It has been calculated that the average time for all trains in 1953 from New York City to Washington, D.C. was *285 minutes* (4 hours and 45 minutes). What do you think

(a) was the time of the slowest train from New York City to Washington in 1953 . . .

1.	337 minutes	(1)	3.	396 minutes	(2)
2.	304 minutes	(0)	4.	483 minutes	(3)

(b) was the time of the fastest train from New York City to Washington in 1953 . . .

1.	236 minutes	(1)	3.	268 minutes	(0)
2.	202 minutes	(2)	4.	145 minutes	(3)

Table 1 – *continued*

12. The average number of births in the world per day during 1955 has been computed to be *27,440*. What do you think

 (a) was the largest number of births in the world in any one day during 1955 . . .

1.	36,501	(2)	3.	49,876	(3)
2.	28,207	(0)	4.	30,023	(1)

 (b) was the smallest number of births in the world in any one day during 1955 . . .

1.	26,340	(0)	3.	14,330	(3)
2.	24,725	(1)	4.	19,704	(2)

13. When all of the world's written languages are considered, linguists tell us that the average number of verbs per language must be somewhere around *15,000*. What do you think

 (a) is the largest number of verbs in any single language . . .

1.	21,000	(1)	3.	50,000	(3)
2.	18,000	(0)	4.	30,000	(2)

 (b) is the smallest number of verbs in any single language . . .

1.	1000	(3)	3.	5000	(2)
2.	13,000	(0)	4.	10,000	(1)

14. The average muzzle to tail length of a sample of 1000 German Shepherd dogs is *40·3 inches*. What do you think

 (a) is the length of the longest Shepherd dog in the sample . . .

1.	60·4 inches	(3)	3.	44·1 inches	(0)
2.	47·8 inches	(1)	4.	54·2 inches	(2)

 (b) is the length of the shortest Shepherd dog in the sample . . .

1.	34·6 inches	(1)	3.	19·7 inches	(3)
2.	28·4 inches	(2)	4.	36·9 inches	(0)

15. The average population of South American countries is approximately *8·6 million* people each. What do you think

 (a) is the population of the most populated country in South America . . .

1.	11·2 million	(0)	3.	23·6 million	(1)
2.	54·7 million	(2)	4.	129·1 million	(3)

 (b) is the population of the least populated country in South America . . .

1.	7000	(3)	3.	2·4 million	(1)
2.	6·2 million	(0)	4.	29,000	(2)

Table 1 – *continued*

16. A Stanford University home economist has estimated that the average American spends around *55 minutes* of his day eating. What do you think

    (a) is the longest eating time of any single American . . .

1.	185 minutes	(2)	3.	245 minutes	(3)
2.	125 minutes	(1)	4.	90 minutes	(0)

    (b) is the shortest eating time of any single American . . .

1.	16 minutes	(2)	3.	38 minutes	(0)
2.	4 minutes	(3)	4.	27 minutes	(1)

17. In 1946 the average number of births per state was *68,000*. What do you think

    (a) was the highest number of births in a single state . . .

1.	87,000	(1)	3.	71,000	(0)
2.	122,000	(2)	4.	254,000	(3)

    (b) was the lowest number of births in a single state . . .

1.	29,000	(1)	3.	14,000	(2)
2.	53,000	(0)	4.	900	(3)

18. Immediately after the Second World War, the average number of submarines owned by the largest seven navies in the world was *58*. What do you think

    (a) was the largest number of submarines owned by *one* of these navies . . .

1.	159	(3)	3.	118	(2)
2.	91	(1)	4.	69	(0)

    (b) was the smallest number of submarines owned by *one* of these navies . . .

1.	22	(2)	3.	36	(1)
2.	9	(3)	4.	47	(0)

19. The average number of churches per religious denomination in the United States is estimated to be *511*. What do you think

    (a) is the largest number of churches of a single religious denomination in the U.S.A. . . .

1.	4833	(2)	3.	1219	(1)
2.	757	(0)	4.	39,801	(3)

Table 1 – *continued*

(b) is the smallest number of churches of a single religious denomination in the U.S.A. ....

| 1. | 313 | (0) | 3. | 1 | (3) |
| 2. | 146 | (1) | 4. | 23 | (2) |

20. In the years 1916 through 1946, according to the U.S. Weather Bureau, there was an average of *140 tornadoes* a year in the United States. What do you think

(a) was the largest number of tornadoes in a single year in the United States during this period ...

| 1. | 154 | (0) | 3. | 312 | (3) |
| 2. | 243 | (2) | 4. | 197 | (1) |

(b) was the smallest number of tornadoes in a single year in the United States during this period ...

| 1. | 103 | (1) | 3. | 61 | (2) |
| 2. | 122 | (0) | 4. | 28 | (3) |

Table 2

Correlations between Category-Width and ACE Scores[1]

Variables	Product-moment r	p
C-W and total ACE	+0·17	<0·05
C-W and ACE L (linguistic)	+0·07	n.s.
C-W and ACE Q (quantitative)	+0·26	<0·01

1. Based on a sample of 200 college undergraduates.

Table 3

Sex and Category-Width Score

Sex	N	C-W mean	Range	SD	t	p	Limits of Distribution's Thirds		
							narrows	mediums	broads
Males	218	71·87	23–117	17·32	4·55	<0·001	0–66	67–78	79–120
Females	116	64·46	34–99	12·04			0–58	59–70	71–120

scale's internal consistency.[3] Over 98 per cent of these relationships are positive, with 87 per cent of these significant at better than the 1 per cent level and with 5 per cent significant at better than the 5 per cent level. The median tetrachoric coefficient is $+0.27$ ($p < 0.01$).

Factorial structure. A 21×21 tetrachoric correlation matrix was constructed for each item score and the Q-score of the ACE of 270 college Ss. Employing Thurstone's complete centroid method (1947) four factors emerge. Orthogonal rotation yields the results in Table 4.[4] It had been expected that the scale would have two important factors: one a verisimilitude factor with heavy loadings on items with categories close to everyday experience, and the other a fantasy factor with heavy loadings on items with categories quite removed from common experience.

Two major factors do evolve, but they bear no close resemblance to the verisimilitude–fantasy differentiation. Rather, they vary in their content and in their relationships with the ACE measure of quantitative ability (Q). Factor I is primarily a time and speed dimension: the scale's four time or speed items – 2, 8, 11 and 16 – all have heavy loadings on it. Moreover, Q is weighted more heavily on factor I than on any of the remaining factors. By contrast, the other major dimension, factor II, is more general in its content and is the least related to Q of all the factors. Most of the items with large factor II loadings – 15, 17, 18 and 19 – require direct judgements (as opposed to indirect judgements in terms of minutes or miles per hour) of such varied categories as births, submarines and churches.

Only slightly related to Q, the smaller factors III and IV tend to have their heaviest loadings on relatively poor items. That is, such items as 3, 4, 7, 9 and 12 have been found to be among those with the least criterion validity (Table 5). It appears, then, that these factors in large part constitute error.

Criterion validity. The scale's criterion is defined as the category width rankings determined from laboratory procedures similar

3. Item dichotomization for the tetrachoric correlations was made by splitting each item as near its median as possible.
4. In the original article a table of unrotated factor loadings is also presented [*Ed.*].

to those employed in the original Bruner and Rodrigues work. Twenty-six undergraduate Ss were individually tested on five categories not contained in the C-W scale. Presented with drawn lines of the average lengths of pheasants and turtles, they chose

Table 4

Rotated Orthogonal Factor Matrix

C-W Items	Factors			
	I	II	III	IV
1	0·28	0·50	−0·14	0·20
2	0·52	0·29	−0·04	0·22
3	0·33	0·00	0·04	0·52
4	−0·01	0·34	0·41	0·55
5	0·33	−0·15	0·41	0·08
6	0·39	0·39	0·51	0·02
7	0·22	0·23	0·41	0·10
8	0·51	0·52	0·29	0·05
9	0·34	0·00	0·47	0·12
10	0·40	0·37	0·29	0·26
11	0·47	0·03	0·24	0·32
12	0·23	0·11	0·56	−0·06
13	0·55	0·08	0·06	0·00
14	0·35	0·10	0·29	0·31
15	0·32	0·46	0·05	−0·04
16	0·73	0·01	−0·05	−0·09
17	0·38	0·60	0·01	0·11
18	0·34	0·61	0·09	−0·03
19	0·46	0·55	0·04	0·25
20	0·50	0·15	0·29	0·04
ACE Q	0·33	0·06	0·25	0·18

between lines drawn on a blackboard the longest and shortest instances of these categories. Similarly, they estimated the weight extremes of ostrich eggs with fixed sets of weights, and the pitch extremes of women's singing voices and factory whistles from fixed alternatives generated by an audio-oscillator. Rankings of the Ss according to their range estimates across these five categories prove to be significantly consistent (Kendall's $W = 0.334$, $p < 0.02$). This provides both a laboratory replication of Bruner and Rodrigues's finding and an independent ranking of the twenty-six Ss according to their category widths for criterion validity purposes.

Table 5

Criterion Validity of C-W Items[1]

Item	Mean of 9 narrows	Mean of 9 broads	t	One-tail p
19	2·11	4·22	2·75	0·01
1	2·33	4·56	2·72	0·01
8	3·33	4·11	2·58	0·02
6	2·67	4·33	2·36	0·02
15	1·78	3·44	2·24	0·02
5	3·33	4·44	2·09	0·05
16	3·00	4·00	2·00	0·05
14	1·67	3·22	1·88	0·05
13	2·89	4·00	1·65	0·10
2	2·67	3·56	1·60	0·10
17	3·33	4·22	1·44	0·10
11	3·11	3·78	1·10	0·15
3	2·78	3·78	1·08	0·15
20	2·78	3·22	0·91	0·20
4	3·22	3·78	0·73	0·25
9	2·44	2·89	0·65	0·30
12	4·22	4·56	0·62	0·30
18	3·67	4·11	0·55	0·30
7	3·44	3·67	0·34	0·40
10	4·00	3·44	−0·05	—

1. The criterion rankings were independently determined by laboratory procedures. The item analysis of this table indicates the discriminatory powers of each C-W item in separating the laboratory's narrow and broad thirds. The total C-W scale yields a rank order correlation with the criterion rankings of $+0.57$, $p < 0.01$.

The Ss were later administered C-W scales. Table 5 presents the item and total scale relationships with the criterion rankings. Of the twenty C-W items, nineteen correctly discriminated between the criterion's broad and narrow thirds, fourteen of these differences surpassing the 20 per cent level of confidence and eight surpassing the 5 per cent level. Many of the poorer items in this table have been noted previously in the factorial structure discussion. The rank order correlation between the total *C-W* scale and the total criterion rankings is $+0.57$ ($p < 0.01$). Allowing for error in both sets of rankings, we may conclude that the *C-W* scale is measuring much the same phenomenon as that originally obtained in the laboratory.

C-W and other cognitive variables. Four other cognitive tasks have been compared with *C-W* in an effort to define more precisely the category width dimension: Rokeach's 'narrow-mindedness' task (1951), a self-concept span instrument, the *F*-scale (Adorno *et al.*, 1950) and the *D*-scale (Rokeach, 1956).

Rokeach has delineated three types of categorizers on his task – comprehensive, narrow and isolated (Rokeach, 1951). Comprehensive categorizers group all of Rokeach's ten political and religious labels under one concept, while narrows use more than one concept, and isolated categorizers omit labels. Those who categorize comprehensively in these terms were predicted to score higher on *C-W* than the narrow and isolated categorizers taken together. Both measures were administered to sixty-eight college *S*s. The thirty-one *S*s who grouped the ten terms comprehensively averaged 73.5 on the *C-W* as compared with the remaining thirty-seven narrow and isolated *S*s' average of 68.9. With a one-tail *t*-test, this difference is significant at the 5 per cent level of confidence.

Mayzner and Tresselt (1955) have studied value concept spans by defining span as the number of words in a standard list checked by the respondent as being related to a particular value area. Employing this definition of span, the 300-word *Gough Adjective Check List* was administered to 106 male student *S*s who had previously taken the *C-W*. The 'self-concept span' – the number of adjectives checked as self-descriptive – was predicted to be related positively to *C-W*. A product-moment correlation of $+0.30$ supports the hypothesis at the 1 per cent level of confidence. The broader the categorizer, the more adjectives he tends to see as related to himself.

The thirty-item forms 40 and 45 of the *F*-scale (Adorno *et al.*, 1950) and the forty-item short form of the *D*-scale (Rokeach, 1956) were administered together with the *C-W* to forty-nine female college *S*s. While the authoritarian *F*-measure correlated $+0.82$

with Rokeach's Dogmatism instrument, neither of these scales correlated significantly with the C-W. F and C-W yielded only a $+0.03$ coefficient, and D and C-W produced only a -0.08 relationship. The category-width and authoritarian variables apparently are quite independent.

Discussion

The scale properties of C-W seem to be very adequate for further research purposes. With both satisfactory reliabilities and substantial criterion validity, this objectively scored measure has but one major limitation. C-W is not a one-dimensional test: it is composed of two important, orthogonal factors – one a moderately quantitative, time-and-speed dimension, the other a non-quantitative, general dimension.

The scale's relationships with quantitative ability and sex have two possible interpretations. They may be artifacts of the procedures. The intensive use of numbers and the particular choice of categories may lead the quantitatively gifted and males to score higher. Alternatively, however, these relationships may indicate that highly quantitative people and males do tend to be more broadly tuned to their environment. As suggested by Wheeler's interesting work (1956), individuals with developed mathematical skills may achieve a uniquely broad sense of category variance. Males, too, may be more reinforced than females in our culture for wide category ranges. Studies by Komarovsky (1950), Diggory (1953), and Sears et al. (1953) hint at such a possibility, and Wallach and Caron's work with children indicates that this sex difference develops early in life (1959). Further work with the scale will be necessary before a choice can be made between these two possibilities.

The comparisons between C-W and the four other cognitive measures aid in determining the nature of category width. Both tasks revealing significant association with C-W – Rokeach's narrow-mindedness technique and the self-concept span measure – involve categorizing behavior, too. Since comprehensive categorizers on Rokeach's instrument tend to have wide category ranges, and C-W broads judge more adjectives on Gough's check list as being self-descriptive, it appears that breadth of categorizing generalizes to a variety of procedures. This finding lends support to the interpretation of category width as a given S's typical equivalence range for classifying objects. Further research might check on this possibility more rigorously by observing how high and low C-W scorers differ in the building-up process of attaining a new category in an experimental setting.

The failure of the F- and D-scales to correlate with C-W indicates that authoritarianism, dogmatism, and their related concept, rigidity, are not helpful in understanding category width. The independence of these dimensions (and how many variables have ever been shown to be *un*related to F?) raises some interesting questions. Perhaps much of the heterogeneity frequently noted among high F-scorers and especially among low F-scorers can be partly accounted for in terms of C-W variance within each of these clusters. Future authoritarianism research could test this possibility by employing both F and C-W to sort their Ss.

The risk-taking interpretation of C-W also deserves further research. Are broad categorizers different from narrow categorizers chiefly in their willingness to accept type I errors and tolerate negative instances? This explanation can be tested with both personality scale work and experimental studies employing C-W and known risk-taking procedures.

Another set of questions revolves around the developmental factors in childhood that make the phenomenon of range consistency possible. Whatever these factors are – independence training, inconsistent training, etc. – they must vary considerably in the training of the sexes. A children's form of the C-W has been constructed now for future research use in this area (Wallach and Caron, 1959).

References

ADORNO, T. W., FRENKEL-BRUNSWIK, E., LEVINSON, D., and SANFORD, N. (1950), *The Authoritarian Personality*, Harper.

BRUNER, J. S., GOODNOW, J., and AUSTIN, G. A. (1956), *A Study of Thinking*, Wiley.

DIGGORY, J. C. (1953), 'Sex differences in the organization of attitudes', *J. Personal.*, vol. 22, pp. 89–100.

HOLZMAN, P. S., and KLEIN, G. S. (1954), 'Cognitive system-principles of leveling and sharpening: individual differences in assimilation effects in visual time-error', *J. Psychol.*, vol. 37, pp. 105–22.

KLEIN, G. S. (1951), 'The personal world through perception', in R. R. Blake and G. V. Ramsey (eds.), *Perception: An Approach to Personality*, Ronald Press, pp. 328–55.

KOMAROVSKY, M. (1950), 'Functional analysis of sex roles', *Amer. soc. Rev.*, vol. 15, pp. 508–16.

MAYZNER, M. S., and TRESSELT, M. (1955), 'Concept span as a composite function of personal values, anxiety, and rigidity', *J. Personal.*, vol. 24, pp. 20–33.

ROKEACH, M. (1951), 'A method for studying individual differences in "narrow-mindedness"', *J. Personal.*, vol. 20, pp. 219–33.

ROKEACH, M. (1956), 'Political and religious dogmatism: an alternative to the authoritarian personality', *Psychol. Monogr.*, vol. 70, no. 18, whole no. 425.

SEARS, R., WHITING, J., NOWLIS, V., and SEARS, P. (1953), 'Some child-rearing antecedents of aggression and dependence in young children', *Genet. Psychol. Monogr.*, vol. 47, pp. 135–236.

THURSTONE, L. L. (1947), *Multiple Factor Analysis*, University of Chicago Press.

WALLACH, M. (1958), 'On psychological similarity', *Psychol. Rev.*, vol. 65, pp. 103–16.

WALLACH, M., and CARON, A. J. (1959), 'Attribute criteriality and sex-linked conservatism as determinants of psychological similarity', *J. abnorm. soc. Psychol.*, vol. 59, pp. 43–50.

WHEELER, J. A. (1956), 'A septet of sibyles: aids in the search for truth', *Scientist*, vol. 44, pp. 360–77.

Part Three **Structural Characteristics**

The three selections presented in Part Three have in common a concern with the definition and measurement of structural characteristics of cognition. They all draw attention to a difference between the content and structure of thought processes, and each introduces its own structural notions.

Reading 7 by Scott is the most general. He examines several concepts under the headings of 'differentiation', 'relatedness' and 'integration'. 'Differentiation' here is in terms of how many different dimensions are employed when a judgement is made. (For this reason it might be referred to as 'dimensional differentiation'.) The notion is similar to, but is operationally distinct from, 'conceptual differentiation' as discussed by Gardner and Schoen and by Glixman in Readings 3 and 4. Reading 8, by Bieri and his colleagues, focuses specifically upon one measure of differentiation as an index of complexity of structure.

Reading 9 by Schroder, Driver and Streufert has as its major interest the assessment of *integrative* complexity. The work discussed in that selection derives partly from the ideas previously developed by Harvey, Hunt and Schroder (1961). Other derivations from that work which might have appeared in Part Three are illustrated instead by Reading 17 commencing on page 315. In Reading 17 Harvey outlines a slightly different approach to the measurement of structural complexity.

Reference
HARVEY, O. J., HUNT, D. E., and SCHRODER, H. M. (1961), *Conceptual Systems and Personality Development*, Wiley.

7 William A. Scott

Conceptualizing and Measuring Structural Properties of Cognition

Excerpts from William A. Scott, 'Conceptualizing and measuring structural properties of cognition', in O. J. Harvey (ed.), *Motivation and Social Interaction: Cognitive Determinants*, Ronald Press, 1963, pp. 266–88.

A structural property may be designated tentatively as one which refers to the relations among components of content, conceived in quasi-systemic fashion, rather than to the elements of content themselves. For example, the strength of an achievement motive is a variable referring to the content of personality, while the degree of compatibility or conflict between this motive and some other represents a structural variable. At the level of cognitive processes the phenomenal object, India, constitutes an element of content while the perceived conflict of interest between India and China represents a relation between two phenomenal objects and, hence, a rudimentary structural property of cognition.

The proposed distinction between content and structure is not as neat as it may appear, for what is one and what the other depends on the level of analysis. Though a structure constitutes a relation among elements, it may itself form an element in some superordinate structure; conversely, the elements of any designated structure may themselves be conceived as complex structures consisting of their own units and interrelations. For the notion of structure to be meaningful, therefore, one must designate explicitly those elements which constitute the structure referred to.

A number of psychologists (e.g. Bieri, 1955; Harvey, Hunt and Schroder, 1961; Kelly, 1955; Rosenberg, 1956; Scott, 1962; Zajonc, 1960) have recently proposed some more or less systematically defined structural properties at a cognitive level of analysis. By cognitive structures I mean those whose elements consist of ideas consciously entertained by the person in his phenomenal view of the world. This concern for structural properties of cognition is commonly based on beliefs such as:

1. The content of experience is organized into structural assemblies from which any element of content derives its significance.

2. The way in which any new experience is received, processed, and interpreted depends on the capabilities and characteristics of the pre-existing cognitive structure into which it is read.

3. While the contents of cognition may be endlessly varied, structural properties can be described in a limited number of genotypic terms, thereby permitting a more parsimonious formulation of psychological processes.

4. The contents of cognition develop from social norms and other fortuitous experience which cannot be well predicted from personality theory; they may be widely shared by different individuals for different reasons and they may fluctuate markedly within a single individual over time. By contrast, the structure of cognition is regarded as more enduring, organism-specific, and invariant over situations; hence structural variables provide better description of the person as conceived in most psychological theories.

The alleged essential, genotypic, characteristic and causative nature of the proposed structural properties has hardly been established empirically; rather these beliefs have, at the moment, the status of assumptions which are tentatively used to justify our focus on structural variables.

No one, I trust, will object to the use of structural concepts simply because they do not correspond to anything in the body. No psychological construct resides in the person, conceived as a biological organism; all theoretical constructs reside in theories; some of them may be attributed to the psychological person, which is itself a complex theoretical construct. Direct translatability into neurophysiological events is not something we demand of our structural concepts. Certain other characteristics, however, can be reasonably expected of them.

1. Structural properties should be conceptualized differently from properties of content; otherwise there is no point in distinguishing the two classes.

2. For each property the elements of the structure should be specified, so that one can know what level of analysis is referred to.

3. The designated structural properties should have different implications for behavior from some more simply formulated content properties; otherwise use of the former is uneconomical or redundant.

4. Any structural property should be empirically assessable; that is, one should be able to elicit behaviors which are epistemically coordinated to the presence or absence, or the magnitude, of the theoretically defined property.

5. The measuring procedures for assessing psychological structure should be distinct from those used to assess psychological content; otherwise any conceptual distinction between content and structure is operationally meaningless.

Some Structural Properties of Cognition

Let us turn now to an extremely tentative discussion of specific structural properties. Each of them is tied to some formal model which bears only a remote and exceedingly abstract correspondence with the psychological domain to which it is coordinated. If any systematic way of measuring the construct has been developed, it is at best crude, and only one of many that might be proposed. Also, one cannot be sure in most cases whether the alleged structural property is empirically distinguishable from some content variable which it is not intended to duplicate, for the validating studies have generally omitted variables which were not of immediate theoretical relevance. Nevertheless, some of the notions, and the preliminary data, seem sufficiently compelling to encourage further exploration that would take into account the considerations offered above.

Structural models

We are indebted to Kurt Lewin (1936) for his compelling suggestions of many structural properties that are conceptualized more precisely today. Another important feature of Lewin's theory was the distinction between two levels of theoretical discourse – the formal and the content. Lewin used topology (or hodology) as a formal model whose components he coordinated to psychological constructs, which were then coordinated to observable phenomena. In this way, the abstract, formal model often served as a guide to the construction of content theory while the latter served as a guide to the measurement and prediction of empirical events. True, in order for the model to be useful in the formulation of content theory, it had to bear some ultimate resemblance to the event domain which was to be comprehended. But, given preliminary grounds for suspecting such a correspondence, one could go ahead on the formal level and elaborate quite economically and precisely relationships which might not have been noticed or which might have been unduly cumbersome to formulate at the level of psychological content theory.

A given formal model can be coordinated to different content theories – dealing, for instance, with cognition or group processes or cultural events – which require different sorts of data for their application. Some of the models used in cognitive theories can potentially serve such multiple functions. Lewin's topology could be applied not only to personality theory, but also to theory of social structure. (The latter was especially developed by J. F. Brown, 1936.) The graph theory, which has been elaborated and transmitted to psychologists by Harary and Norman (1953), finds application at both the psychological and social levels.

A model uniquely appropriate for cognitive structure has been proposed by Abelson and Rosenberg (1958); it is a kind of matrix algebra by which cognitive balance and processes associated with it may be described. Scott (1961b, 1965) suggests a geometrical model of cognition, consisting of a set of points and the lines intersecting them in multidimensional Euclidean space. These elements are coordinated in psychological theory to a person's concepts of objects (called *images*) and his concepts of the attributes which inhere in the phenomenal objects. An object-image is represented by the intersection of multiple dimensions, while an attribute is coordinated to a locus of points representing cognitive objects which embody the attribute to varying degrees. A simple image may be visualized as a point which is intersected by only one or two dimensional lines, whereas a complex image is seen as the intersection of many lines, representing a multitude of attributes. A complexly conceived attribute may be correspondingly represented in the formal model as one which runs through a large number of points that stand for the images that contain the attribute to varying, finely shaded, degrees. A barren attribute, by contrast, runs through few points or else permits few quantitative distinctions by lumping many object-images together in gross categories.

Certain structural concepts of cognition may be formulated within the framework of this model, employing the geometrized notions concerning relations among image-concepts and among attribute-concepts. These may be discussed under the headings of 'Differentiation', 'Relatedness' and 'Integration'.

Differentiation. Basic to any concept of structure is the notion of differentiation, or distinctiveness of the elements which constitute the set. Psychologically this involves an articulation of concepts, an isolability of one idea from another. Without an initial distinction between two cognitive elements, it is meaningless to speak of their relationship. This very word, differentiation, was used by Vera French (1947, 1948) in her discussion of sentiments. Krech and Crutchfield (1948) spoke of the precision of an attitude, defining this in terms of clarity and differentiation. Zajonc's (1960) research on cognitive tuning made use of both the concept and an empirical measure of cognitive differentiation. Harvey, Hunt and Schroder (1961) referred to 'clarity *v.* ambiguity' as an important characteristic of concepts. This property depends on the 'articulation of component parts', so it is appropriate to equate their notion with that of differentiation.

It is not so immediately apparent that differentiation of object concepts is intimately connected with the structural property which has been designated as 'complexity of the attribute concepts'. Bieri (1955) has noted this, and Scott (1960, 1961b) has developed the same point, as follows: in order for two object-images to be distinguished, they must be seen as embodying different attributes; for attributes to be phenomenally different, they must order the object-images in different ways. The degree of differentness in the ordering of objects along two attributes can be represented (inversely) by a correlation coefficient and, correspondingly, by the angle between the attribute-vectors. The

149

greater the difference, the more nearly orthogonal are the vectors; hence the more dimensional space utilized by the pair of attributes. Considering the cognitive domain as a whole, the greater the differentiation among object-images, the greater must be the distinctiveness among the attributes embodied in the objects. So the degree of distinctiveness among elements of either class – images or attributes – amounts to the same thing.

Bieri (1955) used a measure of cognitive complexity which was a simplified analysis of Kelly's (1955) Rep Test.[1] Campbell (1960) applied a non-parametric factor analysis to the same instrument, using the strength of the first factor as a measure of cognitive simplicity – the direct obverse of complexity. Ulehla (1961) developed quite a different measure aimed at the same construct (which he referred to as 'channel capacity'); this consisted of an index of multidimensional information yield adopted from information theory (Attneave, 1959). Scott (1965) has developed yet another measure of dimensional complexity, which is simpler than Kelly's (1955) Rep Test to administer and score. It is based on an object sorting task, which is quite generally acceptable to all kinds of subjects. The measure of complexity represents the information yield from S's category system, or the number of groups-worth of information which S's sorts produce. It has been found to correlate with certain other structural and dynamic characteristics of cognition that will be mentioned presently. [. . .]

Relatedness. Once two cognitive elements can be distinguished, the question 'In what manner are they related?' becomes meaningful. The relationship between two elements may be treated as a primary structural characteristic which forms the basis for more complex structural properties. The relation of 'similarity' has already been treated in the discussion of differentiation. Other terms for this are association, spatial proximity, co-variance and likelihood of simultaneous (or consequent) arousal. All of these similarity relationships may be formally represented either as the angle between two attribute-vectors or as the distance between two object-images in attribute-space.

Another kind of relatedness is of greater interest here. It is what Zajonc (1960) has called dependency – or its obverse,

1. See Reading 8, page 160 [*Ed.*].

determinance. This refers to the phenomenal influence of one element upon another. There remains the problem of determining from S's response whether the phenomenally dependent element, B, is really distinct from, but causally connected with A, or whether it has simply not been differentiated from A. It would probably be helpful to devise some task which would permit S to show that, though A and B tend to co-vary empirically, they can be separated in some hypothetical circumstance.

The *salience* of a particular attribute refers to the likelihood of its being triggered off by environmental cues. Structurally, this may be represented as the number of other concepts with which it is associated in a dependent fashion. There is a tendency for the evaluative dimension to be salient in the cognitive functioning of many people. This may be due either to the failure of other attributes to be distinguished from it or to their being phenomenally connected in a causal fashion.

Other concepts besides evaluation may be salient as well, appearing psychologically as dominant concerns in the person's relation to his environment or in his view of objects. Some people are vigilant with regard to Communism and sedition, others with regard to restriction of individual freedom. When any such characteristic of one's world is repeatedly highlighted and sought where others ignore it, we speak of an obsession with the attribute in question. There is a more general structural notion within which this trait can be framed: it may be called the *dispersion among saliences*. If only one or two attributes appear in equal degrees of salience, there is low dispersion; if many attributes appear in equal degrees of salience, there is high dispersion. In the latter case, the attribute that is aroused will presumably depend more on the environmental cues than on internally generated obsessions. Kluckhohn and Murray (1955) used an apt term when they spoke of the 'regnancy' of a psychological process, referring to possession of one's behavior by a particular determining tendency. In the normal case, any regnancy is of moderate duration, reflecting a structural condition somewhere between maximum and minimum dispersion of saliences. An exceedingly transitory regnancy of all a person's determining tendencies would be manifest as scattered attention and sporadic pursuit of any goal. A particularly long-enduring regnancy, on the other hand, would presumably lead to overly focused concern and to a limitation on free exploration of the environment. Harvey, Hunt and Schroder's (1961) notion of openness-closedness, defined as the degree of receptivity to external events, appears quite related to this structural concept, dispersion of saliences, with its consequent effect on the duration of regnancies.

Integration. While the various terms relating to the differentiation of a psychological structure can all be fairly well reduced to a common meaning, the single term *integration* appears to have a variety of meanings which will probably have to be distinguished before convergent operations are devised. The most common meaning – still rather imprecise in most cases – refers to the connectedness among parts of the structure, a state in which the relations among the various attributes (or concepts) are known and manipulable by the person, so that he can shift as necessary from one to another. Zajonc's (1960) measure of cognitive unity explicitly equals the sum of the dependencies in ratio to the maximum number possible, given the number of cognitive elements to be related. Krech and Crutchfield (1948) had previously defined a property of an attitude or belief which they called 'specificity' or isolation from other belief systems, in contrast to the property of connectedness with other attitudes and beliefs. Harvey, Hunt and Schroder (1961) present the idea of 'compartmentalization *v.* interrelatedness' among concepts; in the latter state all parts of the concept system can be activated in unison, or each part can be activated solo. It would also seem that Vera French's (1947, 1948) designation of the degree of unconscious component of a sentiment is a closely related notion; for 'unconscious' may be interpreted as unverbalizable, inaccessible to awareness, unconnected with other cognitive concepts – the opposite of integration in the present sense.

I am not aware of any very satisfactory objective measure of integration in this general sense of interconnectedness among parts. Zajonc's (1960) assessment of cognitive unity, though not dependent on the researcher's judgement, nevertheless relies heavily on S's introspection concerning the component dependencies. A somewhat more objective measure might be proposed within the framework of the sorting task used by Scott (1961b) to assess cognitive differentiation. Following assignment of the objects to groups, S might be asked, 'Suppose group A did not exist, would that affect any of the other groups? How? What objects would be added to (or subtracted from) group B?' Alternatively one could inquire, 'Which object in group A is the main (defining) object? Suppose it were not in A, would that make it belong in any of the other groups? Which ones?' The intent of such questioning would be to get S actually to manipulate the objects on other attributes as a consequence of their change on the focal one; from his manipulation the researcher could infer the phenomenally causal relations involved. Since the procedure has not yet been tried at this writing, it is impossible to report its actual usefulness, but the features of objectivity and coordination with other structural measures have *a priori* advantages.

Once a satisfactory method (or series of methods) for assessing psychological interconnectedness has been developed, then it will be possible to characterize any given element according to its degree of centrality or peripherality in the structure – i.e. the number of other concepts to which it is connected. These properties can be formally represented by means of graph theory (Harary and Norman, 1953). Harvey, Hunt and Schroder (1961) have supplied psychological content by suggesting that centrality refers to the 'essentialness' of a concept to the self or to a constellation of concepts. [. . .]

In order for Zajonc (1960) to develop his measure of cognitive unity, it was necessary to specify a particular kind of connectedness among the elements, namely 'dependency'. Very likely this will be necessary for any other measure of integration as well, for the general notion of 'connectedness' is probably too vague to suggest any specific operations. It may well be, therefore, that each different variety of connectedness among elements will lead to a different meaning of the concept 'integration'. Two or three relevant notions can be found in current discussions of cognitive structure.

Perhaps the most familiar is that which Heider (1946) called 'structural balance'. Originally he defined this property as follows: 'A balanced state exists if all parts of a unit have the

153

same dynamic character (i.e. if all are positive, or all are negative), and if entities with different dynamic character are segregated from each other' (p. 107). By 'dynamic character' Heider meant affective sign (like or dislike), and by 'unit' he referred to a set of cognitive elements related by 'similarity, proximity, causality, membership, possession or belonging'. Subsequent interpreters have, however, focused on more restricted meanings of 'unit', such as 'other people who are seen as liking each other'.

In a restricted sense, therefore, a balanced state of interpersonal perception exists if one sees his friends as liking each other, his enemies as liking each other, and the two groups as mutually antagonistic. This may appear as one mode of integration, i.e. having elements of like affective sign grouped together. Another perspective, however, suggests that cognitive balance consists essentially of a perfect correspondence between the affective attribute and whatever other cognitive attribute is used as a basis for grouping the elements. In the restricted sense, mutual friendship is the second attribute, while in the original, more general meaning the basis of 'belonging together' constitutes the second attribute. To the extent that any other attribute is highly correlated with the affective dimension, the cognitive structure is thereby simplified, or poorly differentiated. Hence, one would expect to find balanced structures most predominantly in people of low dimensional complexity. Essentially, this is what was found by Campbell (1960) and Scott (1961a) in two quite different attacks on the problem. One might say, then, that structural balance constitutes a simplistic mode of cognitive integration.

Another kind of integration is suggested by the notion *cognitive consistency* (Scott, 1959). When applied to a single attitude, this refers to the degree to which it is 'embedded' in a structure of related values and expectancies. When applied to the structure itself, cognitive consistency suggests that the object of an attitude is perceived in relation to the person's values in such a fashion that its positive and negative features exactly balance at the point on the affective continuum at which his attitude falls. An objective method for measuring varying degrees of cognitive consistency was proposed, based on Rosenberg's (1956) procedure for assessing the cognitive components of an attitude. The major deficiency of the measure lies in its inability to tap what, for any particular subject, constitute all the major values and expectancies relevant to his attitude. Nevertheless, an important consequence of this structural property has been repeatedly found: cognitively consistent attitudes are less subject to change under persuasive attempts than are cognitively inconsistent attitudes. This result is independent of initial attitude strength. The implication of these studies is that that particular kind of integration specified here – namely, consistency of an attitude with its cognitive surround – serves to stabilize the attitude in the face of pressures to change. [. . .]

The Generality of Structural Properties

All of the above characteristics of cognitive structure have been described with respect to a single domain of cognition. Operationally one is restricted, at best, to assessing the degree of differentiation, balance, unity, etc., pertaining to a given set of phenomenal objects that constitute considerably less than the totality of any person's life space. So it seems preferable, at least in the beginning, to restrict the structural notions to a scope that can be encompassed empirically.

There is an even better reason for talking about just one domain of cognition at a time. It is that there is little empirical assurance at present of any generality of these structural properties across cognitive domains. Psychologists are used to assuming a functional unity within a person and within his cognitive processes. This leads them to expect that a structural characteristic encountered in one domain of cognition will be duplicated elsewhere. Yet empirical work to date does not generally support this expectation with respect to the structural attributes referred to here. In Ulehla's (1961) study, the cognitive complexity of nurses in dealing with schizophrenic symptoms was not correlated with their cognitive complexity in defining the nurse's role. Among a group of college students Scott (unpublished data) found no correlation between the cognitive complexity of concepts about nations and of those about people. With respect to the property of cognitive consistency, neither Gochman (1960) nor Scott (unpublished data) has found much consistency of high or low scores across a sample of

155

attitudinal domains. The only study at hand which reports a correlation between structural measures applied to two different areas is that of Bieri and Blacker (1956) concerning the perception of people and of inkblots. However, their operations reflect variability of response, which they relate theoretically to cognitive complexity, rather than measuring the structural property more directly; therefore it is not certain that structural generality has been demonstrated. In any case, one can hardly say that there is overwhelming evidence for the generality of these structural attributes from one domain of cognition to another.

If the results of further studies continue in the same vein, they will pose a problem. Either we must discard our measures in favor of some that are more reliable; or we must suspect that what they are tapping is an ephemeral product of the instruments rather than an inherent quality of cognition; or we must revise our assumptions about the functional unity of cognition which have led us to expect generality in the structural attributes. Since most critics would presumably be prepared to follow the first two lines of attack, let us pursue the third. In the first place, one need not think of total cognitive activity as particularly unified, and in the second place it is not necessarily true that such structural unities as there are will show up in the domains that have been assessed so far.

When one considers past difficulties encountered in developing the traits of 'logical reasoning ability' and 'precise thinking' via the study of Latin and geometry, one may become less sanguine about the prospects of nurturing a particular cognitive style which will be manifest in a wide range of applications. Moreover, to the extent that one takes an empiricist, rather than a nativist, approach to the origins of cognition, one will be reluctant to believe that people are born with ready-made cognitive styles that are quite generally manifest. This is not to deny some striking individual differences in organization and approach to central areas of the life space. But it is quite likely that these modes of organization, and the cognitive structures associated with them, have been built up through specific experiences with the object domains – the way a person is introduced to an area, the amount of time he spends thinking about it, the way in which he uses his knowledge, etc. It would seem altogether possible to maintain a conceptual framework concerning professional activities that is structurally quite different from that relating to family or social life – mainly because the situations in which they are developed and expressed pose quite different functional demands. It would seem unproductive, therefore, to go looking for 'types' of people identifiable by their over-all cognitive structures – the differentiated and undifferentiated, the integrated and unintegrated, and so forth. Maybe extreme cases exist in which all cognitive functioning is of a piece, but they would be so few in number that the typology would have little utility; more likely such people would be found in mental institutions, since the very consistency of their functioning across all domains would severely impede their adaptation.

At present, the appropriate unit of analysis in the study of cognitive styles would seem to be not the total person, but a particular area of his functioning that is associated with an identifiable event-domain.[2] It is, of course, possible that in central areas of a person's life he will tend to develop similar modes of cognitive organization – particularly if those areas are experienced close together in time, space and interpersonal surround. However, the instruments for assessing cognitive structure used so far do not generally tap central features of any particular subject's life. Rather they deal with nations in the world, or a general sample of people that he has encountered, or topics of opinion that are not necessarily of major concern. Perhaps one could assume that it is in these relatively peripheral areas of a person's life space that he will most likely manifest any dominant and central cognitive style (cf. Smith, Bruner and White, 1956). But the opposite assumption seems more compelling at the moment – namely, that dominant, pervasive styles gain expression more readily in the familiar, well-used areas of one's life space. They are likely to differ for different people, so that a single standardized instrument with completely preformed content will not pick up the central content areas nor, therefore, any structural commonalities among them. It will be necessary,

2. It should be recognized that this position is held by most writers. Rokeach's notion of 'dogmatic thinking' (see Reading 2, page 36) is restricted to interpersonal authority domains; and measures of 'cognitive complexity' are usually seen as being specific to (say) one's social environment [Ed.].

rather, to discover for each subject what are his central domains, then proceed to examine them structurally with a generalized instrument that is not tied to any particular content.

It is, of course, not certain that this approach will turn up structural commonalities across different areas of cognition, for the various other sources of differences mentioned above may dominate over any tendency toward similarities. At least for the present there is little ground for distinguishing 'classes of people' by their types of cognitive structure, but only for describing different ways of structuring any selected cognitive domain. Doubts concerning the prospects of wide generalization are raised by past experience with typologies which used the individual as the unit of analysis: usually correlations among the component characteristics are so low that nothing approaching a multimodal distribution of persons can be generated; hence those falling in the 'pure types' constitute such a small sample of the total as to be trivial.

References

ABELSON, R. P., and ROSENBERG, M. J. (1958), 'Symbolic psychologic: a model of attitude recognition', *Behav. Sci.*, vol. 3, pp. 1–13.

ATTNEAVE, F. (1959), *Applications of Information Theory to Psychology*, Holt.

BIERI, J. (1955), 'Cognitive complexity–simplicity and predictive behavior', *J. abnorm. soc. Psychol.*, vol. 51, pp. 263–8.

BIERI, J., and BLACKER, E. (1956), 'The generality of cognitive complexity in the perception of people and inkblots', *J. abnorm. soc. Psychol.*, vol. 53, pp. 112–17.

BROWN, J. F. (1936), *Psychology and the Social Order*, McGraw-Hill.

CAMPBELL, V. N. (1960), Assumed similarity, perceived sociometric balance, and social influence, *Unpublished Ph.D. Dissertation*, *University of Colorado*.

FRENCH, V. (1947, 1948), 'The structure of sentiments', *J. Personal.*, vol. 15, pp. 247–82; vol. 16, pp. 78–100, 209–44.

GOCHMAN, D. S. (1960), Ego-tension, cognitive consistency, and attitude change, *Unpublished Master's Thesis, University of Colorado*.

HARARY, F., and NORMAN, R. Z. (1953), *Graph Theory as a Mathematical Model in Social Science*, Institute for Social Research, Ann Arbor, Michigan.

HARVEY, O. J., HUNT, D. E., and SCHRODER, H. M. (1961), *Conceptual Systems and Personality Development*, Wiley.

HEIDER, F. (1946), 'Attitudes and cognitive organization', *J. Psychol.*, vol. 21, pp. 107–12.

KELLY, G. A. (1955), *A Psychology of Personal Constructs*, Norton.

KLUCKHOHN, C., and MURRAY, H. A. (1955), 'A conception of personality', in C. Kluckhohn, H. A. Murray and D. M. Schneider (eds.), *Personality in Nature, Society, and Culture*, Knopf.

KRECH, D., and CRUTCHFIELD, R. S. (1948), *Theory and Problems of Social Psychology*, McGraw-Hill.

LEWIN, K. (1936), *Principles of Topological Psychology*, McGraw-Hill.

ROSENBERG, M. J. (1956), 'Cognitive structure and attitudinal affect', *J. abnorm. soc. Psychol.*, vol. 53, pp. 367–72.

SCOTT, W. A. (1959), 'Cognitive consistency, response reinforcement, and attitude change', *Sociometry*, vol. 22, pp. 219–29.

SCOTT, W. A. (1960), Properties of cognitive structure, *Paper Read at Meeting of Rocky Mountain Psychological Association*.

SCOTT, W. A. (1961a), Cognitive complexity and cognitive balance, *Unpublished Manuscript*.

SCOTT, W. A. (1961b), Cognitive complexity and cognitive flexibility, *Unpublished Manuscript*.

SCOTT, W. A. (1962) 'Cognitive structure and social structure', in N. F. Washburne (ed.), *Decisions, Values, and Groups*, vol. 2, Pergamon.

SCOTT, W. A. (1965), 'Psychological structure and social correlates of international images', in H. C. Kelman (ed.), *International Behavior*, Holt, Rinehart & Winston.

SMITH, M. B., BRUNER, J. S., and WHITE, R. W. (1956), *Opinions and Personality*, Wiley.

ULEHLA, Z. J. (1961), Individual differences in information yields of raters, *Unpublished Master's Thesis, University of Colorado*.

ZAJONC, R. B. (1960), 'The process of cognitive tuning in communication', *J. abnorm. soc. Psychol.*, vol. 61, pp. 159–67.

8 J. Bieri, A. L. Atkins, S. Briar, R. Lobeck, H. Miller and T. Tripodi

The Nature of Cognitive Structures

Excerpts from J. Bieri, A. L. Atkins, S. Briar, R. Lobeck, H. Miller, and T. Tripodi, *Clinical and Social Judgment*, Wiley, 1966, pp. 184–96.

Basically, a cognitive structure is a hypothetical link between stimulus information and an ensuing judgement which refers to those cognitive processes which mediate the input–output sequence. The conceptualization of cognitive structures has been broached variously in psychological theories, including notions such as *schemata*, as used by Bartlett and Piaget, Tolman's concept of *cognitive maps* and Klein's conception of *cognitive controls*. From a more purely associationistic viewpoint, Mandler (1962) defines structures as '. . . temporal and probabilistic linkages of inputs and behavior which are available in functional units'. He suggests that cognitive structures are '. . . rules of behavior, maps or schemata laid down which connect various behaviors and environmental inputs'. Rapaport (1957), by contrast, has considered cognitive structure in relation to the psychoanalytic theory of autonomous ego functions and has indicated that the concept refers both to relatively enduring means and to the creation of new means for man's organization of the information that he gains from his environment.

Although there are a variety of definitions of cognitive structure that refer to different psychological processes, there are at least two common areas of agreement among cognitive theorists. First, cognitive structures refer to organized systems whose properties are dependent upon the interrelations of the various elements in a given system. Second, knowledge of cognitive structures implies that predictions can be made of the way in which the person copes with his environment.

Contemporary conceptualizations of the properties of cognitive structure have been influenced to a large extent by the analyses of Lewin (1951), especially in relation to the properties of a person's 'life space'. Lewin analyses the various parts of a given life space in terms of their interdependence and organization. Thus, he refers to the *degree of differentiation* of a region as the number of distinct elements within such a region and *hierarchical organization* as a unit of behavior which subsumes different levels of hierarchical behavior. Lewin's attempt to develop a mathematics of hodological space essentially was an effort to define these theoretical concepts in an operational form (Deutsch, 1954). Although theoretical distinctions are made between the concepts of differentiation and organization, investigators have had little success in deriving independent measures of such concepts. One effort is that of Zajonc (1960), who employed measures of differentiation, complexity, unity and organization. However, he too implies there is difficulty in defining such concepts so that they lead to independent measurements.

In our conceptualization of cognitive structure, we are following a point of view which is derived from Kelly's theory of personal constructs (1955) and which incorporates Lewin's concept of degree of differentiation. Our assumption is that each person has a system of dimensions which he uses in construing his social environment, and that the characteristics describing the relations among these dimensions refer to a person's cognitive structure. While little is known concerning the development of cognitive structures, it is commonly assumed that there is an increased differentiation of one's social environment and an increased variety of behavior as this development progresses (Bieri, 1964). The work of Witkin *et al.* (1962) on psychological differentiation and Harvey, Hunt and Schroder (1961) on the development of conceptual systems reflects recent interest in the developmental aspects of cognitive structures.

Cognitive Complexity–Simplicity

The property of cognitive structure upon which we shall focus is that of cognitive complexity–simplicity (Bieri, 1955, 1961). In its most general meaning, cognitive complexity is a construct which is intended to indicate something about the person's structuring of his social world. More specifically, we consider cognitive complexity to be an information processing variable which helps us predict how an individual transforms *specified* behavioral information into social or clinical judgements.

We can begin to identify the nature of this structural variable by noting that cognitive complexity is intended to reflect the relative differentiation of a person's system of dimensions for construing behavior. It should be noted that although cognitive complexity is closely related to the notion of differentiation, we consider a more complex structure to be a more differentiated structure in a particular sense. That is, we are concerned with the differentiation of *dimensions* of judgement, rather than with categories, concepts or regions. Cognitive complexity may be defined as the capacity to construe social behavior in a multi-dimensional way. A more cognitively complex person has available a more differentiated system of dimensions for perceiving others' behavior than does a less cognitively complex individual. As we have noted, an advantage of this approach is that it brings the analysis of the cognitive structural variable into closer systematic relation to the stimulus conditions within which judgement occurs. If we wish to predict differences on a task between judges who differ in cognitive complexity, we believe it is of value to analyse the stimulus in terms of its relative dimensionality.

A Dimensional Theory of Judgement

It is apparent from the preceding discussion that our approach to a dimensional analysis of cognitive structure was influenced by the theory of personality developed by G. A. Kelly (1955), which he calls the *psychology of personal constructs*. [. . .] Kelly's theory is based on the idea that each individual has available a number of personal constructs for cognizing and perceiving events. The foundations of Kelly's theory are centered on his formulation of a fundamental postulate: 'A person's processes are psychologically channelized by the ways in which he anticipates events.' From this postulate a system of corollaries is evolved which emphasizes the nature of constructs and the differences among individuals in the constructs they employ for construing their environment. A construct is conceived of as a dimension for

J. Bieri, A. L. Atkins, S. Briar, R. Lobeck, H. Miller and T. Tripodi

construing the way in which persons are alike and different from others. Constructs are assumed to be bipolar. Kelly's Role Construct Repertory Test (Rep Test), designed to elicit an individual's system of role constructs, will be described in detail subsequently. Although a number of modifications of the original form (Kelly, 1955) of this procedure have been used in research, the basic procedure involves judging a number of persons on a series of construct dimensions. These judgements are cast onto a grid or matrix from which analyses of the judge's dimensional space are carried out. [. . .]

Kelly considers that the process of decision making or judgement follows a cycle of circumspection, pre-emption and control (the C–P–C cycle). In a judgement situation the judge first construes his environment by *circumspection*. He does this by employing a series of propositional constructs to determine what judgement alternatives are available. In effect, the judge perceives the situation in a multidimensional way. Having considered the available alternatives, he narrows the range of alternatives by selecting what he considers the most relevant axis on which to construe his situation. This is the phase of *pre-emption*, where a choice point is set up for the judge. The final phase in the C–P–C cycle is the act of *control*, which is the choice of only one alternative. [. . .]

The Measurement of Cognitive Complexity

No less vexing than the precise delineation of the nature of cognitive structures is the problem of their measurement. An analysis of some of these assessment problems has been presented elsewhere (Bieri, 1964; Scott, 1963), but for the present purpose of providing an introduction to the empirical studies which follow, we shall focus on the measurement of cognitive complexity. [. . .]

We have previously indicated that the measurement of cognitive complexity is based on the Rep Test originated by Kelly (1955).[1] In the group version of the Rep Test the subject is presented with a grid containing spaces for persons to be judged

1. Other students of cognitive complexity do of course use different measurement tools. See, for example, Readings 7 and 17 [*Ed.*].

(columns) and rows for constructs. The list of role titles represents a sampling of individuals presumed to be of personal importance to the subject. These may include parents, friends, teachers, relatives, and so forth, including both positive or liked and negative or disliked persons. After identifying each role person at the top of each of the several columns, the subject is asked to consider three of these persons (delineated by the examiner) at a time. Constructs are formed by having the subject indicate in what way two of these persons are alike and different from the third. Following this, a second triad of persons is considered for each row of the grid, and so on. As each construct is generated, the subject checks the two cells in the matrix under the two similar persons and leaves the cell of the third person void. The construct dimension is entered next to the row and is indicated by a bipolar similarity and contrast. After constructs have been elicited for each row of the grid, the subject is asked to reconsider each dimension and check all those in addition to the two already checked to whom the similarity pole of the construct applies.

A major difference between the Rep Test as originally developed by Kelly and the semantic differential (Osgood, Suci and Tannenbaum, 1957) resides in whether or not the constructs are provided for the subject (as in the semantic differential) or elicited from the subject (as in the Rep Test). In some of the studies of cognitive complexity and judgement to be reported, we have developed a version of the Rep Test grid which employs constructs *provided* by the experimenter rather than the subject's *own* construct dimensions. Such a modification of the Rep Test, which brings it into closer kinship with the semantic differential, assumes that the sampling of personal constructs provided for a judge is representative of that judge's own constructs elicited in describing similarities and differences among people. We shall shortly present several sources of evidence consistent with this assumption.

Figure 1 represents the modified group version of the Rep Test employed in our more recent studies. Each judge is presented with a 10×10 grid. Each of the ten columns is identified by a different role type selected to be representative of the meaningful persons in the judge's social environment. The ten rows of bipolar constructs which are *provided* were selected on the basis of being representative of the dimensions elicited from college-trained subjects. After the judge has listed the name or initials of each of the ten persons who best correspond to the ten role types, he is instructed to use a six-step Likert-type scale in rating all ten

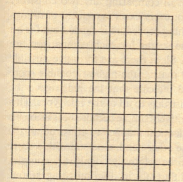

1. Yourself

2. Person you dislike

3. Mother

4. Person you'd like to help

5. Father

6. Friend of same sex

7. Friend of opposite sex (or spouse)

8. Person with whom you feel most uncomfortable

9. Boss

10. Person difficult to understand

+3	+2	+1	-1	-2	-3
interesting	independent	considerate	responsible	cheerful	interested in others	calm	decisive	adjusted	outgoing	shy	maladjusted	indecisive	excitable	self-absorbed	ill-humored	irresponsible	inconsiderate	dependent	dull

Figure 1 Modification of the Rep Test for assessing cognitive complexity

persons he has listed on the first provided construct. For example, the first construct dimension is 'outgoing-shy'. Each judge rates each of the ten persons on a scale of +3(outgoing) to −3(shy). Following this, the judge rates all ten persons on the second construct dimension and so on through all ten rows. Thus each subject makes ten ratings for each of the role types, for a total of 100 ratings.

Cognitive complexity is measured by comparing each rating in a row with the rating directly below it (i.e. for the same person) in the other rows on the matrix. In comparing any two construct rows, a score of one is given for every exact agreement of ratings on any one person. This matching procedure is carried out for all possible comparisons, and the scores for each comparison are added to give one total score. Since there are forty-five possible row comparisons in a 10×10 matrix, the highest possible score is 450. A score of 450 would indicate that the judge gave the same rating on all bipolar constructs to all of the role types. This judge would be relatively cognitively simple because he is using his construct dimensions in an identical manner to construe all the individuals on the grid. On the other hand, a person with a score as low as 100 is presumed to be relatively cognitively complex because he uses constructs differently in discriminating among people.

We mentioned above that the comparability of own and provided constructs as a basis for measuring cognitive complexity has been studied empirically. Tripodi and Bieri (1963) have obtained evidence that supports the assumption that comparable complexity indices are derived from own and provided constructs. Sixteen graduate students in social work were asked to list five bipolar constructs that they would use in judging people who were representative of ten role types. The judges were instructed to rate those people on a six-step Likert scale ranging from $+3$ to -3 for each of their *own* bipolar constructs. Following that, the judges rated the same people on five bipolar constructs that were provided by the experimenter. Each judge therefore filled out two matrices with ten columns and five rows. Two scores of cognitive complexity were derived for each judge, one based on the matrix in which the judge's own constructs were used, the other based on the matrix in which the same constructs were provided for all judges. Wilcoxon's signed-ranks test indicated no significant difference between the two distributions. Furthermore, a significant rank order correlation (rho $= 0.50$, $p < 0.05$) was obtained between the two distributions of complexity scores. Several other studies are in line with these results. Kieferle and

Sechrest (1961) have reported results which indicate that the way in which judges use provided constructs is functionally equivalent to the way in which they use their own constructs.

Jaspars (1964) also reports positive correlations between measures of cognitive structure on the Rep Test using own and provided constructs. Interestingly, Jaspars finds that for subjects who are least neurotic the correlation is 0·78 while for those who are most neurotic (on Eysenck's neuroticism scale) the correlation is only 0·26. These and other results reported by Jaspars suggest that for *clinical* populations, the use of own dimensions may be a more sensitive method of assessing individual differences in cognitive structure. Certainly additional research on this problem seems desirable.

A final method problem in measuring cognitive complexity concerns the metric used. The matching procedure described above which we used in our research is akin to a number of correlational and factor analytic approaches. One of these, a nonparametric factor-analytic method developed by Kelly (1962), allows one to consider the amount of variance *not* explained by the first factor as an index of complexity. This measure seems preferable to using the number of factors extracted, which may be too few for a reliable measure (Pedersen, 1958). The results of Jaspars (1964), in turn, indicate that Kelly's first factor is a good approximation of the first centroid factor. In our own work we have found a correlation of 0·90 between our matching procedure and the factor analytic measure derived from Kelly's procedure when six-category judgements were reduced to two-category judgements.

The use of multidimensional scaling methods offers yet another approach to the measurement of cognitive complexity and has increased in recent years (Torgerson, 1958). Unfortunately, some of the judgement procedures such as paired comparisons or the method of triads used with this approach are quite tedious for the subject. For example, with the group form of the Rep Test grid in Figure 1, a total of 100 judgements are required. However, if one were to use the complete method of triads (Torgerson, 1958), a total of 360 judgements for ten stimulus persons would be necessary $\{n(n-1)(n-2)/2\}$, inasmuch as each person in the triad is compared with the other two persons in that triad. Jaspars (1964) has found in a pilot study an average correlation between the interpoint distances obtained with the Rep Test and the distances found with the complete method of triads of 0·35, a correlation which is significant ($p = 0·01$). The comparability of correlational and multidimensional scaling approaches to cognitive structure remains to be explicated. Methodological studies such as that of Todd and Rappoport (1964) may provide needed answers to questions of method in this area, particularly if the various structural measures which are analysed are in turn systematically related to meaningful variables of behavior.

Cognitive Complexity and Judgement

A number of empirical studies dealing with the relation of cognitive complexity to judgemental behavior have appeared in recent years. An overview of this research may provide us with some understanding of the potential value of this structural variable in a cognitive analysis of behavior. In spite of variations in method concerning the measurement of cognitive complexity, a number of studies have indicated that this variable is related to information processing in social and clinical judgement (Bieri, 1961). For example, if we assume that the more complex judge has a more versatile cognitive structure for construing others' behavior, he should then manifest greater accuracy in his judgements about others. In the first study employing the concept of cognitive complexity, Bieri (1955) found that on a task involving prediction of behavior in common social situations the relation between cognitive complexity and predictive accuracy was significant, although not of a high absolute value. However, when two independent components of the accuracy measure were isolated, cognitive complexity was significantly related to the accurate perception of *differences* between oneself and the other ($r = 0·35$) but was not related to the accurate perception of similarities ($r = 0·02$). Furthermore, cognitively more simple judges tended to perceive unwarranted similarities between themselves and others. These results suggest a difference in mode of processing information between high and low complex judges which continues to be observed in subsequent studies. Thus,

168

Leventhal (1957) found that cognitively complex judges tended to judge another person more accurately than did less complex judges, although this relation was not significant ($p < 0.10$). Complex judges tended, furthermore, to be more accurate in predicting differences while simple judges were more accurate in predicting similarities, although neither trend was statistically significant. Leventhal also found that cognitively simple judges predicted significantly more similarity between others' behavior and their own than did more complex judges. Finally, we may note an unpublished study by Plotnick in 1961 which involved the clinical judgements of 129 graduate social work students concerning the attitudes towards authority of three outpatients in a mental hygiene clinic. Using synopses of clinical histories and diagnostic evaluations, he found that the high complex judges, as a group, predicted the mean attitude toward authority scores of the three patients in the correct rank order, while low complex judges could not discriminate accurately between two of the three patients. Plotnick also observed that judges who were both more cognitively complex and more intelligent (as measured by tests of vocabulary and mathematics) had significantly higher mean accuracy scores for judgements of two of the three clients than did judges who were low on both complexity and intelligence indices. The interested reader will find reports of additional studies on judgemental accuracy and cognitive complexity in the review by Bieri (1961).

A second area of research has been concerned with the relation of cognitive complexity to behavior change. In the research by Leventhal (1957) mentioned previously, the effects of varying amounts of information on judgements were studied as a function of level of cognitive complexity of the judges. With an increase in the amount of information available, less complex judges tended to improve their predictions at a greater rate than did more complex judges. This improvement was observed particularly in relation to the accurate prediction of differences. Because the added information contained self-description material, Leventhal thought that this information served to correct the disposition of less complex judges not to discriminate between themselves and others. Lundy and Berkowitz (1957) predicted that more complex subjects would manifest greater attitude change than less complex subjects, reasoning that additional information must be relevant to existing constructs if it is to be conceptualized differently. Attitude scales in three different areas were administered before and after information which concerned the attitudes of others presumed to be influential was presented. Although Lundy and Berkowitz did find that least change occurred with subjects who were lowest in complexity, the most complex subjects displayed a negative change or boomerang effect in that they *increased* the level of their initial attitudes. Subjects who were moderate in complexity were either more consistently susceptible to change or were more variable on the various subscales.

Perhaps more specific understanding of the relation of cognitive complexity to change in behavior can be found in studies in which there is both an increase in the *amount* of information to be judged as well as a change in the *kind* of information to be judged. Two recent studies have analysed the relation of cognitive complexity to change in judgements following the presentation of information which is inconsistent or contradictory to previous information received. Mayo and Crockett (1964) had one group of judges (selected in terms of being either high or low on cognitive complexity) make judgements based on positive information about a person. Following this, negative information was provided and a second set of judgements was made based upon the pooled information. Another group of judges received the negative information first followed by the positive information. Consistent with their expectations, Mayo and Crockett found that on an adjective check list judgement task, high and low complex judges differed significantly in their resolution of the inconsistent information. While the initial impressions did not differ as a function of judges' complexity, the second impressions of low complex judges revealed striking recency effects whereas high complex judges retained a more ambivalent impression. Presumably, low complex judges attempted to maintain a more univalent impression of the person, and thus manifested greater changes in judgement upon receipt of the subsequent contradictory information. It should be noted that in this study the index of complexity was the number of *verbal* constructs generated rather than the rating-matching procedure.

J. Bieri, A. L. Atkins, S. Briar, R. Lobeck, H. Miller and T. Tripodi

Leventhal and Singer (1964) have also studied the relation between cognitive complexity and resolution of contradictory information in an impression change study. They presented stimulus information which varied in terms of being initially favorable, neutral or unfavorable to judges who were either high, moderate, or low in cognitive complexity as assessed by the row-matching procedure (Bieri, 1955). Judges were asked to react to this initial information in terms of several attitude and social distance items, trait impressions and impression organization as assersed by the method of Zajonc (1960). In addition, each judge was asked to report on such matters as the clarity of his impression and the need for additional information. Following this, inconsistent information about the same person was provided and a new set of judgements was obtained. Although all the results of this detailed study cannot be summarized briefly, it was found that simple judges reported greater clarity on the basis of initial information than did complex judges, especially for the two more emotionally toned figures. Following the presentation of contradictory information, the simple judges showed more change in the unclarity of their impressions, particularly for the two figures about which the greatest clarity existed initially.[2] In terms of changes in attitudes toward the figures, simple judges became more negative than the other complexity groups in relation to the initially most positive figure, a finding consistent with some of the results reported by Mayo and Crockett (1964). Over all, Leventhal and Singer believe that their results support the expectation that cognitively simple judges manifest greater change in impressions than do more complex judges. However, they stress that their clearest findings suggest that simple judges responded more to the outer, normative quality of others' behavior while complex judges search for information concerning inner states such as maladjustment. Such an external *v.* internal orientation had been noted previously in content analyses of personal constructs (Bieri, Bradburn and Galinsky, 1958).

2. Similar findings have been reported by Ware and Harvey. See Reading 20, page 361 [*Ed.*].

References

BIERI, J. (1955), 'Cognitive complexity–simplicity and predictive behavior', *J. abnorm. soc. Psychol.*, vol. 51, pp. 263–8.

BIERI, J. (1961), 'Complexity–simplicity as a personality variable in cognitive and preferential behavior', in D. W. Fiske and S. R. Maddi (eds.), *Functions of Varied Experience*, Dorsey.

BIERI, J. (1964), Cognitive complexity and personality development, *Unpublished Manuscript*.

BIERI, J., BRADBURN, W. M., and GALINSKY, M. D. (1958), 'Sex differences in perceptual behavior', *J. Personal.*, vol. 26, pp. 1–12.

DEUTSCH, M. (1954), 'Field theory in social psychology', in G. Lindzey (ed.), *Handbook of Social Psychology*, vol. 1, Addison-Wesley.

HARVEY, O. J., HUNT, D. E., and SCHRODER, H. M. (1961), *Conceptual Systems and Personality Organization*, Wiley.

JASPARS, J. M. F. (1964), 'Individual cognitive structures', in *Proceedings of the Seventeenth International Congress of Psychology*, North-Holland.

KELLY, G. A. (1955), *The Psychology of Personal Constructs*, vol. 1, Norton.

KELLY, G. A. (1962), A further explanation of factor analysis, *Unpublished Manuscript, Ohio State University*.

KIEFERLE, D. A., and SECHREST, L. (1961), 'Effects in alterations in personal constructs', *J. psychol. Studies*, vol. 12, pp. 173–8.

LEVENTHAL, H. (1957), 'Cognitive processes and interpersonal predictions', *J. abnorm. soc. Psychol.*, vol. 55, pp. 176–80.

LEVENTHAL, H., and SINGER, D. L. (1964), 'Cognitive complexity, impression formation, and impression change', *J. Personal.*, vol. 32, pp. 210–26.

LEWIN, K. (1951), *Field Theory in Social Science*, Harper.

LUNDY, R. M., and BERKOWITZ, L. (1957), 'Cognitive complexity and assimilative projection in attitude change', *J. abnorm. soc. Psychol.*, vol. 55, pp. 34–7.

MANDLER, G. (1962), 'From association to structure', *Psychol. Rev.*, vol. 69, pp. 415–27.

MAYO, C. W., and CROCKETT, W. H. (1964), 'Cognitive complexity and primacy–recency effects in impression formation', *J. abnorm. soc. Psychol.*, vol. 68, pp. 335–8.

OSGOOD, C. E., SUCI, G. J., and TANNENBAUM, P. H. (1957), *The Measurement of Meaning*, University of Illinois Press.

PEDERSEN, F. A. (1958), A consistency study of the R.C.R.T., *Unpublished Master's Thesis, Ohio State University*.

RAPAPORT, D. (1957), 'Cognitive structures', in J. S. Bruner *et al.* (eds.), *Contemporary Approaches to Cognition*, Harvard University Press.

SCOTT, W. A. (1963), 'Conceptualizing and measuring structural properties of cognition', in O. J. Harvey (ed.), *Motivation and Social Interaction*, Ronald Press, pp. 266–88. [See Reading 7.]

J. Bieri, A. L. Atkins, S. Briar, R. Lobeck, H. Miller and T. Tripodi

TODD, F. J., and RAPPOPORT, L. (1964), 'A cognitive structure approach to person perception: a comparison of two models', *J. abnorm. soc. Psychol.*, vol. 68, pp. 469–78.

TORGERSON, W. S. (1958), *Theory and Methods of Scaling*, Wiley.

TRIPODI, T., and BIERI, J. (1963), 'Cognitive complexity as a function of own and provided constructs', *Psychol. Rep.*, vol. 13, p. 26.

WITKIN, H. A., DYK, R. B., FATERSON, H. F., GOODENOUGH, D. R., and KARP, S. A. (1962), *Psychological Differentiation*, Wiley.

ZAJONC, R. B. (1960), 'The process of cognitive tuning in communication', *J. abnorm. soc. Psychol.*, vol. 61, pp. 159–67.

9 H. M. Schroder, M. J. Driver and S. Streufert

Levels of Information Processing

Excerpts from H. M. Schroder, M. J. Driver and S. Streufert, *Human Information Processing*, Holt, Rinehart & Winston, 1967, pp. 4–28.

Relationship between Information-Processing (Structural) Variables and Content Variables

One of the most common observations made about the behavior of organisms, at all points along the evolutionary ladder, is their consistency under similar conditions. Organisms either inherit or develop characteristic modes of thinking, adapting or responding. Such modes or adaptive orientations not only differ among species but are observed as individual differences within species, and change in the same organism as a result of change in environmental conditions.

According to their theoretical preference or problem orientation, psychologists refer to these adaptive strategies as response patterns, attitudes, needs, defense mechanisms, norms, and so on. Much of psychology is directly concerned with the conditions surrounding the development, generalization, and persistence of such orientations. However, two distinct classes of information are relevant to the understanding of adaptation.

'Content variables' provide information about the acquisition, direction, and magnitude of responses, attitudes, norms, needs, and so on. From this standpoint, we are interested in what and how much a person learns, how long it is remembered, what attitudes or needs he holds, and how intense they are. Here the criterion or metric for describing adaptive orientations is the behavioral outcome measured in terms of the components involved, their magnitude (how much), and their direction (which stimuli are evaluated negatively or positively).

'Structural variables' provide a metric for measuring the way a person *combines* information perceived from the outside world as well as internally generated information, for adaptive purposes

It is here maintained that an adaptive orientation acts, first, like a set of filters – selecting certain kinds of information from the environment – and, second, like a program or set of rules which combines these items of information in specific ways. The first aspect is the component or content variable, and the second aspect is the structural or information-processing variable. [. . .]

We shall emphasize the contribution of structural variables to the understanding of development, personality, attitudes, intelligence, performance, and interpersonal and intergroup relations. The emphasis will be upon *how* a person thinks or uses an attitude as a structure for processing new information, as opposed to an emphasis upon content, upon *what* a person thinks, what his attitudes are, and so forth.

Instead of treating differences in information processing as error, we hope to show that if the same informational components are processed in different ways – regardless of the content of the outcome – different adaptive consequences follow. For example, two persons may reach the same conclusion in a situation or hold the same attitude, but if the conclusion or judgement was reached by a different thought process or if the same attitude is used in a different way for processing information, then very different adaptive consequences would be expected to follow. [. . .]

General Characteristics of Information Processing

Let us turn more explicitly to the identification of, and the operations for, various gradations (levels) of information processing in persons. Information processing refers to the nature and interdependence of conceptual rules available for organizing dimensional values. One problem is to determine the number of dimensional attributes processed in an environment, and if two or more dimensional attributes of information are perceived, the next problem is to determine the degrees of freedom involved in the rules of combination.

For example, in thinking about international stimuli, one person may perceive two dimensions (capitalism–socialism and military strength–weakness) and another, three dimensions (adding autocracy–democracy). The second person perceives an additional dimensional scale value of information about a

175

nation. But the number of dimensional attributes of information perceived has only a low-order relationship to the level of information processing involved, and it can only be used as an operation under special circumstances. A person using two dimensions may be able to use them conjointly, combine them in different ways and compare outcomes, while a person using three dimensions may use them independently in a compartmentalized way. The number of dimensions, taken alone, then, has no necessary relationship to the level of information processing; but given complex combinatory rules, the potential for generating new attributes of information is higher, and the degree to which one stimulus can be discriminated from another is increased as the number of perceived dimensions increases.

For the purposes of this chapter, we will assume a gradual increase in the number of dimensions with higher structural levels. This state of affairs is probable but not inevitable.

Further, we shall assume that the structural properties of the person are relatively unchanged by the impingement of external forces. Although such a state of affairs may never actually occur, we shall later describe research which shows that structural properties over a given range of stimuli are relatively stable.[1] These studies also show that, under certain conditions of stress, system functioning becomes less complex. The more a structure either remains stable or undergoes regression under conditions that permit abstract functioning, the more it is described as being closed. Many gradations or structural levels could be described along the conceptual–complexity dimension; however, in the pages to follow, we will describe only four: low, moderately low, moderately high and high integration indices. We would like to emphasize that these are merely points on a somewhat continuous dimension which have been selected solely for purposes of communication. For an identification of these four conceptual levels see Figures 1, 2, 3 and 4.

Simple (concrete) intervening structures are characterized by compartmentalization and by a hierarchical integration of parts (rules). Regardless of the number of dimensions or the number of rules and procedures involved, the integrating structure is

1. For this research the reader should turn to the book from which the present selection is taken [*Ed.*].

absolute. It lacks sets of alternate interacting parts. When the structure is hierarchical, the dimensional 'readings' of a range of stimuli are organized in a fixed way.

A number of implications concerning the functioning of concrete structure (low degrees of freedom) can be derived from these characteristics: (a) At any given time, stimuli are 'read' or interpreted unidimensionally. Such a system identifies and organizes stimuli in a fixed way, and the rules derived from existing

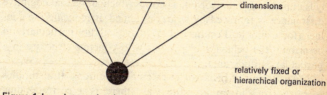

Figure 1 Low integration index

schemata are explicit in defining this one way. (b) Comparatively few degrees of freedom exist. The more undifferentiated the schemata, the lower the potential for generating conflict or ambiguity or for resolving ambiguity by means other than exclusion. (c) Dimensions are dichotomous with respect to the distribution of stimuli. A single hierarchy or rules for stimulus placement in a given category, which is compartmentalized so as to be independent of other subrules, has little potential for developing scaled dimensions. Stimuli are matched against yes–no categories, which they either do or do not fit. Less categorical discriminations will emerge (stimuli are discriminated more finely) when schemata are present for the generation of several simultaneous interpretations of a given range of stimuli. [. . .]

What are some of the familiar behavioral patterns generated by low integration index properties, regardless of the particular population of stimuli or content area?

These general characteristics of behavior include:

1. Categorical, black–white thinking. The discrimination of stimuli along dimensions is minimally graduated; for example, if a person holds an extremely concrete attitude toward Negroes, and 'Negroes' are categorized in a single way, it follows that

all Negroes will tend to be lumped into one category (for example, 'bad') and contrasted with others. A structure that depends upon a single fixed rule of integration reduces the individual's ability to think in terms of relativeness, of 'grays' and 'degrees'.

2. Minimizing of conflict. Stimuli either fit into a category or are excluded from consideration. There is no conceptual apparatus that can generate alternatives; the result is fast 'closure' in choice or conflict situations. When conflict is introduced (as with the presentation of attitudinal refutation or dissonance), it quickly is minimized and resolved. Theories which argue that cognitive dissonance is followed by strategies aimed at reducing the conflict (for example, Festinger, 1957) have validity particularly in describing the behavior of persons with concrete structure in a particular attitude area.

3. Anchoring of behavior in external conditions. If a stimulus is categorized in an absolute way, there is a corresponding restriction of internal integrative processes, and alternate resolutions or interpretations fail to arise. In structures with a low integration index, behavior is maximally controlled by external stimulus conditions. With increasing conceptual level, alternative perspectives and interrelationships can be generated from the same dimensional values of information. This represents an increase in the concept of 'self' as an agent, a going beyond any single or externally given interpretation, and an increase in the conception of internal causation.

4. The more absolute the rules of integration, the greater the generalization of functioning within a certain range, and the more abrupt or compartmentalized the change when it occurs. For example, if a stimulus person is categorized as holding the same attitude as the self, this perception (of agreement) will persist unchanged as the degree or nature of agreement becomes less or more complex. Conflicting attitudes tend to be misperceived or 'warded off' because of the absoluteness of the stimulus categorization and the lack of alternate schemata for 'sensing' shades of difference. In this sense, the perception of the other person is overgeneralized. When a person continues to perceive the world completely in terms of his own schemata, ignoring subtle situational changes and the alternate interpretations of others around him, he is 'projecting'. Thus, projection may be con-

sidered to be a defense mechanism commonly used by individuals low in integrative complexity. If the changes in the situation exceed a certain limit (which is defined in terms of the conditional rules for categorizing stimuli), the categorization of the stimulus person will change rather abruptly, and he will be perceived in a drastically different way. Another compartmentalized hierarchical set of rules negatively related to the first takes over.

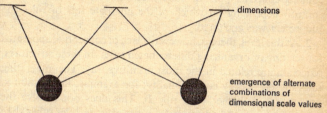

dimensions

emergence of alternate combinations of dimensional scale values

Figure 2 Moderately low integration index

Many transitional systems could be described as the level of structure increases. Generally, the most significant aspect of change is the extent to which the system becomes less determinate. Increasing abstractness implies an increasing number of degrees of freedom. The system must itself generate conflict and ambiguity if it is to evolve beyond an adaptation characterized by fixed rules; for example, although a digital computer program may generate complex solutions, the rules are explicated, fixed and externally determined. The program cannot change itself in the face of a changing environment. It is thus incapable of the behavior that most strikingly characterizes higher organisms.

One of the major requirements for the evolvement of abstract properties is the potential to generate alternate interpretations of a stimulus on any one dimension at a particular time (see Figure 2). It is one thing to categorize a stimulus on one dimension under one set of conditions, but it is a different matter to interpret the same stimulus at two places on the same dimension by using alternate rules at the same time. In more abstract structure, more information is generated and evaluations are less fixed. Decisions can be – and are – made on the basis of more information, yet there is less certainty owing to the presence of conflict.

179

The major characteristics of this second structural level are:

1. The presence of a conceptual apparatus that is able to generate alternate organizations of dimensions. That is, if there are three dimensions, such a structure would provide at least two possible rules for combining these dimensions. A given stimulus could be placed at two different points on any or all of the dimensions. For example, a mother helping a child to dress could be coded as 'plus' or 'minus' on a given dimension (such as control) depending on which of the alternate sets of rules the judgement was anchored.

2. At this level, there is, however, a lack of conceptual apparatus for relating or organizing differentiated rules. In these structures, schemata are related in the most primitive way. The integrating rules loosely specify conditionality; for example, in situation x, weight rule A higher than rule B. This does not involve the simultaneous use of schemata by superordinate rules other than conditional principles. In this sense, once a rule is engaged, moderately low integration index structure functions much like low integration index structure except that other schemata are available.

This moderately low level of organization is characterized by the delineation of several alternative ways of structuring the world. Although such conceptual properties are not effective for relating or organizing differentiated sets of rules for decision-making processes, they do usher in the problem of choice and probability. The generation of alternatives or of uncertainty is an important step in increasing abstractness, but at this level the system is characterized by ambivalence. Unlike low-level structure, for which the problem of choice is minimal, moderately low structure generates alternate interpretations without a fixed basis for choice or organization. For example, there is no fixed rule for what is right or wrong. Here conditions affect the choice not only of dimensions, as is the case in structures with a low integration index, but also of schemata. [. . .]

Some of the consequences of moderately low structural properties include:

1. A movement away from absolutism. Because of the availability of alternate schemata, 'right' and 'wrong' are not fixed as they were in structures with low integration index.

2. The emergence of primitive internal causation. A fixed system, based on a rigid set of absolutes, requires and expresses no internal processes. There is no freedom of choice. When alternates are available, the individual must make choices; internal processes, however minimal, begin to emerge. At the second level, the internal processes are mainly conditional, and in this sense they are primitive compared to the internal processes of more abstract structures.

3. Instability and noncommitment. In the absence of both absolute ways of evaluating environments and complex rules for integrating alternate schemata, there is ambivalence and lack of consistency in decision making and judgement. From the observer's point of view, conditional rules may appear inconsistent, and their application may indicate lack of commitment. In psychoanalytic terms, the person might be described as having a weak superego.

4. A form of rigidity still present, as in the first level. Rigidity there was used in the sense that external stimuli are perceived in a minimally differentiated and complex way; thus, the richness and range of experience is small. At this second structural level, the rigidity is due to the fact that, after the selection of a given schemata when one perceptual organization has been accepted, alternate schemata are almost completely ineffective. Information that could have entered the system via the rejected schemata is not available. There is, consequently, a failure to consider certain environmental pressures under some conditions.

5. A 'pushing against' or negative orientation. When alternate schemata can be selected by a set of conditional rules, the person is able to generate and understand two or more ways of perceiving a given situation. But since the two evaluations are used in a compartmentalized manner, failure to utilize one schema can be interpreted by an outside viewer as 'negativism'. Further, the process of generating alternate schemata itself implies a 'pushing against' present or alternate schemata and can again be viewed as an expression of negativism. [. . .]

Increasing levels of information processing involve the emergence of more complex and interrelated schemata. In turn, more dimensions are generated, and discrimination between stimuli becomes more linear. If the adaptive significance of moderately low structure is the delineation of alternate rules, the significance of moderately high structure may be described as the initial emergence of rules for identifying more complex relations than alternation (see Figure 3).

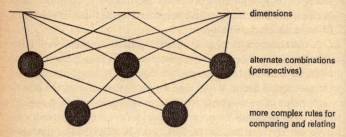

Figure 3 Moderately high integration index

At this level, the person is able to combine schemata. In moderately low structure, the rules could not be effectively combined. The arrangement of stimuli generated by each alternate set of rules was relatively fixed. However, the delineation of alternate schemata increased the level of uncertainty and decreased the fixity of outcomes. This shift from absoluteness to the generation of alternatives increases the amount of functional information available at a given time. Uncertainty increases with the presence of more abstract properties, not in the sense that the world is more chaotic, but rather in the sense that alternatives exist. Much more information is sought before resolutions are made; when they have been made, these resolutions are less fixed and the system remains open to the perception and effects of alternatives.

At the minimum, moderately high levels of structure require rules for matching, comparing and relating pairs of schemata. Each of these three processes utilizes *both* 'readings' for arriving at decisions or resolutions. In low-level structure, the rules determine conditions that govern the choice of stimulus categories; in moderately low-level structure, additional rules specify conditions under which alternate schemata are used; and at the third level, additional rules specify various ways in which schemata are compared. The process is one of 'comparing' or 'matching' in such a way that alternate schemata become organized more or less independently of other organizations.

A number of important behavioral implications are associated with moderately abstract properties:

1. The system is less deterministic. Combining and using two alternate systems of interpretation greatly increases the number of alternative resolutions that can be generated. Even when the individual closes on a particular decision, he is still open to a number of alternative pressures. At this level, abstractness (that is, lack of fixity) becomes a formal rule of the system.

2. When system properties begin to permit the simultaneous utilization of two schemata, the environment can be tracked in many more ways. While moderately low integration index structure permits different ways of tracking or interpreting an environment at different times moderately high integration index structure can vary combinations of alternate schemata. A person who is functioning at this level may view a social situation in terms of two points of view, see one in relationship to the other, perceive the effects of one upon the other. He is able to generate strategic adjustment processes, in which the effects of behavior from one standpoint are seen as influencing the situation viewed from another vantage point. This implies, for example, that a person can observe the effects of his own behavior from several points of view; he can simultaneously weigh the effects of taking different views. The adaptive utilization of alternate schemata here is much less compartmentalized than at moderately low levels.

3. The presence of choice makes possible the use of internal processes. Such processes emerge in a rudimentary way in moderately low-level structure. However, the 'comparing' or 'relating' function, which is entirely an internal process, is characteristic of more integratively complex levels than the second. At the third level, structure is potentially self-reflective. The awareness of 'self' (and the 'self' as a causative agent) is greatly enhanced, although it does not reach its climax until the development of high-level structure. In moderately high levels of integrative complexity, rules are minimally fixed. They are no

longer completely anchored in the past. When relationships are not thus anchored, the process of relating alternate schemata to each other is a highly internal one. It is internal in the sense that it is not anchored in established rules, in the sense that it represents a projection into the future, and in the sense that many different interactions can be generated in the same external situation. Functioning is decreasingly dependent upon immediate external stimulus conditions, and behavior is decreasingly predictable from a knowledge of the individual's past. In order to predict behavior, it becomes increasingly important to understand the internal processes of the structure.

While moderately high structure generates rules for comparing and combining the effects of specific pairs (or small groups) of schemata at a time, high-level structure includes additional and more complex potentialities for organizing additional schemata in alternate ways. At the fourth level, comparison rules can be further integrated. Alternate complex combinations provide the potential for relating and comparing different systems of interacting variables. As with other system differences, the difference between the moderately high and the high levels is one of degree. In the latter, the potential to organize different structures of interacting schemata opens up the possibility of highly abstract functions (see Figure 4).

In a very loose sense, and by analogy, the difference between moderately high and high levels may be described as the difference between an empirical and a theoretical outlook. At the moderately high level, a number of classes of empirical relationships are possible; in high-level functioning, it is possible to generate or apply general laws that systematize a large and differentiated body of information generated by simpler schemata in various related ways. Unlike the low level, which consists of a hierarchical set of established rules and procedures, high-level functioning (which again reaches a form of unity in the system) is characterized by the ability to generate the rules of the theory, the complex relations and alternate schemata, as well as the relationships between the various structures. It has the potential to generate alternate patterns of complex interactions.

As with other levels, an increase in the number and complexity of the parts of the mediating structure is accompanied by (a) an increase in the degree of diversity the system can generate and handle, in the number of schemata and dimensions, and in the complexity of their organization; (b) greater discrimination between stimuli within dimensions; and (c) an increased potential for the structure to generate alternate patterns of interaction and new schemata without the imposition of new external conditions. Internal processes can produce alternate organizations of rules for viewing the world. These schemata can then be tested by exploration. [. . .]

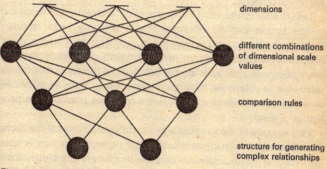

dimensions

different combinations of dimensional scale values

comparison rules

structure for generating complex relationships

Figure 4 High integration index

Tests and Behavioral Operations for Levels of Information Processing

The following is a brief summary of the measures used in our research.

Measures of differentiation

The problem here is to determine the number of dimensional units of information generated by a person when he 'perceives' an array of stimuli. A dimension is defined as a unique arrangement of stimuli. When a person makes a decision or a judgement of 'agreement' or 'good' or 'similar', we ask how many unique dimensions of information are involved in the judgement. If a person is asked to sort objects into categories or groups, the number of categories does not necessarily represent the number of unique dimensions since categories may be identical or overlapping. For example, two categories, 'long objects' and 'short objects', represent two scale values on the same dimension.

In general, measures that utilize object or stimulus sorting are only partially satisfactory as measures of differentiation. In our research experience, the technique that seems to hold most promise is multidimensional scaling (e.g. Torgerson, 1958). In this method, the subject makes similarity judgements between all pairs of the stimuli involved. The analysis then consists of calculating the number of dimensions required to reproduce the judgement matrix.[2]

Less precise estimates of the degree of differentiation in behavior or perception can be obtained from 'tracking' and 'rating' tasks. In the games used in our studies, many kinds of information became available at certain times (through combining various units of input). By observing the behavior of the participants, we were able to determine how many dimensional units of information and what kinds of information were being tracked by a person or a team.

Perhaps one of the simplest ways to determine gross differences in differentiation (such as whether the perceptual space is unidimensional or multidimensional) is to observe the consistency of ratings. In the 'least preferred person' technique of Fiedler (1962), subjects are asked to select the person with whom they would least prefer to work in a group. This person is then rated on a number of characteristics. The more a subject rates a disliked person positively on some characteristics, the more likely it is that several dimensions are involved in perception and judgement. It further indicates that discrepant perspectives (or multidimensional units of information) can be generated and tolerated.

Measures of discrimination

The capacity of the conceptual structure to distinguish among stimuli is called discrimination. The more integratively complex the structure, the more ways there are in which a stimulus can be perceived. Providing these 'ways of perceiving' can be related (as in high integration–index structure), one stimulus can be

2. See also Reading 18, page 334 [*Ed.*].

discriminated finely from another. Thus, the more integratively complex the structure: (a) the greater the number of stimuli that can be judged or assimilated by a given dimension; (b) the more perspectives (combinations of dimensional scale values) a person can generate and integrate about each stimulus (stimuli are finely discriminated); (c) the more the individual delays final decisions concerning the stimulus; and (d) the more open the structure is to change (since the stimulus can be 'read' in more ways).

Measures of discrimination parallel the above four aspects. These include: (a) measures of stimulus range or category width to determine the number of stimuli that can be ordered by a dimension; (b) measures of fineness of the gradations of intra-category distances (gradations can vary from gross 'yes–no' dichotomies to complex ratio scales with an infinite number of values and the potential for discriminating among an infinite number of stimuli); (c) measures of certainty of placement, or of delay, which can be used to determine the extent to which discrimination implies the analysis of more information; and (d) measures of flexibility of rules for including certain stimuli in a dimension. The less fixed the rules of admission, the more stimuli will be included and the more finely such stimuli can be discriminated. Consequently, new information about any aspect of a stimulus would be associated with greater probability of change in the placement of that stimulus on dimensions.

Measures of integrative complexity

Integration in behavior measures the extent to which dimensional units of information can be interrelated in different ways in order to generate new and discrepant perspectives about stimuli. The direct measurement of this characteristic remains a goal for the future. However, since this is the most central and important behavioral referent from our point of view, it is fortunate that there are a number of 'signs' or associated characteristics which can be reliably inferred and measured. These measures can be classified into three broad groups: projective, scaling and behavioral.

Projective measures. The research to be presented typically involves the selection of specific groups of individuals varying in level of structure in some stimulus area. Since our experiments were primarily in the area of social interaction, we attempted to develop relatively standardized paper-and-pencil tests to measure structure in this area. Up to this point, we have had the most success with two semiprojective measures: the paragraph completion and the impression formation tests.

In the Paragraph Completion Test, the subject is asked to write a short paragraph (three to four sentences) to complete various sentence stems (for example, 'When I am in doubt . . .'; 'When I am criticized . . .'; 'Rules . . .'). The second measure, the impression formation test, presents slightly incongruous adjectives and asks the subject to write a paragraph describing a person with those characteristics. Raters then are asked to assess the degree of integrative complexity demonstrated by the response; that is, the level of structure that generated the response. Ideal completions representing various levels of personality structure have been simplified and used in an objective forced-choice test (the situational interpretation test). However, this form of the test is much less satisfactory and its use is not recommended.[3]

The referents indicating more concrete responses on these tests include such categories as (a) overgeneralization of response, (b) hierarchical organization, (c) absoluteness of response, (d) inability to generate conflict or diversity, (e) inability to view a situation from another person's point of view and to see it in relationship to one's own, (f) inability to generate alternate perceptions and outcomes, and (g) tendency to seek structure, avoid delay, to close fast, and so forth.

Measures of abstractness of structure based on the paragraph completion and impression formation tests: (a) are highly intercorrelated; (b) produce a significant but low-order correlation with the objective situational interpretation test; (c) correlate significantly (negatively, about $0.2-0.5$ over various samples) with F- (authoritarianism) scores (Adorno *et al.*, 1950); (d) show correlations of borderline significance (negative) with the dogmatism scale (Rokeach, 1960); (e) are significantly positively related to intelligence ($0.15-0.45$); and (f) are unrelated to social

3. Tests, manuals and empirical data are presented in an appendix to the book from which this selection is taken [*Ed.*].

desirability (Edwards, 1957) and verbal fluency (estimated from the number of words used in sentence completion).

Scaling measures. Although no precise scaling technique has been developed for measuring the flexibility of integration involved in behavior, Driver (1962) has established construct validity in a particular experimental setting for a dimensional weighting procedure. Having discovered the number of dimensions generated and used by a person or a group in reference to some range of stimuli (such as people, groups or objects), Driver reasoned that the more evenly each dimension was weighted in any given set of judgements or perceptions, the greater the probability that the response was generated by a integratively complex structure. Conversely, the more uneven the weighting (for example, one dimension contributing 95 per cent and another 4 per cent), the more categorical the utilization of the dimensions (for example, one dimension would be used under some conditions and another dimension under other conditions). Thus, uneven 'weighting' scores for dimensions that have been self-generated by a person in a particular situation may indicate comparatively low-level structure. [. . .]

Behavioral measures. A number of referents may be used to assess the degree of integrative complexity in natural social situations. Laboratory environments can be designed in order to bring these characteristics of behavior more clearly into focus.

One example of such a behavioral measure is the number of alternate 'hypotheses' or perceptions a person or a group generates on the basis of feedback, and the degree to which alternate constructions of past and present feedback are combined and reorganized in decision making. Another example is the use of measures of generalization across situations. The less change there is in behavior as the situation changes, the more concrete the intervening structure. And yet, as we have indicated n low-level structures, behavior is increasingly anchored in external stimuli – it is more 'stimulus bound'. In low-level structure, once a perceptual perspective is established, it tends o persist regardless of the more subtle situational changes. Further, the situation is not perceived in relationship to other

189

events. Also, the lower the level of information processing: (a) the smaller the range and the less the diversity of the information being processed about a situation; (b) the more highly correlated (less dissonant) or hierarchically structured the informational units; and (c) the greater the tendency to 'ward off' informational units that are not highly salient and that do not fit into the attitude. That is, when nonsalient conflicting information produces little effect on attitudes or functioning, low levels of integrative complexity may be inferred.

Conversely, if new or discrepant information can be made highly salient (as by authority, or by strong emphasis on discrepant information as exemplified by intensive group pressure) and consequent change in attitude or behavior occurs in a categorical way, a low level of integration may be inferred. Low integrative complexity is inferred whenever a narrow band of highly salient information becomes the basis for attitudes or decisions, and when marked changes in salience lead to categorical changes. When high levels of complexity are involved in behavior, less salient aspects of the informational field have an interactive effect. This results in less categorical change, a reduction in the 'funneling' effect in behavior and less 'blackness–whiteness' of attitudes and decisions.

Measures of integration in group structure also may be used as behavioral indices. Groups are described in terms of the arrangements of parts (group members) when the group, as a system, is engaged in information processing and action. As in personality structure, the 'arrangement of parts' refers to the differentiation and integrative complexity of the units (the members of groups), and, as indicated earlier, the same analysis of levels of structure can be used (Schroder and Harvey, 1963). Concrete group structure is characterized by hierarchical (autocratic) organization, minimal interchangeability of parts, and fixed rule relationships. In turn, these properties of concrete group structure would be expressed in categorical norms, great reliance on a narrow band of highly salient information, lack of complexity of integration in group decision making, little generation of new and discrepant information, and so on. [. . .]

References

ADORNO, T. W., FRENKEL-BRUNSWIK, E., LEVINSON, D. J., and SANFORD, R. N. (1950), *The Authoritarian Personality*, Harper.

DRIVER, M. J. (1962), Conceptual structure and group processes in an internation simulation. Part one: the perception of simulated nations, *Educational Testing Service Research Bulletin*, RB 62-15.

EDWARDS, A. L. (1957), *The Social Desirability Variable in Personality Assessment and Research*, Holt, Rinehart & Winston.

FESTINGER, L. (1957), *A Theory of Cognitive Dissonance*, Harper

FIEDLER, F. E. (1962), 'Leader attitudes, group climate, and group creativity', *J. abnorm. soc. Psychol.*, vol. 65, p. 308.

ROKEACH, M. (1960), *The Open and Closed Mind*, Basic Books.

SCHRODER, H. M., and HARVEY, O. J. (1963), 'Conceptual organization and group structure', in O. J. Harvey (ed.), *Motivation and Social Interaction-Cognitive Determinants*, Ronald Press, pp. 134–66.

TORGERSON, W. S. (1958), *Theory and Methods of Scaling*, Wiley.

Part Four Psychological Differentiation

Since this book is largely concerned with relationships between cognitive elements, it is not surprising that 'differentiation' is a recurrent term. We have come upon 'conceptual differentiation' in Part Two and 'dimensional differentiation' in Part Three, and we look now at a similar, though bolder, concept – that of 'psychological differentiation'.

This concept is closely associated with the work of Witkin (Witkin *et al.*, 1954; 1962), and it is appropriate that one of the two Readings in Part Four is a paper in which he summarizes the ideas behind this work. Psychological differentiation is seen as a general personality characteristic which can be observed directly in cognitive style measures. Witkin discusses several such measures – of perceptual field dependence, of articulation of body concept, and so on.

The other paper in Part Four – one by Corah – contrasts with Witkin's article in that it deals specifically with one circumscribed issue: parent–child similarities in psychological differentiation. The results of Corah's study point to the influence of a child's opposite-sexed parent as a determinant of differentiation. Similar findings emerge from other studies exploring social antecedents of differentiation level in a variety of cultures (Witkin, 1967).

References

WITKIN, H. A. (1967), 'A cognitive style approach to cross-cultural research', *Int. J. Psychol.*, vol. 2, pp. 233–50.

WITKIN, H. A., DYK, R. B., FATERSON, H. F., GOODENOUGH, D. R., and KARP, S. A. (1962), *Psychological Differentiation*, Wiley.

WITKIN, H. A., LEWIS, H. B., HERTZMAN, M., MACHOVER, K., MEISSNER, P. B., and WAPNER, S. (1954), *Personality through Perception*, Harper.

10 Herman A. Witkin

Psychological Differentiation

Excerpt from Herman A. Witkin, 'Psychological differentiation and forms of pathology', *Journal of Abnormal Psychology*, vol. 70, 1965, pp. 317–36.

Recent research has demonstrated that people show character-istic, self-consistent ways of functioning in their perceptual and intellectual activities. These cognitive styles, as they have come to be called, appear to be manifestations, in the cognitive sphere, of still broader dimensions of personal functioning which cut across diverse psychological areas. The fact that these broader dimensions may be 'picked up' in the person's cognitive activities, in the form of cognitive styles, has an important methodological advantage. Cognitive styles may be evaluated by controlled laboratory procedures, thereby providing an experimental, objective approach to personality study and assessment.

It is of interest, too, that the dimensions of personal function-ing that have been identified through the cognitive-style work represent different ways of cutting the personality 'pie' from those traditionally used. New ways of looking at personality organization are thus being suggested. Even if the personality dimensions that are now being explored as outgrowths of the cognitive-style work, prove, in time, to be congruent with our more traditional dimensions, the outcome will be to deepen and enrich our understanding of these traditional dimensions.

The approach to cognitive activity followed in the research on cognitive styles has been a functional one. A primary concern has been with the adaptive function of cognitive processes in the psy-chological economy of the individual. This has led to a search for connexions and consistencies across psychological areas. An outcome of this research enterprise has been to demonstrate further that the conventional categories often used in describing man's psychological life are not as separate as once believed. A by-product of the cognitive-style research has thus been its contribution to a more integrated, holistic view of personality.

In these and other ways the recent extensive research on cognitive style has significant implications for personality theory, for the methodology of personality research, and for some of the practical problems encountered by the clinician in his work on diagnosis and therapy. Some of these implications may be demonstrated by considering, as illustrative, the particular cognitive style with which we have been concerned in our laboratory (Witkin *et al.*, 1954, 1962).

Indicators of Extent of Differentiation

Articulated v. global dimension of cognitive functioning

We first identified this cognitive style, and the dimension of personal functioning of which it is a part, in perception, where we called it 'field dependence–independence'. In a field-dependent mode of perceiving, perception is strongly dominated by the over-all organization of the field, and parts of the field are experienced as 'fused'. In a field-independent mode of perceiving, parts of the field are experienced as discrete from organized background. There is now considerable evidence that a tendency toward one or the other ways of perceiving is a consistent, pervasive characteristic of an individual's perception.

From our studies of the field dependence–independence dimension there has emerged a variety of perceptual tests for evaluating individual differences along this dimension. In all of these tests the issue is whether or not the person is able to keep an object separate from organized field in perception. In one test, the 'object' is the person's own body; in another, it is a stick; in still another, it is a simple geometric design. A brief account of these tests will make clearer the nature of the perceptual dimension they assess.

One test, the Body-Adjustment Test, is concerned with perception of the position of the body in space. The test evaluates the person's ability to perceive his body apart from the surrounding visual field, through reference to sensations of body position. The apparatus for this test consists of a small room, which can be tilted left or right, within which is a chair, which can also be tilted left or right. The subject's task is to make his body straight while the room around him is tilted. Some persons, in carrying out this task, move their bodies into alignment with the tilted room, and in that position report that they are straight, though objectively tilted as much as thirty-five degrees, or even more. In this kind of performance, which we call 'field dependent', perception of body position is dictated by the relation between the body and surrounding world. There seems to be a fusion between body and field in experience. At the other extreme of the performance range, we find subjects who, regardless of the position of the surrounding room, are able to bring their bodies close to the true upright. Persons who perform in this fashion – we call it a 'field-independent' performance – seem to have an immediate sense of the separateness of their bodies from the surrounding world.

Another of our tests of field dependence again involves perception of the upright, but the object of perception is a neutral external object, a stick, instead of the body. The apparatus for this test consists of a luminous rod and frame, the only objects visible to the subject in the completely darkened room. With the frame tilted, the subject is required to adjust the rod to the upright. Some subjects perceive the rod as straight only when it is fully aligned with the tilted frame around it. For these field-dependent persons perception of rod position is dictated by the context provided by the axes of the surrounding frame. They cannot keep rod separate from frame; in this sense their perception is global. Other subjects, at the opposite extreme, are able to adjust the rod more or less to the true upright, independently of frame position. These field-independent persons are able to perceive a part of the field as discrete from the field; in this sense, their perception is analytical.

Still another test of field dependence, the Embedded-Figures Test, requires the subject to locate a simple figure in a complex design which is so organized as to conceal the simple figure. For some persons the simple figure almost 'pops out' of the complex design. Their perception is field independent. Others are not able to find the simple figure within the five minutes allowed. Their perception is field dependent.

People tend to perform in a consistent fashion in these three tests. The individual who cannot separate the simple figure from the complex embedding design also cannot keep his body apart from the surrounding tilted room or the rod apart from the surrounding frame. Going beyond the particular tests I have described, this same individual is unable to keep item apart from context in a wide variety of other perceptual situations (including such classical ones as the constancies, illusions, reversible perspective) and in situations involving other sense modalities, as touch (Axelrod and Cohen, 1961). Such consistency is indicative of a stylistic tendency in perception.

The particular stylistic tendencies we have been considering are not limited to a person's perception; they manifest themselves, in congruent form, in his intellectual activities as well. Thus, persons whose perception is field dependent do less well at solving problems which require isolating essential elements from the context in which they are presented and using them in different contexts, as, for example, the tasks employed by Duncker in his studies of functional fixity.

It is because these stylistic tendencies extend across both perception, where we are dealing with an immediately present stimulus configuration, and intellectual functioning, where we are dealing with symbolic representations, that we refer to them as *cognitive* styles. The particular cognitive style we have been considering may be described as follows: at one extreme there is a consistent tendency for experience to be global and diffuse – the organization of the field as a whole dictates the manner in which its parts are experienced. At the other extreme there is a tendency for experience to be delineated and structured – parts of a field are experienced as discrete and the field as a whole organized. To these opposite poles of the cognitive style we may apply the labels 'global' and 'articulated'. As with the dimension of perceptual field dependence, there is no implication here that the world is peopled by two kinds of human beings. Scores for any large group on tests of this cognitive style show a continuous distribution.

I may add that a more global or more articulated quality is a stable characteristic of an individual's cognitive functioning over time. There are also consistent sex differences in the articulation-global cognitive dimension. Boys and men show greater articulation than girls and women. Small but consistent sex differences in tests of field dependence have been found with groups in the United States, in a number of western European countries (see e.g., Andrieux, 1955; Bennett, 1956; Chateau, 1959; Franks, 1956; Wit, 1955), and in Hong Kong,[1] Israel[2] and Sierra Leone, Africa (Dawson, 1963) as well.

Evidence that the global-articulated style of cognitive functioning is part of a still broader dimension of personal functioning has come from studies of the relation of this cognitive style to nature of the body concept, of the self and of controls and defenses.

Articulation of body concept

Let me consider first our studies of the body concept – that is to say, the systematic impression an individual has of his body, cognitive and affective, conscious and unconscious. Our concern has been with the cognitive, rather than the libidinal aspects of the body concept, and with the articulated-global dimension in particular. In turning to the body concept, we are in effect shifting the spotlight from experience which has its primary source 'out there', our main concern to this point, to experience which has its primary source 'within'. There is now considerable evidence that children and adults who show an articulated cognitive style in their performance in perceptual and intellectual tasks of the kind we have been considering are also likely to have an articulated body concept – that is to say, they experience their bodies as having definite limits or boundaries and the parts within as discrete yet interrelated and formed into a definite structure.

Performance in the Body-Adjustment Test itself permits some inference about articulation of the body concept. Take, for example, the person who, in order to perceive his body as upright, aligns it with the tilted room, and in that position reports no experience of tilt. Such a fusion of body and field in experi-

1. Personal communication from Robert Goodnow.
2. Personal communication from Martin Rothman and Joel H. Kaplan.

ence, or inability to keep body and field separate, suggests a lack of clear body boundaries.

In another, more familiar approach to study of the body concept, we have used the figure-drawing technique. To evaluate extent of articulation of drawings of human figures, made in response to the request to draw a person and then to draw a person of the opposite sex, a five-point sophistication-of-body-concept scale was devised. This scale does not follow the usual projective uses of the figure-drawing technique but rather considers directly characteristics of the figures drawn. Three areas of the drawings are considered in making ratings: form level, identity or role and sex differentiation and level of detailing. In a number of studies, scores for the figure-drawing test have been shown to relate significantly to measures of cognitive style. In the drawings of field-dependent children, we find very little detail and unrealistic representation of proportioning and of body parts. Sexual characteristics are shown minimally or not at all, so that in some pairs of drawings it is difficult to tell which is male and which is female. In most cases, there is no attempt at role representation. On the other hand, in the drawings of children whose perceptual performance is at the field-independent extreme we find the body drawn in realistic proportion. Parts of the body are presented in some detail and fairly realistically. There is clear representation of sex and sex differences. Aside from indication of sex through body characteristics, the sex of the figure is also indicated by such externals as clothing. We also find attempts at role representation, suggesting a sense of the uses to which the body may be put. These differences among children in the way in which they represent the body on paper are significantly related to how they perform in the cognitive tests in the laboratory.

It may appear from the description of the kinds of drawings they make that field-dependent children, who tend to make relatively unarticulated drawings, are just not as bright as field-independent children, who tend to make highly articulated drawings. Significant correlations are in fact found between figure-drawing articulation scores and total I.Q. Several studies have shown, however, that this relation is carried mainly by particular subtests of standard intelligence tests which, like the cognitive tests we use, have the task requirement of separating item from context. These subtests are block design, picture completion and object assembly which in past factor analytic studies of the Wechsler were shown to load what we would designate an 'analytical factor' (Cohen, 1957, 1959). There are only low, non-significant relations between figure-drawing articulation scores and scores for the Wechsler vocabulary, information and comprehension subtests which have been shown to define a 'verbal-comprehension factor'. I should mention that scores for tests of field dependence, similarly, relate very highly to scores for the triumvirate of block design, picture completion and object assembly; and they do not relate to scores for the triumvirate of vocabulary, information, and comprehension (Goodenough and Karp, 1961; Karp, 1963).

The sophistication-of-body-concept scale is easily learned and applied, even by persons without experience in the figure-drawing technique. Checks on interjudge agreement in a number of studies have shown good reliability. And, as we have just seen, scores based on the scale relate well to scores of tests of the articulated-global cognitive dimension. These characteristics of the scale, together with the ease of obtaining figure drawings from subjects, make the scale a useful assessment technique.

Let me interpolate that other studies, using more experimental means to evaluate articulation, have confirmed the relation between articulation of body concept and cognitive style (Epstein, 1957; Silverman *et al.*, 1961).

Sense of separate identity

To continue, persons with a more articulated or more global mode of cognitive functioning also differ in an important aspect of the self, namely, sense of separate identity. Persons with an articulated cognitive style give evidence of a developed sense of separate identity – that is to say, they have an awareness of needs, feelings, attributes which they recognize as their own and which they identify as distinct from those of others. Sense of separate identity implies experience of the self as segregated. It also implies experience of the self as structured; internal frames of reference have been formed and are available as guides for definition of the self. The less developed sense of separate identity of persons with a global cognitive style manifests itself in reliance on external sources for definition of their attitudes, judgements, sentiments and of their views of themselves.

The nature of this relation may be made clearer by considering a few studies from among the many that have been done in this area.

Konstadt and Forman (1965) observed that children with a global cognitive style, when taking a test under stress and so concerned about their performance, looked up at the *face* of the adult examiner about twice as often as children with an articulated cognitive style. Similarly, Crutchfield, Woodworth and Albrecht (1958) found that persons with a global cognitive style were relatively better at recognizing and recalling faces of people they had been with earlier. Messick and Damarin (1964) observed that field-dependent subjects showed greater incidental learning than field-independent subjects when the incidental material consisted of human faces; the relation is in the opposite direction with nonhuman incidental material (Witkin *et al.*, 1962). These studies suggest that persons with a global style are particularly attentive to faces, the major source of cues as to what others are feeling and thinking. The reliance of persons with a global cognitive style on external sources for self-definition was demonstrated in quite a different way by Linton (1955). She found that in an autokinetic situation, such persons more often changed their judgement about movement of the point of light in conformance with the suggestion of a planted confederate. The results of these and numerous other studies may be summarized by saying that the person for whom the frame around the rod, or the room around his body, strongly influence the manner in which rod and body are experienced, is, similarly, strongly influenced by the immediate social context in his experience of himself.

I would like to mention here a recently completed study by Winestine (1964) on the 'twinning reaction' of boy twins because of the particularly direct way in which sense of separate identity was evaluated. The twinning reaction, assessed by interview, was rated as strong for a given twin if in his specific attitudes, feelings and actions he showed that he experienced himself as an integral part of the twinship rather than as individuated.

Twins rated high on the twinning reaction were strikingly more field dependent and their representation of the body in their figure drawings much more global. In fact, so specific a characteristic as whether the twins dressed alike or differently proved to be significantly discriminating with regard to both perceptual field dependence and nature of body concept in figure drawings. It would be of interest to study the parents of twins in relation to strength of the twinning reaction. We might expect that mothers of twins who show a weak twinning reaction and who are field independent to perceive their twins as separate individuals, rather than as a unit; to have a distinct relation with each child; and to foster the separation of the twins. These expectations are based on an earlier finding that mothers of more field-independent children, in their interactions with them, give their children greater opportunity for separation (Witkin *et al.*, 1962).

Differences between field-dependent and field-independent persons, as a function of difference in sense of separate identity, have even been observed in characteristics of their dreams. In an experimental study of dreaming, using rapid eye movements and Stage-1 EEG sleep as indicators of the dream state, Lewis *et al.* (1966) observed that field-dependent subjects more often dreamed overtly about the laboratory situation. Moreover, in a recent analysis of the data from that study we found a difference between field-dependent and field-independent subjects in the kinds of incorporation they made. Field-dependent subjects more often had dreams concerned with their relation to the experimenter. Apparently these subjects get 'caught up' more with another person in the laboratory situation, as we have found they do in general, and these feelings are carried over into the dream.

Specialization of defenses

Finally, let me comment on the relation between cognitive style and nature of defenses. Studies have shown that persons who experience in articulated fashion tend to use specialized defenses, as isolation. In contrast, persons with a global cognitive style tend to use such defenses as massive repression and primitive denial. These latter defenses involve an indiscriminate, total blotting out of memory for past experiences and of perception of stimuli. Compared to such mechanisms as isolation, they represent relatively nonspecific ways of functioning.

The contrasting kinds of defenses used by persons with a more global or more articulated cognitive style may be conceived in terms similar to those we used earlier in characterizing their cognitive functioning. In the last analysis, defenses help determine the content of a person's experience – what enters into consciousness and what is put aside. They do this, in part, through regulating the interrelation between affect, on the one hand, and ideation and perception, on the other. It seems true of persons with a global cognitive style that feelings strongly influence thought and perception, in other words, that feelings are not kept sufficiently discrete from thoughts and percepts. This is congruent with what we saw happen within their perception, where again they are unable to 'keep things separate' – as body separate from field, rod separate from frame or simply figure separate from organized ground. Persons with an articulated cognitive style, in their use of isolation, maintain the discreteness of feelings and ideas, although the feeling component may be 'split off'.

This view of communality in mode of functioning in the areas of cognition and of defenses may be made more evident by considering a few representative studies.

Bertini (1961) carried out a study of the relation between cognitive style and defenses, following this view. He considered that the 'capacity' to separate and isolate an idea from its emotional content, involved in the mechanism of isolation, parallels the capacity in field-independent perception to 'separate several elements from the phenomenal field in isolating them from a context'. To assess the use of isolation as a defense, Bertini relied on the Rorschach, basing his analysis on the work of Schafer (1954). The expectation that the tendency to use isolation would go with field-independent perception was confirmed.

A recent study by Minard[3] on perceptual defense effectively complements Bertini's study. Words matched in structure and previously found in a free-association test to be neutral or charged for the particular subject, were presented tachistoscopically. Persons who were field dependent showed a considerable perceptual-defense effect; their speed of perception of

3. Personal communication from James Minard.

words was markedly affected by whether or not the word carried an emotional connotation for them. Percept and feeling were, in other words, not kept separate. Field-independent persons showed no difference in speed of perception of neutral and charged words, suggesting discreteness of percept and feeling. In their use of denial and repression as characteristic defenses, persons with a global cognitive style are in effect showing a particularly extreme influence of feeling on percepts and memories. In these instances the total experience, including both its cognitive and affective components, is 'split off'.

A particularly striking example of this kind of complete blotting out of experience by field-dependent persons is found in their tendency to forget their dreams, presumably because of their use of repression as a characteristic defense. A connexion between field dependence and dream recall has been found by Eagle[4] in one study of ten year olds and in another study of seventeen year olds. It has been observed by Linton[5] and Schonbar (1964) with groups of college students. More recently it was found again in an analysis we made of data from the study of Lewis et al. (1966). Eight subjects at each extreme of the field-dependence dimension were picked from their total group of forty-six college students. Considering frequency of dream reports in a home dream diary these subjects kept, seven of the eight most field-dependent subjects and only one of the eight most field-independent subjects were found to be 'non-reporters' – that is, failed to recall dreams. Recent evidence from studies using rapid eye movement and Stage-1 EEG sleep as indicators of dreaming makes it entirely clear that everyone dreams a number of times each night (Aserinsky and Kleitman, 1953; Dement and Kleitman, 1957). A lack of dream reports is therefore indicative of a failure to recall dreams rather than a failure to dream.

The hypothesis that the failure of field-dependent persons to remember their dreams is, in part at least, a function of repression, is being tested in a study Donald Goodenough, Helen Lewis, Arthur Shapiro and I are carrying out. This study is making use of a technique Helen Lewis and I developed in an earlier preliminary study (Witkin and Lewis, 1965). The technique consists

4. Personal communication from Carol Eagle.
5. Personal communication from Harriet Linton.

of creating an important psychological event for the person just before he goes to sleep and obtaining his subsequent dreams by awakening him during each period of rapid eye movement and Stage-1 EEG. The pre-sleep event we use consists, on some occasions, of viewing an emotionally charged film; on other occasions, viewing a neutral film; and on still other occasions, an encounter with another person through the medium of suggestion. The results of the preliminary study showed, first of all, that the pre-sleep event often found expression in the subject's subsequent dreams in a clearly identifiable way. Further, reports from subjects that they had been dreaming, but could not remember the dream, occurred more often on awakenings following the exciting pre-sleep event than on awakenings following the neutral pre-sleep event. We anticipated this outcome on the premise that the exciting pre-sleep event, by 'charging' subsequent dreams, would make these dreams better 'candidates for repression' and so reduce dream recall. In the study Goodenough, Lewis, Shapiro and I are now doing we are following this same procedure of pre-sleep stimulation, using field-dependent and field-independent persons as our subjects. It is our expectation that field-dependent persons will be more likely to 'lose' dreams charged by an exciting pre-sleep experience. Such an outcome would lend further support to the view that field-dependent persons tend to use repression as a typical mode of defense.

Summary of indicators of differentiation

Reviewing the evidence considered to this point, a tendency toward a more global or more articulated cognitive style has been shown to be associated with differences in body concept, in sense of separate identity and in nature of defenses. It is now our view that the characteristics which make up the contrasting constellations described may be conceived as diverse manifestations of more developed or less developed psychological differentiation. Thus, we consider it more differentiated if, in his perception of the world, the person perceives parts of the field as discrete and the field as structured. We consider it more differentiated if, in his concept of his body, the person has a definite sense of the boundaries of the body and of the interrelation among its parts. We consider it more differentiated if the person has a feeling of himself as an individual distinct from others and has internalized, developed standards to guide his view of the world and of himself. We consider it more differentiated if the defenses the person uses are specialized. It is our view that these various characteristics, which we have found to cluster together, are not the end-products of development in separate channels, but are diverse expressions of an underlying process of development toward greater psychological complexity. 'Level of differentiation' is a concept which encourages us to look across psychological areas and provides a basis for thinking about self-consistency in individual psychological make-up.

The level of differentiation at which a person functions may be assessed in different areas. For clinical evaluation one or several areas may be considered. It is perhaps best assessed through the person's cognitive style where, as noted earlier, objective experimental means of evaluation may be used. In this sense a person's cognitive style, in the articulated-global dimension, may be considered a 'tracer element'. Certainly, assessment of psychological differentiation need not be limited to the cognitive sphere. It may also be assessed effectively, for example, in the area of the body concept, by means of the figure-drawing sophistication-of-body-concept scale which I described earlier. In our own work, when we want to make a rapid assessment with regard to differentiation we use the Embedded-Figures Test and Figure-Drawing Test, both of which are easily administered and scored, but time permitting, we like to use the Rod-and-Frame Test as well. If the Wechsler has been given, we use the score for the block-design subtest, which, as we saw, is very similar in its requirements to the tests of field dependence and is in fact a good test of field dependence.[6]

References

ALEXANDER, F. (1950), *Psychosomatic Medicine*, Norton.
ANDRIEUX, C. (1955), 'Contribution à l'étude des différences entre hommes et femmes dans la perception spatiale', *L'Année Psychol.*, vol. 55, pp. 41–60.

6. The remainder of this paper deals specifically with psychopathology and is presented in the Part of the book dealing with that area. See Reading 23 [*Ed.*].

ASERINSKY, E., and KLEITMAN, N. (1953), 'Regularly occurring periods of eye motility and concomitant phenomena during sleep', *Science*, vol. 118, p. 273.

AXELROD, S., and COHEN, L. D. (1961), 'Senescence and embedded-figures performance in vision and touch', *Percept. mot. Skills*, vol. 12, pp. 283–8.

BAUMAN, G. (1951), The stability of the individual's mode of perception, and of perception–personality relationships, *Unpublished Doctoral Dissertation, New York University*.

BENNETT, D. H. (1956), 'Perception of the upright in relation to the body image', *J. ment. Sci.*, vol. 102, pp. 487–506.

BERTINI, M. (1961), 'Il tratto difensivo dell'isolamento nella sua determinazione dinamica e strutturale', *Contributi dell'Istituto di Psicologica*, vol. 25.

BERTINI, M., LEWIS, H. B., and WITKIN, H. A. (1964), 'Some preliminary observations with an experimental procedure for the study of hypnagogic and related phenomena', *Archivio di Psicologia, Neurologia e Psichiatria*, vol. 25, pp. 495–534.

BOUND, M. M. (1951), A study of the relationship between Witkin's indices of field dependency and Eysenck's indices of neuroticism, *Unpublished Doctoral Dissertation, Purdue University*.

BRYANT, A. R. (1961), An investigation of process-reactive schizophrenia with relation to perception of visual space, *Unpublished Doctoral Dissertation, University of Utah*.

CANCRO, R. (1962), A comparison of process and reactive schizophrenia, *Unpublished Doctoral Dissertation, State University of New York Downstate Medical Center*.

CHATEAU, J. (1959), 'Le test de structuration spatiale TIB. I.', *Le Travail humain*, vol. 22, pp. 281–97.

COHEN, J. (1957), 'The factorial structure of the WAIS between early adulthood and old age', *J. consult. Psychol.*, vol. 21, pp. 283–90.

COHEN, J. (1959), 'The factorial structure of the WISC at ages 7–6, 10–6, and 13–6', *J. consult. Psychol.*, vol. 23, pp. 285–99.

CRUTCHFIELD, R. S., WOODWORTH, D. G., and ALBRECHT, R. E. (1958), Perceptual performance and the effective person, *USAF WADC Technical Note*, no. 58–60, Lackland Air Force Base, Texas.

DAWSON, J. L. M. (1963), Psychological effects of social change in a West African community, *Unpublished Doctorial Dissertation, University of Oxford*.

DEMENT, W., and KLEITMAN, N. (1957), 'The relations of eye movements during sleep to dream activity: an objective method for the study of dreaming', *J. exp. Psychol.*, vol. 53, pp. 339–46.

EPSTEIN, L. (1957), The relationship of certain aspects of the body image to the perception of the upright, *Unpublished Doctoral Dissertation, New York University*.

FISHBEIN, G. M. (1963), 'Perceptual modes and asthmatic symptoms: an application of Witkin's hypothesis', *J. consult. Psychol.*, vol. 27, pp. 54–8.

FRANKS, C. M. (1956), 'Différences déterminées par la personalité dans la perception visuelle de la verticalité', *Rev. Psychol. appl.*, vol. 6, pp. 235–46.

FREEDMAN, N. (1962), The process of symptom modification in psychopharmacological therapy, *Paper Presented at a Department of Psychiatry Meeting, State University of New York Downstate Medical Center*.

GOODENOUGH, D. R., and KARP, S. A. (1961), 'Field dependence and intellectual functioning', *J. abnorm. soc. Psychol.*, vol. 63, pp. 241–6.

GORDON, B. (1953), An experimental study of dependence–independence in a social and a laboratory setting, *Unpublished Doctoral Dissertation, University of Southern California*.

GRUEN, A. (1955), 'The relation of dancing experience and personality to perception', *Psychol. Monogr.*, vol. 69, no. 14, whole no. 399.

HOLT, R. R., and GOLDBERGER, L. (1959), Personological correlates of reactions to perceptual isolation, *W A D C Technical Report*, no. 59–735.

JACKSON, D. N. (1955), Stability in resistance to field forces, *Unpublished Doctoral Dissertation, Purdue University*.

JANUCCI, G. I. (1964), Size constancy in schizophrenia: a study of subgroup differences, *Unpublished Doctoral Dissertation, Rutgers State University*.

KARP, S. A. (1963), 'Field dependence and overcoming embeddedness', *J. consult. Psychol.*, vol. 27, pp. 294–302.

KONSTADT, N., and FORMAN, E. (1965), 'Field dependence and external directedness', *J. Personal. soc. Psychol.*, vol. 1, pp. 490–93.

KRAIDMAN, E. (1959), Developmental analysis of conceptual and perceptual functioning under stress and non-stress conditions, *Unpublished Doctoral Dissertation, Clark University*.

LEWIS, H. B., GOODENOUGH, D. R., SHAPIRO, A., and SLESER, I. (1966), 'Individual differences in dream recall', *J. abnorm. Psychol.*, vol. 71, pp. 52–9.

LINTON, H. B. (1952), Relation between mode of perception and tendency to conform, *Unpublished Doctoral Dissertation, Yale University*.

LINTON, H. B. (1955), 'Dependence on external influence: correlates in perception, attitudes, and judgement', *J. abnorm. soc. Psychol.*, vol. 51, pp. 502–7.

MESSICK, S., and DAMARIN, F. (1964), 'Cognitive styles and memory for faces', *J. abnorm. soc. Psychol.*, vol. 69, pp. 313–18. [See Reading 22.]

PARDES, H., and KARP, S. A. (1965), 'Field dependence in obese women', *Psychosom. Med.*, vol. 27, pp. 238–44.

PEREZ, P. (1955), Experimental instructions and stimulus content as variables in the size constancy perception of schizophrenics and normals, *Unpublished Doctoral Dissertation, New York University*.

POLLACK, I. W., and KIEV, A. (1963), 'Spatial orientation and psycotherapy: an experimental study of perception', *J. nerv. ment. Dis.*, vol. 137, pp. 93–7.

POLLACK, M., KAHN, R. L., KARP, S. A., and FINK, M. (1960), Individual differences in the perception of the upright in hospitalized psychiatric patients, *Paper Read at the Eastern Psychological Association*, New York.

POWELL, B. J. (1964), A study of the perceptual field approach of normal subjects and schizophrenic patients under conditions of an oversize stimulus, *Unpublished Doctoral Dissertation, Washington University*.

ROSENBLUM, L. A., WITKIN, H. A., KAUFMAN, I. C., and BROSGOLE, L. (1965), 'Perceptual disembedding in monkeys: a note on method and preliminary findings', *Percept. mot. Skills*, vol. 20, pp. 729–36.

RUDIN, S. A., and STAGNER, R. (1958), 'Figure-ground phenomena in the perception of physical and social stimuli', *J. Psychol.*, vol. 55, pp. 213–25.

SCHAFER, R. (1954), *Psychoanalytical Interpretation in Rorschach Testing*, Grune & Stratton.

SCHONBAR, R. A. (1964), 'Some dimensions of sensitivity of recallers and nonrecallers of dreams', in Dream research and theory, *Symposium Presented at the Post-Graduate Center for Mental Health*.

SHAFER, J. W. (1962), 'A specific cognitive deficit observed in gonadal aplasia (Turner's Syndrome)', *J. clin. Psychol.*, vol. 18, pp. 403–6.

SILVERMAN, A. J., COHEN, S. I., SHMAVONIAN, B. M., and GREENBERG, G. (1961), 'Psychophysical investigations in sensory deprivation: the body-field dimension', *Psychosom. Med.*, vol. 23, pp. 48–61.

SOLL, J. (1963), The effect of frustration on functional cardiac disorder as related to field orientation, *Unpublished Doctoral Dissertation, Adelphi University*.

STAFFORD, A. E. (1963), An investigation in parent–child test scores for evidence of hereditary components, *Unpublished Doctoral Dissertation, Princeton University*.

TAYLOR, J. M. (1956), A comparison of delusional and hallucinatory individuals using field dependency as a measure, *Unpublished Doctoral Dissertation, Purdue University*.

WINESTINE, M. C. (1964), Twinship and psychological differentiation, *Unpublished Doctoral Dissertation, New York University*.

WIT, O. C. (1955), Sex differences in perception, *Unpublished Master's Thesis, University of Utrecht*.

WITKIN, H. A. (1948), The effect of training of structural aids on performance in three tests of space orientation, *CAA Div. Res. Rep.*, no. 80.

WITKIN, H. A. (1965), Cognitive patterning in congenitally blind children, *Paper Presented at the Symposium on Cognitive Structure and Personality, American Psychological Association, Chicago*.

WITKIN, H. A., and LEWIS, H. B. (1965), 'The relation of experimentally induced pre-sleep experiences to dreams: a report on method and preliminary findings', *J. Amer. Psychoanal. Assoc.*, vol. 13, pp. 819–49.

WITKIN, H. A., FATERSON, H. F., GOODENOUGH, D. R., and
BIRNBAUM, J. (1966), 'Cognitive patterning in mildly retarded boys',
Child Devel., vol. 17, pp. 301–16.

WITKIN, H. A., DYK, R. B., FATERSON, H. F., GOODENOUGH, D. R.,
and KARP, S. A. (1962), *Psychological Differentiation*, Wiley.

WITKIN, H. A., LEWIS, H. B., HERTZMAN, M., MACHOVER, K.,
MEISSNER, P. B., and WAPNER, S. (1954), *Personality through
Perception*, Harper.

ZUKMANN, L. (1957), Hysteric compulsive factors in perceptual
organization, *Unpublished Doctoral Dissertation, New School for Social
Research*.

11 Norman L. Corah

Differentiation in Children and their Parents

Excerpts from Norman L. Corah, 'Differentiation in children and their parents', *Journal of Personality*, vol. 33, 1965, pp. 300–308.

Witkin *et al.* (1962) have used the concept of psychological differentiation in relation to a variety of perceptual and cognitive functions. Thus, field independence or analytic functioning in perception is related to modes of structuring experience, articulation-of-the-body concept and sense of separate identity, and the nature of the individual's controls and defenses.

These authors have also attempted to deal with the origin of differences in level of differentiation. Study of a group of boys and their mothers led these investigators to stress the importance of early mother–child interaction in the development of differentiation in the child. An independent unpublished study by Seder (cited in Witkin *et al.*, 1962, pp. 351–5) which included boys and girls and utilized maternal interviews tended to confirm the Witkin group's findings. However, it may be noted that the role of the child's father was not directly investigated in either of these studies.

Witkin (1964) and Witkin *et al.* (1962) have stressed the role of the mother's own level of differentiation in fostering the development of this characteristic in the child. Their results indicate that a relatively 'differentiated mother' will have a 'differentiated child'. Significant relationships were found between several measures of differentiation in the mothers and boys.

The present study is an attempt to extend these findings to include both mothers and fathers. In addition, the admonition of Zigler (1963a and b) was followed and the role of verbal intelligence was assessed and controlled. While most of the relationships between measures of differentiation and verbal intelligence presented by Witkin *et al.* (1962) were low or non-significant, a recent study by Powell (1964) found significant correlations between Vocabulary scores from the Wechsler Adult Intelligence Scale (Wechsler, 1956) and two measures of differentiation in adults. These findings might suggest that there are different relationships in children and adults between verbal intelligence and measures of differentiation.

Method

Subjects

A total of sixty families were studied. There were thirty boys and thirty girls between the ages of eight and eleven years. None was an adoptive child. All came from middle and upper-middle class backgrounds. In cultural background, the Ss were fairly homogeneous. Of the families forty-seven were Jewish, eleven Protestant, and two were Catholic.

Procedure

[. . .]

The general intent of the procedure was to use measures which were as nearly identical as possible for all family members. Verbal intelligence was assessed in parents and children with the Full-Range Picture Vocabulary Test, Form A (Ammons and Ammons, 1948), and I.Q. equivalents were obtained.

Two measures of differentiation were obtained from each child, mother, and father. The Children's Embedded Figures Test (CEFT) was administered to the children (Karp and Konstadt, 1963). The adults were given the first twelve figures of Witkin's (1950) Embedded-Figures Test (EFT) with a three-minute instead of five-minute time limit as recommended by Witkin *et al.* (1962, pp. 40–41). The second measure of differentiation was obtained from human figure drawings made by each S. The usual instructions for the Draw-A-Person Test (Machover, 1949) were modified as follows: 'Draw a person, draw a whole person; draw the *best* person you can.' This change in instructions was deemed necessary after some pre-testing to insure that S put forth his best effort.

The drawings were rated according to the sophistication-of-body-concept scales developed by Witkin *et al.* (1962). A more complete account of the adult form of the sophistication scale

is given in Karp, Poster and Goodman (1963). The figure drawings of the boys, girls, mothers and fathers were rated independently by three graduate student raters for each group. The
average correlations for inter-rater agreement were: boys,
0·76; girls, 0·80; mothers, 0·77; fathers, 0·86. These values are
approximately the same as those reported by Witkin *et al.*
(1962).

Results

The ages and I.Q.s of the subject groups are given in Table 1.
There were no differences between mothers of boys and mothers
of girls or between the fathers of the two groups in age and I.Q.
Consequently, the same-sexed parents from both groups were
combined as in Table 1, for all analyses that did not include the
children. The vocabulary I.Q.s of all groups are clearly above
average. The boys' I.Q.s are significantly higher than those of
the girls ($t = 2.574$, $p < 0.02$). This sex difference is also reflected
in the parents where the fathers obtained higher I.Q.s than did
the mothers ($t = 2.260$, $p < 0.05$).

Table 1

Age and I.Q. of the Subject Groups

Group	N	Age in Years		I.Q.	
		Mean	SD	Mean	SD
Boys	30	9·57	0·68	133·93	14·75
Girls	30	9·48	0·48	125·53	10·09
Mothers	60	35·50	4·88	108·82	10·80
Fathers	60	39·75	5·98	113·17	10·28

The relationship of embedded-figures scores and figure drawing scores (FD) to age and I.Q. are presented in Table 2. The
signs of correlations with EFT scores have been reversed in this
and all subsequent analyses since high scores on this measure
have the same meaning as low scores on the other measure of
differentiation.

All of the correlations between measures of differentiation and

I.Q. are in the expected direction and most of them are significant or near-significant. Although none of the correlations with age are significant, they are consistently positive for the children's measures and consistently negative for the adult measures. In terms of the major purpose of the study, both age and I.Q. were

Table 2

Correlations between Differentiation Measures and Age and I.Q.

Group	Measure	N	Correlation	
			Age	I.Q.
Boys	CEFT	30	0·20	0·03
	FD	30	0·27	0·10
Girls	CEFT	30	0·20	0·32
	FD	30	0·16	0·36*
Mothers	EFT	60	−0·15	0·45**
	FD	60	−0·14	0·34**
Fathers	EFT	60	−0·19	0·55**
	FD	60	−0·06	0·39**

* $p < 0.05$. ** $p < 0.01$.

irrelevant variables. Consequently, the regression weights for age and I.Q. in relation to each of the measures of differentiation in each group were obtained and their effects were partialled out of the embedded figures and FD scores.

Table 3

Differentiation Measures Corrected for Age and I.Q.

Measure	Boys		Girls		Mothers		Fathers	
	Mean	SD	Mean	SD	Mean	SD	Mean	SD
Embedded figures	20·90	3·74	20·80	3·47	65·60	31·90	45·30	23·13
FD	2·60	1·02	3·23	1·01	2·95	1·00	2·75	1·06

The residualized differentiation measures for each group are presented in Table 3. Again, there were no differences on either measure between same sexed parents of boys and girls, and these measures are presented for the total of parent groups. There was no difference between CEFT scores for the boys and girls. Girls did achieve significantly higher FD scores than did boys ($t = 2.405$, $p < 0.05$). The fathers obtained EFT solutions significantly faster than did mothers ($t = 3.991$, $p < 0.001$). The parents did not significantly differ in their FD scores although the mothers tended to receive higher scores. This result is consistent with that obtained for the children.

Table 4

Correlations between Children's and Parents' Measures of Differentiation

Group	Measure	Mothers		Fathers	
		EFT	FD	EFT	FD
Boys	CEFT	0.31	0.38*	0.18	0.38*
	FD	−0.05	0.39*	0.03	0.11
Girls	CEFT	0.02	0.06	0.28	0.16
	FD	0.07	−0.15	0.38*	0.08
Mothers	EFT			0.14	0.01
	FD			0.04	0.22

* $p < 0.05$.

The correlations between the children's and parents' residualized scores from the differentiation measures are given in Table 4. The boys' scores are significantly related to the mothers' FD scores while the correlation between CEFT and mothers' FD falls just short of significance. There is only one significant correlation between boys and their fathers.

A different pattern of relationships exists for girls and their parents. There were no significant correlations between girls' scores and those of their mothers. The only significant relationship exists between girls' FD and fathers' EFT. The correlation between this latter measure and girls' CEFT is in the same direction but falls short of significance.

The correlations between embedded-figures scores and FD scores within each group were: boys, 0.40; girls, 0.02; mothers, 0.41; fathers, 0.35. All of these correlations except that for the girls are significant ($p < 0.05$).

Since Witkin *et al.* (1962) have used an index score based on their perceptual measures as a stable estimate of field dependence, a similar measure was obtained in the present study. The residualized embedded figures and FD scores for each group were converted to standard scores and a mean calculated for each S. It was assumed that this index score would give a more reliable estimate of an S's relative position in his group on the differentiation dimension than would one or the other of the single measures.

Table 5

Intercorrelations of Index Scores

Group	Mothers	Fathers
Boys	0·39*	0·25
Girls	0·00	0·41*
Mothers		0·15

* $p < 0.05$.

The intercorrelations of the index scores are given in Table 5. There are two significant correlations. Boys' scores are significantly related to those of their mothers while girls' scores are significantly related to those of their fathers.

Discussion

The relationship between the measures of differentiation and the measure of verbal intelligence used in the present study raises an interesting problem. The nonsignificant correlations for the boys are consistent with those obtained by Witkin *et al.* (1962). However, the results for the other groups, especially the adults, are consistent with Powell's (1964) data. Consequently, it would appear that inclusion of a measure of verbal intelligence is warranted in studies of differentiation so that its effects may be assessed and controlled.

The relationship between boys and their mothers on measures of differentiation found in the present study is consistent with the earlier findings of Witkin *et al.* (1962). However, the results for the girls raise another problem. It must be concluded that level of differentiation in girls is related to that of their fathers but not to that of their mothers or that these results are spurious.

Several points might be raised in support of the latter conclusion. First, it might be argued that the samples differ in characteristics other than the sex of the children. Although every effort was made to insure comparable groups (most of the children came from the same neighborhoods), some chance differences may have occurred. It may be noted that the I.Q.s of the boys are significantly higher than those of the girls. However, this sex difference in I.Q. exists for the parents of both groups as well and may be considered a function of either the entire population studied or the test itself.

The results of the differentiation measures themselves, it could be argued, do not reflect the usual sex differences favoring males that have been found in the earlier studies (Witkin *et al.*, 1954, 1962). If the measures are considered separately, this conclusion is open to doubt. First, the parents clearly differ in their EFT scores. There is a very slight, but not significant, tendency in the CEFT scores for the boys to perform better than the girls. However, in their developmental studies, the Witkin group found trends for sex differences on EFT measures in children as young as ten years of age but they were not significant except in groups seventeen years of age and older (Witkin *et al.*, 1954). Moreover, the data presented in the CEFT Manual (Karp and Konstadt, 1963) would suggest that no significant sex difference would be obtained with this test.

The FD scores present a somewhat different picture. The present study is, to the best of the writer's knowledge, the first to present FD data from both sexes at the same time. The trend in the adult data for mothers to achieve higher scores than fathers and the significantly higher FD scores for girls would suggest that this measure is likely to produce sex differences opposite from those obtained with other measures of differentiation. Further exploration of sex differences with this measure appears to be warranted.

Another point which could be raised is the lack of consistency between embedded figures and FD scores for the girls while the correlations between these two measures are fairly consistent for the other groups. Witkin *et al.* (1954) have also noted that a greater variability characterizes the performance of women on different measures of differentiation. In the present study, this lack of consistency in the girls' measures, if it were of importance in influencing the correlations with the parents' scores, should have led to a reduced correlation with their fathers' scores after the index scores were formed. However, this correlation was slightly higher than any which were obtained from the single measures.

It would appear, then, that boys and girls show different patterns of relationships with their parents on the differentiation dimension, i.e. the child's level of differentiation tends to be more consistent with that of his opposite-sexed parent than with the same-sexed parent. If level of parental differentiation may be considered an important determiner for the development of differentiation in the child, the results of this study suggest that this development is in some way contingent upon the opposite-sexed parent.

This reasoning would suggest that the role of parent–child relationships in the development of differentiation is somewhat more complex than the data of Witkin *et al.* (1962) would imply. The Witkin group tended to emphasize the degree to which the mother fostered autonomy on the child's development. The present results might indicate that it is the opposite-sexed parent who plays the important role in this process. In addition, this process may be mediated by the efforts of the opposite-sexed parent to foster the appropriate sexual identification in the child. These speculations have been offered in the hope of directing further research efforts on this problem.

References

AMMONS, R. B., and AMMONS, H. S. (1948), *Full-Range Picture Vocabulary Test*, Psychological Test Specialists.

KARP, S. A., and KONSTADT, N. L. (1963), *Children's Embedded-Figures Test*, Cognitive Tests.

KARP, S. A., POSTER, D. C., and GOODMAN, A. (1963), 'Differentiation in alcoholic women', *J. Personal.*, vol. 31, pp. 386–93.

MACHOVER, K. (1949), *Personality Projection in the Drawing of the Human Figure*, C. C. Thomas.

POWELL, B. J. (1964), A study of the perceptual field approach of normal subjects and schizophrenic patients under conditions of an aversive stimulus, *Unpublished Doctoral Dissertation, Washington University*.

WECHSLER, D. (1956), *Wechsler Adult Intelligence Scale*, Psychological Corporation.

WITKIN, H. A. (1950), 'Individual differences in ease of perception of embedded figures', *J. Personal.*, vol. 19, pp. 1–15.

WITKIN, H. A. (1964), 'Origins of cognitive style', in C. Scheerer (ed.), *Cognition: Theory, Research, Promise*, Harper, pp. 172–205.

WITKIN, H. A., DYK, R. B., FATERSON, H. F., GOODENOUGH, D. R., and KARP, S. A. (1962), *Psychological Differentiation: Studies of Development*, Wiley.

WITKIN, H. A., LEWIS, H. B., HERTZMAN, M., MACHOVER, K., MEISSNER, P. B., and WAPNER, S. (1954), *Personality through Perception: An Experimental and Clinical Study*, Harper.

ZIGLER, E. (1963a), 'A measure in search of a theory?', *Contemp. Psychol.*, vol. 8, pp. 133–5.

ZIGLER, E. (1963b), 'Zigler stands firm', *Contemp. Psychol.*, vol. 8, pp. 459–61.

Part Five **Other Cognitive Styles**

We have so far examined a number of approaches to the way people differ in their styles of information processing. The conceptualizations we have examined are all fruitful and productive ones, but they do not exhaust the range of concepts used by psychologists in this area. Other cognitive styles have been described and studied, and some of these are considered here in Part Five. Still different treatments may be found in papers referred to on page 431.

In Part Five there are articles by Gardner, by Kagan and by Vick and Jackson. Gardner (Reading 12) discusses in general terms (and with extensive references) work carried out at the Menninger Foundation into several aspects of cognition. He introduces, for example, two important 'controls of attention' – extensiveness of scanning and selectiveness of attention. Kagan's interest is in the degree of stimulus analysis and of reflection which occurs before an item is classified. His paper (Reading 13) discusses the nature and measurement of 'conceptual tempo', and summarizes information from a number of studies of children's thinking. Reading 14 – by Vick and Jackson – is more detailed and methodologically oriented. In a critical empirical study they examine the style of levelling–sharpening. From their investigation they conclude that such a style is indeed important, but that it is probably not a unitary dimension.

12 Riley W. Gardner

Differences in Cognitive Structures

Excerpts from Riley W. Gardner, 'The development of cognitive structures', in C. Scheerer (ed.), *Cognition: Theory, Research, Promise*, Harper & Row, 1964, pp. 147–59, 167–71.

Introduction

The discussion of the development of cognitive structures that follows is based at a number of points on two groups of studies of individual differences in cognitive structures and of relationships between different forms or aspects of structure conducted at the Menninger Foundation during the past several years. The first group dealt with individual differences in a variety of cognitive structures in adults. The second dealt with relations between these and other structures in children.

Before going further, let me point out that the ensuing discussion refers primarily to the specific class of structures comprised of enduring *arrangements* of cognitive processes that shape the expression of intentions under particular types of environmental conditions. Several forms or aspects of structure in this sense will be considered, including cognitive controls, defense mechanisms, and intellectual structures. Findings concerning relations between structures within this general class and between members of this class and other aspects of cognitive structuring will also be considered. The term, *cognitive control*, was originally applied by George Klein (1954) to a group of enduring arrangements, patterns or programs of cognitive functions whose formation and operation may be relatively independent of conflict between drives, and which therefore seem to be different from defensive structures in at least one important way. It is entirely possible, however, as indicated in several earlier publications (e.g. Gardner *et al.*, 1959), that, following the first stages of structure formation, every cognitive structure serves both defensive and nondefensive purposes. The terms cognitive control, defense, intellectual structure, and so on, may actually, therefore, be

223

most appropriately considered as useful rubrics referring to different facets of the structural complexity of any bit of cognitive behavior.

The specific studies referred to were designed and the results interpreted within the broad general framework provided by psychoanalytic theory, including the many recent developments in the ego-psychological aspects of this theory. We have employed this general theoretical framework because we feel that ultimate understanding of cognitive structures *per se* and of the inter-action of various cognitive structures in development will be accomplished only within a conceptual framework that makes full provision, from the outset, for the importance of unconscious factors to structure formation, for the unconscious conflicts that lead to the formation of particular kinds of structures and for the integral relationship between cognitive structures and the organization of the total personality.

Hartmann (1951, pp. 35–6) has summarized some of the relevant recent developments within psychoanalytic theory as follows:

The most incisive change which took place in Freud's model of psychic personality can be pictured as adding to its description as a series of layers its representation as a (more or less) integrated whole, sub-divisible in centers of mental functioning – these substructures being defined by their functions, and their demarcation being based on the fact that empirically he found greater coherence among some functions than among others. . . . This facilitates a multidimensional approach and, so far as psychoanalytic psychology and therapy goes, it has been rather generally accepted as being more useful in giving account of the dynamic and economic properties of mental life.

The importance of understanding relationships between cognitive structures has been emphasized by Hartmann (1951), L. B. Murphy (1957), Rapaport (1959), and others. [. . .] Beginning with Freud's (1937) re-emphasis upon the importance of inherited factors in the determination of defense structures, and continuing through the elaboration by Hartmann (1939) and others of the importance of constitutional characteristics of the conflict-free apparatuses involved in defensive and other cognitive functions, the ego-psychological movement has contained an important place for genic, as well as experiential factors in the complex of interactions that lead to the emergence of various types of cognitive structures.

In our earlier publications (e.g. Gardner *et al.*, 1959), we ourselves have emphasized – in considering the relationship between cognitive controls and defense structures – that some controls, which may be heavily determined by genic factors, may serve as essential preconditions for the development of certain defense mechanisms.

Lest my emphasis upon the adequacy of this general theoretical framework for dealing with the problem of cognitive structuring and its development appear overly exclusive, let me emphasize that we have been particularly interested in relationships between defenses, controls, intellectual abilities and other structures and the vast array of valuable information concerning specific cognitive functions provided by a large group of earlier experimenters who neither employed this theoretical framework nor conceived of their studies in terms of their relevance to the problem of individual differences in cognitive structures. The work of Köhler and Lauenstein on memory formation, for example, provided valuable new information concerning assimilation effects in the registration of sequential stimulation. The work of Jean Piaget, both on the development of intellectual structures and on the development of the attentional structures involved in perception, serves as another representative example. But valuable as it is, earlier work on *general* laws of cognition provides only steppingstones for an approach to the organization of cognitive structures within the individual. As Gordon Allport (1937, p. vii) pointed out so effectively:

As a rule, science regards the individual as a mere bothersome accident. Psychology, too, ordinarily treats him as something to be brushed aside so the main business of accounting for the uniformity of events can get under way. The result is that on all sides we see psychologists enthusiastically at work upon a somewhat shadowy portrait entitled 'the generalized human mind'. Though serving well a certain purpose, this portrait is not altogether satisfying to those who compare it with the living individual models from which it is drawn. It seems unreal and esoteric, devoid of locus, self-consciousness, and organic unity – all essential characteristics of the minds we know.

With the intention of supplementing this abstract portrait by one that is more life-like, a new movement within psychological science has gradually grown up. It attempts to depict and account for the manifest individuality of mind. This new movement has come to be known . . . as the *psychology of personality*.

As I shall attempt to elucidate in the remarks that follow, our investigations of relationships between different types of cognitive structures in adults, and the formation of these structures during development, seem to indicate that the problem is even more complicated than Allport suggested. Not only the general laws of adult cognitive behavior, but also the general developmental curves for cognitive functions, seem to tell us little or nothing of their relationship in the cognitive organization of a single individual.

Studies of the Cognitive Organizations of Adults

One of our enduring interests has been in the ways people categorize their experience. Recently, we have focused our attention on relationships between the differentiation adults impose upon heterogeneous arrays of objects, persons, events, etc., the level of abstraction at which they *prefer* to function in such categorizing situations, and their capacity to abstract. You will recognize the last of these three aspects of concept formation as one which has in the past received consistent attention from psychologists interested in the laws of concept formation and of the development of concept formation. Relevant to these studies are, of course, the brilliant pioneer work of Vygotsky (1934); the contributions of Inhelder and Piaget, whose monograph on the development of comprehension and abstraction (Piaget and Inhelder, 1959) caps years of study; the work of Bruner and his associates (Bruner, Goodnow and Austin, 1956); and the contributions of a large number of other investigators.

Relevant, too, are the significant contributions to our understanding of concept formation by our friend and valued consultant in this work, Martin Scheerer. Not only in his earlier work with Goldstein (Goldstein and Scheerer, 1941), but also in his later publications (e.g. 1949, 1959), his devotion to the general problem of concept formation is worthy of special note. In this area, as in many others, his contributions to the literature, his discussions with his students and his consultations with our research group, were all marked by his keen eye for the dissimilarities among superficially similar phenomena, as well as the similarities linking superficially different phenomena. These qualities of his thinking were evident, for example, in his paper on performance analysis (Scheerer, 1946), in which he carefully and thoroughly detailed the value of thoughtful participation by psychologists in the procedure they employ, and of thoughtful reflection on the processes involved. [. . .]

Let us turn now to the studies of adult individual consistencies in concept formation referred to earlier, and then proceed to some of the other areas we have explored and the developmental studies that have occupied us recently. Our recent studies of adult concept formation (Gardner and Schoen, 1962) have impressed us once again with the remarkable complexity of the structures involved in cognitive behavior. Individual differences in conceptual differentiation, which we have studied in a number of contexts over the years (Gardner, 1953; Gardner, Jackson and Messick, 1960; Gardner et al., 1959), are relatively stable over time (Gardner and Long, 1960e) and show considerable situational generality – provided, of course, that both the stimulus conditions and the intention invoked in the subject are appropriate to this particular principle of cognitive control. But, surprisingly enough, this dimension of individual differences in conceptual differentiation is independent not only of the level of abstraction at which the person momentarily chooses to perform in relatively free categorizing tasks, but also of his capacity to abstract, at least as measured by various indices of intelligence, including similarities tests designed to assess one aspect of the capacity to abstract. In addition, the level of abstraction at which the individual prefers to function in these situations is remarkably independent of his capacity to abstract, assessed in the ways just referred to. Note here the complexity of the cognitive structures involved in a relatively limited segment of the vast area of concept formation. D. Rapaport, Gill and Schafer (1945) have pointed out that concept formation may be the ultimate basis of thought functioning, and that it finds representation in a vast array of psychological phenomena ranging from largely drive-determined arrangements of ideas that are unconscious to certain conversion symptoms. The studies referred to above touch only three facets of a much larger realm of behavior involving concept formation.

Our recent work has also included a series of studies of the controls of attention, not because we feel that attention is the central or dominant variable in cognitive functioning or personality organization, but because attention and the controls of attention, which have been severely neglected in American psychology, represent the point of contact between the individual and both external and internal reality. Our explorations of attention have been devoted to three general areas: the selectiveness with which the individual can attend, for example, to relevant stimuli in the face of impelling irrelevant stimuli of various kinds; the extensiveness of the individual's scanning in free scanning situations leading to decisions about the relative characteristics of stimuli (Gardner, 1961a; Gardner and Long, 1962a and b); and the intensity of attention, as it affects assimilation in the registration and recall of sequential stimuli (Gardner and Lohrenz, 1961). We recently performed further studies of the differential effects on perception of selectiveness on the one hand and extensiveness of scanning on the other in a single set of test situations (Gardner and Long, 1962b). Our results once again demonstrate the multiplicity of cognitive structures involved in superficially similar performances. We find, for example, that, using speed in finding embedded figures in Witkin's test as a criterion measure of the selectiveness of attention, we can predict performances in other situations in which (a) the relevant stimulus is embedded in a larger context that, as it were, 'competes' with it for attention; (b) the relevant stimulus is the surround rather than the embedded item, which in this case becomes the irrelevant stimulus; or (c) the relevant stimulus appears among irrelevant stimuli that do not combine with it to form a superordinate Gestalt organization, and in which organized part–whole relations do not obtain. We find, also, that measures of the extensiveness with which adults scan certain stimuli allow prediction, to a modest degree, of the experienced apparent magnitude of stimuli. Here, our work (Gardner and Long, 1960a and b, 1962a and b) directly touches the studies of relations between attention and perception performed over a period of twenty years by Piaget and his associates and summarized in a recent monograph (Piaget, 1961). Even, however, when we obtain measures of the extensiveness of scanning and of the selectiveness of attention to relevant *v.* compelling irrelevant stimuli from the same test judgements, these dimensions of individual consistency remain both logically and statistically independent of each other.

What, then, are the relationships between these two aspects of attention deployment – provided, of course, that our working hypotheses for certain laboratory situations ultimately prove tenable – and the individual consistencies in conceptual differentiation and levels of abstraction referred to earlier? Our findings suggest that all of these cognitive variables are essentially independent, in both adults and children.

We have also been intensely interested in the relationship of individual consistencies in field dependence, or field articulation, massively explored and documented by Witkin and others (see Witkin *et al.*, 1962), and a dimension of individual consistencies in assimilation among new percepts and related memories of earlier percepts, which Holzman and Klein (1954; Holzman, 1954) referred to as 'leveling–sharpening'. Their work has been extended in a number of subsequent studies (e.g. Gardner *et al.*, 1959, 1960; Gardner and Lohrenz, 1960; Gardner and Long, 1960c–e; Gardner, Jackson and Messick, 1960; Gardner *et al.*, 1959; Holzman and Gardner, 1959). Adequate measures of assimilation are difficult to achieve. We feel, however, that the procedures we have employed more recently are clear enough in their implications to provide tentative answers to one or two crucial questions concerning relationships between different cognitive structures representing a single general type of structure. We find, for example, that performance in the criterion tests of field articulation developed by Witkin and his associates allows prediction of certain aspects of learning and recall, but only in particular types of learning situations (Gardner and Long, 1961; Long, 1962). Knowledge of individual differences in a criterion test of leveling–sharpening allows prediction of other, nonoverlapping, aspects of performance in the same kind of test situation (Gardner and Long, 1960c). In other learning and recall situations – for example, when the similarity of items is low – no

229

such relationships obtain for either criterion. Once again it is apparent that cognitive controls are enduring patterns of cognitive functioning that mediate the expression of particular intentions when the individual is confronted with particular stimulus conditions (cf. Gardner *et al.*, 1959).

In a recent series of experiments, we employed procedures that seem to pinpoint the meaning of these earlier tests. We have developed two superficially similar tests in which designs are presented to subjects sequentially in such a way as to invoke the operation of both cognitive control principles, field articulation and leveling–sharpening. The first of these tests seems to maximize the effects of leveling–sharpening on the registration of similar sequential stimuli, the second to maximize the independent effects of selective attention upon the recall of similar stimuli. Both tests, however, were designed to involve both sets of controls. Only the balance of assimilation-selectivity is different in the two situations. Under these two sets of conditions, the two cognitive controls *appear* to have similar effects upon reproduction of the designs. The hypothesized difference between the effects of the two criterion variables on performance is appropriately tested by means of an analysis of variance that reveals the interaction between the citeria as predictors of performance in the two situations. In a recent sample, this interaction is significant. It could probably be made still more significant by increasing the unique properties of the two tests. These results are not unusual in our laboratory. We have performed other studies of the relationship between field articulation and leveling–sharpening as determinants of learning and recall that confirm these findings. We have, over a period of years, also explored relations between these and other cognitive controls and kinesthetic and visual aftereffects (Gardner, 1961b). Once again, although assimilation theory and aftereffect theory could potentially account for many of the same performances, measures of individual differences in these cognitive variables are related neither to each other nor to any of the cognitive control variables we have dealt with.

Let me turn now to some of the other areas of adult cognition that we have concerned ourselves with over the years. I shall refer first to an aspect of cognition that has very different implications from those of the three control principles I have referred to thus far. We have described our findings concerning this aspect of cognitive organization in terms of a dimension of individual consistencies in tolerance for unrealistic experiences (Klein, Gardner and Schlesinger, 1962). You will readily see that this dimension of cognitive functioning implies no specific set of cognitive processes, but rather represents a general characteristic of the ego-as-a-whole in the constant interplay between unconscious determinants of behavior on the one hand and the dictates of external reality on the other. I mention this body of work briefly here only to indicate the varied approaches we have taken to the cognitive organization of the individual. Our purpose in continuing to sample widely different forms or aspects of cognitive structure ranging from the specific to the general is to achieve a more adequate sampling of the still larger panorama of cognitive structures. As in our studies of individuality in other aspects of cognitive organization, we find that individuals are consistent in this aspect of their cognitive functioning in a wide variety of situations. A study by Snyder and Scheerer (1961), who used similar procedures, produced very similar results. Knowing the degree to which a person's perception is altered by proximal cues at variance with what he knows to be true, we can predict his approach to the Rorschach test and related situations with reasonable accuracy.

In our recent studies, we have also attempted to evaluate several other general aspects of the individual's cognitive organization. Following Rapaport, we are attempting to assess the relative autonomy of the individual's total array of cognitive structures from drive-determined, primary-process thinking, on the one hand, and from external reality, on the other (D. Rapaport, 1951, 1958). This variable probably bears a curvilinear relationship to tolerance for unreality. In our recent studies focused on relations between various facets of cognitive structuring, we have also attempted clinical assessments of the basic integrity and psychological health represented by the total pattern of the individual's defensive and intellectual structures. Among the intriguing preliminary results with the latter measure is its relation to performance in the Color-Word Test.

I have referred thus far primarily to a cluster of specific and more general aspects of the cognitive organization of individual

231

adults that we have conceptualized as principles of cognitive control. But my initial remarks implied that we are particularly interested in *relations* between various control structures and between these and distinctly different forms or aspects of cognitive structure. In one study, we explored, with generally predictable results, relations between various dimensions of cognitive control and the intellectual abilities defined by Thurstone and his successors (Gardner, Jackson and Messick, 1960). We are now exploring relations between a cluster of cognitive control principles and performance in the Wechsler intelligence tests by groups of normal adults and by groups of adults whose psychopathology is of sufficient intensity to have required hospitalization. In these current studies, we are focusing with particular care upon relations between cognitive controls, intellectual structures, defense structures and general properties of cognitive organization. In working with a patient group, we are, of course, also exploring relations between complex patterns of cognitive structuring and types of severities of symptomatology. These recent studies are based on a group of earlier studies aimed at relations between particular aspects of control in adults and particular defenses. To mention a few of these, we have demonstrated a special type of relationship between leveling and generalized repressiveness (Gardner *et al.*, 1959; Holzman and Gardner, 1959), and between extensiveness of scanning and the strength of the defense of isolation in adults (Gardner and Long, 1962a). Although we were not surprised at these results, they may in some ways increase our understanding of the cognitive processes involved in the employment of defenses. Let me point out here that although certain defenses are relatively easy to observe in the clinic, and although defenses have vast implications for the cognitive functioning of the individual, we as yet know extremely little about the actual cognitive processes involved in these enduring aspects of personality organization.[1] [. . .]

1. In the original article Gardner went on to discuss some of the developmental findings obtained from a group of sixty pre-adolescent children. This study was subsequently reported in more detail by Gardner and Moriarty (1968) [*Ed.*].

References

ACKERMANN, N. (1958), *The Psychodynamics of Family Life: Diagnosis Treatment of Family Relationships*, Basic Books.

ACKERMANN, N., and BEHRENS, M. L., (1955), 'Child and family psychopathy: problems of correlation', in P. H. Hoch and J. Zubin (eds.), *Psychopathology in Childhood*, Grune & Stratton, pp. 77–96.

ALLPORT, F. H. (1955), *Theories of Perception and the Concept of Structure*, Wiley.

ALLPORT, F. H. (1962), 'A structuronomic conception of behavior: individual and collective', *J. abnorm. soc. Psychol.*, vol. 64, pp. 3–30.

ALLPORT, G. W. (1937), *Personality: A Psychological Interpretation*, Holt, Rinehart & Winston.

BARKER, R. G. (1960), 'Comments on the papers by Dr Taylor and Dr Toman', in M. R. Jones (ed.), *Nebraska Symposium on Motivation*, University of Nebraska Press, pp. 95–6.

BRODY, S. (1956), *Patterns of Mothering*, International Universities Press.

BRUNER, J. S., GOODNOW, J. J., and AUSTIN, G. A. (1956), *A Study of Thinking*, Wiley.

COHEN, J. (1959), 'The factorial structure of the WISC at ages of 7–6, 10–6, and 13–6', *J. consult. Psychol.*, vol. 23, pp. 285–99.

COMALLI, P. E., JR, WAPNER, S., and WERNER, H. (1962), 'Interference effects of Stroop color-word test in childhood, adulthood, and aging', *J. genet. Psychol.*, vol. 100, pp. 47–53.

FREUD, A. (1954), 'Psychoanalysis and education', *N.Y. Acad. of Med.*, May 5.

FREUD, S. (1923), *The Ego and the Id*, translated and edited by J. Strachey, Norton, 1961.

FREUD, S. (1937), 'Analysis terminable and interminable', *Collected Papers*, vol. 5, Hogarth, 1950, pp. 316–57.

GARDNER, R. W. (1953), 'Cognitive styles and categorizing behavior', *J. Personal.*, vol. 22, pp. 214–33.

GARDNER, R. W. (1961a), 'Cognitive controls of attention deployment as determinants of visual illusions', *J. abnorm. soc. Psychol.*, vol. 62, pp. 120–27.

GARDNER, R. W. (1961b), 'Individual differences in figural after-effects and response to reversible figures', *Brit. J. Psychol.*, vol. 52, pp. 269–72.

GARDNER, R. W. (1961c), Personality organization and the nature of consciousness, *Paper read at Conference on Problems of Consciousness and Perception*, Wayne State University, February.

GARDNER, R. W. (1962), 'Cognitive controls and adaptation: research and measurement', in S. Messick and J. Ross (eds.), *Measurement in Personality and Cognition*, Wiley, pp. 183–98.

GARDNER, R. W., and LOHRENZ, L. J. (1960), 'Leveling–sharpening and serial reproduction of a story', *Bull. Menninger Clin.*, vol. 24, pp. 295–304.

GARDNER, R. W., and LOHRENZ, L. J. (1961), 'Attention and assimilation', *Amer. J. Psychol.*, vol. 74, pp. 607–11.

GARDNER, R. W., and LONG, R. I. (1960a), 'Errors of the standard and illusion effects with the inverted-T', *Percept. mot. Skills*, vol. 10, pp. 47–54.

GARDNER, R. W., and LONG, R. I. (1960b), 'Errors of the standard and illusion effects with L-shaped figures', *Percept. mot. Skills*, vol. 10, pp. 107–9.

GARDNER, R. W., and LONG, R. I. (1960c), 'Leveling–sharpening and serial learning', *Percept. mot. Skills*, vol. 10, pp. 179–85.

GARDNER, R. W., and LONG, R. I. (1960d), 'Cognitive controls as determinants of learning and remembering', *Psychologia*, vol. 3, pp. 165–71.

GARDNER, R. W., and LONG, R. I. (1960e), 'The stability of cognitive controls', *J. abnorm. soc. Psychol.*, vol. 61, pp. 485–7.

GARDNER, R. W., and LONG, R. I. (1961), 'Field-articulation in recall', *Psychol. Rec.*, vol. 11, pp. 305–10.

GARDNER, R. W., and LONG, R. I. (1962a), 'Control, defence, and centration effect: a study of scanning behavior', *Brit. J. Psychol.*, vol. 53, pp. 129–40.

GARDNER, R. W., and LONG, R. I. (1962b), 'Cognitive controls of attention and inhibition', *Brit. J. Psychol.*, vol. 53, pp. 381–8.

GARDNER, R. W., and MORIARTY, A. (1968), *Personality Development at Pre-Adolescence: Exploration in Structure Formation*, University of Washington Press.

GARDNER, R. W., and SCHOEN, R. A. (1962), 'Differentiation and abstraction in concept formation', *Psychol. Monogr.*, vol. 76, no. 41, whole no. 560. [See Reading 3.]

GARDNER, R. W., JACKSON, D. N., and MESSICK, S. J. (1960), 'Personality organization in cognitive controls and intellectual abilities', *Psychol. Issues*, vol. 2, no. 4, whole no. 8.

GARDNER, R. W., HOLZMAN, P. S., KLEIN, G. S., LINTON, H. B., and SPENCE, D. P. (1959), 'Cognitive control', *Psychol. Issues*, vol. 1, no. 4.

GOLDSTEIN, K., and SCHEERER, M. (1941), 'Abstract and concrete behavior: an experimental study with special tests', *Psychol. Monogr.*, vol. 53, whole no. 239, pp. 1–151.

HARTMANN, H. (1939), *Ego Psychology and the Problem of Adaptation*, trans. D. Rapaport, International Universities Press.

HARTMANN, H. (1951), 'Technical implications of ego psychology', *Psychoanalyt. Quart.*, vol. 20, pp. 31–43.

HOLTZMAN, W. H., THORPE, J. S., SWARTZ, J. D., and HERRON, E. W. (1961), *Inkblot Perception and Personality*, University of Texas Press.

HOLZMAN, P. S. (1954), 'The relation of assimilation tendencies in visual, auditory, and kinesthetic time-error to cognitive attitudes of leveling and sharpening', *J. Personal.*, vol. 22, pp. 375–94.

HOLZMAN, P. S., and GARDNER, R. W. (1959), 'Leveling and repression', *J. abnorm. soc. Psychol.*, vol. 59, pp. 151–5.

HOLZMAN, P. S., and KLEIN, G. S. (1954), 'Cognitive system-principle of leveling and sharpening: individual differences in assimilation effects in visual time-error', *J. Psychol.*, vol. 37, pp. 105–22.

KLEIN, G. S. (1954), 'Need and regulation', in M. R. Jones (ed.), *Nebraska Symposium on Motivation: 1954*, University of Nebraska Press, pp. 224–74.

KLEIN, G. S., GARDNER, R. W., and SCHLESINGER, H. J. (1962), 'Tolerance for unrealistic experiences: a study of the generality of a cognitive control', *Brit. J. Psychol.*, vol. 53, pp. 41–55.

LONG, R. I. (1962), 'Field-articulation as a factor in verbal learning and recall', *Percept. mot. Skills*, vol. 15, pp. 151–8.

MERCADO, S. J., DIAZ GUERRERO, R., and GARDNER, R. W. (1963), 'Cognitive control in children of Mexico and the United States', *J. soc. Psychol.*, vol. 59, pp. 199–208.

MURPHY, G. (1960), 'Organism and quantity: a study of organic structure as a quantitative problem', in B. Kaplan and S. Wapner (eds.), *Perspectives in Psychological Theory*, International Universities Press, pp. 179–208.

MURPHY, L. B. (1957), 'Psychoanalysis and child development. Part II', *Bull. Menninger Clin.*, vol. 21, pp. 248–58.

PIAGET, J. (1936), *The Origins of Intelligence in Children*, International Universities Press (reprinted 1952).

PIAGET, J. (1961), *Les Mécanismes Perceptifs*, Presses Universitaires de France.

PIAGET, J. (1962), 'The stages of the intellectual development of the child', *Bull. Menninger Clin.*, vol. 26, pp. 120–28.

PIAGET, J., and INHELDER, B. (1959), *La Genèse des Structures logiques Elémentaires: Classifications et Serations*, Delachaux & Niestlé, Neuchâtel.

RAPAPORT, D. (1951), 'The autonomy of the ego', *Bull. Menninger Clin.*, vol. 15, pp. 113–23. (Reprinted in R. P. Knight and C. R. Friedman (eds.), *Psychoanalytic Psychiatry and Psychology*, International Universities Press, 1954, pp. 248–58.)

RAPAPORT, D. (1958), 'The theory of ego autonomy: a generalization', *Bull. Menninger Clin.*, vol. 22, pp. 13–35.

RAPAPORT, D. (1959), 'The structure of psychoanalytic theory: a systematizing attempt', in S. Koch (ed.), *Psychology: A Study of a Science, Study I. Conceptual and Systematic. Vol. 3. Formulations of the Person and the Social Context*, McGraw-Hill, pp. 55–183. (Reprinted in *Psychol. Issues*, vol. 2, 1960, no. 2, whole no. 6.)

RAPAPORT, D. (1960), 'Psychoanalysis as a developmental psychology', in B. Kaplan and S. Wapner (eds.), *Perspectives in Psychological Theory*, International Universities Press, pp. 209–55.

RAPAPORT, D., GILL, M., and SCHAFER, R. (1945), *Diagnostic Psychological Testing*, vol. 1, Year Book Medical Publishers.

REIFF, R., and SCHEERER, M. (1959), *Memory and Hypnotic Age Regression. Developmental Aspects of Cognitive Function Explored through Hypnosis*, International Universities Press.

SCHEERER, M. (1946), 'Problems of performance analysis in the study of personality', *Ann. N.Y. Acad. Sciences*, vol. 46, pp. 653–78.

SCHEERER, M. (1949), (with the collaboration of Ludwig Immergluck and Morris Buchman), 'An experiment in abstraction', *Confinia Neurologica*, vol. 9, pp. 232–54.

SCHEERER, M. (1953), 'Personality functioning and cognitive psychology', *J. Personal.*, vol. 22, pp. 1–16.

SCHEERER, M. (1959), 'Spheres of meaning: an analysis of stages from perception to abstract thinking'. *J. indiv. Psychol.*, vol. 15, pp. 50–61.

SCHEERER, M., and HULING, M. D. (1960), 'Cognitive embeddedness in problem solving: a theoretical and experimental analysis', in B. Kaplan and S. Wapner (eds.), *Perspectives in Psychological Theory*, International Universities Press, pp. 256–302.

SNYDER, R., and SCHEERER, M. (1961), 'Interrelationships between personality, skeleto-muscular, and perceptual functioning', in W. H. Ittelson and S. G. Kutash (eds.), *Perceptual Changes in Psychopathology*, Rutgers University Press, pp. 166–210.

VYGOTSKY, L. S. (1934), *Thought and Language*, M.I.T. Press and Wiley, 1962.

WHITE, R. W. (1959) 'Motivation reconsidered: the concept of competence', *Psychol. Rev.*, vol. 66, pp. 297–333.

WHITE, R. W. (1960), 'Competence and the psychosexual stages of development', in M. R. Jones (ed.), *Nebraska Symposium on Motivation*, University of Nebraska Press, pp. 97–141.

WITKIN, H. A., DYK, R. B., FATERSON, H. F., GOODENOUGH, D. R., and KARP, S. A. (1962), *Psychological Differentiation*, Wiley.

13 Jerome Kagan

Developmental Studies in Reflection and Analysis

Excerpts from Jerome Kagan, 'Developmental studies in reflection and analysis', in A. H. Kidd and J. L. Rivoire (eds.), *Perceptual Development in Children*, University of London Press, 1966, pp. 487–505, 517–22.

The varied and murky phenomena implied by the word cognition range from the unrestrained racing of images and words to the more orderly, goal-directed sequence of mediated steps that are activated by the desire to solve a problem or acquire a new cognitive structure. This chapter restricts itself to the latter domain of cognitive events, specifically to the processes of stimulus classification and hypothesis selection. Three sequential operations typically occur when a person is confronted with a problem – an initial categorization of the relevant information, storage of the coded categorization and, finally, the imposing of transformations (formal algorithms or mediational elaborations) upon the encoded data. The nature of the categorization, transformation or elaborative mediation is governed, of course, by the nature of the problem. Students of cognitive development have generally assumed that the striking differences among the intellectual products of children of different ages or among children of the same age were attributable primarily to differences in the availability of vocabulary, possession of deductive or inductive rules and mediational diversity. In essence, the superior intellectual performance of older, in comparison to younger, children has been ascribed to the greater knowledge repertoire of the older children. This supposition is intuitively attractive and empirically verified. It is not surprising, therefore, that psychologists have not seriously entertained the possibility that other factors may contribute to age and individual differences in the form and quality of cognitive products. Specifically, there has been a tendency to ignore the relevance of differences in two aspects of information processing – differences in the degree of stimulus analysis that precedes initial coding, and the degree of reflection attendant upon classification and hypothesis selection. It now appears that children and adults have clear preference hierarchies with respect to these two variables. The empirical work described in this essay is an inquiry into the significance of these two variables that are so intimately involved in the initial classification phase of problem solving, the phase during which external information is given its first symbolic coding, and the best possible solution sequence is selected.

To preview the heart of the chapter, we have discerned two stable dimensions upon which children and adults are distributed. The first is called reflection–impulsivity and describes the degree to which the child reflects upon alternative classifications of a stimulus or alternative solution hypotheses in situations in which many response possibilities (i.e. classifications or solution hypotheses) are available simultaneously. In these situations some children have a fast conceptual tempo; they impulsively report the first classification that occurs to them or carry out the first solution sequence that appears appropriate. The reflective children, on the other hand, characteristically delay before reporting a classification or carrying out a solution hypothesis. They actively consider the alternatives available to them and compare their validity. The reflective child behaves as if he cared that his first response be as close to correct as possible.

The reader is urged to withhold any premature tendency to stereotype the reflective child as excessively cautious or frightened, and the impulsive child as daring, divergent or creative. The evidence to be presented does not allow such a glib evaluative template to be placed upon this class of behaviour. We enjoin the reader to be reflective, and to withhold evaluation of the 'goodness' of this predisposition until all the evidence has been considered.

A second dimension, called visual analysis, describes the child's tendency to analyse complex stimuli into their component parts. Some children fractionate a stimulus into small subunits; others label and react to a larger stimulus chunk. Analysis is relatively independent of reflection, and each of these variables contributes variance to a variety of cognitive products.

History

This line of inquiry was originally stimulated by an observation that piqued our curiosity because it did not agree with contemporary ideas concerning modal classification and conceptualization habits among normal subjects. Specifically, we found that when adult subjects were asked to select, from a large array of human figures, 'a group of figures that went together on some conceptual basis', a sizeable number grouped these paper figures on the basis of a shared objective element that was a component part of the total stimulus (e.g. 'These three men go together because *they have no hair*', or 'These people are all *holding an object in their hands*'). We called this class of concepts *analytic* because the basis for the grouping always involved a differentiated component of a set of diverse stimuli. What was more surprising, however, were the behavioral characteristics of the men who preferred this class of concepts to the more popular conceptual categories of abstract-inferential or thematic. The men who preferred analytic concepts were behaviorally more independent, more concerned with intellectual mastery, slightly more intelligent, more desirous of social recognition and displayed more spontaneous sudomotor activity at rest than men who did not report many analytic concepts (Kagan, Moss and Sigel, 1963). This cluster of attributes elicited cognitive dissonance, for we would have thought that ambitious, bright, independent men would prefer elegant, abstract concepts (i.e. happy soldiers, poverty-stricken people, creative artists) to the more stimulus-bound concepts classified as analytic.

Most of the work during the last four years has involved school-age children and has attempted to amplify our understanding of the significance of the analytic conceptual response and to discover its immediate and historical antecedents. The results indicate that spontaneous analytic concepts are the product of the joint action of the two more fundamental variables of reflection and visual analysis.

There is, at present, more information on the stability and significance of the reflection–impulsivity dimension than there is on the variable of visual analysis. The data are persuasive in indicating that the child's tendency to reflect on alternative responses (in situations where several alternatives are available simultaneously) generalizes across varied problem situations, and shows remarkable intraindividual stability over periods ranging from two to twenty months. The operational definition of the reflection variable is response time in problem situations in which the subject is presented with a standard stimulus and an array containing the standard and five to ten highly similar variants. The child is required to select the one stimulus in the array that is identical to the standard. There is typically a negative correlation between response time and number of errors (i.e. incorrect selections) in these problem situations. Children who delay before offering their first answer makes fewer errors. The adjective 'reflective' is most descriptive of the child who has long response times and few errors.

Reflection and Analysis: Measurement and Developmental Changes

This section describes the test situations used most frequently with children to assess the reflection and analysis variables, and the relations among the major variables derived from these tests.

Conceptual Style Test (CST)

This test consists of thirty stimuli, each illustrating line drawings of three familiar objects. The child is asked to select two pictures that are alike in some way and to state the reason for his grouping. The items were constructed so that an analytic concept (i.e. a concept based on similarity in an objective element that was a differentiated component of only two of the stimuli) competed with an indifferential-abstract or thematic concept. The analytic concept typically was a less obvious conceptual association to the stimulus card than an inferential or thematic concept. The two major variables derived from this test were the number of analytic concepts and the average response time to concept selection. Figure 1 illustrates three stimuli from this test.

The most common analytic concept to the watch–man–ruler item was: 'The watch and ruler have numbers'; to the zebra–

shirt–striped-shirt item: 'These two have stripes'; to the house–
match–pipe item: 'The house and pipe have smoke coming from
them.' These concepts were called analytic because the numbers,
stripes and smoke were objective, differentiated components of
the total stimulus.

Figure 1 Sample items from C S T

Delayed Recall of Designs (D R T)

In this test a simple design was presented for five seconds. This
standard was then removed, and after fifteen seconds an array
of eight, nine or ten stimuli was presented. The S selected the
one design that was identical to the standard. The major variables

derived were number of errors (a secondary distinction was made between major and minor errors) and average response time. Figure 2 illustrates a sample item.

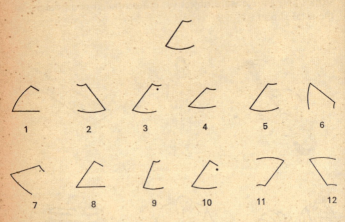

Figure 2 Sample item from DRT

Matching Familiar Figures (*MFF*)

This task was basically similar to the DRT, but illustrated familiar objects rather than geometric designs and, unlike DRT, contained no memory requirement. The *S* was shown a picture (the standard) and six similar stimuli, only one of which was identical to the standard. The *S* selected the one stimulus that was identical to the standard. The standard and variations were always available to the subject. The major variables scored were number of errors, and average response time to first selection. Figure 3 illustrates a sample item.

Haptic-Visual Matching (*HVM*)

In this task, the child first explored with his fingers a wooden form (approximately three inches square) to which he had no visual access. He was allowed an unlimited time to explore the form, and when he withdrew his hands, he was presented with a visual array of five stimuli, one of which illustrated the form he had explored haptically. The twenty-item test contained geometric

242

forms as well as familiar objects and yielded three variables: errors, response time and palpation time (i.e. time *S* devoted to tactual exploration of the wooden form). Figure 4 illustrates a sample item.

Figure 3 Sample item from M FF

Visual analysis

This task assessed the degree to which the child attached a new label to component parts of a visual stimulus while associating the new label with the whole stimulus pattern. This task was regarded as a measure of a visually analytic attitude. The

Figure 4 Sample item from HVM

stimuli were designs that contained three distinct components: background, figural form and element. The background component was a repetitive pattern; the figural component referred to the shape into which the discrete elements fell. That is, the elements were small, discrete geometric forms that traced out the figural pattern. Figure 5 illustrates a sample item.

The design in the upper left corner of the illustration was the stimulus to which the child associated a nonsense syllable. The semicircles were the background components, the triangles were the element components, and the 'staircase' pattern was the figural component.

In the administration of this task, the child first learned four different nonsense syllables to each of four different complex designs. When the child reached criterion (eight consecutive correct trials) he was given a response-transfer task. In this transfer task he was shown separate illustrations of the background, element and figural components, each without any perceptual

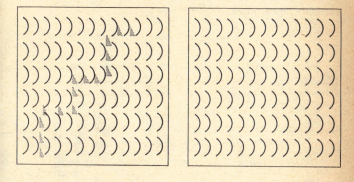

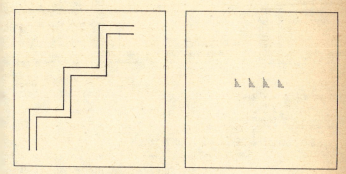

Figure 5 Sample item from visual analysis task

support from the other two aspects of the original design. Thus, with reference to Figure 5, the child would be shown the semi-circles, the triangles or the 'staircase' and asked to apply the correct nonsense syllable. The transfer task contained two illustrations of each of the three components for each of the four designs (twenty-four items in all). During the transfer series the four nonsense syllables, which were printed on cards, were always available to the child to insure that incorrect labelling of the separate components would not be due to forgetting of the newly acquired labels. After a short recess, a second set of four different designs was presented, and the child was asked to perform a similar task. The major variables derived from these tasks were number of ground, figural and element components labelled correctly on each task.

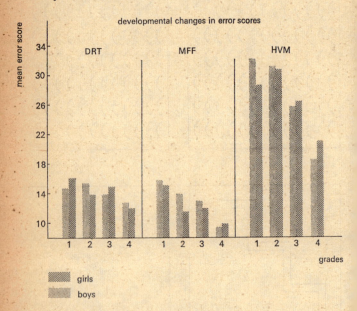

Figure 6 Developmental changes in error scores

The five tests described above have been administered to children in grades 1 to 4 [ages six to nine] from a variety of schools (a minimum of fifty boys and fifty girls at each grade level). Figures 6, 7 and 8 illustrate the changes in errors, response time, and level of visual analysis over these four grades.

The developmental trends indicate that, with age, there is a linear increase in analytic concepts on the CST, a decrease in errors and an increase in response time on DRT, MFF and HVM. The visual-analysis data are more complex, but provocative. There is a marked increase, with age, in correct labelling of the figural component, accompanied by poorer recognition of the background components. Moreover, with age, boys have higher recognition scores for ground and element components than do girls, suggesting that the boys are visually more analytic.

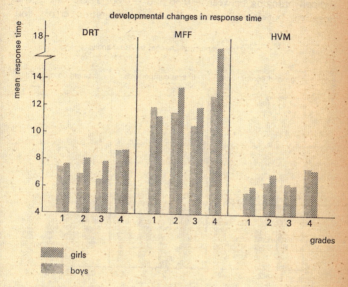

Figure 7 Developmental changes in response time

Since the DRT, MFF and HVM tasks are easier for older children, and the older children make fewer errors, the correlation between response time and age suggests that a disposition favoring reflection over alternative solution hypotheses grows stronger as the child matures. Supplementary data from other studies support this conclusion.

Relationships among Response Time, Recognition Errors and Verbal Ability

The three perceptual recognition tasks (DRT, MFF and HVM) were similar in their psychological requirements, and all yielded the two variables of recognition errors and response time. In almost every sample studied there has been a negative relationship between frequency of recognition errors and average response time (i.e. the latency between presentation of the array of alternatives and the child's first selection), the coefficients typically ranging between −0·30 and −0·60. There was also a negative, but lower, relation between recognition errors and

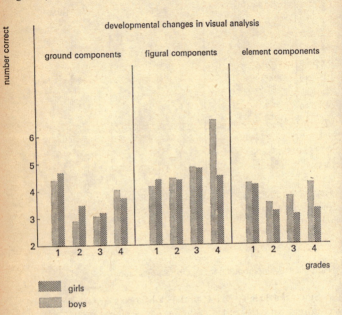

Figure 8 D evelopmental changes in visual analysis

verbal ability (mean score on three verbal subtests of the WISC: vocabulary, information and similarities). The relation between errors and verbal ability was typically lower for boys than for girls. Response time to these tasks, however, was independent of verbal ability, the correlations typically falling below 0·20. Thus, the reflection–impulsivity dimension appeared to be relatively orthogonal to the traditional construct of verbal intelligence. The moderate relation between recognition errors and verbal skills, in girls especially, suggests that the basic cognitive processes implied by the phrase 'high verbal intelligence' (e.g. richer verbal resources, greater self-confidence, problem-solving skills, stronger motivation to perform with competence) have some relevance for accuracy in perceptual recognition tasks among school-age children. Multiple correlation coefficients with recognition errors as the criterion and verbal ability and response time as the two predictors have yielded coefficients in the seventies.

There was remarkable consistency of recognition-error scores across the three tasks (coefficients typically ranged from 0·30 to 0·60 for different groups), and even higher intertask consistency for response times across the three tasks. Moreover, average response time on one task (DRT, for example) predicted not only response time but also errors on a second recognition task (MFF or HVM). Finally, both recognition errors and response time on DRT were highly stable over short (nine weeks) and long (seventeen months) periods. In sum, response time appears to be a critical conceptual variable; it shows generality over tasks, stability over time, and is relatively independent of verbal skills. The occurrence of recognition errors is a more complex variable, for it is related both to response time and to the multiple factors associated with verbal skills.

Psychological Correlates of Analytic Concepts

Numerous studies early in the research attempted to explore the psychological correlates of analytic concepts on the CST (Kagan, Moss and Sigel, 1963; Kagan *et al.*, 1964; Lee, Kagan and Rabson, 1963). The early work on reflective and analytic attitudes used the CST because we were not yet aware of the role of the fundamental variables of response time and visual analysis. We realized only recently that the production of analytic concepts is a joint function of these two variables. Analytic concepts are most likely to occur when the child pauses to consider alternative conceptual groupings on the CST and has a penchant for analysing visual stimuli into smaller components. This section summarizes some salient characteristics of children who report a large number of analytic concepts, a response disposition that involves the reflection–impulsivity dimension.

It will be recalled that the frequency of analytic concepts increased with age and this disposition showed stability over a one-year period (r ranged from 0·47 to 0·73).

An impressionistically consistent cluster of characteristics was possessed by seven- to ten-year-old boys who reported many analytic concepts. These boys were less distractible in the classroom, less likely to display task-irrelevant gross motor behavior on the playground or in a restrictive laboratory setting and less likely to report many incorrect solutions. They were more likely to become involved in sedentary tasks requiring long periods of concentration, more likely to prefer intellectual vocations that required motoric passivity (e.g. scientist, writer), and typically produced more complete drawings of objects. One of the most objective demonstrations of the relationship between motoric restlessness and analytic attitude was contained in the positive association between analytic concepts and regular, non-variable respiratory rhythms during episodes of rest and episodes when the boy was attending to simple visual or auditory stimuli (Kagan and Rosman, 1964). Moreover, boys with many analytic concepts demonstrated greater cardiac deceleration when asked to attend to external stimuli. Cardiac deceleration and regular respiration rates have been shown to be reliable indexes of the degree to which a person invests attention in external stimuli (Lacey, 1959). It appears, therefore, that young boys who prefer analytic concepts are more capable of sustained attention to visual inputs than less analytic youngsters.

Analytic concepts were positively associated with long response times to the CST and DRT and with correct labelling of the element components in the visual analysis task, but negatively related to recognition errors on the DRT. Moreover, children who produced large numbers of analytic concepts, in contrast to those with few concepts, manifested earlier acquisition (in a standard concept-formation task) of concepts requiring visual analysis. Examples of such concepts are 'objects with a missing leg', and 'objects with a black band around them'. However, the analytic child did not show easier acquisition of concepts that did not require visual analysis (Lee, Kagan and Rabson, 1963). Finally, there was a moderate relationship, among girls, between rejection of traditional sex-role interests and analytic concepts. There was no such relationship among boys.

Study of all the data gathered so far suggests the following interpretation of analytic concepts on the CST. To almost every item on the CST the most obvious way of grouping two pictures involves a thematic relation between the pair (see Figure 1). For example, the compelling associational tendency to the item illustrating a wrist watch, a man and a ruler is to link the watch and the man functionally (e.g. the man wears the watch). The pre-potent association to the house with smoke coming from the chimney, the matches and the pipe is a functional link between the matches and pipe. If the child is to produce an analytic concept he must suppress these initially strong, culturally popular associations, and reflect on alternative groupings. He must display response uncertainty. If, in addition to the tendency to reflect over alternative responses, he also has a disposition favoring visual analysis, he is likely to produce an analytic concept. The capacity to delay in the service of reflection, together with a predisposition to visual analysis, appear to be the critical determinants of analytic concepts.

Psychological Correlates of Recognition Errors and Response Time

The early work with the CST led quickly to an appreciation of the variable of reflection in problems presenting multiple-answer possibilities. This realization prompted the investigations with the DRT, and later with the MFF and HVM tasks. It was noted earlier that recognition errors and response time on DRT were highly stable over time and were correlated with errors and response time on the MFF and HVM. Recognition errors and response times differ in their patterns of relations in several respects. First, response time was typically orthogonal to verbal ability for both sexes, whereas error scores usually had a low but significant negative correlation with verbal skills. Moreover, visual-analysis scores (i.e. correct labelling of figure and element components) were negatively related to recognition errors, but not to response time. Finally, response time usually manifested more consistent intertask generality and greater stability over time than the error scores. In one elaborate study, the average response time to 108 tachistoscopic exposures (six different pictures) was positively related to response time on MFF (average $r = 0.40$). We have coined the phrase 'conceptual tempo' to describe the connotative meaning we assign to the reflection variable. Some children consistently spew out the first reasonable hypothesis that occurs to them without pausing to reflect on its probable validity. Their strategy of problem solving has a shotgun character; the child fires a fusillade of answers in the hope that one will be correct, or, perhaps, because he needs immediate feedback from the environment to inform him of the quality of his performance. This child contrasts with one who characteristically pauses to consider the differential validity of several hypotheses. This child behaves as if he had a strong desire to be as correct as possible on his first attempt, and he is able to tolerate the ambiguity and tension inherent in the period of silence that is an inevitable concomitant of response selection. Two qualifications are in order. These general statements about the significance of long response times apply only to those problem situations in which all the alternatives are available simultaneously (either in visual form as in the DRT, or as mental images).[1] These conclusions do not apply to problems for which the child has no immediate solution hypothesis (e.g. What is the cube root of 810?), or to situations in which the child is so afraid of failure that he is reluctant to offer any answer. We believe that our test situations minimize the latter possibility, but are exploring ways of detecting the excessively fearful child who may show long response times. We are currently working on a method to detect two small groups of subjects for whom the above generalizations about response times may not always apply. There is, on the one hand, a small group of bright subjects who can have relatively fast response times on easy tasks (like DRT) but make few errors. These children do not have fast response time on the MFF because this task is more difficult than the DRT. It is crucial to use tasks that are of optimum difficulty for each age level to guarantee that fast response times typically lead to high

1. The assumption that response time is a sensitive index of response uncertainty was well demonstrated in a recent study by Morin and Forrin (1963).

error scores. A second anomalous group, also small, contains children whose long response times result from extreme fear. These children may have high error scores, for they are not reflecting upon alternative possibilities during the long delay. They fail to respond quickly because they have no idea what to say and are afraid of offering any answer. It is likely that elimination of children who show both excessively long response times and high error scores will permit us to understand with greater clarity the antecedents of the reflection variable.

When recognition errors or response time on DRT or MFF were used as indexes of the reflection–impulsivity dimension, an impressionistically consistent set of relationships to other behaviors emerged. Impulsive children (i.e. high errors and fast response times) showed a marked increase in errors of commission on a serial learning task (i.e. reporting words not originally present on the list) after being told that their performance on the serial learning task was inadequate. The more impulsive the child prior to the learning task, the greater his increase in errors of commission following this threat.[2]

There is much similarity between recognition errors on DRT, HVM or MFF, and orthographic errors in reading. One might expect these two classes of errors to be related in young children learning to read. In a recently completed study of 130 first-grade children we found a strong positive relationship between errors in recognizing three-letter words (i.e. big, dog, cat, nap) and errors on DRT, MFF or HVM. However, there was a minimal relationship between the accuracy of recognition of single letters and errors on DRT, MFF or HVM. To illustrate, the correlation for sixty-five boys between HVM errors and word errors was 0·47 (p < 0·001); the correlation with single-letter errors was only 0·19. It appears that the tendency to read *log* for *dog*, *cat* for *pot*, or *eat* for *ear* is related to a disposition toward impulsive selection of hypotheses, even when the child has mastered the individual graphemes of his language.

It should be noted, finally, that recognition errors and response times are not influenced appreciably by the degree of acceptance or warmth displayed by an examiner. A carefully controlled

2. Comprehensive evidence for this statement may be found in the original paper from which this selection is excerpted [*Ed.*].

experiment in which examiner rapport was manipulated (warm v. impersonal, cold approach to the child) did not allow rejection of the null hypothesis (Kagan *et al.*, 1964).

The Significance of Visual Analysis

Systematic work on visual analysis has only recently begun, and less information is available on the significance of this variable. As noted earlier, there is a developmental shift in preferred perceptual focus. First-grade children initially recognize the solitary background components with greater accuracy than second-, third- or fourth-grade children. The older children are more accurate in recognizing the solitary figural components. Second, accurate recognition of the element components was associated with early recognition of tachistoscopically presented scenes that contained incongruous elements. This is a reasonable association, for a disposition toward visual analysis should facilitate early recognition of pictures that contain one or two incongruous elements (e.g. person in a woman's dress smoking a pipe; living room with a tree). Finally, recognition of figural and element components was associated with low error scores on DRT, MFF and HVM, and with analytic concepts on CST. But these visual-analysis variables were orthogonal to response times and verbal skills.[3] [. . .]

Discussion and Summary

The accumulated evidence from a dozen investigations of children in the first four grades is remarkably univocal in its message. Reflection over alternative solution possibilities and visual analysis are fundamental cognitive dispositions that are independent of each other and of the richness of the child's language repertoire. Moreover, each of these dimensions influences the occurrence of the more complex cognitive products of analytic conceptual groupings (on CST) and recognition errors (on

3. In the original article Kagan went on to discuss in detail a longitudinal study of reflection–impulsivity. This investigation followed up children between the ages of seven and nine to examine the stability and interrelationships of the indices discussed previously [*Ed.*].

DRT, MFF or HVM). The complementary role of visual analysis and reflection in predicting infrequent recognition errors is reasonable, for in order to select the correct variant on the first attempt one must analyse each stimulus into its components, inhibit the immediate reporting of initial hypotheses, and evaluate alternative solution possibilities. A reflective disposition displays a stability over time and a generality across tasks that is unusual for psychological attributes, and tempts one to conclude that this response tendency must be a basic component of the individual's behavioral organization.

The points of contact between these two dispositions and basic theory and research in intellectual processes are not yet clear. Witkin and his colleagues (1962) have been concerned with the dimension of field independence and have used performance on the Embedded Figures and Spatial Orientation Tests as the operational indexes of this variable. We have found no strong relation between reflection and solution time on Witkin's version of the Embedded-Figures Test (Kagan *et al.*, 1964). But reflective children offer far fewer incorrect solution hypotheses prior to achieving solution. We have not assessed the relation between visual analysis and field independence, but expect it to be moderately positive.

Basic theory in intellectual development has been concerned mainly with the growth of mediational systems and the acquisition of operations (or transformation rules) that allow more complex deductive and inductive reasoning. Both European and American investigators have been fascinated by the behavior of cognitive structures, how they are born, grow and die. They have been indifferent to those processes that mark the beginning and end of a problem-solving sequence, namely, the initial processing of external information and the characteristics of the response classes involved in the overt reporting of a completed cognitive product. The growing interest in information processing in both adult and child should amplify our understanding of these aspects of mental activity.

Antecedents of reflection–impulsivity

A search for the historical and immediate antecedents of a reflective versus impulsive attitude should consider at least three possibilities, none of which is mutually exclusive of the others. These three are constitutional predispositions, involvement in the task and anxiety over task competence. There is some evidence favoring the idea that excessive motor restlessness and distractibility at age eight have their anlage in congenital deficit resulting from minimal and subtle brain damage during the peri-natal or early post-natal period. Since the extremely impulsive boys in our studies were also excessively restless and distractible, it is possible that these children suffered subtle cerebral damage early in life. It is possible, of course, that biological variables, unrelated to central nervous system deficit, predispose some infants and pre-school children to hyperactivity and impulsive reactions. Schaefer and Bayley (1963) have found that extremely active one-year-old infants were minimally attentive to intellectual problems at five and six years of age. The Fels longitudinal study has yielded similar results. Ratings of hyperkinesis during ages three to six were inversely correlated with ratings of involvement in intellectual activity during adolescence and adulthood (Kagan and Moss, 1962). Moreover, ratings of hyperactivity during ages four through eight were negatively related to analytic concepts among ten-year-old boys (Kagan et al., 1964). This relationship suggests that signs prognostic of the development of an impulsive conceptual attitude may be manifest early in development.

In sum, there are tantalizing scraps of evidence from several laboratories that lend some credibility to the idea that children who are extremely active during the opening years of development are more likely to be conceptually impulsive during the school years than those who are motorically more quiescent. We are now conducting an intensive longitudinal study of a group of infants who were seen first at eight weeks of age and who are thirteen months old at the time of this writing. Preliminary analyses indicate marked stability of the attributes of *motor activity and duration of sustained attention to external stimuli* over this forty-eight-week period, with the activity and attention variables inversely correlated with each other.

A second class of factors that might influence reflection deals with the degree of involvement in the task. A child with high standards of performance should be more likely to reflect on alternative hypotheses and more likely to want his first answer to be correct than a child who is minimally concerned with the quality of his performance. We have found that girls who rejected traditional feminine interests were more reflective than girls with traditional feminine standards. There is a positive relation, among girls, between degree of rejection of sex-typed activities and involvement in intellectual mastery (Kagan and Moss, 1962), and this relation furnishes indirect evidence for the proposition that reflective girls may have been more highly involved in our tasks.

A final hypothesis deals with the child's anxiety over his ability to perform adequately in tasks like DRT or MFF. Let us assume that most children have a desire to do well on these tests and to convince the examiner that they are able to perform adequately. Let us look closely at the psychology of the inter-personal situation the moment the examiner presents the problem to the child. The child who is anxious about his ability to perform adequately should be less able to tolerate the period of silence that must occur if he is to reflect over various hypotheses. He may fear that his failure to respond immediately will be inter-preted as an indication of his inadequacy and he may be pre-disposed to offer an answer quickly. The confident child, on the other hand, should be more able to tolerate the delay between presentation of the problem and the offering of a solution. The fact that children show increased response times with age suggests that reflection gains strength with development. It is difficult to determine, however, whether this increased penchant for reflec-tion is the product of greater confidence, a stronger need to avoid reporting incorrect answers, the ability to generate more solution possibilities, or, perhaps, variables we have not yet recognized.

Our current belief, held with only moderate confidence, is that a child's position on the reflection–impulsivity dimension can be the result of either constitutional or experiential factors, with the former most relevant for children at the extreme end of the impulsivity continuum.

Methodological implications

Responses to all psychological tests are, first of all, cognitive responses. The interpretation of an inkblot, the telling of a story to a TAT picture, or the selection of an answer on a multiple-choice test all involve the selection of one best response from a set of alternatives. The reflection–impulsivity dimension should affect the manner in which external information is classified and organized, and the content and form of the final response. It is reasonable to expect that production of motivational content variables on selected 'personality tests' (e.g. aggressive or sexual imagery to inkblots or pictures) may be the partial result of tendencies toward impulsivity or reflection. For example, there is a marked association between the production of inkblot imagery that would be coded as aggressive or sexual in content and the production of a response containing movement components. Movement responses characteristically require longer response times than nonmovement responses and typically require analysis of a component of the total stimulus. It is likely, therefore, that reflective children will produce more movement responses and, by so doing, also report a percept that has motivational content. It is reasonable to defend the idea that a penchant for reflection is one critical determinant of an 'aggressive' inkblot interpretation.

A second implication for method concerns certain factor-analytic approaches to understanding intellectual functioning. Group-administered tests of mental abilities do not obtain response-time data and, therefore, cannot evaluate the reflection–impulsivity variable. If this disposition is as critical as these data suggest, it is unwarranted to assume that one can discover the basic factors of mental activity through factor analysis of these scores.

Implications for problem solving

A second set of implications concerns problem-solving efficiency and the gradual establishing of permanent attitudes toward problem solving. In problems with alternate routes to solution, reflection and evaluation of the validity of solution sequences are critical for eventual success. The child who does not reflect upon the probable validity of alternative-solution sequences is likely to follow through on the first idea that occurs to him. This strategy is more likely to end up in failure than one which involves reflection. The impulsive child who reaches a cul-de-sac in a problem-solving sequence, and recognizes that he has not solved the problem, is likely to become more anxious than he was initially. As a result of the increased anxiety his selection of a second solution path is likely to be impaired and the probability of success attenuated. This maladaptive cycle may become entrenched with time, and after four or five years of experiencing the sequence: problem $\longrightarrow$ impulsive selection of invalid solution $\longrightarrow$ failure $\longrightarrow$ anxiety $\longrightarrow$ selection of second solution $\longrightarrow$ failure, etc., the child may gradually withdraw from problem situations, and apathy and hostility may become characteristic reactions toward intellectual situations.

We do not wish to paint the reflective child as necessarily the better or brighter child. It is likely that efficient learning and creative problem solving will occasionally be facilitated by a reflective approach, occasionally by an impulsive approach. Indeed, a recent study (Lee, Kagan and Rabson, 1963) demonstrated this last point clearly. Some of the academic contents children must master require reflection and analysis, for instance, mathematics and the physical sciences. But maximal productiveness and mastery of principles in aspects of the arts, social studies and humanities may be hampered by an excessively reflective orientation. New pedagogical procedures should acknowledge this interaction between the preferred strategy of the learner and the material to be acquired and tailor the presentation of materials to the psychological requirements of the task and the cognitive predisposition of the learner.

References

KAGAN, J., and MOSS, H. A. (1962), *From Birth to Maturity: A Study in Psychological Development*, Wiley.

KAGAN, J., and ROSMAN, B. L. (1964), 'Cardiac and respiratory correlates of attention and an analytic attitude', *J. exp. child Psychol.*, vol. 1, pp. 50–63.

KAGAN, J., MOSS, H. A., and SIGEL, I. E. (1963), 'Psychological significance of styles of conceptualization in basic cognitive processes in children', *Monogr. Soc. Res. Child Devel.*, vol. 28, no. 2.

KAGAN, J., ROSMAN, B. L., DAY, D., ALBERT, J., and PHILLIPS, W. (1964), 'Information processing in the child', *Psychol. Monogr.*, vol. 78, no. 578.

LACEY, J. I. (1959), 'Psychophysiological approaches to the evaluation of psychotherapeutic process and outcome', in E. A. Rubenstein and M. B. Parloff (eds.), *Research in Psycho-Therapy*, National Publishing Co., pp. 160–208.

Other Cognitive Styles

LEE, C. L., KAGAN, J., and RABSON, A. (1963), 'The influence of a preference for analytic categorization upon concept acquisition', *Child Devel.*, vol. 34, pp. 433–42.

MORIN, R. E., and FORRIN, B. (1963), 'Response equivocation and reaction time', *J. exp. Psychol.*, vol. 66, pp. 30–36.

SCHAEFER, E. A., and BAYLEY, N. (1963), 'Maternal behavior, child behavior and their intercorrelations from infancy through adolescence', *Monogr. Soc. Res. Child Devel.*, vol. 28, no. 3.

WITKIN, H. A., DYK, R. B., FATERSON, H. F., GOODENOUGH, D. R., and KARP, S. A. (1962), *Psychological Differentiation*, Wiley.

14 Odin C. Vick and Douglas N. Jackson

Cognitive Styles in the Schematizing Process

Odin C. Vick and Douglas N. Jackson, 'Cognitive styles in the schematizing process: a critical evaluation', *Educational and Psychological Measurement*, vol. 27, 1967, pp. 267–86.

In psychophysical judgement, as in interpersonal situations, individuals differ in the degree to which they notice small differences and changes in sequences of stimuli. Some Ss, termed 'levelers', seem to be relatively insensitive to differences between similar stimuli, while others, termed 'sharpeners', tend to emphasize these differences. Each approach probably has both functional and dysfunctional aspects. Thus, the sharpener might have his counterpart in lay personality theory in either the incisive critic or the individual who ruins his eyes splitting hairs. In contrast, the leveler might be the eclectic theoretician quick to see the consistencies in diverse positions or, on the other hand, the muddle-headed bungler who constantly confuses distinct alternatives.

The present study is a systematic attempt to define, to measure, and to examine personality correlates of certain consistent individual differences in the areas of perception and cognition previously identified as leveling–sharpening. In this attempt we have paid particular attention to contemporary approaches to construct validation (Cronbach and Meehl, 1955; Loevinger, 1957), as well as to certain elementary concepts of classical test theory. The problem of defining individual consistencies in cognition as an approach to the study of personality is both a challenging and a hazardous undertaking. Our understanding of the manner in which personality structure manifests itself in diverse perceptual and cognitive processes has been greatly broadened by the pioneering efforts of such research workers as Thurstone (1944), Witkin (1950) and the Menninger group. However, here, as elsewhere in science it is important to avoid the dangers of allowing enthusiasm with initial results to outstrip careful refinement of procedures and of allowing hypothesis and theory elaboration to overwhelm the equally important challenge of empirical validation. While there have been notable exceptions to this tendency (Witkin *et al.*, 1954, 1962), this research area, even more than most, requires the most painstaking, even tedious, analysis of the properties of measures, if its initial promise is to be repaid with hard currency.

The terms 'leveling' and 'sharpening' were first described by Wulf (1938; cf. Koffka, 1935) as referring to different ways in which a memory trace might change over time. Leveling involved a loss of detail, a tendency for certain prominent aspects of the figure to become less salient or to disappear; conversely, sharpening represented modification of the original percept in the direction of emphasizing and elaborating details. Allport and Postman (1958) used these terms to describe similar systematic changes occuring in the transmission of rumor.

In a series of studies conducted at the Menninger Foundation, Gardner *et al.* (1959), Holzman (1954) and Holzman and Klein (1951) sought to define the leveling–sharpening dimension. Poles of this dimension were defined in terms of two opposite hypothetical modes of perceptual and memory organization, having relevance to consistent individual differences in cognition and personality. The experimental definition of leveling–sharpening was based upon performance in the Schematizing Test. This test, an adaptation of the Squares Test used for other purposes by Hollingworth (1913), requires Ss to judge the absolute size of squares projected on a screen one at a time. Squares of fourteen different sizes are arranged in subsets of five, the five smallest squares forming the first subset. Each succeeding set of five squares is formed by eliminating the smallest of the preceding set and adding the next larger square that has not yet appeared in the test. The squares of each subset are presented to the Ss first in order of ascending size and then in two fixed, predetermined random orders. The squares are presented in a series with no extra time break between the subsets. Thus, as the test proceeds, there is a gradual but irregular increase in the size of squares.

Two styles of responding to the test, presumably a bipolar dimension, have been identified: *leveling*, the general and progressive failure to keep up with the trend of increasing size of the squares; and *sharpening*, the absence or minimization of that lag or the anticipation of the trend of change. Leveling and sharpening tendencies are thought to be revealed in another respect, namely 'ranking accuracy'. When the ranks of the absolute size judgements of each S within each of the subsets are compared with the ranks of the size of the stimuli of each set, 'ranking accuracy' scores may be obtained. These scores have served as indicants for assigning Ss to sharpening or leveling categories (Holzman, 1954; Holzman and Klein, 1954).

The problems in leveling–sharpening begin with the Schematizing Test, which is tedious for Ss and expensive to administer and score, thus discouraging some investigators from undertaking research in the area at all, while others study samples of inadequate size. The notable lack of system or clear rationale in scoring has given rise to numerous problems, several of which have been carefully explicated by Krathwohl and Cronbach (1956). Neither the appropriate measurement operations nor the hypothesized underlying processes have been unequivocally spelled out. Scores based both on variations in lag and on ranking accuracy have been used as criteria for selecting groups of levelers and sharpeners, often without specifying which type of score was used or how multiple scores were combined (Holzman, 1954; Holzman and Gardner, 1959; Holzman and Klein, 1954). This fact renders the research findings very ambiguous, since such correlations as have been reported between lag and ranking accuracy have not been sufficiently high to justify interchanging the scores (cf. Gardner, Jackson and Messick, 1960). Indeed, the unavailability of experimentally independent scores of accuracy and lag make any obtained correlations and factor patterns difficult to interpret.

Both as a cause and as a result of equivocal research findings, the conceptualization of leveling–sharpening with regard to basic processes and perceptual, cognitive and personality correlates has at times lacked clarity and denotative specificity. The principal process hypothesis, which ascribes leveling to perceptual assimilation and sharpening either to less assimilation or to contrast tendencies (Holzman and Klein, 1950; Klein, 1951), has received some support as regards time error assimilation effects (Gardner *et al.*, 1959; Holzman, 1954; Holzman and Klein, 1951, 1954), but in other studies the assimilation hypothesis has not received unequivocal support (Gardner *et al.*, 1959; Holzman, 1954; Murney, 1955).

Some evidence has been found for the importance of leveling–sharpening both in immediate memory organization (Gardner and Lohrenz, 1960), and delayed memory organization (Holzman and Gardner, 1960). In addition, suggestive evidence of a relation to repression (Gardner *et al.*, 1959; Holzman and Gardner, 1959; Lachmann, Lapkin and Handelman, 1962) has been found. Holzman and Klein (1950) and Klein (1951) reported that levelers were judged by psychiatrists to be passive, constricted, rigid, avoidant of competition and naïve, as compared to sharpeners. In addition, they have suggested (Holzman, 1954; Klein, 1951) that sharpeners may show greater cognitive complexity than levelers. Tear and Guthrie (1955) found levelers nominated more often as cooperative, and sharpeners as competitive, by their fraternity brothers. Krathwohl and Cronbach (1956) found sharpeners tended toward greater rigidity in questionnaire responses, but Murney (1955) obtained no significant differences between levelers and sharpeners on Q-sorts of self-descriptive items. Although Holzman and Klein (1950) reported a relationship between sharpening and Embedded-Figures Test performance, subsequent studies have failed to support this finding (Gardner, Jackson and Messick, 1960; Murney, 1955); indeed, such tests define a quite different perceptual and personality dimension, field independence (Jackson, Messick and Myers, 1964; Witkin *et al.*, 1954, 1962).

In approaching the problems of defining cognitive styles in the schematizing process, we considered it essential to use more than one score to measure components of this hypothetical dimension (cf. Campbell and Fiske, 1959). Therefore, different simplified group-administered test forms of the schematizing process were designed (cf. Vick and Jackson, 1964), permitting both an evaluation of internal consistency and cross-method correlation of components. The validation process included an appraisal of the correlations of these leveling–sharpening component scores with measures of: (a) perceptual-cognitive contrast tendencies, i.e criticalness (Frederiksen and Messick, 1959), perceptual critical ness (Vick and Jackson, 1964) and category width (Pettigrew 1958); (b) art judgement complexity; and (c) selected personality traits, as measured by trait ratings. To assess discriminant validity, correlations with certain mental abilities, field independence, age, sex and academic performance were obtained. Finally, the data were examined for information as to the consistency and generality of leveling–sharpening tendencies.

Method

Subjects

Subjects were volunteers recruited from introductory psychology classes. Of 204 tested, eight had at least one unscorable test and were not included in the analysis. The final sample consisted of 196 Ss, 109 men and eighty-seven women. The age range was seventeen to twenty-six years, with a mean of 19·0 and a standard deviation of 1·3 years.

Procedure

Each S served in one of four identical three-hour sessions, during which twelve tests were administered. The tests used are described below together with the variables they measured and reasons for their inclusion.

The Squares Lag Test and Dots Lag Test were designed for this study on the basis of previous results (Vick and Jackson, 1964), the former in an effort to represent previously used methods of measuring leveling–sharpening, and the latter in order to assess the generality of the dimension. Both tests were analogous to the Holzman–Klein Schematizing Test, but shorter and simpler, requiring Ss to make sixty-eight absolute judgements (size of squares or number of dots) of twenty stimuli. In each test the stimuli were projected on a motion picture screen singly and successively, three seconds on and six seconds off. Each test commenced with the smallest four stimuli, shown once in random order. In each test succeeding sets were formed by dropping the smallest (or least numerous) stimulus from the preceding set and incorporating the stimulus next larger (or more numerous) than any previously presented. Thus, seventeen sets of four stimuli were formed for each test. Adjacent stimuli in the basic squares series were discriminably different by paired comparisons; adjacent dots stimuli were not. Instructions stressed accuracy and alertness. In each test the first four slides were for demonstration purposes; they were shown in a separate random order forward and backward, while E labeled each stimulus as to size of squares or number of dots. Judgements were made by circling fixed categories on a prepared answer sheet, a modified successive intervals procedure. Three extra categories below and eleven above the actual limits of the stimulus series were provided.

Four scores were obtained which reflected the lag-anticipation tendencies described by Holzman and Klein (1951); these were termed Early Slope, Late Slope, Over-all Slope and Increment. The first three represented the slope of the regression of judgement totals on stimulus totals for the first eight, last eight, and all seventeen sets of stimuli, respectively. Increment was a simplified version of Increment Error (Gardner *et al.*, 1959) in which certain mathematically constant values were eliminated. The four scores will be referred to as lag scores, although scored in the direction of anticipation.

Two additional scores representing ranking accuracy and ranking error were obtained. The Accuracy score (the former Ranking Accuracy score) was the number of agreements between judgement ranks and stimulus ranks within sets of stimuli. The Error score was refined somewhat to take account of the magnitude, as well as the frequency, of ranking errors. Error was the sum of the absolute values of discrepancies between intraset stimulus and judgement ranks.

The Alternative Expressions Test was used to measure critical-ness response set (Frederiksen and Messick, 1959), on the hypothesis that criticalness and leveling are negatively related. It requires Ss to judge whether the meaning of each of seventy sentences would be changed in any practical way by substituting a given word or phrase for one indicated in the sentence. The response set score D, number of judgements 'different', was used.

The Angles and Squares Similarity–Difference Tests were designed to test the generality of criticalness over simple perceptual judgements and were tentatively labeled tests of 'perceptual criticalness'. Each stimulus for the Angles Test was a slide showing two straight black lines, joined at one end to form an acute angle. All angles were oriented the same way, with the base line horizontal. Squares stimuli were the same as for the Squares Lag Test. Each test comprised twenty pairs of stimuli, presented on a screen singly and successively for three seconds each, with intervals of one and a half seconds between pair members and six seconds between pairs. Ss were to judge whether the stimuli in each pair were the same or different. The members of half the pairs in each test were discriminably different by paired comparisons; members of the remaining pairs in each test were identical. Scores were obtained separately for the Angles and the Squares Similarity–Difference Tests and combined for a total; they were the number of correct judgements ($R+$), and the number of judgements of 'different' (D).

The Estimation Questionnaire (Pettigrew, 1958), a measure of category width, requires Ss to estimate the upper and lower extremes of the frequencies when given the average frequency of some event.[1] On the hypothesis that Ss who tend to exaggerate differences between stimuli would use narrower categories than those who tend to minimize differences, this test was expected to correlate with sharpening and with criticalness. Scoring followed Pettigrew's (1958) procedure.

The Figure Choices Test was used to appraise the hypothesis that habitual leveling results in a generally impoverished, simplified cognitive structure. Barron (1953, 1955) used the Barron–Welsh Art Scale (Barron and Welsh, 1952) as a measure of preference for complexity or simplicity. A forced-choice form of the test was developed by Sechrest and Jackson (1961) to reduce response set variance. Figure Choices is a forced-choice booklet form of the Barron–Welsh scale prepared by Messick and Kogan. It is scored for the number of preferences S expresses for the more complex member of pairs of figures.

A group-administered Embedded-Figures Test, a measure of field independence (Witkin *et al.*, 1954), was included, in the light of the status of field independence as a separate cognitive style, to provide data relevant to the discriminant validity of the lag tests as measures of leveling–sharpening. The embedded-figures form was designed by Jackson, Messick and Myers (1964) to minimize the role of memory organization in performance and to provide for convenient group administration. The test was administered

1. See Reading 6, page 127 [*Ed.*].

with a twelve-minute time limit and scored for the number of simple figures correctly identified in the test figures.

The Trait Rating Form was used to test hypotheses concerning relationships between leveling–sharpening and certain personality variables. This instrument, developed by Jackson, is designed to assess personality through Ss' judgements of desirability of 300 traits which were chosen to represent eleven of Murray's need concepts, as well as desirability response bias, with twenty-five items in each scale. Ratings of traits were on a nine-point scale. Scores were based on the sum of the ratings.

Advanced Vocabulary, Mathematics Aptitude and Perceptual Speed Tests were included as a further check on the discriminant validity of the Squares Lag Test. The Advanced Vocabulary and Mathematics Aptitude Tests were taken from French's (1954) kit of factored tests; they are classified as measures of verbal knowledge and general reasoning, respectively. The Perceptual Speed Test is from the Guilford–Zimmerman Aptitude Survey (1947). The ability test scores were the number of correct responses.

Age, *Sex* and academic *Grade Point Average* were obtained from each S so that the correlation of these variables with leveling–sharpening might be appraised.

Results and Discussion

The means and SDs of leveling–sharpening measures are presented in Table 1. Note that the lag scores and Accuracy are higher, and Error lower in the Squares Lag Test than in the Dots Lag Test. These differences reflect the fact that the smallest difference between squares was easily discriminable, whereas this was not the case for the dots.

Table 2 shows the corrected odd–even reliability coefficients of the measures. Of special interest are the estimates of internal consistency for the Squares and Dots Lag Test scores. The score X represents the sum of judgements within each set of four stimuli in the lag tests. Thus the reliabilities of X for the two lag tests represent the internal consistencies of the scores upon which Increment and Over-all Slope are based, and may be taken as estimates of the reliabilities of Increment and Over-all Slope. The uncorrected odd–even reliability coefficients for X in the two tests

Table 1

Means and Standard Deviations of Leveling–Sharpening Scores ($N = 196$)

Variable	Lag Test			
	Squares		Dots	
	Mean	SD	Mean	SD
Early Slope	0·85	0·68	0·54	0·57
Late Slope	0·75	0·75	0·12	0·49
Over-all Slope	0·76	0·65	0·35	0·42
Increment	2·13	0·82	1·10	0·10
Accuracy	38·18	7·64	16·08	5·42
Error	26·90	8·67	66·84	10·59

Table 2

Corrected Odd–Even Reliabilities of Test Score Variables ($N = 196$)

Variable	r	Variable	r
Squares Lag Test		Estimation Questionnaire	0·83
X[1]	0·99	Embedded Figures	0·79
Accuracy	0·56	Figure Choices	0·91
Error	0·56	Mathematics Aptitude	0·78
Dots Lag Test		Advanced Vocabulary	0·70
X[1]	0·98	Trait Rating Form	
Accuracy	0·33	n Achievement	0·91
Error	0·38	n Impulsion	0·64
Similarity Difference Tests[2]		n Dominance	0·86
Angles R+	0·05	n Understanding	0·82
Angles D	0·37	n Autonomy	0·83
Squares R+	−0·05	n Aggression	0·88
Squares D	0·23	n Abasement	0·83
Total R+	−0·07	n Rejection	0·84
Total D	0·46	n Harmavoidance	0·79
		n Exhibition	0·81
Alternative Expressions	0·81	n Affiliation	0·90

Note: Correlations required for significance at 0·05 and 0·01 levels: 0·14 and 0·19 respectively.
1. X is sum of judgements within sets.
2. $R+$ is number correct; D is number judged different.

may be considered to be estimates of the reliability of Early Slope and Late Slope. The correlations indicate that trends in judgements are very consistent from one set of stimuli to the next.

Although less consistent than the lag scores, both Accuracy and Error show reliabilities in the moderate range, significant well beyond the 0·01 level. Both Accuracy and Error are somewhat less reliable in the Dots than in the Squares Lag Test. This difference probably resulted from the difference in discriminability of stimuli.

These data for the lag tests make it apparent that all the lag measures possess satisfactory internal consistency, and that the Accuracy and Error scores, though less reliable, are sufficiently high so as to be of further interest. The data support the conclusion that on both tasks, Ss show the individual differences in judgements that have been labeled leveling and sharpening by the Menninger investigators.

In the Similarity–Difference Test the reliabilities of $R+$ (total number of correct judgements) were not significantly different from zero, while those of D (number of judgements 'different') were all greater than zero at better than the 0·01 level of significance, though low to moderate in magnitude. Thus, in Similarity–Difference Test scores, simple accuracy of judgement was not consistent for a given S from one item to the next, despite the composition of the tests which insured the discriminability of the members of the pairs keyed 'different'. The data indicate that this type of test evokes a set to respond 'different' which is more consistent than the tendency to judge differences accurately. The various scales of the Trait Rating Form generally displayed substantial internal consistency. The reliabilities of seven of the scales were in the 0·80s, with three lower and two higher, the median being 0·83. These are moderate to high reliabilities for personality scales.

Intercorrelations of variables

Pearson product-moment correlations were obtained between all relevant pairs of variables.

Lag scores. Lag or anticipation (Slope and Increment scores) appears to be a fairly consistent set of individual differences within in each of the lag tests, but is more complex than was revealed in

previous research (e.g. Gardner *et al.*, 1959). Intercorrelations of
lag scores were generally high (Tables 3 and 4), but not so high as
to suggest their interchangeability. In both tests, the lowest cor-

Table 3

Intercorrelations of Squares Lag Test Scores ($N = 196$)

Score	Early Slope	Late Slope	Over-all Slope	Increment	Accuracy
Late Slope	0·41				
Over-all Slope	0·62	0·87			
Increment	0·77	0·76	0·92		
Accuracy	0·18	0·16	0·20	0·22	
Error	−0·06	−0·05	−0·06	−0·06	−0·84

Note: Correlations required for significance at the 0·05 and 0·01 levels:
0·14 and 0·19 respectively.

relations among lag measures were between Early Slope and Late
Slope. The latter results, although not reproducing exactly the
findings of Krathwohl and Cronbach (1956) because the present

Table 4

Intercorrelations of Dots Lag Test Scores ($N = 196$)

Score	Early Slope	Late Slope	Over-all Slope	Increment	Accuracy
Late Slope	0·17				
Over-all Slope	0·67	0·62			
Increment	0·72	0·39	0·77		
Accuracy	0·14	−0·03	0·04	0·14	
Error	0·04	0·00	0·05	0·07	−0·57

Note: Correlations required for significance at the 0·05 and 0·01 levels:
0·14 and 0·19 respectively.

correlations were statistically significant, do lend support to the
conclusion of those investigators that Early Slope and Late Slope
contain different information. All the lag scores will probably
prove useful in further analytical work on leveling–sharpening,

though one may question the unique value of a separate Increment score because of its high correlation with Over-all Slope.

The hypothesis that lag is an adaptation-level or frame of reference phenomenon receives some support from the correlations of Squares Lag Test scores with their counterparts in the Dots Lag Test. Table 5 shows that lag scores generally held up fairly well

Table 5

Correlations of Scores across Lag Tests ($N = 196$)

Dots Test	Squares Test					
	Early Slope	Late Slope	Over-all Slope	Incre-ment	Accu-racy	Error
Early Slope	*0·43*	0·42	0·48	0·49	0·16	−0·04
Late Slope	−0·06	*0·12*	0·11	0·06	0·06	−0·05
Over-all Slope	0·29	0·38	*0·42*	0·41	0·06	0·02
Increment	0·31	0·34	0·38	*0·38*	0·06	0·01
Accuracy	0·18	0·08	0·08	0·11	*0·12*	−0·09
Error	−0·02	0·20	0·15	0·10	−0·06	*0·11*

Note: Correlations required for significance at the 0·05 and 0·01 levels: 0·14 and 0·19 respectively.

across the two tests, considering the rather marked differences between the tests in type and discriminability of stimuli and type of judgement required, as well as the probable operation of sequence effects. Of considerable interest is the exception to this rule – Dots Late Slope – which was correlated about zero with all Squares Lag Test scores. In contrast, Dots Early Slope was correlated about as well with all Squares Lag Test lag scores as each of the latter correlated with its own Dots Lag Test counterpart. These results suggest strongly that a mode of responding adopted in the Squares Lag Test carried over well into the Dots Lag Test for most Ss, and was then abandoned by them. Only further research can clarify the reasons for these results, but the data suggest that the phenomena involved may be individual differences in anchoring effects in judgements (Sherif and Hovland, 1961).

Lag and Accuracy. Apparently lag is only slightly related to ranking Accuracy, although these two aspects of performance have been used rather indiscriminately as referents of 'leveling–sharpening'. The data (Tables 3 and 4) did not permit the rejection of the null hypothesis as regards a relationship between lag *v.* Error, but did permit its rejection for lag scores *v.* Accuracy in the Squares Lag Test and for Dots Early Slope and Increment. The importance of this finding derives from the fact that the assumption, made by some previous investigators, that the two types of scores are measuring essentially the same trait of leveling–sharpening was one basis for conceptualizing leveling–sharpening in terms of assimilation *v.* contrast. That is, lag was regarded as a consequence of the operation of assimilation tendencies in sequential judgements (Holzman, 1954). The present correlations, however, do not support the equivalence of lag and accuracy scores. Moreover, it appears that the measures of accuracy are more susceptible than the lag scores to change in situational or task variables. Neither Accuracy nor Error in the Squares Lag Test correlated significantly with its analogous score in the Dots Lag Test (Table 5).

Further data must be examined before much can be said about the nature of the Accuracy variable itself. However, the data in Tables 3, 4 and 5 are sufficient to cast serious doubt on the functional unity of leveling–sharpening as previously defined. The latter statement holds whether one is referring to defining operations or to the hypotheses relevant to this cognitive style. It is at least clear that a more careful analysis of the leveling–sharpening formulation is needed and probable that it will have to be drastically redefined. Research aimed at further clarification of the concept will need to use the data from all *S*s, not merely that from extreme groups (Holzman, 1954). The practice of using extreme groups may have produced statistically significant differences in the predicted directions which lack both practical and theoretical importance because of low relationships between the variables when all the data are considered (cf. Bolles and Messick, 1958).

Lag v. other variables. Discussion of the correlates of leveling–sharpening will be confined to relationships involving scores on the Squares Lag Test. The latter shows a higher and clearer patterning of correlations than does the Dots Lag Test, a finding probably attributable to the higher reliability of the Squares Lag Test.

Little evidence was obtained that lag is related to age, sex or academic achievement or ability variables. None of the correlations between lag scores and age, grade point average or the Mathematics Aptitude Test was significant, which offers some evidence for the discriminant validity of lag scores. On the other hand, Advanced Vocabulary was correlated significantly at the 0·05 level with Early Slope and nearly so with Increment; Perceptual Speed was correlated with Over-all Slope and Increment at the 0·05 level; and sex was correlated with Early Slope at the 0·01 level and with Increment at the 0·05 level of significance. These correlations may best be regarded as leads for further research rather than as a basis for firm conclusions.

The assimilation v. contrast hypothesis received little support in this study as an explanation of lag. Lag scores were not significantly correlated with Similarity–Difference Test or Alternative Expressions Test D-scores, or with the Estimation Questionnaire. In fact, no evidence was obtained for a general trait of perceptual contrast. The Similarity–Difference tests were designed for the study and the Alternative Expressions Test and Estimation Questionnaire were included in the study because performance on those tests could be conceptualized readily in terms of a style of perceptual contrast. However, although the Similarity–Difference Test D-scores were correlated significantly at the 0·01 level (0·32), lending some support to the contrast trait, neither of those scores was correlated significantly with the Alternative Expressions Test D (a measure of criticalness) or with the Estimation Questionnaire (category width), nor were the latter two tests significantly correlated.

Only one of the four correlations between lag scores and Figure Choices (Early Slope) was significant at the 0·05 level so that, while a suggestion of a relationship worth following up in future research exists, caution is called for. Evidence linking lag and ability to extract items from context as in the Embedded-Figures Test was not obtained. This is in line with most previous findings and supports the discriminant validity of the lag scores. Furthermore, the present data offer little support for the hypothesis that lag is related to personality variables as measured by the Trait Rating Form.

Accuracy and Error scores. As noted above, the safest conclusion to be made from these and previously published results is that ranking Accuracy and lag are different variables, although somewhat correlated. The next question to be answered is: what is the nature of the process (or processes) reflected in the Accuracy and Error scores? The data in Tables 3 and 4 make clear the fact that Accuracy and Error, though not identical, measure something very similar. They were correlated -0.84 in the Squares Lag Test and -0.57 in the Dots Lag Test. Neither score showed statistically significant stability over tests (Table 5). A revision of the Dots Lag Test, with the stimulus series arranged more like that of the Squares Lag Test might increase the stability of these scores across the tests to an acceptable level.

Accuracy v. other variables. Accuracy appears to be related to general reasoning (Mathematics Aptitude Test) and possibly to perceptual speed and age, but not to verbal ability, sex, or academic performance. Table 6 shows that the Mathematics Aptitude Test was significantly correlated with both Accuracy and Error, positively with the former and negatively with the latter. French (1954) classified this test as one of general reasoning, but one is reluctant to interpret the present correlations as indicating that accuracy scores would load on that factor; more probably perceptual accuracy, or carefulness in performing tasks, contribute to both the Mathematics Aptitude and accuracy scores. It is tempting to interpret the near-significant correlations of age and perceptual speed with the accuracy scores, but in the interest of caution it is probably best to regard them as merely indicating a possible relationship worthy of further attention.

The question was raised earlier as to whether ranking accuracy represents an aspect of accuracy of perceiving, or a set such as perceptual criticalness or contrast. Table 6 contains the data relevant this question; none of the correlations is high enough to justify in conclusions, but several are statistically significant. The most striking feature of these correlations is that Accuracy was correlated positively and Error negatively with *all* scores (except $R+$ the Angles Test) of the Similarity–Difference Tests, both those

Table 6

Correlations of Accuracy and Error Scores with Ability Tests, Age, Sex, Academic Achievement and Cognitive Variables ($N = 196$)

Variable	Accuracy	Error	Variable	Accuracy	Error
Mathematics Aptitude	0·20	0·21	Similarity–Difference Tests[1]		
Advanced Vocabulary	0·03	0·05	Angles R+	−0·03	0·05
Perceptual Speed	0·14	−0·11	Angles D	0·11	0·02
Age	0·11	−0·13	Squares R+	0·15	−0·19
Sex	−0·01	0·05	Squares D	0·20	−0·12
Grade Point Average	0·05	−0·07	Total R+	0·10	−0·15
Alternative Expressions	0·12	−0·12	Total D	0·18	−0·08
Embedded Figures	0·16	−0·12	Estimation	0·10	−0·07
			Questionnaire	−0·01	0·09
			Figure Choices		

Note: Accuracy and Error are from Squares Lag Test. Correlations required for significance at the 0·05 and 0·01 levels: 0·14 and 0·19 respectively.

1. $R+$ is judgements correct; D is judgements 'different'.

designed to measure accuracy of perception and those reflecting consistent tendencies to judge stimuli to be different. This pattern included the Alternative Expressions Test *D*-score, and the Embedded Figures Test as well. It seems likely, considering all these results together, that both keenness of discrimination and set to respond 'different' to pairs of stimuli may contribute to Accuracy and Error, but do not account for a large proportion of the variance in ranking accuracy.

Accuracy was correlated with *n* Autonomy, and Error was correlated with *n* Autonomy and with *n* Impulsion, all significant at the 0·05 level, but none accounting for much variance. It is noteworthy that the correlations with *n* Autonomy represent a reversal of the findings of Klein (1951). There were no other significant correlations with personality variables, but in every case where there was a directional prediction from Klein's results, the direction was reversed in the present results. The correlations with *n* Autonomy and *n* Impulsion suggest again that accuracy represents acceptance of instructions and carefulness in performance. Considering the rather monotonous nature of the judgement tasks, which required prolonged and careful attention to detail, these significant correlations are not surprising. It would be of some interest to manipulate task variables such as adaptive consequences of perceptual accuracy and of task boredom as these affect relationships with personality variables.

One conclusion to be drawn from these data is that individual differences in lag or anticipation can be measured with high internal consistency using briefer procedures than the Holzman–Klein Schematizing Test. The new methods also provide moderately reliable measures of the ranking accuracy variable. However, further refinement of the tests and simpler scoring procedures are still desirable.

The major conclusion of this research is that 'leveling–sharpening' is badly in need of further analytical research and reformulation. It is doubtful that leveling–sharpening refers to a unitary dimension in behavior. Rather, it appears to comprise phenomena which are operationally complex and to involve a set of hypotheses so loosely formulated and interrelated as to compound the usual difficulties of operational specification and appraisal of validity for describing or predicting behavior.

Accuracy and lag tendencies do not share enough variance to be regarded as measures of the same dimension. Hence lumping these two measures together would appear to be illogical. Because only ranking accuracy, and not lag, showed any sign of correlating significantly with variables supposedly related to leveling–sharpening, the possibility exists that many previous findings reported in the literature were primarily attributable to accuracy and not to lag. In any event, some decision must be made concerning what is to be the referent of 'leveling–sharpening'. Further research will be required to determine which of the components is the most useful referent, considering all the ways these terms have been used in the past.

Research is needed to obtain better measures of the processes involved in Accuracy, and to explore the nature of the relation between Accuracy and Error. Research should also be aimed at explicating the relationship between lag and anchoring or frame of reference effects, a question raised by the present and previous data. The similarities between these two groups of phenomena are compelling, and in fact the terms 'assimilation' and 'contrast' have been used to describe anchoring effects, although with different operational referents than those given these terms by the Menninger group (cf. Sherif and Hovland, 1961).

The hypothesis that leveling–sharpening cognitive styles relate substantially to major personality variables is not unequivocally established. In the present study, the suggestion is that most of the previously reported relationships may possibly involve accuracy, but not lag, and some of them may not be in the direction predicted by Holzman and Klein. In any case, further studies of correlations between accuracy and/or lag and personality tendencies need to make use of multiple indicants of the personality variables involved, as well as experimental manipulation of such factors as the adaptive consequences of accuracy, the role of boredom, and other influences upon the social psychology of the assessee (cf. Riecken, 1962).

Although the results of this research are discouraging to the view either that leveling–sharpening is a unitary dimension or that it enjoys substantial correlations with personality variables, much more research needs to be done before efforts to understand it can be justifiably abandoned. The ubiquity of behavior like leveling and sharpening in studies of memory (Allport, 1930; Wulf, 1938), judgement (Sherif and Hovland, 1961) and rumor (Allport and Postman, 1958), suggest that with further operational clarification some variable or variables like leveling and sharpening will prove to be of value in psychology. What is important is to demand that care in development of experimental measures keep pace with theory and to determine the nature of the basic processes involved before putting so much emphasis on the correlates of a putative variable which is itself so little understood. The concept 'leveling–sharpening' like any other, must have some fairly clear referent if interest in its relationship to other concepts is to be justified.

References

ALLPORT, G. W. (1930), 'Change and decay in the visual memory image', *Brit. J. Psychol.*, vol. 21, pp. 138–48.

ALLPORT, G. W., and POSTMAN, L. (1958), 'The basic psychology of rumor', in E. E. Maccoby, T. M. Newcomb and E. L. Hartley (eds.), *Readings in Social Psychology*, Holt, Rinehart & Winston.

BARRON, F. (1953), 'Complexity–simplicity as a personality dimension', *J. abnorm. soc. Psychol.*, vol. 48, pp. 163–72.

BARRON, F. (1955), 'The disposition towards originality', *J. abnorm. soc. Psychol.*, vol. 51, pp. 478–85.

BARRON, F., and WELSH, G. S. (1952), 'Artistic perception as a factor in personality style: its measurement by a figure-preference test', *J. Psychol.*, vol. 33, pp. 199–203.

BOLLES, R., and MESSICK, S. (1958), 'Statistical utility in experimental inference', *Psychol. Rep.*, vol. 4, pp. 223–7.

CAMPBELL, D. T., and FISKE, D. W. (1959), 'Convergent and discriminant validation in the multitrait-multimethod matrix', *Psychol. Bull.*, vol. 56, pp. 81–105.

CRONBACH, L. J., and MEEHL, P. E. (1955), 'Construct validity in psychological tests', *Psychol. Bull.*, vol. 52, pp. 281–302.

FREDERIKSEN, N., and MESSICK, S. J. (1959), 'Response set as a measure of personality', *Educ. psychol. Measmt*, vol. 19, pp. 137–57.

FRENCH, J. W. (ed.) (1954), *Manual for Kit of Selected Tests for Reference Aptitude and Achievement Factors*, Educational Testing Service.

GARDNER, R. W., and LOHRENZ, L. J. (1960), 'Leveling–sharpening and serial reproduction of a story', *Bull. Menninger Clin.*, vol. 24, pp. 295–304.

GARDNER, R. W., JACKSON, D. N., and MESSICK, S. J. (1960), 'Personality organization in cognitive controls and intellectual abilities', *Psychol. Issues*, vol. 2, no. 8.

Other Cognitive Styles

GARDNER, R. W., HOLZMAN, P. S., KLEIN, G. S., LINTON, H. B., and SPENCE, D. P. (1959), 'Cognitive control: a study of individual consistencies in cognitive behavior', *Psychol. Issues*, vol. 1, no. 4.

GUILFORD, J. P., and ZIMMERMAN, W. S. (1947), *Guilford–Zimmerman Aptitude Survey*, Sheridan Supply Co.

HOLLINGWORTH, H. S. (1913), 'Experimental studies in judgment', *Arch. Psychol.*, vol. 29, pp. 44–52.

HOLZMAN, P. S. (1954), 'The relations of assimilation tendencies in visual, auditory, and kinesthetic time-error to cognitive attitudes of leveling and sharpening', *J. Personal.*, vol. 22, pp. 375–94.

HOLZMAN, P. S., and GARDNER, R. W. (1959), 'Leveling and repression', *J. abnorm. soc. Psychol.*, vol. 59, pp. 151–5.

HOLZMAN, P. S., and GARDNER, R. W. (1960), 'Leveling–sharpening and memory organization', *J. abnorm. Psychol.*, vol. 61, pp. 176–80.

HOLZMAN, P. S., and KLEIN, G. S. (1950), 'The schematizing process: perceptual attitudes and personality qualities in sensitivity to change', *Amer. Psychol.*, vol. 5, p. 312 (abstract).

HOLZMAN, P. S., and KLEIN, G. S. (1951), 'Perceptual attitudes of "leveling" and "sharpening": relation to individual differences in time error', *Amer. Psychol.*, vol. 6, p. 257 (abstract).

HOLZMAN, P. S., and KLEIN, G. S. (1954), 'Cognitive system-principles of leveling and sharpening: individual differences in assimilation effects in visual time-error', *J. Psychol.*, vol. 37, pp. 105–22.

JACKSON, D. N., MESSICK, S., and MYERS, C. T. (1964), 'Evaluation of group and individual embedded figures measures of field independence', *Educ. psychol. Measmt*, vol. 24, pp. 177–92.

KLEIN, G. S. (1951), 'The personal world through perception', in R. R. Blake and G. V. Ramsey (eds.), *Perception: An Approach to Personality*, Ronald Press.

KOFFKA, K. (1935), *Principles of Gestalt Psychology*, Harcourt, Brace.

KRATHWOHL, D. R., and CRONBACH, L. J. (1956), 'Suggestions regarding a possible measure of personality: the squares test', *Educ. psychol. Measmt*, vol. 16, pp. 305–16.

LACHMANN, F. M., LAPKIN, B., and HANDELMAN, N. S. (1962), 'The recall of dreams: its relation to repression and cognitive controls', *J. abnorm. soc. Psychol.*, vol. 64, pp. 160–62.

LOEVINGER, J. (1957), 'Objective tests as instruments of psychological theory', *Psychol. Rep.*, vol. 3, pp. 635–95.

MURNEY, R. J. (1955), An investigation of the cognitive system-principles of leveling and sharpening and their relationship to selected personality variables, *Ph.D. Dissertation, Catholic University Press*.

PETTIGREW, T. F. (1958), 'The measurement and correlates of category width as a cognitive variable', *J. Personal.*, vol. 26, pp. 532–44. [See Reading 6.]

RIECKEN, H. A. (1962), 'A program of research on experiments in social psychology', in N. F. Washburne (ed.), *Decisions, Values, and Groups*, vol. 2, Pergamon Press, pp. 25–41.

SECHREST, L., and JACKSON, D. N. (1961), 'Social intelligence and accuracy in interpersonal predictions', *J. Personal.*, vol. 29, pp. 167–82.

SHERIF, M., and HOVLAND, C. I. (1961), *Social Judgment*, Yale University Press.

TEAR, D. G., and GUTHRIE, G. M. (1955), 'The relationship of cooperation to the sharpening–leveling continuum', *J. soc. Psychol.*, vol. 42, pp. 203–8.

THURSTONE, L. L. (1944), *A Factorial Study of Perception*, University of Chicago Press.

VICK, O. C., and JACKSON, D. N. (1964), Leveling–sharpening as a cognitive style: appraisal of alternative methods of measurement, *Research Bulletin, Stanford University*.

WITKIN, H. A. (1950), 'The perception of the upright', *Sci. Amer.*, vol. 200, pp. 50–56.

WITKIN, H. A., DYK, R. B., FATERSON, H. F., GOODENOUGH, D. R., and KARP, S. A. (1962), *Psychological Differentiation*, Wiley.

WITKIN, H. A., LEWIS, H. B., HERTZMAN, M., MACHOVER, K., MEISSNER, P. B., and WAPNER, S. (1954), *Personality through Perception*, Harper.

WULF, F. (1938), 'Tendencies in figural variation', in W. D. Ellis (ed.), *A Source Book of Gestalt Psychology*, Routledge & Kegan Paul. (A translation of parts of F. Wulf, 'Über die Veränderungen von Vorstellen (Gedächtnis und Gestalt)', *Psychol. Forsch.*, vol. 1, 1922, pp. 333–73.)

Part Six Studies of Interpersonal Behaviour

The previous five Parts of this book have dealt with particular styles of information processing and with some structural interpretations of these styles. The remaining Parts each look at how these stylistic and structural interpretations have been applied in different areas of psychology.

In Part Six are presented two studies of interpersonal behaviour. These illustrate clearly how social activities are mediated by group members' cognitive habits. In Reading 15 by Stager it is shown that group structure, role differentiation, information search, and so on are dependent upon members' integrative complexity. A related paper by Streufert (1966) shows how this same information-processing characteristic partly determines subjects' reactions to deviant and conforming group members. In Reading 16 Steiner and Johnson examine the relationship between category width and social conformity, taking as their starting point the assumption that people who employ wide categories should see little difference between their own views and the divergent opinions of respected associates.

Reference

STREUFERT, S. (1966), 'Conceptual structure, communicator importance and interpersonal attitudes toward conforming and deviant group members', *J. Personal. soc. Psychol.*, vol. 4, pp. 100–103.

15 Paul Stager

Conceptual Level as a Composition Variable in Small-Group Decision Making

Excerpts from Paul Stager, 'Conceptual level as a composition variable in small-group decision making', *Journal of Personality and Social Psychology*, vol. 5, 1967, pp. 152–61.

Small groups active in the decision-making process are concerned with the three distinct but interrelated functions of information acquisition, information processing and subsequent decision making. The effectiveness of the decision-making process in the groups would seem to depend upon the quality of the differentiated component processes and the degree to which the three functions are integrated within the groups.

There is considerable evidence in the small-group literature (Bass, 1960; Collins and Guetzkow, 1964; Steiner, 1964) that heterogeneity of group composition may in some instances facilitate and, in others, be detrimental to the integration of group processes. The level of performance on certain tasks is frequently a function of the extent to which group processes are integrated. The effect of group composition on performance is dependent upon the type of situation or task confronting the groups and upon the composition variables. There is a definite interaction effect between personality and situational variables. Both sets of variables act as intervening variables in mediating human performance and have been viewed as variable 'complexes' (Ware, 1964).

One critical personality and composition variable which has been shown to be a determinant of performance in decision-making tasks is the conceptual level dimension (Schroder, Driver and Streufert, 1967); this dimension describes the integrative complexity of a group member's conceptual structure. The term conceptual structure refers to a set of cognitive mediating links which produce a relatively stable group of techniques by which the individual receives, processes, and transmits information. The integrative complexity of the conceptual structure is a function of the number of dimensions along which stimuli are ordered, the number of different schemata with which the perceived dimensions of information are organized and the complexity of the organization. Individuals whose information processing is characterized by the use of few dimensions of information and few or fixed schemata in a given domain are described as having a *low conceptual level*; individuals who typically perceive many dimensions of information and utilize many alternate combinatory schemata are described as having a *high conceptual level*. Although the level of information processing tends to increase with an increase in the level of conceptual structure, the former can vary as a function of various forms of environmental stress.

The previous studies which have used conceptual level as a composition variable (Stager and Kennedy, 1965; Tuckman, 1964, 1966) focused primarily upon group performance rather than group processes. Since there is an interaction effect between personality or composition variables and situational variables, it becomes necessary to examine differences in group processes when considering performance differences. Tuckman (1966) has attempted to relate the composition variable, heterogeneity, to group performance. The manner in which composition heterogeneity affects group processes, however, remains to be clarified. If certain task situations require decision-making groups to structure themselves in certain ways, then it is necessary to know what type of group information-processing structures will emerge in given group compositions. [. . .]

The present study was directed toward differences in group functioning in an attempt to relate the conceptual level dimension to the emergent group information-processing structures and the characteristic predecisional subprocesses. Four specific hypotheses, derived from conceptual systems theory (Schroder, Driver and Streufert, 1967), are presented in the following paragraphs.

Hypotheses

Hypothesis I. With an increase in the *percentage of members of a high conceptual level* in the group, there is an increase in the role flexibility or, conversely, a decrease in structuring and more functional role uncertainty.

Theoretically, high conceptual level members are able to cope with a higher level of uncertainty in their environment and are more adaptable to environmental demands than low conceptual level members. Whereas high conceptual level members may be aware of considerable uncertainty in a situation, without attempting to increase the amount of structuring (reduce uncertainty – Sieber and Lanzetta, 1964), low conceptual level members tend to simplify and structure their environment; for example, groups homogeneously composed of low conceptual level members form hierarchical group structures (Tuckman, 1964). In groups comprised of members with different levels of conceptual structure (heterogeneous groups), clearly defined boundaries between subgroups or parts are likely to develop. If differentiation occurs on the basis of functional roles or task boundaries, heterogeneous groups should be characterized by a high degree of functional role centrality (Hutte, 1965), particularly when there is a low percentage of members of a high conceptual level in the group. The uncertainty in the functional role structure (the amount of uncertainty in the group information-processing structure), therefore, was predicted to increase as the percentage of high conceptual level members in the group increased.

Hypothesis II. Groups in which the members are all of a high conceptual level (100 per cent) generate more interpersonal (substantive) conflict than groups in which the members differ in conceptual level.

Individuals of a high conceptual level characteristically generate diversity and conflict in their processing of information (Schroder, Driver and Streufert, 1967). For high conceptual level group members, '... reality is defined as being possessed of multiple alternatives and hence diversity is sought as a means of enhancing validation' (Schroder and Harvey, 1963, p. 150). Similarly, Bennis and Shepard (1956) have noted that in groups which are advanced in their development conflict is undisturbingly present; conflict is generated from a delineation of substantive issues.

Hypothesis III. The extent to which generated conflict is utilized in the synthesis of decisions increases with an increasing percentage of members of a high conceptual level in the group. With an increasing percentage of high conceptual level members, there is increasingly more synthesizing of generated alternatives and evaluating of alternatives in the predecisional phase.

The second and third hypotheses are interdependent since the capacity to synthesize alternatives is concomitant with the capacity to cope with diversity and conflict in the generation of alternatives. Although low conceptual level members may generate numerous essentially unrelated alternatives, they are not able to evaluate them as extensively as the high members. Since the former are less sensitive to the extent to which diversity is being generated, in groups with low percentages of members of a high conceptual level, diversity and conflict are less likely to be maintained at optimal levels. In other words, there is likely to be a super-optimal level of diversity with little integration or evaluation of discrepant information. When groups are functioning at a higher conceptual level, they act as effective integrative instruments (Martin and Hill, 1957), in which there is utilization of differences and collaboration among members (Hearn, 1955). Schroder and Harvey (1963) have stated that group functioning, at a high conceptual level, is characterized by a consensus which is the result of rational discussion rather than a compulsive attempt at unanimity.

In groups comprised of predominantly low conceptual level members, the development of a hierarchical group structure prevents fluidity of the functional role structure and minimizes the possibility of there being conflicting and divergent alternatives generated, or at least evaluated. Moreover, since low conceptual level members, unlike high level members, are not characterized by the ability to make multiple discriminations or to assume different perspectives in regard to give discrepant units of information, the prediction was made that evaluation and synthesis would characterize the participation of high conceptual level members.

Hypothesis IV. The extent of search for novel information increases as the percentage of members of a high conceptual level in the group increases, whereas total information search is not dependent upon group composition.

Since high conceptual level members are able to cope with more uncertainty, to generate additional information from that already in memory storage, and to utilize a more complex dimensional structure in the perception of the environment (Schroder, Driver and Streufert, 1967), the assumption was made that groups with a higher percentage of high conceptual level members would exhibit less extensive searching for other than specifically novel information.

Lanzetta (1963) has explored the relationship between environmental uncertainty and information-search behavior, suggesting that information search is elicited by a response conflict engendered by response uncertainty; the greater the degree of uncertainty, the stronger is the conflict and the stronger the instigation to search. Intuitively, it would seem that individuals seek information until they reach some optimal level of uncertainty, at which they make a decision, the level being a function of the level of initial uncertainty, the rate of uncertainty reduction, and the level of conceptual structure. The inability of low conceptual level members to cope with higher levels of uncertainty would tend to require more extensive information search before decisions could be made [. . .]

Method

Subjects

Subjects were eighty male university undergraduate and graduate students. The subjects were selected from among approximately 500 volunteers on the basis of the measures subsequently described.

Subject selection

The subjects were administered the following tests:

1. The Paragraph Completion Test of Conceptual Level (Schroder, Driver and Streufert, 1967). The Paragraph Completion Test is a projective test of several sentence stems designed for the assessment of the level of conceptual structure. On the basis of previously acquired norms, subjects were classified as low in the level of conceptual structure if they obtained scores of 3 or less, and high in the level of conceptual structure if they obtained scores which were greater than 7.

2. The *n* Dominance scale of the Edwards Personal Preference Schedule (Edwards, 1959). The need for dominance items reflects

the desire to be a leader, to give advice, to make decisions, and to defend one's own position. For purposes of comparison, the scale was administered in the same form as used by Tuckman (1966); in order to reduce the visibility of the scale, it was given with the n Affiliation scale of the Edwards Personal Preference Schedule, and the items from the two scales were interspersed. n Dominance scores were converted to quartile scores, based on norms derived from a sample of approximately 200 individuals; subjects were classified as *high* on n Dominance if they scored in the highest quartile, *intermediate* if they scored in either of the two intermediate quartiles, and *low* if they scored in the lowest quartile. This breakdown was used since the research design required half of the subjects to be intermediate on this measure, with half of the remaining subjects high and the other half low.

Group composition

Those subjects classified as high or low in the level of conceptual structure were considered for further selection; all others were rejected. There was no difference in the levels of intelligence, as measured by the Wonderlic Personnel Test, between the high and low conceptual level subjects. The subjects were further subdivided into high, intermediate and low n Dominance groupings. Twenty four-man groups were composed to yield four combinations of conceptual level. Each of the four combinations was represented by five groups. The group compositions were defined with respect to the dimension of an increasing percentage of members of a high conceptual level in the group. The homogeneous composition comprised four members who were of an equally high conceptual level (100 per cent). The other types of composition comprised groups in which three, two or one of the members, in each type of composition respectively, had a high level of conceptual structure. The groups, therefore, were considered as being equally spaced along this dimension. The 100 per cent group was homogeneous in composition and the 25, 50 and 75 per cent groups were heterogeneous with respect to the conceptual level dimension. Member n Dominance was controlled by systematically varying the distribution of high, intermediate and low n Dominance members across members of each group composition. Each group comprised one high, one low and two intermediate n

Dominance members. In each instance, at least one of the high conceptual level members in the group was of intermediate n Dominance. Groups were matched, as closely as possible, on intelligence.

Experimental decision environment

Each group participated in a complex simulated tactical decision-making situation (Streufert *et al.*, 1965). The groups were confronted with a model of an island which they were to assume was held by an enemy force of unknown strength and location. Acting as four members of equal status on a military field staff, they were instructed to engage the enemy and to secure the island. The groups received information about the enemy movements and the effects of their own decisions by providing for acquisition of such information through the deployment of their own forces. Responses to their decisions were provided by a preprogrammed input (Karlins, Schroder and Streufert, 1965), which was perceived by the groups as realistically dynamic and responsive. The fixed-input program was initially designed for the purpose of providing a controlled and standardized input of information to subjects participating in the tactical situation. The duration of the tactical decision situation comprised seven half-hour periods.

Coding and rating scales

Preceding the experiment, a coding scheme was derived and found, after continuous refinement, to yield reliable functional categorization of individual and group behaviour. The final coding and rating scheme was prepared in the form of a manual which could be used by the observers.

Verbal behavior of the groups was coded according to the predefined catories of perceiving and proposing the problem, requesting information, supplying information, suggesting alternatives, evaluating alternatives, autocratically deciding, and confirming decisions through consensus. Each category was considered as a functional role in the decision-making process; scoring, therefore, was concerned with the changes of a group member from one role to another. In order to provide additional analysis, the frequencies with which (a) new or novel information search was requested, (b) different alternatives were proposed or

(c) evaluations of different alternatives were given, while members were in the respective functional roles, were noted.

Groups were rated with respect to their utilization or synthesizing of conflicting alternatives, the degree to which interpersonal conflict was present, and the number of effective communication channels which were available to the group members (i.e. communication complexity).

The reliability of coding and rating, across all of the measures, was determined by computing the Pearson product-moment correlation coefficient of the independent assessments. The reliabilities, based on the assessments of two trained observers, ranged between 0·79 and 0·96 for the first eleven experimental groups. The median reliability coefficient, 0·91, was taken as justification for the assumption that observations by a single observer would be reliable for the remaining nine groups. Although both observers were aware of the theoretical assumptions, the fact that one observer was not informed of the group composition and the rapidity with which the coding had to be done were assumed to minimize confounding between assessments and the group composition variables.

Assessment of group structure

Two methods were used to assess the structuring which emerged in the different group compositions. *Group information-processing structure* was construed in terms of the amount of uncertainty, existing within the group, with respect to the frequency with which the different group members tended to perform various decision-making functions (i.e. assume different functional roles). The group information-processing structure, construed in this manner, was tractable by the information measure of uncertainty (H). If it is assumed that the different functional roles represent different categories of events, then by noting the frequency with which the different functional roles are assumed, a frequency or probability distribution for the categories can be generated. The uncertainty involved in the distribution is obtained by applying the Shannon measure of average information (see Garner, 1962). The formula for computing the average information is as follows:

$$H = -\sum^{i} p_i \log p_i.$$

In the formula, i represents any one of the individual alternatives (functional roles) available. Maximum uncertainty for any distribution occurs when all categories are associated with equal probabilities. In reference to the total group uncertainty, the uncertainty or H value for each member's participation can be determined and then summed with the H values for the other members, thus providing a total H value for the group. A higher value of H for a group would be obtained when the members tend to exhibit 'flexibility' by assuming different roles at different times in sequential decision making. Groups, alternatively, could reduce the amount of uncertainty in their information-processing structure, or interpersonal environment, by organizing into a decision-making structure in which the different members assume different functional roles consistently. It is important to note, at this point, that the uncertainty involved in a member's participation resides not in the transmitter (the member concerned), but in the receivers (the remaining group members and the external observer); the computed uncertainty for a given member's participation may not correspond to his subjective uncertainty. The latter assumption is not critical, however, in the present conceptualization.

The first measure applied to the data concerning group participation was, therefore, the Shannon measure of uncertainty. The second measure was the role-centrality index which has previously been described by Hutte (1965). The centrality index is a value, between 1 and 0, which indicates the extent to which only one member assumes a given functional role (indicated by an index value of 1), or all of the members assume a given functional role equally often (indicated by an index value of 0). The degree of role centrality is determined by applying the formula,

$$C = \frac{(t-1)d_h - (d_{h-1} + d_{h-2} + d_{h-3})}{(t-1)D},$$

where t is the total number of group members, D is the total number of contributions in the decision category (or functional role) concerned, d_h is the number of contributions by the most active member (i.e. the highest score) and d_{h-1} represents the second highest score. For each group, the centrality indexes for each functional role were summed across the different roles, thus yielding a *total structural index*.

Procedure

Each of the twenty four-man groups participated in the tactical decision-making situation with the assumption that the enemy was represented by another group. The group interaction, generated by the task, was tape-recorded and observed through one-way observation screens. The members' participation was recorded by means of individual throat microphones connected to separate tape recorders. During the three-and-a-half-hour session, the group interaction was coded continuously according to the described categories or functional roles. Groups were rated, at the end of each half-hour session, on the behaviors previously listed. Each of the orders drafted and submitted by the groups was retained for further analysis.

Results

Group structuring

Figure 1 presents the mean values of the total group uncertainty H for each type of group composition. An analysis of variance indicated that the composition effect was significant ($F = 12.9$, $df = 3, 16, p < 0.001$); the increase in H, with an increasing percentage of members of a high conceptual level, was significantly linear (with a trend analysis yielding $F = 37.3$, $df = 1, 16$, $p < 0.001$). The trend analysis applied to the data assumed equal distances between the different compositions. The assumption is defensible since the different compositions were derived by replacing one additional low conceptual level member with one high conceptual level member at successive intervals along the group-composition dimension. Figure 1 also presents the mean values of the total structural index. As illustrated, the uncertainty measure H and the structural index appear to provide comparable assessments of the degree of group structuring. The composition effects were significant ($F = 4.5$, $df = 3, 16, p < 0.05$), the increase in group structuring (as measured by the structural index), with an increasing percentage of high conceptual level members also being significantly linear ($F = 17.6$, $df = 1, 16, p < 0.001$). Total group structuring, as reflected in the total structural index, correlated significantly ($p < 0.01$, $df = 18$, one-tailed test) with group uncertainty H ($r = -0.62$). The latter correlation provides a more accurate representation of the relationship between group uncertainty and the total structural index than Figure 1 itself. The points plotted in Figure 1 are, as indicated, based on means of five

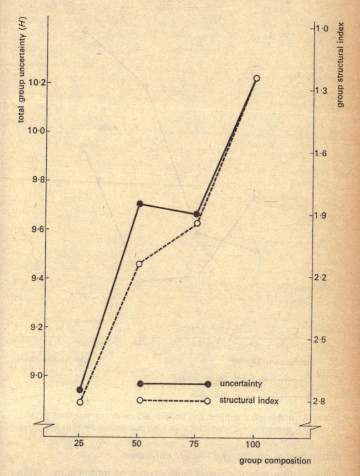

Figure 1 Group uncertainty (H) and structural index as functions of an increasing percentage of members of a high conceptual level in the group

groups each and are intentionally scaled to correspond as closely as possible, in order to emphasize the comparable trends which were observed in the data.

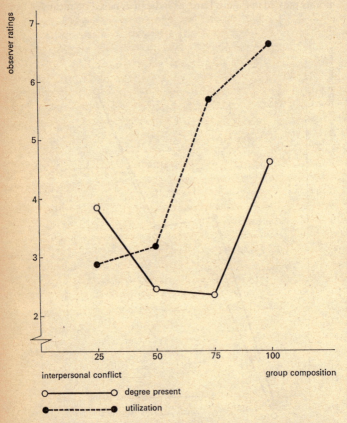

Figure 2 Interpersonal conflict and conflict utilization as functions of an increasing percentage of members of a high conceptual level in the group

Interpersonal conflict and conflict utilization

Composition means derived from ratings of interpersonal (substantive) conflict and utilizations of conflict in the synthesis of decisions are presented in Figure 2. The degree of interpersonal conflict present in the group interaction was curvilinearly related to group composition (a quadratic trend analysis yielding a significant $F = 13 \cdot 0$, $df = 1$, 16, $p < 0 \cdot 01$); the rated utilization of generated conflict increased linearly (linear trend analysis $F = 66 \cdot 3$, $df = 1$, 16, $p < 0 \cdot 001$) with an increase in the percentage of highs in the group. An analysis of variance indicated that the composition effects for interpersonal conflict were significant ($F = 4 \cdot 7$, $df = 3$, 16, $p < 0 \cdot 05$); the homogeneous (100 per cent highs) groups generated significantly more conflict ($p < 0 \cdot 05$ in a *post hoc* comparison of means) than any of the other compositions. Similarly, composition effects, with respect to the utilization of generated conflict were significant ($F = 23 \cdot 8$, $df = 3$, 16, $p < 0 \cdot 01$).

Generation of suggestions or alternatives did not vary significantly with different group compositions; the number of evaluations, however, and hence, the ratio of suggestions to evaluations (S/E), was subject to composition effects (Figure 3). Analysis of variance yielded a significant F in both instances (evaluations, $F = 3 \cdot 4$, $df = 3$, 16, $p < 0 \cdot 05$; S/E ratio, $F = 15 \cdot 9$, $df = 3$, 16, $p < 0 \cdot 01$). A trend analysis indicated that the S/E ratio involved both linear and quadratic components ($Fs = 135 \cdot 0$, $8 \cdot 3$, $df = 1$, 16, $p < 0 \cdot 01$, $p < 0 \cdot 025$, respectively); the number of evaluations increased linearly ($F = 9 \cdot 9$, $df = 1$, 16, $p < 0 \cdot 01$).

Figure 3 also illustrates the linear increase in the complexity of group communication (linear trend $F = 10 \cdot 1$, $df = 1$, 16, $p < 0 \cdot 01$) that occurred as the proportion of highs in the group increased. Rated communication complexity or, alternatively, openness of communication channels, correlated significantly ($p < 0 \cdot 01$, $df = 18$) with the rated utilization of generated conflict ($r = 0 \cdot 95$), the S/E ratio ($r = -0 \cdot 67$) and the number of evaluations made by the group ($r = 0 \cdot 53$). Total group structuring (structural index) also correlated significantly ($p < 0 \cdot 01$, $df = 18$, one-tailed test) with the S/E ratio ($r = 0 \cdot 59$) and the rated utilization of conflict ($r = -0 \cdot 63$). The partial correlation coefficient for group structure (structural index) and the S/E ratio, with the effect of communication removed, was not significant. A variance interpretation of the coefficients indicated that some 86 per cent of the association of the latter three variables resulted from the effect of communication. Communication ratings

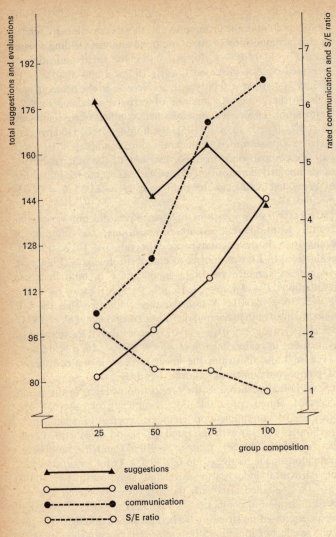

Figure 3 The effect of an increasing percentage of members of a high conceptual level in the group on the generation of alternatives, evaluation of alternatives, communication complexity and S/E ratio

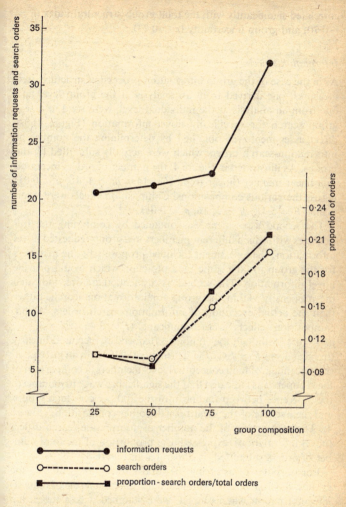

Figure 4 Information requests, search orders and proportion of search orders for novel information as functions of an increasing percentage of members of a high conceptual level in the group

correlated significantly with the total group structural index ($r = -0.70$) and group uncertainty ($r = 0.73$).

Information search

As in the case of the group information-processing structure, two measures, one derived from an analysis at the group level and one from an analysis at the individual level, were used to assess group search for specifically novel information (Figure 4). A direct assessment was obtained by determining the number of information-search orders which were actually submitted by the groups. As illustrated in Figure 4, the number of orders increased in a linear manner (linear trend $F = 14.0$, $df = 1, 16$, $p < 0.01$) across the various compositions. Composition effects were significant ($F = 5.41$, $df = 3, 16$, $p < 0.01$).

The second assessment was obtained by combining the frequencies with which different members in a group requested novel information; the assessment included proposals by the members for the group to take some kind of action which would provide novel information. The second assessment, therefore, indicated the propensity within the group for information search, rather than the actual execution of information-search orders. Again, composition effects were significant ($F = 3.46$, $df = 3, 16$, $p < 0.05$). Although the combined frequencies increased linearly (trend analysis $F = 7.4$, $df = 1, 16$, $p < 0.025$) with an increase in the percentage of high conceptual level members, a comparison of the group means indicated that the significance was attributable to the difference between the mean of the 100 per cent high groups and the average of the means for the other compositions (Figure 4). The relationship of the number of information-search orders (novel information), expressed as a proportion of the total number of orders submitted, is illustrated in Figure 4.

For purposes of assessing the total information search in the groups, the frequencies, with which the functional role of requesting information was assumed, were summed across the group members; no significant differences between the various compositions were obtained.

Discussion

The results confirmed the hypothesis (I) that group structuring and role differentiation decrease with an increase in the percentage of high conceptual level members in the group. Since the focus of the present study was upon group processes, the relation of the observed group functioning to group performance is uncertain. French (1951), however, noted that equal participation of group members was positively related to group performance; a negative relationship existed between the degree of centralization and the level of performance. Similarly, Hutte (1965) has recently reported that groups performed more effectively when there was less leadership in regard to decision making.

Guetzkow's (1960) analysis of role differentiation and emergence of interlocking structures was based upon research involving communication nets. Effective performance in the various communication designs required role differentiation and, more importantly, the development of an interlocking organizational structure in the system, but, as Hutte has pointed out, the communication net research has been characterized by a topological channeling of information – a factor which was not present in the approach taken by Hutte or the present study and which may be one determinant of performance differences.

The underlying point here, then, is that different environments or task situations require different structural responses with respect to group organization. Granting that the task demands of the environment partially determine the structuring of the group, the present results suggest that the conceptual level of the group members is probably a limiting factor. The need for a low level of uncertainty, on the part of low conceptual level members in a complex environment, is reflected in the reduction of uncertainty with respect to differentiation and centralization of functional roles. The structural response may, then, be one source of personality-situation interaction effects.

The results of the present study confirmed the hypothesis (II) that groups in which all of the members are of a high conceptual level generate more interpersonal conflict than groups in which the members differ in conceptual level. Although there was a curvilinear relationship between generated conflict and the conceptual level dimension, the high levels of conflict represented by the end points of the curve appeared to be related to different processes. In the 100 per cent high groups, the level of conflict was a function of the extensive evaluation of alternatives; although there was an *initial* increase in the level of conflict when members attempted to support their proposals, extensive evaluation was conducive to conflict resolution. The conflict in the 25 per cent high groups, on the other hand, was a function of the diversity generated; conflict resolution was attempted through persistent efforts on the part of the members to have their respective proposals accepted. The various alternatives were seldom assessed by other members or by the members responsible for them. Since the levels of conflict in the two different groups were similar but functions of different processes, differences in the extent to which the interpersonal conflict is utilized in decision making would not be unexpected (Hypothesis III).

The process of synthesizing or integrating perhaps relevant but discrepant information would seemingly have to be preceded by the process of evaluation. The increase in evaluation, which occurred with a decrease in group structuring, was paralleled by a linear increase in the group communication-channel complexity. A multichanneled communication network would be expected to facilitate reciprocal evaluation. Communication complexity consistently correlated highly with the rated utilization of conflicting information, the frequency of evaluation, and (negatively) with the S/E ratio. Although group structuring also correlated highly with these variables, the association was primarily attributable to the effects of communication complexity. It would seem that flexibility in performing different functions is a necessary but not a sufficient requirement for effective decision making; an openness to multiple sources of information is required on the part of each group member.

Another factor, which could be involved in the decrease of the S/E ratio with an increase in the proportion of highs, is the tendency of low conceptual level members to consider single rather than multiple alternatives, particularly under various stress conditions. This type of information processing provides a means of simplifying a situation to the point where it is possible for some action to be taken.

The hypothesis (IV) that the extent of novel information search increases with an increase in the proportion of highs in the group, was confirmed by the results. (See also Suedfeld and Streufert, 1966.) The increase in the proportion of information-search orders clearly paralleled the increase in the absolute number of search orders. Since the total number of decision orders did not significantly vary with group composition, a lower proportion of search orders for novel information would possibly indicate that the respective groups were more redundant in their search and retaliatory in their decisions; in other words, with a decrease in the percentage of members of a high conceptual level in the groups, there was a decrease in the use of long-range strategies. Informal observations would seem to be consistent with this interpretation.

References

BASS, B. M. (1960), *Leadership, Psychology, and Organizational Behavior*, Harper.

BENNIS, E. G., and SHEPARD, H. A. (1956), 'A theory of group development', *Hum. Rel.*, vol. 9, pp. 415–37.

COLLINS, B. E., and GUETZKOW, H. (1964), *A Social Psychology of Group Processes for Decision-Making*, Wiley.

EDWARDS, A. L. (1959), *Edwards Personal Preference Schedule*, Psychological Corporation.

FRENCH, J. R. P. (1951), 'Group productivity', in H. Guetzkow (ed.), *Groups, Leadership, and Men*, Carnegie Institute of Technology Press, pp. 44–54.

GARNER, W. R. (1962), *Uncertainty and Structure as Psychological Concepts*, Wiley.

GUETZKOW, H. (1960), 'Differentiation of roles in task-oriented groups', in D. Cartwright and A. Zander (eds.), *Group Dynamics: Research and Theory*, Row, Peterson, pp. 683–704.

HEARN, G. (1963), The process of group development, Cassidy Lecture, University of Toronto. (Cited in O. J. Harvey, ed., *Motivation and Social Interaction: Cognitive Determinants*, Ronald Press, 1963, p. 150.)

HUTTE, H. (1965), 'Decision-taking in a management game', *Hum. Rel.*, vol. 18, pp. 5–20.

KARLINS, M., SCHRODER, H. M., and STREUFERT, S. (1965), 'Controlled input program for a tactical war game', *American Documentation Institute*, no. 8621, Washington.

LANZETTA, J. T. (1963), 'Information acquisition in decision making', in O. J. Harvey (ed.), *Motivation and Social Interaction: Cognitive Determinants*, Ronald Press, pp. 239–65.

MARTIN, E., and HILL, W. F. (1957), 'Toward a theory of group development: six phases of therapy group development', *Intern. J. group Psychother.*, no. 1. (Cited in O. J. Harvey, ed., *Motivation and Social Interaction: Cognitive Determinants*, Ronald Press, p. 149.)

SCHRODER, H. M., DRIVER, M. J., and STREUFERT, S. (1967), *Human Information Processing*, Holt, Rinehart & Winston. [See Reading 9.]

SCHRODER, H. M., and HARVEY, O. J. (1963), 'Conceptual organization and group structure', in O. J. Harvey (ed.), *Motivation and Social Interaction: Cognitive Determinants*, Ronald Press, pp. 134–66.

SIEBER, J. E., and LANZETTA, J. T. (1964), 'Conflict and conceptual structure as determinants of decision-making behavior', *J. Personal.*, vol. 32, pp. 622–41.

STAGER, P., and KENNEDY, J. L. (1965), Decision making and performance in heterogeneous and homogeneous groups, *Technical Report, Office of Naval Research, Princeton University*, no. 6.

STEINER, I. D. (1964), 'Group dynamics', *Ann. Rev. Psychol.*, vol. 15, pp. 421–46.

STREUFERT, S., CLARDY, M. A., DRIVER, M. J., KARLINS, M., SCHRODER, H. M., and SUEDFELD, P. A. (1965), 'A tactical game for the analysis of complex decision making in individuals and groups', *Psychol. Rep.*, vol. 17, pp. 723–9.

SUEDFELD, P., and STREUFERT, S. (1966), 'Information search as a function of conceptual and environmental complexity', *Psychonom. Sci.*, vol. 4, pp. 351–2.

TUCKMAN, B. W. (1964), 'Personality structure, group composition, and group functioning', *Sociometry*, vol. 27, pp. 469–87.

TUCKMAN, B. W. (1966), The effects of group composition and task differences on group performance, *Paper Read at Eastern Psychological Association, New York*.

WARE, C. T., JR (1964), 'Individual and situational variables affecting human performance', *Hum. Fact.*, vol. 6, pp. 673–4.

16 Ivan D. Steiner and Homer H. Johnson

Category Width and Responses to Interpersonal
Disagreements

Ivan D. Steiner and Homer H. Johnson, 'Category width and
responses to interpersonal disagreements', *Journal of Personality and
Social Psychology*, vol. 2, 1965, pp. 290–92.

Research by Gardner (1953) and Pettigrew (1958)[1] suggests that
there are reliable individual differences in the widths of the cognitive categories people employ when they judge phenomena. Some
people regard rather diverse events as equivalent, whereas other
people do not.

The concept of category width appears to have considerable
relevance for studies of conformity behavior. People who employ
wide categories should see little difference between their own
views and the divergent opinions of their respected associates.
And because conformity tends to be positively related to the perceived discrepancy between one's own views and those advocated
by others (Harvey, 1962; Sherif and Hovland, 1961; Weiss,
1958), people who use wide categories should be less inclined to
conform than are people who use narrow categories. On the other
hand, wide categorizers should be prone to minimize or under-
recall disagreements. As Berkowitz (1960) has suggested, they
should 'assimilate' differences.

The present research employs the Pettigrew (1958) Category
Width Scale as a tool for measuring category width. Rosen (1961)
found that male subjects who were identified by this scale as
narrow categorizers were significantly more prone to employ a
dissonance-reducing response (seek information which supported
their decisions) than were wide categorizers. And in a preliminary
investigation the present authors obtained a significant negative
correlation between the Pettigrew scale and Fiedler's ASo Scale.

---

1. As was suggested in the introduction to Part Two of this book, it is
in fact helpful to distinguish between Gardner's approach (which does not
specify which dimensions a subject is to use) and that of Pettigrew (which
provides dimensions for the judge) [*Ed.*].

The latter findings suggests that wide categorizers are especially prone to minimize differences when making judgements about people.

Procedure

Subjects

The experimental subjects were sixty-four male undergraduate students enrolled in the introductory psychology course at the University of Illinois. Twenty-three additional male students from this course served as control subjects. All subjects received research credit for their participation.

Preliminary sessions

The experimental subjects reported to a classroom in groups of ten to twenty students. At these sessions they responded to the Pettigrew scale. Only the ten items which Pettigrew had found to correlate most highly with laboratory tests of category width were used in the present study. Scores based on these ten items ranged from 5 to 49 with a mean of 34·1.

Experimental treatments

At a designated time during the two weeks which followed the administration of the Pettigrew scale each subject reported to the laboratory where he met two other students who were serving as accomplices of the experimenter. The same two male students served as accomplices for all experimental sessions. Subjects were randomly designated to receive one of two experimental treatments. Thirty-two subjects received each treatment.

Treatment 1. In response to oral questions by the experimenter one accomplice reported that he was a pre-medical student, a junior and had an academic average higher than B. The other accomplice reported that he was a physics major, a junior and also had an average higher than B. A previous study (Steiner and Johnson, 1963) has indicated that subjects who receive this bogus information are almost invariably convinced that their associates are highly competent and resourceful persons.

After the naïve subject had reported his major, class at the university and academic average, the experimenter announced that he would administer a test which would be answered orally. Participants were urged to pay attention to one another's answers so that they might improve the 'accuracy of their interpersonal perceptions'. The test to which they were subjected consisted of thirty-two multiple-choice questions which called for judgements about political and social events, the characteristics of animals, the sizes and shapes of geometrical figures and number series which had been included in I.Q. tests. Each question was printed, along with three possible answers, on a card approximately nine by eleven inches in size. Each card was presented for a period of thirty seconds and participants were requested to announce their answers orally. The experimenter suggested that it was much easier for him to record the answers if participants always adhered to the same order when announcing their replies. He then instructed the 'pre-medical student' to give his answers first and asked the 'physics student' to announce his answers second.

The accomplices had been coached to give a predetermined set of answers. In Treatment 1 the two accomplices gave identical answers to twenty-eight questions, nineteen of these being the replies which had most often been given by twenty-three control-group subjects who had responded privately to the questions without any knowledge of other people's replies. Nine of the answers given by the accomplices were those which had least frequently been given by members of the control group. To the four remaining questions each accomplice gave two 'most popular' answers and two which had been second most popular among members of the control group. Consequently, the two accomplices disagreed with one another a total of four times, but each gave twenty-one answers which were most popular, nine which were least popular and two which were intermediate in popularity among members of the control group.

After all thirty-two cards had been exposed the subject and the accomplices were asked to provide written estimates of the number of times they had disagreed with one another.

Treatment 2. Except for the answers which the accomplices gave to the thirty-two questions, this treatment was exactly like Treatment 1. Each accomplice again gave twenty-one popular answers, nine least popular answers and two answers which were intermediate in popularity. But the questions to which the 'physics student' gave least popular answers were always different from those to which he had given least popular answers in Treatment 1, while the 'pre-medical student' gave exactly the same answers he had given in Treatment 1. Consequently the two accomplices disagreed with one another twenty-two times instead of four, but each gave the same number of most popular answers he had given in Treatment 1.

Response measures. A *conformity score* was computed for each subject by counting the number of times he had agreed with the two accomplices. Agreements with one accomplice were added to agreements with the other accomplice. For Treatment 1 the mean score was 45·4 and the standard deviation was 5·1. For Treatment 2 the mean was 34·6 and the standard deviation was 2·0.

Subjects' estimates of the number of disagreements with each accomplice were subtracted from the actual number of disagreements to yield an index of *under-recall of disagreements with the accomplices.* This score indicates the degree to which the subject under-recalled his disagreements with the two accomplices. The means and standard deviations were 5·9 and 4·1 for subjects who received Treatment 1, and 11·6 and 7·5 for subjects who received Treatment 2.

A score indicating the subject's tendency to *under-recall disagreements between his associates* was obtained by subtracting his estimate of the number of times such disagreements had occurred from the actual number of such disagreements. For Treatment 1 the mean score was 0 and the standard deviation was 5·0. For Treatment 2 the comparable statistics were 12·0 and 5·1.

Results

Table 1 reports relationships between category width and scores on conformity and under-recall.

Subjects who received Treatment 1 were free to conform, and the data indicate that narrow categorizers did so to a significantly greater degree than did wide categorizers. In Treatment 2 the accomplices disagreed with one another so many times that it was virtually impossible for a subject to earn a high conformity score or for one subject to conform much more often than another. (The standard deviation of the scores was only 2·0.) Under these very restrictive circumstances there was no relationship between category width and conformity.

Table 1

Correlations between Category-Width Scores and Responses in Experimental Sessions

Responses	Treatment 1 (N = 32)	Treatment 2 (N = 32)
Conformity to accomplices	−0·78*	0·02
Under-recall of disagreements with accomplices	−0·10	0·51*
Under-recall of disagreements between accomplices	−0·10	0·28

* $p < 0.01$.

Among subjects who received Treatment 2, under-recall of disagreements with the accomplices was significantly greater for wide categorizers than it was for narrow categorizers. However, in the case of subjects who received Treatment 1 the anticipated positive relationship was not obtained.

Among subjects who received Treatment 2, wide categorizers were more inclined than were narrow categorizers to under-recall disagreements between accomplices ($p < 0.12$). In Treatment 1 the accomplices actually disagreed with one another only four times and the subject's freedom to under-recall was seriously restricted. Under these conditions a very low negative relationship was obtained.

Discussion

The experimental conditions seriously limited the freedom of subjects to conform in Treatment 2 and to under-recall disagreements among accomplices in Treatment 1. Consequently it seems reasonable to suggest that only four of the six correlations presented in Table 1 should be regarded as evidence bearing on the effects of category width. Three of these four correlations are in the anticipated direction and two of them are significant at the 0·01 level.

The fact that wide categorizers did not show a special proneness to under-recall disagreements with the accomplices in Treatment 1 seems to contradict the thesis of this paper. However, it should be noted that in Treatment 1 neither the wide nor the narrow categorizers showed much tendency to under-recall disagreements with the accomplices. The mean under-recall score was only about half as large as it was for subjects who received Treatment 2. In Treatment 1 the predominant response was conformity; in Treatment 2 it was under-recall. And in both treatments category width was related to the predominant response in the manner demanded by our thesis.

Under-recall of disagreements *with* the accomplices was significantly related to category width in Treatment 2, but under-recall of disagreements *between* accomplices was not ($p < 0.12$). The failure of the latter correlation to reach an acceptable level of significance may indicate that disagreements between associates are less anxiety provoking than are disagreements between one's self and one's associates. If such is the case even narrow categorizers may tend to ignore or 'assimilate' differences between associates while concentrating on the more important differences between themselves and their associates.

However, an alternative explanation seems more plausible. The range and standard deviation of the scores for under-recall of disagreements *with* accomplices are larger than they are for under-recall of disagreements *between* accomplices. Inspection of the scatterplots indicates that a few extreme cases contributed markedly to the correlation between category width and under-recall of disagreements with accomplices, whereas this was not 'rue for the other correlation. In order to minimize the effect of extreme cases Kendall's tau was employed in a reappraisal of the correlations. The obtained tau values were 0·29 and 0·28, both significant at the 0·05 level. In view of these findings it seems probable that category width had very similar effects on the two types of under-recall examined in this study.

310

The theories of Berkowitz (1960) and Manis (1961) suggest that there may be conditions under which narrow categorizers will experience 'contrast effects'. Thus if a narrow categorizer's views are frequently and emphatically contradicted by a person of questionable competence, he may tend to *over-recall* disagreements. There is no evidence in the present study that this reaction occurred, but the high prestige of the accomplices and the relatively mild disagreements they created could scarcely be expected to encourage this response. If our accomplices had been introduced as less prestigeful persons and if they had expressed more extreme views, we would have expected them to be rejected by narrow categorizers. Under such conditions over-recall of disagreements might have occurred.

References

BERKOWITZ, L. (1960), 'The judgmental process in personality functioning', *Psychol. Rev.*, vol. 67, pp. 130–42.

GARDNER, R. (1953), 'Cognitive styles in categorizing behavior', *J. Personal.*, vol. 22, pp. 214–33.

HARVEY, O. J. (1962), 'Personality factors in resolution of conceptual incongruities', *Sociometry*, vol. 25, pp. 336–52.

MANIS, M. (1961), 'The interpretation of opinion statements as a function of message ambiguities and recipient attitude', *J. abnorm. soc. Psychol.*, vol. 63, pp. 76–86.

PETTIGREW, T. F. (1958), 'The measurement and correlates of category width as a cognitive variable', *J. Personal.*, vol. 26, pp. 532–44. [See Reading 6.]

ROSEN, S. (1961), 'Postdecision affinity for incompatible information', *J. abnorm. soc. Psychol.*, vol. 63, pp. 188–90.

SHERIF, M., and HOVLAND, C. (1961), *Social Judgment*, Yale University Press.

STEINER, L. D., and JOHNSON, H. H. (1963), 'Authoritarianism and "tolerance of trait inconsistency"', *J. abnorm. soc. Psychol.*, vol. 67 pp. 388–91.

WEISS, W. (1958), 'The relationship between judgments and a communicator's position and extent of opinion change', *J. abnorm. soc. Psychol.*, vol. 56, pp. 380–84.

Part Seven Studies of Attitude and Belief

In this Part of the book we turn to style and structure approaches to attitudes and beliefs. There are two main issues to be covered here:

1. Can we increase our understanding of attitude and belief systems by applying structural concepts? Recent work by McGuire, Rosenberg and others (summarized in Feldman, 1966; Fishbein, 1967; Insko, 1967) makes it clear that in general this is worth-while, but much of the research discussed by these authors is predominantly from the standpoint of a student of attitudes. The question may also be approached from a more personality-oriented position.

2. Can we relate differences between people in their attitudes to differences in their (independently measured) styles of thinking? From what has been examined on previous pages this seems to be very likely.

The first selection to be presented here is addressed to both these questions. Harvey (Reading 17) shows how a conceptual systems approach to personality has fruitful relevance to studies of attitude and attitude change. (Incidentally, Harvey's paper can usefully be read in conjunction with those general accounts of cognitive structure which were set out in Part Three.) Reading 18, by Warr, Schroder and Blackman, is an illustration of how some structural aspects of belief may be measured. As such it exemplifies the first question noted above. The final paper in this Part (Reading 19) deals with an aspect of the second question: Wolitzky shows how indices of a cognitive control of interference-proneness are predictive of cigarette smokers' assimilation of 'interfering' facts about smoking and lung cancer. Both Wolitzky and Harvey bring out very clearly that orthodox conceptualizations of cognitive dissonance, balance, etc. require modification by the inclusion of propositions about individual differences.

References
FELDMAN, D. (ed.) (1966), *Cognitive Consistency*, Academic Press.
FISHBEIN, M. (ed.) (1967), *Readings in Attitude Theory and Measurement*, Wiley.
INSKO, C. A. (1967), *Theories of Attitude Change*, Appleton-Century-Crofts.

17 O. J. Harvey

Conceptual Systems and Attitude Change

Excerpts from O. J. Harvey, 'Conceptual systems and attitude change', in C. W. Sherif and M. Sherif (eds.), *Attitude, Ego-Involvement and Change*, Wiley, 1967, pp. 205-18, 222-6.

Structural Variation: Differences in Concreteness–Abstractness

Of the many structural attributes of conceptual systems, our concentration has been on concreteness–abstractness, a quality of *how* the individual articulates and organizes his concepts of relevant aspects of his environment (Harvey and Schroder, 1963; Harvey, Hunt and Schroder, 1961). Concreteness–abstractness, as we have characterized and validated the construct, refers to a superordinate conceptual dimension encompassing such more molecular organizational properties as the degree of differentiation, articulation, integration and centrality of the cognitive elements. Being more generic and qualitative, variation in concreteness–abstractness rests upon differences in patterning or organization and not in differences in algebraic quantity of these subordinate characteristics. Different syndromes of interpretive, affective and behavioral tendencies accompany or underlie concrete and abstract functioning.

More concrete functioning is expressed at the behavioral level by high stimulus–response requiredness, the extreme of which could be illustrated by such one-to-one correspondence as that between the stimulus of a light and the taxic response of a moth. More abstract functioning, on the other hand, because of a more enriched and complex mediational system and a greater ability to transcend and depart from the immediate and perceptual characteristics of the impingements, results in less absolutism, that is, greater relativism in thought and action.

From a series of studies we have found greater concreteness, in contrast to greater abstractness, to be manifested in several ways, including:

1. A simpler cognitive structure, comprised of fewer differentiations and more incomplete integrations within more central and ego-involving domains *but not within domains of low involvement* (Harvey, 1966; Harvey, Reich and Wyer, 1966; Harvey, Wyer and Hautaluoma, 1963).

2. A greater tendency toward more extreme and more polarized evaluations, namely, good–bad, right–wrong, black–white (Adams, Harvey and Heslin, 1966; Campbell, 1960; Ware and Harvey, 1967; White and Harvey, 1965).

3. A greater dependence on status and authority-related cues as guidelines to belief and action (Crockett, 1958; Harvey, 1964, 1966; Harvey and Beverly, 1961; Kritzberg, 1965; Tiemann, 1965).

4. A greater intolerance of ambiguity expressed in higher scores on such measures as the *F*-Scale and Dogmatism Scale and in the tendency to form judgements of novel situations more quickly (Harvey, 1966; Reich, 1966).

5. A greater need for or tendency toward cognitive consistency and greater arousal and change from the experience of cognitive dissonance (Harvey, 1965; Harvey and Ware, 1966; Ware and Harvey, 1967).

6. A greater inability to change set and hence greater stereotypy in the solution of more complex and changing problems (Felknor and Harvey, 1963; Harvey, 1966; Harvey and Ware, 1966; Reich, 1966).

7. A poorer delineation between means and ends and hence a paucity of different methods of solving a problem or achieving a goal (Harvey, 1966).

8. A greater insensitivity to subtle and minimal cues and hence a greater susceptibility to false but obtrusive cues (Harvey, 1966).

9. A poorer capacity to 'act as if', to assume the role of the other or to think and act in terms of a hypothetical situation (Harvey, 1963a; Harvey and Kline, 1965).

10. The holding of opinions with greater strength and certainty that the opinions will not change with time (Hoffmeister, 1965).

11. A higher score on the factor of dictatorialness reflected in

such behavioral characteristics as high need for structure, low flexibility, high rule orientation, high dictation of procedure, high frequency of the usage or unexplained rules, high punitiveness, low diversity of activities and low encouragement of individual responsibility (Harvey *et al.*, 1966).

12. A lower score on the factor of task orientation (Harvey *et al.*, 1966).

13. A greater tendency to form and generalize impressions of other people from highly incomplete information (Ware and Harvey, 1967).

Greater abstractness has been found to accompany reverse quantities on the above dimensions.

Content Differences in Conceptual Systems

In the process of achieving its goals, evolving and transmitting its values, each society comes to delineate and formally or informally codify the referents or social objects of greatest significance to it. Differences in such referents, through their reciprocal influence upon and influence from social norms, are among the attributes that differentiate most sharply among societies.

Although membership in a given society disposes toward a common content in the conceptual or self-systems of the members (this being fairly synonymous with what has traditionally been referred to as the social self), variation exists among individual members in their *personal ordering of significance* of these referents. Some referents of socially designated significance are thus more central to some individuals whereas other individuals commit themselves more strongly to other social objects.

Although the content and structure of self-systems are theoretically independent, we have generated a set of developmental assumptions that led to our positing a high relationship between an individual's level of abstractness and the content of his *more central* concepts. It should be stressed that such a relationship is assumed *not to obtain for concept referents of low centrality and involvement*. In support of this assumption, the results of several of our experiments in which involvement was varied have made it clear that system differences such as those to be noted later

317

hold for the higher but not the lower levels of involvement or centrality.

Specific self-systems

From the interaction between conceptual content and structure several patterns may be theoretically deduced in which the tendency to make certain objects central is accompanied by a particular level of concreteness–abstractness. Although in our earlier work (Harvey, Hunt and Schroder, 1961), several such patterns or self-systems were deduced, my major theoretical and research interest has centered around the four summarized below.

System 1. This most concrete mode of relating to and construing the world best fits the description of concrete functioning described earlier. It is assumed to evolve from a developmental history in which the individual has been restricted in the exploration of that part of his world concerned with values, power relations and social causality. Along with minimal exposure to diversity in these domains, the rewards and punishments of the developing individual and his feelings of acceptance as a 'good person' have been contingent upon his ideas and approaches to problems conforming catechismically to the omnipotently and omnisciently imposed standards of the parent or controlling authority. More than any other method of inculcation, the socialization techniques surrounding System 1 development follows the conditioning model of S–R psychology, generating concepts through trial and error and fostering the internalization of values without insight and the ritualistic adherence to rules without understanding. System 1 functioning consequently manifests itself in such characteristics as high superstition, high religiosity, high absolutism and closedness of beliefs, high evaluativeness, high *positive* ties with and dependence on representatives of institutional authority – especially those of more nearly unimpeachable validity, such as God and religion – high identification with social roles and status positions, high conventionality and high ethnocentrism or strong beliefs that the values of one's own country should be adopted as a model by the rest of the world.

System 2. This self-system, somewhat more abstract than System 1, is thought to result from experience with an authority who, in addition to acting omnipotently and omnisciently, is also capricious in the control of rewards and punishments, administering these in such unpredictable fashions that the child (or any other recipient for that matter) is always unsure of the course of action that will enhance positive feedback and minimize the chances of punishment and rejection. Owing to their failure to provide any stable or predictable guidelines in an unstructured world, such vacilating practices present the developing child with diversity far in excess of the optimal. Although such variation in treatment tends to result in higher abstractness than in System 1 because of rejection of authority and consequent forced independence, it also produces deep feelings of uncertainty, distrust of authority and rebellion against the more socially approved guides of behavior. System 2 representatives, more than persons of any of the other self-systems, seem to be in a psychological vacuum, guided more by rejection of social prescriptions and avoidance of dependency on God and other representations of institutional authority that serve as positive guides for System 1 than by positive adherence to personally derived standards.

System 3. This mode of functioning is next to the highest level of abstractness treated by Harvey, Hunt and Schroder (1961). It is assumed to be the consequence of overindulgence by one or both parents, which, by preventing exploration of the physical world and by encouraging manipulation of the parents, produces in the developing child inflated notions of esteem and social power alongside the feeling of inability to cope with problems except by the control of others through dependency. Because of their domination of their parent(s), representatives of this system are much less oriented toward institutional power and authority than either persons from System 1, with their attitudes of deference and acquiescence, or individuals from System 2, with their orientation of negative independence and social rebellion. System 3 representatives, more than representatives of any of the other systems, are concerned with establishing friendships, intra-group consensus and dependence relations in order to avert the feeling of helplessness and social isolation that would result from being forced to be on their own. Through the use of highly developed skills of manipulation, particularly through exploitation of dependencies, System 3 functioning tends to favor success in effecting desired outcomes in the social sphere.

System 4. The most abstract of the four systems, this mode of construal and behaving is viewed as the consequences of childhood freedom to explore both the social and physical aspects of one's own experience and thought and to solve problems and evolve solutions without fear of punishment for deviating from established truth and the social imperatives. This developmental history eventuates in a high task orientation, information seeking, exploratory behavior, risk taking and independence.

In summary, System 1 is characterized by the lowest level of abstractness and a positive orientation toward extrapersonal referents, such as God and institutional authority. System 2 is slightly more abstract and negatively oriented toward the same social objects. System 3 is next to the highest in abstractness and is oriented toward establishing and maintaining intragroup consensus as a step toward dependency and control of others. And System 4 is the most abstract, more impersonal and more oriented toward information seeking and problem solving for intrinsic rather than extrinsic rewards.

An understanding of the specific functioning of the four systems may be enhanced by a description of the method by which we have assessed them.

Measures of Conceptual or Self-Systems

Several scales exist which, singly or in some combinations, can be used as a measure of a facet of one or more of the systems.

For example, the *F*-Scale, as well as other measures of authoritarianism, provides a fairly reliable measure of System 1 functioning but not of the other systems. Although F scores correlate highly with the System 1 orientation, a low F score does not correlate very highly with the orientation of System 4 because low scorers on F are comprised of both System 4 and System 2 representatives. Before developing a more appropriate measure of conceptual systems, we did employ the F-Scale, however, as one measure of concrete functioning. Some of the results to be discussed later were obtained through use of this instrument.

Rokeach's Dogmatism (D) Scale (1960) correlates significantly with the dimension of abstractness but does not sufficiently distinguish effectively between systems. A combination of the F- and D-Scales discriminate more accurately among systems than does either instrument alone. With scores from both scales split into high, middle, and low thirds, System 1 subjects tend to fall in the cell of high authoritarianism–high dogmatism, System 2 individuals to be in the cell of low authoritarianism–high dogmatism, System 3 representatives to fall in the middle authoritarianism–middle dogmatism group and System 4 persons to fall in the cell of low authoritarianism–low dogmatism.

We have developed two instruments specifically as measures of conceptual systems. The 'This I Believe' Test, a semiprojective sentence completion test, has been used most extensively and successfully. The Conceptual Systems Test is an objective scale only recently developed and still being perfected and validated.

The This I Believe (TIB) Test

This instrument aims at providing a basis of dimensionalizing an individual's more central concepts or beliefs according to the criteria implicit in the characterization of the four systems. Thus the sentences to be completed have to do with significant personal and social referents. Subjects are asked to indicate their beliefs about these referents by completing in two or three sentences the phrase; 'This I believe about —,' the blank being replaced successively by one of the following referents: friendship, the American way of life, guilt, marriage, myself, religion, sin, majority opinion, people, compromise, the future and the past. As can be seen, some of these referents are relevant mainly to one system whereas the relevance of others is more general.

As detailed in earlier publications (Harvey, 1964, 1965, 1966; Ware and Harvey, 1967; White and Harvey, 1965), the completions are scored both in terms of their positive and their negative orientations toward the referents and their absolutism evaluativeness, multiplicity of alternatives, triteness, and normativeness. In the more than thirty studies in which it has been used at the

University of Colorado and other universities, the TIB has been found to predict accurately and reliably to a wide range of both paper and pencil tests and experimentally induced behavior. Many of these between-systems differences from tests and behavioral situations have been described elsewhere (Harvey, 1966).

The Conceptual Systems Test (CST)

The items in the CST were derived from statements made by subjects in their completions of the TIB and from certain other tests purporting to measure personality aspects related to dimensions of conceptual systems. Factor analysis of each of the five revisions of the CST by Tryon's method of cluster analysis (Tryon and Bailey, 1965, 1966) has yielded seven theoretically meaningful and replicated factors from the five independent samples of respondents. These factors, as we have tentatively labeled them, together with some of their representative items, are:

1. Divine Fate Control (DFC) is assessed by such items as, 'There are some things which God will never permit man to know,' 'In the final analysis, events in the world will be in line with the master plan of God' and 'I believe that to attain my goals it is only necessary for me to live as God would have me live.'

2. Need for Simplicity-Consistency (NS-C) is inferred from response to such statements as 'I dislike having to change my plans in the middle of a task,' 'It is annoying to listen to a lecturer who cannot seem to make up his mind as to what he really believes' and 'A group which tolerates extreme differences of opinion among its own members cannot exist for long.'

3. Need for Structure-Order (NS-O) is derived from such items as 'I don't like to work on a problem unless there is a possibility of coming out with a clear-cut, definite answer,' 'I don't like for things to be uncertain and unpredictable' and 'I like to have a place for everything and everything in its place.'

4. Distrust of Social Authority (DSO) is tapped by such items as 'Most public officials are really interested in the poor man's problems' (negatively loaded), 'Government officials are as

interested in serving the poor as others' (negatively loaded) and 'A lot of people in positions of respect don't deserve as much respect as they receive.'

5. Friendship Absolutism (FA) is assessed by such statements as 'I do not enjoy arguing with my friends,' 'I cannot believe that a friend of mine could be guilty of stealing' and 'Sometimes I don't like any of my friends' (negatively loaded).

6. Moral Absolutism (MA) is revealed through answer to such items as 'I think I am stricter about right and wrong than most people,' 'Friendship is of greater value than adhering to a morally righteous cause' (negatively loaded) and 'It is less important to get along with others than to follow a code of conduct.'

7. General Pessimism (GP) is measured by such items as 'The world is run by a few people in power and there isn't much one can do about it,' 'Most people don't really care what happens to the other fellow' and 'You sometimes can't help wondering whether anything is worth-while anymore.'

The mean score of each of the four systems, as measured by the TIB, on each of these CST factors is presented in Figure 1. It can be seen that these system profiles conform closely to the theoretical attributes described earlier.

Self-systems and attitude change

With the self-systems depicted, we can now turn briefly to the question of how their variation relates to each of two related facets of attitude change: (a) source characteristics and behavior that foster change and (b) responses in addition to or in lieu of change evoked by conceptual refutation and/or attempts at change.

Characteristics of an effective source. The descriptions of System 1 imply that if a source is to be a 'significant other' in the eyes of System 1 representatives and if he can influence them in a direction counter to their own beliefs, he must be of high formal status, behave in accordance with clear-cut role definitions and issue highly structured and rule-oriented messages.

In line with this hypothesis, Crockett (1958) found more

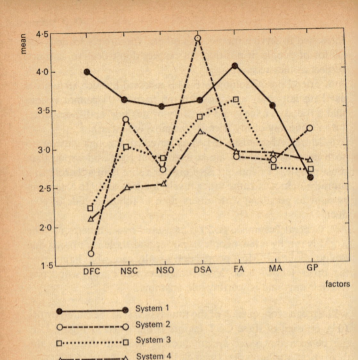

Figure 1 Mean score of each system as determined by T I B on the Conceptual Systems Test. D F C is divine fate control; N S C is need for simplicity-consistency; N S O is need for structure-order; D S A is distrust of social authority; F A is friendship absolutism; M A is moral absolutism; G P is general pessimism

authoritarian soldiers to prefer more autocratic leaders. And in an unreported study, Harvey found that college students representing System 1, to a greater extent than representatives of the other systems, preferred instructors who were high in academic rank, gave precise and highly structured assignments, made the criteria for grading very explicit and gave lectures of greater absolutism and simplicity, that is, of fewer contingencies, more 'facts' and fewer theoretical interrelationships.

In further accord with this reasoning are the findings from several experiments that authoritarianism tends to be positively correlated with attitude change (e.g. Christie and Cook, 1958;

Crutchfield, 1955; Harvey, 1963c; Harvey and Beverly, 1961; Titus and Hollander, 1957; Wagman, 1955; Wright and Harvey, 1965). Significantly, the relationship between authoritarianism and attitude change holds only for a high status source. As we have suggested, 'Authoritarianism is positively related to opinion change when the source of the incongruous input is of high status and the target concept is of low involvement. But it is negatively related to change when the source is of low status and the target concept is of high involvement' (Wright and Harvey, 1965, p. 180). Presumably for the same reason – that is, warding off conflicting inputs from all but a high status source – authoritarianism relates negatively to change in concepts of heaviness of weights and distance between lights produced by discrepant anchor weights and lights (Harvey, 1963c).

Evidence that an autocratic approach is more effective than its counterpart in producing concept change among more authoritarian individuals is provided in an experiment by Wright and Harvey (1965). Subjects varying in authoritarianism were tested on their attitudes toward several referents, following which they were criticized to the point of derogation by a high status source (their instructor) and retested.

With the exception of the ratings of professions, upon which derogation occurred, persons high on authoritarianism were high on pretreatment dependent variable scores and became still higher after treatment. Persons low in authoritarianism remained low on the dependent variable or became still lower. . . . Instead of a displacement theory, as suggested by Adorno *et al.* (1950), these results suggest that high authoritarianism disposes one toward expecting (and accepting as proper) extreme treatment from authority. Rather than frustration and negative affect, it appears such treatment may result in the opposite effects for more authoritarian individuals (Wright and Harvey, 1965, p. 180).

In a somewhat related experiment, Harvey and Rutherford (1958) found that more authoritarian individuals changed their concepts of light movement more from an absolute than a gradual approach, that is, from an approach in which the source made all of his judgements differ a fixed amount from those of the subject instead of first making his judgement match those of the subject and then gradually deviating from them.

That authoritarianism sensitizes an individual toward formal status and power rather than information may be inferred from the study by Harvey and Beverly (1961). Following refutation of their pre-assessed attitudes toward alcohol by a high status and powerful source, subjects varying in authoritarianism were asked to reproduce the main arguments the speaker (who was both their instructor and minister of their church) had made in favor of alcohol. Despite changing their opinion more in the direction of the communication, the more authoritarian subjects were able to reproduce fewer of the speaker's points than were the persons lower in authoritarianism. Thus the more authoritarian individuals appear to have changed their opinions more because of the status of the source than from their grasp of the reasons he advanced for change.

Although four of our experiments have shown that formal status is a characteristic of differential significance to individuals of the four systems (Harvey, 1963a, 1964; Kritzberg, 1965; Tiemann, 1965), only one study has been concerned directly with systems' influence on source effectiveness. In that study (Harvey, 1964) representatives of each of the four self-systems, among other tasks, judged the contents of sixteen projected slides of varying clarity following exposure to a pre-recorded narration that described the contents of each slide in a general way. The contents of the *nine more ambiguous* slides were incorrectly depicted whereas the contents of the seven slides of *greater clarity* were correctly described. The narration accompanying the projection of the slides was attributed to either an undergraduate student interested in photography (*low status* source) or to a professor of psychology interested in the slides as experimental stimuli (*high status* source). As hypothesized, the number of incorrect descriptions accepted in identification of the slides under the high status condition was greater for System 1 than any other system.

The assumed history of concept acquisition by System 1 representatives, especially of those concepts representing more central values and beliefs, suggests several important leads as to the most effective approach for modifying the more central concepts of these individuals. If indeed these concepts have been acquired through ways that approximate the S–R conditioning model, as we proposed earlier, then this basic behavioristic assumption may be applied to deduce notions of conceptual, or at least behavioral, modification. One obvious implication is that – since individuals of System 1 have only rudimentary mediational linkages between stimulus impingements and response, their connexions between S and R are more of classical conditioning than of insight learning, and they are more autonomic and affective than central – such persons would not be receptive to an informational approach to change of their central concepts. On the other hand, they should be more receptive to an approach that relies on deconditioning or some other application of S–R theory aimed at lessening the affective strength of the S–R bond. This could be done, theoretically, by repeated pairing of the emotion-producing stimulus with the response under conditions in which the autonomic system was not aroused. Repeated presentation of the stimulus unaccompanied by the reinforcement of negative affect could lead the individual to more freely explore the formerly negative object and to accept different definitions of it. Role playing and the use of tranquilizer-type drugs may provide ways of by-passing or neutralizing the autonomic system of the more concrete individual and through so doing of allowing him to engage central processes and become more receptive to an informational approach. One vein of our research hopes to pursue these possibilities.

Systems 2, 3 and 4 will be considered together because of the paucity of data specifically relevant to the question of what kind of source characteristics are most effective for each of these systems. Since, as noted earlier, both Systems 2 and 4 score low on authoritarianism scales, the responses of the low authoritarians, in contrast to the high authoritarians considered in the preceding section, cast little light on either System 2 or 4.

The earlier depiction of System 2 would indicate a negative orientation toward authority sources by its representatives and presumably a negative weighting by them of cues emanating from authority. In line with this and presumably reflective of the fear and distrust of authority, System 2 individuals performed the most poorly of the four systems on a role-playing task under the instruction that their performance was to be evaluated by a curriculum committee from the university (Harvey, 1963a); but when led to believe that no one, including the experimenter, would ever hear how they played the role, these same individuals outperformed individuals of both Systems 1 and 3. In the study noted earlier (Harvey, 1964), in which no mention was made of the possibility of their performance being evaluated by an authority person, System 2 representatives were significantly more influenced by a low status than by a high status source in the number of incorrect descriptions of the slides they accepted, the opposite of System 1. As will be noted later, whether the System 2 individual adheres to or rejects suggestions from authority depends to a great extent upon the degree of fate control the authority has over him and whether the response occurs in the presence or absence of authority surveillance.

The study that found representatives of Systems 1 and 2 to be strongly influenced by the status of the source in their acceptance of falsely depicted slides found individuals from Systems 3 and 4 to be only slightly influenced.

The acceptance of false descriptions by System 3 individuals, high under the low authority condition, was only slightly increased under the high authority variation; and System 4 representatives, who accepted a relatively low number of false depictions under the low authority condition, accepted only a fraction more under the high authority treatment (Harvey, 1964, p. 220).

Another part of the same study suggests that System 3 individuals are more susceptible to peer groups than to authority influences. Representatives of each of the four systems, in addition to being asked to identify the contents of the sixteen slides, judged the distance between twelve pairs of dots, first in the presence of a falsely calibrated but authentic appearing ruler, and then in the absence of the ruler but with the knowledge of the judgements of two other members of a temporary triad. Judgements in the social context were made under instructions that either made no reference to conformity or specifically depicted the experiment as one in conformity. As predicted, the degree of social influence, as measured by the difference between an individual's judgement before and after group discussion, was greatest for System 3 in the condition that made no reference to conformity. This finding is consistent with other findings that

System 3 individuals score higher than representatives of the other systems on need for affiliation, as assessed both by French's Scale and Edward's Personal Preference Schedule.

As a partial aside, it may be noted that specific reference to the experiments as a study in conformity reduced the social influence only slightly on Systems 1, 3 and 4 but lessened it markedly on representatives of System 2, implying a greater tendency toward negative independence on the part of these last individuals.

A second experiment relevant to the interaction of source characteristics and self systems is that of Adams, Harvey and Heslin (1966). In a study aimed at telescoping developmental histories, representatives of each of the four systems were hypnotized, their own pasts removed through suggestion and one of the four childhood pasts assumed to accompany each system of functioning was hypnotically implanted. Subjects performed the same tasks under each of the four hypnotic sets or pasts. The one task aimed at measuring social influenceability required each subject, as in Sherif's early experiment (1935), to form a personal norm of autokinetic movement by first judging the phenomenon alone, then to judge the movements in the presence of discrepant judgements by Dr Brainard, a source of both formal status and expertise, and lastly to judge again the movement of the light alone.

Because of their assumed experience of controlling authority more than being controlled by it, representatives of System 3 were the least influenced of the four systems when judging in the presence of Dr Brainard; and because of their assumed positive orientation toward expertise, System 4 individuals were the most influenced by Brainard's judgements. We conjectured that if the source

had been depicted as a policeman, minister, judge or a representative of an institutionalized position, it is likely that subjects would have been significantly more influenced by his judgements under the System 1 than under the System 2 induction. Moreover, it is also likely that had the source been of the latter variety, without special accomplishments or expertise in the particular area, subjects under the System 4 set would have been influenced appreciably less by his judgement (Adams, Harvey and Heslin, 1966, p. 232).

[. . .]

Continuous versus Discontinuous Response to System-Event Disparities

Without its having been made explicit, theories of attitude change are based on either of two assumptions: that if change occurs it may do so in any gradation, that is, change is continuous; or that change, if it occurs, will be in an either–or, discontinuous fashion.

Most theories of change and reaction to concept refutation are based upon the assumption of response continuity. Those that are not are theories that have sprung directly from notions of field theory and thermodynamics, alluded to in an earlier section of this chapter. Even some of the theories that have evolved from thermodynamics do not assume complete discontinuity in the response repertory of the individual; among these are such theories of balance and consistency as those of Heider (1946, 1958), Newcomb (1961) and others, all of whom allow for the restoration of balance through a kind of fusion of or compromise between the conflicting cognitive elements, such as change toward both the target concept and the source of the disparate event.

The theory based most heavily on the assumption of response discontinuity is Festinger's notion of dissonance (e.g. Brehm and Cohen, 1962; Festinger, 1957). Dissonance exists, according to these theorists, when the existence of one cognitive element implies the obverse of the other. Faced with this polarity of opposites, the respondent is forced to choose one extreme or the other. And once having chosen, the subject is supposed to act in ways to further increase the psychological distance between the former response alternatives by extolling one and derogating the other. Based on notions of inherency and a closed system, dissonance theory makes no allowances for individual differences in response to conceptual conflict.

However, whether an individual responds continuously or discontinuously to conflict in cognitive elements depends, among other things, upon the conceptual system that mediates between input and output and underlies the quality and frequency of response alternatives. Undifferentiated and bifurcated conceptual systems, such as those possessed by more concretely functioning individuals, are likely to eventuate in polarized and discontinuous responses, such as those stressed by dissonance theorists. At the same time, more differentiated conceptual systems, like those of more abstractly functioning persons, provide the bases for fine discriminations and accompanying continuities in response. Thus, it appears that although the assumptions of dissonance theory have some validity for concretely functioning individuals, they are considerably less valid for the more abstractly functioning persons.

References

ADAMS, D. K., HARVEY, O. J., and HESLIN, R. E. (1966), 'Variation of flexibility and creativity as a function of hypnotically induced past histories', in O. J. Harvey (ed.), *Experience, Structure and Adaptability*, Springer, New York, pp. 217–34.

ADORNO, T. W., FRENKEL-BRUNSWIK, E., LEVINSON, D. J., and SANFORD, R. N. (1950), *The Authoritarian Personality*, Harper.

BERLYNE, D. E. (1960), *Conflict, Arousal and Curiosity*, McGraw-Hill.

BREHM, J. W., and COHEN, A. R. (1962), *Explorations in Cognitive Dissonance*, Wiley.

CAMPBELL, V. N. (1960), Assumed similarity, perceived sociometric balance, and social influence, *Doctoral Dissertation, University of Colorado*.

CANNON, W. B. (1932), *The Wisdom of the Body*, Norton.

CHRISTIE, R., and COOK, P. (1958), 'A guide to published literature relating to authoritarian personality through 1956', *J. Psychol.*, vol. 45, pp. 171–99.

CROCKETT, E. P. (1958), Authoritarianism and leader acceptance, *ONR Technical Report, Vanderbilt University*, no. 5.

CRUTCHFIELD, R. S. (1955), 'Conformity and character', *Amer. Psychol.*, vol. 10, pp. 191–9.

FELKNOR, C., and HARVEY, O. J. (1963), Cognitive determinants of concept formation and attainment, *Technical Report, University of Colorado*, no. 10.

FESTINGER, L. (1957), *A Theory of Cognitive Dissonance*, Row, Peterson.

FISKE, D. W., and MADDI, S. R. (eds.) (1961), *Functions of Varied Experience*, Dorsey.

GLANZER, M. (1958), 'Curiosity, exploratory drive and stimulus satiation', *Psychol. Bull.*, vol. 55, pp. 302–15.

HARVEY, O. J. (1963a), Cognitive determinants of role playing, *Technical Report, University of Colorado*, no. 3.

HARVEY, O. J. (1963b), 'Current status of the incongruity hypothesis', in O. J. Harvey (ed.), *Motivation and Social Interaction*, Ronald Press, pp. 289–300.

HARVEY, O. J. (1963c), 'Authoritarianism and conceptual function in varied conditions', *J. Personal.*, vol. 31, pp. 462–70.

HARVEY, O. J. (1964), 'Some cognitive determinants of influenceability', *Sociometry*, vol. 27, pp. 208–21.

HARVEY, O. J. (1965), 'Cognitive aspects of affective arousal', in S. S. Tomkins and C. E. Izard (eds.), *Affect, Cognition and Personality*, Springer, New York, pp. 242–62.

HARVEY, O. J. (1966), 'System structure, flexibility, and creativity', in O. J. Harvey (ed.), *Experience, Structure and Adaptability*, Springer, New York, pp. 39–65.

HARVEY, O. J., and BEVERLY, G. D. (1961), 'Some personality correlates of concept change through role playing', *J. abnorm. soc. Psychol.*, vol. 63, pp. 125–30.

HARVEY, O. J., and KLINE, J. A. (1965), 'Some situational and cognitive determinants of role playing: a replication and extension', *Technical Report, University of Colorado*, no. 15.

HARVEY, O. J., and RUTHERFORD, J. (1958), 'Gradual and absolute approaches to attitude change', *Sociometry*, vol. 21, pp. 61–8.

HARVEY, O. J., and SCHRODER, H. M. (1963), 'Cognitive aspects of self and motivation', in O. J. Harvey (ed.), *Motivation and Social Interaction*, Ronald Press, pp. 95–133.

HARVEY, O. J., and WARE, R. (1966), 'Personality differences in dissonance reduction', *Technical Report, University of Colorado*, no. 18.

HARVEY, O. J., HUNT, D. E., and SCHRODER, H. M. (1961), *Conceptual Systems and Personality Organization*, Wiley.

HARVEY, O. J., REICH, J., and WYER, R. S. (1966), Affective and personality determinants of differentiation, *Unpublished Manuscript, University of Colorado*.

HARVEY, O. J., WHITE, B. J., PRATHER, M., ALTER, R., and HOFFMEISTER, J. K. (1966), 'Teachers' beliefs and preschool atmospheres', *J. educ. Psychol.*, vol. 57, pp. 373–81.

HARVEY, O. J., WYER, R. S., and HAUTALUOMA, J. E. (1963), 'Some cognitive and affective determinants of differentiation and integration', *Technical Report, University of Colorado*, no. 8.

HEBB, D. O. (1949), *The Organization of Behavior*, Wiley.

HEBB, D. O. (1955), 'Drives and the C.N.S. (conceptual nervous system)', *Psychol. Rev.*, vol. 62, pp. 243–54.

HEIDER, F. (1946), 'Attitudes and cognitive organization', *J. Psychol.*, vol. 21, pp. 107–12.

HEIDER, F. (1958), *The Psychology of Interpersonal Relations*, Wiley.

HOFFMEISTER, J. K. (1965), Conceptual determinants of strength and certainty of beliefs, *Unpublished Manuscript, University of Colorado*.

JAMES, W. (1890), *Principles of Psychology*, vol. 2, Holt.

KRITZBERG, S. F. (1965), 'Conceptual systems and behavior styles', *Technical Report, University of Colorado*, no. 13.

NEWCOMB, T. M. (1961), *The Acquaintance Process*, Holt, Rinehart & Winston.

RICHTER, C. P. (1927), 'Animal behavior and internal drives', *Quart. Rev. Biol.*, vol. 2, pp. 307–43.

RICHTER, C. P. (1936), 'Increased salt appetite in adrenalectomized rats', *Amer. J. Psychol.*, vol. 115, pp. 155–67.

RICHTER, C. P. (1942), 'Total self-regulatory functions in animals and human beings', *Harvey Lecture Series*, vol. 38, pp. 63–103.

RICHTER, C. P., and ECKERT, J. F. (1939), 'Mineral appetite of parathyroidectomized rats', *Amer. J. med. Sci.*, vol. 198, pp. 9–16.

REICH, J. (1966), Conceptual systems and group performance, *Unpublished Manuscript, University of Colorado*.

ROKEACH, M. (1960), *The Open and Closed Mind*, Basic Books.

SCOTT, W. A. (1959), 'Empirical assessment of values and ideologies', *Amer. sociol. Rev.*, vol. 24, pp. 299–310.

SCOTT, W. A. (1964), *Values and Organizations: A Study of Fraternities and Sororities*, Rand-McNally.

SHERIF, M. (1935), 'Some social factors in perception', *Arch. Psychol.*, *N.Y.*, vol. 27, whole no. 187.

TIEMANN, H. A. (1965), 'Some social and personality determinants of reaction to sensory deprivation', *Technical Report, University of Colorado*, no. 14.

TITUS, H. E., and HOLLANDER, E. P. (1957), 'The California F Scale in psychological research', *Psychol. Bull.*, vol. 54, pp. 61–8.

TRYON, R. C., and BAILEY, D. E. (1965), *Try User's Manual*, University of Colorado Computing Center.

TRYON, R. C., and BAILEY, D. E. (1966), *The B. C. Try System of Cluster and Factor Analysis*, University of Colorado.

WAGMAN, M. (1955), 'Attitude change and authoritarian personality', *J. Psychol.*, vol. 40, pp. 3–24.

WARE, R., and HARVEY, O. J. (1967), 'A cognitive determinant of impression formation', *J. Personal. soc. Psychol.*, vol. 5, pp. 38–44.

WHITE, B. J., and HARVEY, O. J. (1965), 'Effects of personality and own stand on judgment and production of statements about a central issue', *J. exp. soc. Psychol.*, vol. 1, pp. 334–47.

WEBSTER, H., SANFORD, N., and FREEDMAN, M. A. (1955), 'A new instrument for studying authoritarianism', *J. Psychol.*, vol. 40, pp. 73–84.

WRIGHT, J. M., and HARVEY, O. J. (1965), 'Attitude change as a function of authoritarianism and punitiveness', *J. Personal. soc. Psychol.*, vol. 1, pp. 177–81.

YOUNG, P. T. (1961), *Motivation and Emotion*, Wiley.

18 Peter B. Warr, H. M. Schroder and S. Blackman

The Structure of Political Judgement

Excerpts from Peter B. Warr, H. M. Schroder and S. Blackman, 'The structure of political judgement', *British Journal of Social and Clinical Psychology*, vol. 8, 1969, pp. 32–43.

There have been many attempts to distinguish between the kinds of judgements made by individuals of different political leanings. On the whole these have successfully shown that political orientation is related to the nature of personal and social judgement. Quite understandably, for example, members of different political parties view politicians themselves in very different ways. (Studies of these differences are reviewed by Warr and Knapper, 1968.) But rather more widespread variations have also been demonstrated: thus political orientation is in a general way linked to authoritarianism (e.g. Adorno *et al.*, 1950; Leventhal, Jacobs and Kudirka, 1964), tough-mindedness (Eysenck, 1954) and to ethnocentrism (e.g. Warr, Faust and Harrison, 1967). These more clearly central personality factors are themselves manifested in fairly well-established syndromes of judgemental behaviour which encompass a wide range of social and personal life.

All these studies have, however, been concerned more with the content of judgements rather than with their structure. Emphasis in the present investigation is given to structural aspects of judgement, and some account of the notion of structure should therefore introduce the study. Perhaps this can most readily be achieved by contrasting the characteristics of authoritarianism and of dogmatism (Rokeach, 1954, 1960). Authoritarianism is fairly clearly a 'content variable' in that a person's degree of authoritarianism is assessed in terms of *what* he believes; a high *F*-scale scorer is someone who holds beliefs, attitudes, values, etc. which have a specified content. Dogmatism on the other hand is much more a 'structural variable'. This means that it is concerned with the organization of belief–disbelief systems of many kinds, rather than with the content of only a few systems. Dogmatic thinking is necessarily manifested in terms of some content, and in empirical practice we are of course not able to completely separate a system's content from its structure.

Nevertheless the concept of structure can itself be discussed in isolation. Thus Rokeach (1954, p. 195) indicates that 'the total structure of a belief–disbelief system can be described as varying along a continuum from open to closed', and that this continuum derives from several structural characteristics. Amongst these are the degree of interdependence among the parts, the system's openness to new information, the existence of contradictions within the system, and so on. It is clear that we can view personality in terms of its structure in this way, and that in doing so we are de-emphasizing the particular content of a person's beliefs and values. The same conceptual approach may be adopted in studying attitudes. Thus Kerlinger (1967) has argued for a structural theory employing terms like 'duality', 'bipolarity' and 'orthogonality'. Several other structural concepts are now in fairly common use by students of attitudes; amongst these we might include the notions of latitudes of acceptance, rejection and non-commitment (Sherif and Hovland, 1961), determinance (Zajonc, 1960), multiplexity (Krech, Crutchfield and Ballachey, 1962), centrality (e.g. Sherif and Cantril, 1947), as well as the several formulations of consistency, congruence, consonance and balance.

What these structural approaches have in common is an interest in the number of psychological components and in their inter-relationships; they are not exclusively concerned with the content of a personality, an attitude or a judgement. This is also the major theme of theories of cognitive complexity–simplicity. The complexity of a person's cognitive structure is a function of the number of dimensions he employs, the way he employs them, and the way he combines them to form unified judgements. It is helpful to describe these three structural aspects as 'differentiation', 'articulation' and 'integration'.

'Differentiation' refers to the number of different dimensions a person has available to him, so that a highly differentiated perceptual structure is one made up of a lot of judgemental dimensions. 'Articulation' is the fineness of discrimination along individual dimensions; a dichotomy (e.g. old–young) is an unarticulated scale, whereas old–middle-aged–young, and very old–old–middle-aged–young adult–teenager–child are each more articulated. Thirdly, the way the available dimensions are combined may be called 'integration'; this is only partly dependent upon the actual number of dimensions. Although there are several formulations of the idea of cognitive complexity, they can all be viewed in terms of these three components. Thus the approaches of Bannister (e.g. 1962) and Bieri *et al.* (1966), deriving from Kelly's (1955) work, give major emphasis to differentiation; some studies of cognitive styles (e.g. Sloane, Gorlow and Jackson, 1963) are more concerned with articulation; and the integrative aspects of cognitive structure are particularly stressed by Harvey (1967), Harvey, Hunt and Schroder (1961) and Schroder, Driver and Streufert (1967).

Although this is still a fairly open question, the assumption is usually made that the complexity of a person's structure is to some extent domain-specific. This means that the nature of the structure used to process information about a certain stimulus domain (religion, alcoholic beverages, railway engines and so on) may be unrelated to the complexity of the structure employed in another domain. But as far as single particular domains are concerned, a number of hypotheses are readily testable. We might, for example, wonder how ego-involvement and structure are associated (Coffman, 1967), or how structure is influenced by environmental stress (Schroder, Driver and Streufert, 1967).

Within the domain of political stimuli we might wonder how different is the cognitive structure of members of different political parties. We have hints that this structure does vary; Rokeach (1960), for example, observed differences in dogmatism-scale score which were related to political affiliation. The present investigation is concerned with this question, but utilizes more direct measures of one aspect of cognitive structure. The study examines several measures of differentiation and contrasts the structural differentiation of groups with varying political orientation. The emphasis is on learning about the number and nature of dimensions used to conceptualize this stimulus domain. For this purpose we have employed measures rather different from those used in more content-orientated studies.

Method

Subjects and stimulus material

The investigation was carried out in the summer of 1966, and subjects were eighty-six undergraduate students from Sheffield University. Twenty-four of the subjects were members of left-wing political organizations (Young Socialists, Marxists, etc.) and thirty-one were of right-wing orientation, being members of the Young Conservatives. The remaining subjects were uncommitted to any political party, and we may refer to these as the 'centre' group.

Respondents were asked to complete a number of paper-and-pencil measures. These all pertained to ten national governments. It was considered unlikely that all the subjects would be well-acquainted with any standard set of ten stimuli which we might suggest, so we adopted a more flexible procedure. Seven of the stimulus governments were specified for all subjects, but each person provided another three of his own choosing. Subjects were asked to note down three governments (not countries) with which they were familiar and which were not present in the standard list. That list contained the following: the governments of (mainland) China, France, Russia, Spain, U.K., U.S.A. and West Germany.

Measuring instruments

The measures themselves were presented in a sequence progressing from completely open-ended to completely specified. The aim here was to give each subject the opportunity in early tasks to make responses from which we could infer the dimensions he himself thought to be the important ones. As he moved on to later measures, we came to specify scales he should use. This was for two reasons: first, to obtain responses which would help us interpret earlier material, and second, to carry out factor analytic and other analyses of a more orthodox kind.

The instruments themselves may now be described. They all involve judgements of some type, and they are set down in the order in which they were administered.

Multidimensional scaling

Subjects' responses for multidimensional scaling (MDS) analysis are comparisons of pairs of stimuli. Two stimuli (governments in this case) are presented together, and a subject is requested to indicate on a numerical scale (1 to 9) how similar are the two members of the pair. All possible combinations of two stimuli are presented, so that with this set of ten governments we elicited forty-five, i.e. $\frac{1}{2}n(n-1)$, similarity estimates. The responses of each subject were analysed separately to learn about the dimensions underlying his judgements.

In carrying out eighty-six separate analyses (rather than analysing group averages) we were concerned with Jackson and Messick's (1963) observation that 'a generalized "average person" may not, in fact, represent anyone'. The aim in these analyses was to obtain separate measures of differentiation for each subject, so that these separate measures could *later* be averaged in whatever ways proved necessary.

Several related procedures are available for MDS analyses. In the present study a non-metric technique was applied (Kruskal, 1964a and b; Shepard, 1962a and b). This involves factoring the judged distances between stimuli to ascertain the most economic underlying structure; and the outcome of the operations is that the distances between stimuli become represented in a space, the dimensions of which correspond to the several ways in which the stimuli are perceived to differ. The points in the space represent the stimuli, and their projections on the obtained dimensions are the scale values for the several attributes thought to underlie the similarity judgements. The minimum *number* of dimensions necessary to account for the judge's responses is determined by ascertaining 'stress' values according to procedures outlined by Kruskal (1964a and b).

It can be seen that from this procedure are available measures of differentiation (the number of dimensions deemed to best account for the similarity judgements) and also of the placement of each stimulus on each dimension. The nature of the dimensions themselves has to be identified *post hoc*. In the present investigation this was achieved by obtaining much additional material from each subject and interpreting the MDS dimensions in the light of this material. This aspect of the study is described later.

Free descriptive responses

This second measure was also an open-ended one, intended to generate information from which to ascertain the number and nature of judgemental dimensions used by each subject. Judges were asked to note down five aspects of each stimulus government which to them seemed to be of major importance. The name of each government appeared on a separate page, and the order of presentation of stimuli was randomized across subjects.

From this procedure fifty descriptions (ten stimuli, five responses to each) are obtained. The investigator now has to classify these responses according to a standard scheme. Once this has been achieved several interesting measures are available. Most obvious is the potential index of differentiation. This is simply the number of classes of responses in a judge's descriptions. It may be, for example, that his fifty descriptions are really somewhat repetitive in that he uses the same concept on several occasions. In scoring the fifty descriptions we are interested in how many *different* concepts or dimensions appear in the responses, so that we might conclude that the subject is in fact using, say, seven separate dimensions in his fifty descriptions. Another subject may make responses which differ more widely, and we might conclude that he is using, say, fifteen different dimensions.

If free descriptive responding (FDR) generates a measure of differentiation, it might be asked how it differs from MDS. There is one very important difference which makes essential the concurrent use of the two procedures. The dimensions generated by MDS are *general* ones, in that they are relevant to all the stimuli in a set. FDR can reveal general dimensions, but in addition this second procedure generates dimensions which are stimulus-specific.

For example, if we conclude from the MDS analysis that strong–weak is a dimension which a particular subject uses to conceptualize governments, then we have to make it clear that we mean that this is a dimension which he applies to *all* the stimuli in the set: he thinks of all the governments in these terms. FDR, on the other hand, can tell us about dimensions which a judge applies only to one or a few governments. Thus he might respond that the British government is 'keen to join the Common Market' or that the Spanish government is 'dominated by Franco'. These dimensions are applied specifically to individual stimuli and would not emerge at all from the MDS analysis.

This means that FDR is a more sensitive instrument. We can derive estimates of general dimensions (those applied to all stimuli), but also of specific ones (those applied to less than all stimuli). These derivations do of course depend upon the availability of an appropriate classification scheme. For this project a manual for coding FDR data about governments has been developed.[1] This embraces nine very broad categories of response, each of which is subdivided into several dimensions of judgement. The nine broad categories are: (a) governmental structure in general, (b) specific aspects of structure, (c) internal policies in general, (d) internal policies in specific, (e) internal characteristics, (f) position in the world, (g) foreign policies, (h) alliances and ties to other governments, (i) external characteristics. The total number of specific dimensions covering these nine groups is fifty-three. For example, seven separate dimensions make up the first broad category (governmental structure in general); these are (a) autocratic–democratic, (b) constitutional status, (c) capitalist–communist, (d) nature of leadership, (e) nature of legislative body, (f) internal organizational characteristics, (g) presence of ideology.

In analysing the FDR material each of a subject's fifty descriptions is coded as one of these fifty-three dimensions. The dimension *autocratic–democratic*, for example, subsumes responses to do with the extent of governmental control. In this way it embraces most comments about élitism, oligarchy, despotism, autocracy, dictatorship, and so on. Using the coding scheme in this way provides immediate information about the number and nature of a subject's judgemental dimensions, and also allows conclusions to be drawn about the relative importance to each subject of his dimensions.

1. Copies of this manual may be obtained from Professor H. M. Schroder, Department of Psychology, Princeton University, Princeton, New Jersey 08540, U.S.A.

Assessment of national goals

The third set of responses concerned national goals which each subject thought to be important. Judges were first asked to note down three different goals which a government should pursue. They were then requested to indicate (on a scale from 1 to 10) each government's potential to attain each of these goals. It will be noted that this third task is also an open-ended one; subjects individually select the aspects of governments which to them are important.

Semantic differential forms

Subjects' final task was to complete ten semantic differential forms – one for each government. Responses were on nine-point scales and the same scales were employed for each stimulus. These were selected on the basis of pilot studies of dimensions thought to be relevant, and several scales of a clearly evaluative nature were also included. The scales employed were: flexible–inflexible, sensitive to its people's needs–insensitive to its people's needs, strong–weak, fair–unfair, capitalist–communist, wise–foolish, unique–typical, representative of its people–unrepresentative of its people, honest–dishonest, independent of other governments–dependent on other governments. Four versions of the forms were used, each with a different sequence of scales. Scales were in all cases laid out so that the position of the positive term (left or right on the page) was varied randomly.

Results

From these tasks we have available measures of differentiation for each subject, as well as some indication of the *nature* of the dimensions each one is employing. We also have data pertaining to the content of judgements on dimensions we ourselves have specified; that is, the semantic differential material. Results will be set out under these headings – number of dimensions, nature of dimensions, other content measures.[2]

2. The section under 'other content measures' has not been included in this excerpt [*Ed.*].

Number of dimensions

Consider first the MDS analyses of similarity–dissimilarity judgements. Each judge's responses were analysed separately to produce a four-dimensional, a three-dimensional, a two-dimensional and a one-dimensional space. The decision about the number of dimensions required to account most economically for the original judgements was made (without knowledge of the subject's political affiliation) on the basis of the 'stress' values derived by Kruskal's (1964a and b) procedure.

No subject was deemed to have employed more than three dimensions, and the average number of dimensions across all eighty-six judges was 2·09. Does this measure of structural differentiation vary with political orientation? Apparently not, since the mean numbers of dimensions required to account for the judgements of the left-wing, centre and right-wing groups did not differ significantly. These values were 2·04, 2·19 and 2·00 respectively. [. . .]

When we turn to the FDR material, we again find that political orientation is not reflected significantly in differentiation. As previously described, this measure is the number of classes of responses into which a judge's fifty judgements fall. Since this FDR index covers specific dimensions as well as general ones, we expect that the average number of observed dimensions will be much greater than the MDS average. In fact, the average number of FDR dimensions used was 19·30. For the left-wing, centre and right-wing groups the mean numbers of dimensions employed were 17·71, 19·03 and 20·31 respectively.

These figures emphasize the use of stimulus-specific dimensions, in that if a particular response category was used only once this was assumed to be a judgemental dimension for the subject, just as if it were used two or three times over ten stimuli. Using a category only once entails that this category is stimulus-specific. We may ask about the more general dimensions in the FDR material. A general dimension for a subject is one which he applies to many of the stimuli within a domain. Although there are no differences between political groups in the FDR values cited above, it is logically possible for one group still to give major emphasis to general dimensions. To test this possibility the FDR judgements have been examined according to several criteria of usage. If the criterion for describing a dimension as 'general' is taken to be its application to, say, more than half of the stimuli in a set, then the general dimensions in this present analysis are those applied to more than five of the governments.

Do the political groups differ in their use of general FDR dimensions? Table 1 presents information about three criteria of usage. The first row in this table contains the values cited

Table 1

Mean Number of Dimensions Used in the FDR Task by Members of Each Group

Criterion of usage	Left-wing	Centre	Right-wing
Present once or more	17·71	19·03	20·31
Present twice or more	9·29	9·90	10·83
Present five times or more	2·17	2·03	1·93

previously, and the third row contains information about more general dimensions. An intermediate criterion is also displayed. In no cases do the measures of differentiation vary significantly between the groups.

For a final measure of differentiation the semantic differential responses may be examined. If the responses from the three political groups are factor analysed, the number of factors present in each group's responses might indicate the complexity of judgemental structure. This measure is unsatisfactory in several respects, not least that it cannot produce an index for each subject. Nevertheless the picture it reveals corresponds well with the analyses already described. Two significant factors are present in the responses of each group; and the percentage of variance attributable to these factors is much the same for all the groups. We must conclude then that the number of dimensions used to conceptualize this judgemental domain does not differ according to a subject's political orientation. This conclusion is suggested by each of the three different comparisons made here.

Nature of dimensions

But the three groups may in fact still use *different* dimensions, and an examination of the nature of these is called for. As far as the FDR task is concerned this is very straightforward. The

343

proportion of each group's responses falling into each of the fifty-three conceptual categories has to be calculated, and the significance of differences between groups has to be determined. Results of these calculations are available, but before they are presented some details of the dimensions important to judges as a whole would be helpful.

Table 2

Percentage of Responses on those FDR Dimensions on which Significant Inter-Group Differences are Present

Dimension title	Left-wing	Centre	Right-wing	F	P<
Autocratic–democratic	12·23	15·87	11·20	3·34	0·05
Constitutional status	1·94	1·50	0·40	4·69	0·02
Capitalist–communist	9·03	7·02	8·37	6·76	0·01
Government structure	4·22	2·69	2·02	2·85	0·10
Role of tradition	2·11	2·08	0·67	3·84	0·02
Particular leader	1·26	1·70	2·83	2·71	0·10
Extensiveness of control	8·27	4·00	2·56	7·94	0·01
Censorship	1·94	0·13	0·47	4·11	0·02
Emphasis on science	0·42	0·06	1·01	3·37	0·05
Maturity	0·16	0·98	1·28	3·67	0·05
Initiative	0·67	4·65	1·82	5·48	0·01
Specific foreign policies	1·35	2·09	3·78	3·37	0·05
Bilateral ties	0·67	1·11	2·63	5·72	0·01
World view	0·59	2·03	1·14	3·01	0·05

In conceptualizing national governments the most important dimension for these subjects was autocratic–democratic. Across all subjects 13·22 per cent of responses were of this kind. The separate category of capitalist–communist was also regularly used (9·52 per cent), as was the dimension extensiveness of governmental control (4·70 per cent). Other widely used dimensions were aggressiveness (3·38 per cent), governmental organization (2·88 per cent), party system (2·86 per cent), stability (2·79 per cent), efficiency (2·62 per cent) and social policies (2·22 per cent). Of the fifty-three different categories in the coding system, a third revealed differences between the political groups. These fourteen categories are presented in Table 2. It can be seen that the left-wing subjects were more likely to utilize the dimensions capitalist–communist, government structure, role of tradition, extensiveness of control and censorship. The right-wing judges made more use of dimensions like maturity, particular leader, and bilateral ties, whilst the centre group predominantly emphasized democratic–autocratic, initiative and world view.

Table 3

Percentage of Each Subject Group Employing the Major Dimensions in MDS Analyses

Dimension title	Left-wing	Centre	Right-wing
Autocratic–democratic	70·8	86·7	74·1
Capitalist–communist	29·3	10·0	19·3
Distribution of power	20·8	3·3	16·1
General competence	16·7	30·0	9·7
Social concern	12·5	3·3	3·3
External influence	4·2	13·3	16·1

Although, therefore, the three political groups employ the same number of dimensions in completing the FDR task, the nature of these dimensions can vary between the groups. This same point is brought out in the interpretative analysis of MDS dimensions. To identify the nature of these general dimensions we have to utilize a subject's other responses in a somewhat clinical fashion. The procedure adopted was to examine the placement of the ten stimuli on each obtained dimension and to relate these placements to the subject's other responses. This interpretation was carried out for each judge by an investigator not familiar with the FDR coding scheme. Several interesting differences emerged between the nature of the general dimensions employed by the three political groups. These differences are laid out in Table 3. It can be seen once again that left-wing judges are more likely to view governments in terms of capitalist–communist, distribution of power and social concern, whereas right-wing subjects emphasize external influence and the centre group stress autocratic–democratic and general competence.

It is obvious that judgements of governments and other social institutions contain a strong evaluative component. This evaluative component is often revealed when subjects make similarity–dissimilarity judgements of the kind here submitted to MDS analysis. For example, Warr and Knapper (1968, ch. 2) have reported correlations exceeding $+0.90$ between judges' first MDS dimension and their responses to evaluative semantic differential scales. In the present investigation the MDS first dimension was also found to be strongly associated with evaluative factor scores from the semantic differential task. Taking all subjects together, the correlation between these two values is $+0.75$. It is interesting to inquire how this relation differs between the three political groups. For the left-wing subjects the product-moment correlation is $+0.55$, for the centre group it is $+0.86$ and for the right-wing judges it is $+0.89$. Further details of this aspect of the study have been reported elsewhere (Warr, Schroder and Blackman, 1969), and it is clear from the several indices reported there that for the right-wing judges the major MDS dimension has a more strongly emphasized evaluative component. Once again it can be seen that, although the number of dimensions used by the three groups does not differ, the nature of these dimensions does vary significantly. [. . .]

Discussion

These results clearly indicate that judgemental structure (as here measured in terms of differentiation) does not vary as a function of political orientation. This study has concerned only one stimulus domain, but since this was the one most relevant to political belief, it was perhaps the most likely to reveal any existing differences. But although the *number* of dimensions used by the three groups does not differ, the *nature* of these dimensions varies significantly.

This observation has of course some intrinsic empirical interest, but it is also important for practical reasons. In examining the way people make judgements it has been usual to specify in advance the dimensions which are to be used. Much valuable material has been obtained by this procedure, but the methodological assumptions underlying it may be questioned. It is assumed that all the scales set down are relevant to all subjects and that there are no others which in addition are relevant ones. Particularly noteworthy is the fact that the more usual technique rules out possible idiosyncratic differences between judges. We may be correct in assuming that a particular dimension (say, capitalist–communist) is an important average dimension. But to many it is irrelevant; knowledge of only the average tells us nothing about the dimensions which underlie judgements by a particular individual.

References

ADORNO, T. W., FRENKEL-BRUNSWIK, E., LEVINSON, D. J., and SANFORD, R. N. (1950), *The Authoritarian Personality*, Harper.

BANNISTER, D. (1962), 'The nature and measurement of schizophrenic thought disorder', *J. ment. Sci.*, vol. 108, pp. 825–42.

BIERI, J., ATKINS, A. L., BRIAR, S., LEAMAN, R. L., MILLER, H., and TRIPODI, T. (1966), *Clinical and Social Judgment: The Discrimination of Behavioral Information*, Wiley. [See Reading 8.]

COFFMAN, T. L. (1967), Personality structure, involvement and the consequences of taking a stand, *Unpublished Doctoral Dissertation, Princeton University*.

EYSENCK, H. J. (1954), *The Psychology of Politics*, Routledge & Kegan Paul.

HARVEY, O. J. (1967), 'Conceptual systems and attitude change', in C. W. Sherif and M. Sherif (eds.), *Attitude, Ego-Involvement and Change*, Wiley. [See Reading 17.]

HARVEY, O. J., HUNT, D. E., and SCHRODER, H. M. (1961), *Conceptual Systems and Personality Organization*, Wiley.

JACKSON, D. N., and MESSICK, S. (1963), 'Individual differences in social perception', *Brit. J. soc. clin. Psychol.*, vol. 2, pp. 1–10.

KELLY, G. A. (1955), *The Psychology of Personal Constructs*, Norton.

KERLINGER, F. N. (1967), 'Social attitudes and their criterial referents: a structural theory', *Psychol. Rev.*, vol. 74, pp. 110–22.

KRECH, D., CRUTCHFIELD, R. S., and BALLACHEY, E. L. (1962), *Individual in Society*, McGraw-Hill.

KRUSKAL, J. B. (1964a), 'Multidimensional scaling by optimizing goodness of fit to a non-metric hypothesis', *Psychometrika*, vol. 29, pp. 1–27.

KRUSKAL, J. B. (1964b), 'Nonmetric multidimensional scaling: a numerical method', *Psychometrika*, vol. 29, pp. 115–29.

LEVENTHAL, H., JACOBS, R. L., and KUDIRKA, N. Z. (1964), 'Authoritarianism, ideology and political candidate choice', *J. abnorm. soc. Psychol.*, vol. 69, pp. 539–49.

ROKEACH, M. (1954), 'The nature and meaning of dogmatism', *Psychol. Rev.*, vol. 61, pp. 194–205.

ROKEACH, M. (1960), *The Open and Closed Mind*, Basic Books.

SCHRODER, H. M., DRIVER, M. J., and STREUFERT, S. (1967), *Human Information Processing: Individuals and Groups functioning in Complex Social Situations*, Holt, Rinehart & Winston. [See Reading 9.]

SHEPARD, R. N. (1962a), 'The analysis of proximities: multidimensional scaling with an unknown distance function: I', *Psychometrika*, vol. 27, pp. 125–40.

SHEPARD, R. N. (1962b), 'The analysis of proximities: multidimensional scaling with an unknown distance function: II', *Psychometrika*, vol. 27, pp. 219–46.

SHERIF, M., and CANTRIL, H. (1947), *The Psychology of Ego-Involvements*, Wiley.

SHERIF, M., and HOVLAND, C. I. (1961), *Social Judgment*, Yale University Press.

SLOANE, H. N., GORLOW, L., and JACKSON, D. N. (1963), 'Cognitive styles in equivalence range', *Percept. mot. Skills*, vol. 16, pp. 389–404.

WARR, P. B., and KNAPPER, C. (1968), *The Perception of People and Events*, Wiley.

WARR, P. B., FAUST, J., and HARRISON, G. J. (1967), 'A British ethnocentrism scale', *Brit. J. soc. clin. Psychol.*, vol. 6, pp. 267–77.

WARR, P. B., SCHRODER, H. M., and BLACKMAN, S. (1969), 'A comparison of two techniques for the measurement of international judgment', *Int. J. Psychol.*, vol. 4, pp. 135–40.

ZAJONC, R. B. (1960), 'The process of cognitive tuning in communication', *J. abnorm. soc. Psychol.*, vol. 61, pp. 159–65.

19 David L. Wolitzky

Cognitive Control and Cognitive Dissonance

Excerpts from David L. Wolitzky, 'Cognitive control and cognitive dissonance', *Journal of Personality and Social Psychology*, vol. 5, 1967, pp. 486–90.

Festinger (1957) defined cognitive dissonance as psychologically uncomfortable tension arising from contradictory cognitions. People are motivated to avoid dissonance and to reduce it when it occurs. A similar emphasis on the tendency towards consonance among cognitions is contained in the concepts of congruity (Osgood and Tannenbaum, 1955) and balance (Heider, 1958).

The numerous studies based on dissonance theory (see Glass, 1965, for a recent review) have tended to neglect individual differences in the perception and tolerance of dissonance and in the modes of dissonance reduction. A similar neglect was evident in the early days of the 'new look' in perception until it was realized that a more precise evaluation of experimental results required attention to individual differences (e.g. Klein, Schlesinger and Meister, 1951). The present study attempts to link the theory of cognitive dissonance with the concept of cognitive controls. Cognitive controls refer to an individual's relatively enduring modes or strategies of processing information and reacting to situations. They are considered to be developmentally stabilized, conflict-free structures which operate consistently despite shifts in situational conditions. With this conception of cognitive control, Klein (1954) demonstrated that the direction and degree of influence exerted by a need (thirst) upon a variety of perceptual cognitive tasks differed in 'constricted' and 'flexible' subjects. The constricted–flexible control dimension refers to individual differences in proneness to interference on a color-word task which requires the subject to ignore compelling, irrelevant stimuli.

Interference proneness seems relevant to dissonance studies in which the subject has the option either of ignoring or denying a dissonance-arousing cognition. For instance, high-interference-prone (constricted) individuals should find it hard to avoid or deny an insistent but dissonant cognition in their efforts to maintain cognitive consistency; those less subject to interference (flexible subjects) should be more facile in this respect.

To test this notion, an early study cited by Festinger (1957) was selected as a point of departure. Festinger reported that cigarette smokers, compared with nonsmokers, did not believe that cigarette smoking was related to lung cancer. Such a belief, according to Festinger, would conflict or be dissonant with the smokers' desire to continue smoking and to remain healthy. Some smokers did, however, admit a smoking–cancer link. In more recent studies, the percentage of smokers who reported belief in a smoking–cancer link ranged from 48 per cent (Horn, 1963) to 67 per cent (Baer, 1966). How can one account for these variations? Perhaps smokers are able to deny a smoking–cancer link only to the extent that they are generally able to ignore intrusive, inconsistent information.

It should be noted that the climate of opinion surrounding smoking and cancer has changed considerably since the time of Festinger's study. Mounting evidence and recent legislative action have made the smoking–cancer relationship less ambiguous and more difficult to deny. Therefore, smoking should provoke greater dissonance than it did in the past. Despite these changes, the following hypothesis can still be tested: Smokers who are characterized by constricted cognitive control will admit that a link exists between cigarette smoking and lung cancer, while smokers characterized by flexible cognitive control will tend to deny it.

Method

Subjects

Seventy-eight male undergraduates (fifty-eight cigarette smokers and twenty nonsmokers) at New York University served as volunteers in individual sessions.

Procedure

Stroop Color-Word Test (*CWT*). Part I: the testing began with a warm-up page of color names (red, blue, green, yellow) typed in black ink; subjects called out the names of colors as quickly and as accurately as possible. Part II: after a one-minute rest, the subjects were shown a page of colored strips of asterisks and asked to read aloud the colors as quickly and as accurately as possible. Part III: the third and main part of the task consisted of color names printed in incongruous colors (e.g. the word 'red' printed in blue, 'green' printed in yellow, etc.). Subjects were told to ignore the *words* and to read aloud the *colors* as quickly and as accurately as possible.

In each of the three sections of the task, the page contained 100 stimuli, ten to a line. Time scores were recorded as the index of performance (Gardner *et al.*, 1959).

Smoking questionnaire. Following the CWT, subjects were asked about their smoking habits: (a) whether they smoked cigarettes, cigars or a pipe,[1] (b) how many packs a day they smoked currently, (c) whether and by how much they had cut down or increased their smoking within the past year, and (d) the extent to which they believed that a relationship exists between cigarette smoking and lung cancer. Degree of belief was expressed on a four-point rating scale: 1 – not at all convinced; 2 – partially convinced; 3 – pretty sure; 4 – certain.

Results

The correlation, based on all seventy-eight subjects, between the time scores on Part II (colors alone) and Part III (color-word incongruence) was 0.56 ($p < 0.01$). Part III scores were therefore adjusted by means of a regression formula in order to obtain an interference score which was independent of color-coding time. The resulting scores were ranked and divided at the median to form constricted (high-interference) and flexible (low-interference) groups. The difference between the two groups with respect to degree of belief in a smoking-cancer link was then assessed. The mean for the constricted group was 3.24 compared with 2.62 for the flexible group ($t = 3.40$, $p < 0.002$), thereby supporting the hypothesis.

1. Cigar and pipe smokers were excluded from the study.

Festinger (1957) reasoned that heavy smokers had more dissonance to reduce than light smokers. In accord with this assumption, he found that amount of cigarette smoking was directly related to the extent of denial of a smoking–cancer link. It was necessary, therefore, to ascertain that the observed difference in belief was not simply due to different amounts of smoking in the flexible and constricted groups. The mean number of packs smoked each day (questionnaire item b) in the constricted group was 1·16, versus 0·86 in the flexible group ($t = 3·26$, $p < 0·002$). The greater denial of a smoking–cancer link found to be typical of flexible subjects cannot then be attributed to amount of smoking since, in fact, they were the lighter smokers of the total sample.

In addition to dissonance created by amount of current smoking, recent *changes* in the smoking habit might affect the magnitude of dissonance. It has been found, for example, that the more recent the choice between attractive alternatives, the greater the dissonance (Ehrlich *et al.*, 1957). Therefore, a recent increase in smoking might raise the level of dissonance, while a recent decrease might lower it. If those who increased smoking were mainly flexible subjects and if those who decreased were mainly constricted subjects, the difference in belief could be attributed to a difference in magnitude of dissonance. In actual fact, when the proportion of decreasers in each group is compared, the results show that 41 per cent of the constricted subjects decreased their smoking, compared with 24 per cent of the flexible subjects ($z = 1·72$, $p = 0·08$, two-tailed test).[2] Thus, the stronger belief in a smoking–cancer link in the constricted group might be due to the use of an alternative mode of dissonance reduction, namely, decreased smoking.

In order to rule out this possible artifact, subjects whose smoking habits had changed were eliminated from the data analysis, leaving only subjects who reported that their smoking habits had remained *stable* for at least one year prior to the study. The respective mean belief score of 3·33 for the constricted group and 2·40 for the flexible group was significantly different ($t = 3·21$, $df = 25$, $p < 0·001$). As in the original analysis, flexible

2. There was no significant difference in the proportion of subjects who increased in each group.

smokers denied a smoking–cancer link. In this group of stable smokers, constricted subjects still smoked significantly more than flexible subjects (1·29 versus 0·90, $t = 3·00$, $df = 25$, $p < 0·05$), again suggesting that, while constricted subjects presumably had more dissonance to reduce, they nonetheless expressed a stronger belief in a smoking–cancer link. On the basis of these analyses, the greater denial in flexible subjects cannot be attributed to greater dissonance in these subjects.

Table 1

Smoking, Interference Score and Belief in Smoking–Cancer Link

	Constricted (high-interference scorers)	Flexible (low-interference scorers)	M
Smokers	3·24[1]	2·62[1]	2·93
Nonsmokers	2·80[2]	3·10[2]	2·95
M	3·13	2·74	

1. $N = 29$.　2. $N = 10$.

Another possible artifact in these results is the possibility of response bias. Perhaps constricted subjects tend to select more extreme points on a rating scale. A check on this possibility was offered by the group of twenty *nonsmokers* who were run through the same procedure. The mean belief rating of the constricted subjects was 2·80, compared with 3·10 for flexible subjects. This is a reversal of the direction found among constricted and flexible smokers and indicates the absence of a response bias.

After having ruled out various possible artifacts, the belief scores of all subjects were subjected to a 2×2 analysis of variance for unequal cell frequencies (Winer, 1962). There was no main effect of constricted–flexible control of smokers–nonsmokers. However, the interaction was significant ($F = 5·22$, $df = 1,74$, $p < 0·05$) and again indicates that the constricted–flexible distinction is relevant only among smokers (see Table 1).

The true relationship between the key variables in this study (constricted–flexible control and belief in a smoking–cancer link) might be confounded by the fact that constricted and flexible smokers differ slightly, but significantly, in amount of current smoking and almost significantly in recent decreases in amount of smoking. Partial correlations were computed, therefore, based on the total sample of fifty-eight smokers and on the subsample of twenty-seven smokers whose smoking habits had remained stable for at least one year. The original correlations between constricted–flexible control and belief in a smoking–cancer link were 0.414 ($N = 58$, $p < 0.01$) and 0.541 ($N = 27$, $p < 0.01$). After partialling out amount of smoking as a variable, the comparable correlations dropped negligibly to 0.381 and 0.516, still significant at $p < 0.01$.

It is noteworthy that the correlation between amount of smoking in the total sample of smokers and degree of belief in a smoking–cancer link is 0.177, a trend contrary to the straightforward dissonance-theory expectation that heavier smokers would tend to deny a smoking–cancer link. A similar lack of support for the dissonance-theory prediction is seen in the failure of smokers to show greater denial than nonsmokers. The mean belief score of the nonsmokers was 2.95, compared with 2.93 for the smokers (see Table 1).

Discussion

The results support the initial hypothesis: Smokers with constricted cognitive control tend to admit a smoking–cancer link; smokers with flexible control, even though they smoke less, tend to deny such a link. These differences were statistically significant whether one included or eliminated subjects whose smoking habits had changed within the year prior to testing. In addition, constricted compared with flexible subjects showed a near-significant trend toward decreased smoking in the year prior to study. The pattern that emerges, then, is that flexible smokers smoke less than constricted smokers, deny a smoking–cancer link and maintain their level of smoking, while constricted smokers smoke more, admit a smoking–cancer link, and tend to cut down on their smoking.

Constricted–flexible cognitive control and belief in a smoking–cancer link

The results regarding belief differences suggest that belief in a smoking–cancer link is quite closely tied in with a person's *ability to deal with discrepant information or intrusive cognitions*. If a smoker is asked to report his belief in a smoking–cancer link, a strong belief in such a link constitutes an intrusive idea with respect to his desire to continue smoking and to remain healthy. It is thus an unwanted but compelling cognition, analogous to the subject's difficulty in ignoring words while naming colors on the color-word task. In dissonance terms, it could be said that the words represent dissonant cognitions. It would seem then that facility in ignoring or withstanding the disruption provoked by the words in the color-word task extends to the area of beliefs. This strategy of dissonance reduction is less available to constricted smokers, and they are forced to either tolerate the dissonance or reduce their smoking.

It should be noted that there are certain difficulties in attempts to account for individual differences in dissonance experiments in terms of cognitive controls or other subject characteristics. These problems have been discussed at length by Brehm and Cohen (1962) and Glass (1965). Briefly, the basic point is that since dissonance can only be measured indirectly (i.e. via efforts to reduce it), it becomes difficult to specify whether the obtained individual differences are due to differences in the perception, tolerance, and/or manner and degree of dissonance reduction. This problem might eventually be solved by including subject variables which have specific relevance to different phases of the dissonance arousal-reduction sequence. On the basis of the present data, one cannot definitively indicate which aspect of the dissonant situation is related to the constricted–flexible cognitive-control dimension. Tentatively, it is assumed that all smokers cannot very readily avoid exposure to (i.e. perception of) information linking smoking and cancer (Feather, 1963). Furthermore there is no reason to assume that constricted subjects, who as a group smoke more than flexible subjects, are more tolerant of dissonance or experience less of it. Rather, it appears that the cognitive resolution via denial is simply less available to constricted subjects so that constricted and flexible subjects differ in the *manner* of dissonance reduction.

It has been suggested (Gardner *et al.*, 1959) that cognitive controls and defenses might involve similar structures which serve adaptive or defensive aims, respectively. Applying this conception to the present data, it is proposed that while resistiveness to intrusive cognitions manifests itself *adaptively* on the color-word task (i.e. is conducive to effective performance), it serves as a defense (perhaps denial or isolation of affect) on the smoking questionnaire insofar as it indicates a failure or unwillingness to acknowledge a reality. Constricted subjects, being more vulnerable to intrusive information, either have to tolerate the dissonance or resort to other ways of resolving the situation (e.g. decreased smoking). It is interesting to note, however, that in contrast to most other studies (e.g. Holt, 1960; Loomis and Moskowitz, 1958) this study showed that a *generally* more adaptive control (viz. flexible control) can, in certain situations, possibly have maladaptive effects (i.e. denial of the reality of a smoking–cancer link).

Relevance of individual differences in the study of dissonance

The present study is an example of how the assessment of stable cognitive characteristics can increase the predictive accuracy of the dissonance model. If the nonsmokers had been compared with the smokers without regard to the constricted–flexible distinction, there would have been no difference in mean belief. Granted an undersized sample of nonsmokers, there was not even a noticeable trend in the direction of the dissonance-theory prediction that smokers would exhibit greater denial. It might be argued that the increasing evidence linking smoking and cancer makes it difficult to deny such a link without flagrant disregard for reality. That this is not the case is indicated by the significant belief difference between constricted and flexible smokers.

Simple varying treatment conditions, then, could have readily obscured individual differences in the impact of a given condition and would have led to the erroneous conclusion that denial was no longer a feasible means of reducing dissonance based on smoking. This point is applicable to a recent study by Pervin and Yatko (1965), where negligible differences were found between smokers and nonsmokers on such variables as contact with and selective recall of relevant information, and estimates of the dangers of smoking. Assessment of relevant subject variables might have produced clear differences among the smokers.

The selection of subject characteristics for assessment should be clearly related to the experimental situation. For example, the constricted–flexible cognitive-control dimension is probably most relevant when the reality of the dissonant situation is unambiguous, for that is when individual differences in denial are likely to come into play. Thus, it probably would have been easier for constricted smokers to deny the unpleasurable aspects of smoking than it was for them to deny the link between smoking and cancer. Similarly, at the time of Festinger's study, more than ten years ago, the evidence linking cigarette smoking and lung cancer was less definitive, and the constricted–flexible distinction might not have been related to difference in belief at that time.

References

BAER, D. J. (1966), 'Smoking attitude, behavior, and beliefs of college males', *J. soc. Psychol.*, vol. 68, pp. 65–78.

BREHM, J. W., and COHEN, A. R. (1962), *Explorations in Cognitive Dissonance*, Wiley.

EHRLICH, D., GUTTMAN, I., SCHÖNBACH, P., and MILLS, J. (1957), 'Postdecision exposure to relevant information', *J. abnorm. soc. Psychol.*, vol. 54, pp. 98–102.

FEATHER, N. T. (1963), 'Cognitive dissonance, sensitivity, and evaluation', *J. abnorm. soc. Psychol.*, vol. 66, pp. 157–63.

FESTINGER, L. (1957), *A Theory of Cognitive Dissonance*, Row, Peterson.

GARDNER, R. W., HOLZMAN, P. S., KLEIN, G. S., LINTON, H. B. and SPENCE, D. P. (1959), 'A study of individual consistencies in cognitive behavior', *Psychol. Issues*, vol. 1.

GLASS, D. C. (1965), 'Theories of consistency and the study of personality', in E. F. Borgatta and W. W. Lambert (eds.), *Handbook of Personality Theory and Research*, Rand McNally.

HEIDER, F. (1958), *The Psychology of Interpersonal Relations*, Wiley.

HOLT, R. R. (1960), 'Cognitive controls and primary processes', *J. psychol. Res.*, vol. 4, pp. 1–8.

HORN, D. (1963), 'Behavioral aspects of cigarette smoking', *J. chron. Dis.*, vol. 16, pp. 383–95.

KLEIN, G. S. (1954), 'Need and regulation', in M. R. Jones (ed.), *Nebraska Symposium on Motivation: 1954*, University of Nebraska Press, pp. 224–80.

KLEIN, G. S., SCHLESINGER, H. J., and MEISTER, D. E. (1951), 'The effects of personal values on perception: an experimental critique', *Psychol. Rev.*, vol. 58, pp. 96–112.

LOOMIS, H., and MOSKOWITZ, S. (1958), 'Cognitive style and stimulus ambiguity', *J. Personal.*, vol. 26, pp. 349–64.

OSGOOD, C. E., and TANNENBAUM, P. H. (1955), 'The principle of congruity in the prediction of attitude change', *Psychol. Rev.*, vol. 62, pp. 42–55.

PERVIN, L. A., and YATKO, R. J. (1965), 'Cigarette smoking and alternative methods of reducing dissonance', *J. Personal. soc. Psychol.*, vol. 2, pp. 30–36.

WINER, B. J. (1962), *Statistical Principles in Experimental Design*, McGraw-Hill.

Part Eight **Studies of Perception and Memory**

The three Readings in this Part illustrate the importance in studies of perception and memory of differences between subjects' styles of thinking. Ware and Harvey (Reading 20) examine judgements of people and show that a judge's conceptual system is associated with his willingness to make extensive inferences and the certainty with which these inferences are made. Lo Sciuto and Hartley (Reading 21) describe a small study of what might be termed 'input selection' in the perception of religious stimuli. They find that dogmatism is related to the tendency to select only those inputs which are consistent with one's own religious ideology. In Reading 22 Messick and Damarin report differences in memory for faces which are related to psychological differentiation and to category width.

It will be noted that all these studies are of perception and memory of a somewhat 'social' kind. Research by 'experimental' (in its restricted sense) psychologists into perception and memory still tends to assume that individual differences between subjects are best treated as 'error variance'. This is surely unfortunate; perhaps the examples set down here will encourage some experimental psychologists to incorporate information processing style into their research designs.

20 Robert Ware and O. J. Harvey

A Cognitive Determinant of Impression Formation

Excerpts from Robert Ware and O. J. Harvey, 'A cognitive determinant of impression formation', *Journal of Personality and Social Psychology*, vol. 5, 1967, pp. 38–44.

While several studies have considered the role of personality factors in the accuracy of person perception and the attribution of certain characteristics to others (see Shrauger and Altrocchi, 1964, for a review of such studies), seemingly few, if any, have been concerned specifically with the influence of personality on the amount of information sought about another person before forming an impression of him or on the certainty with which an inference is made. It is with these related questions that the present study deals. [. . .]

Of the many predispositional factors that should affect certainty and extent of impression generated by controlled amounts of information, the degree of concreteness–abstractness of the conceptual system through which inputs are mediated and transmuted into psychological significance should be among the more important. The more abstract and cognitively complex individual, with his greater tendency toward processing and construing the world multidimensionally, should seek more information than the more concrete and cognitively simple person before forming an impression of high certainty about an object person. Applied to the method of the present study, this suggests that the more abstract person, from controlled amounts of information, should generalize less and hold more tentative and less certain impressions of the object person than the more concrete individual. A test of this general hypothesis was the primary concern of the study; it had the dual objective of simultaneously contributing to the accumulating information on the role of personality factors in person perception and testing some of the basic propositions underlying the theory of Harvey, Hunt and Schroder (1961). [. . .]

This theory's characterizations of concreteness–abstractness[1] suggest clearly that, if left free to seek as much information as they wish before forming an impression of another person at some criterion level of generalization and certainty, more concrete individuals will seek less information than the more abstract persons. This should mean that when, instead of providing each person with the information he seeks, all subjects are exposed to equivalent but less than maximal amounts of information, as in the present study, more concrete individuals will form more generalized and more certain impressions of the object person than will more abstract individuals. The validity of this latter assumption, however, is clearly contingent upon the level of information at which impressions are assessed.

Results from the numerous studies of the effects of intra-organismic variables upon cognition indicate that the influence of concreteness–abstractness should be greater under the ambiguity resulting from little information than under the stimulus compulsion embodied in very large amounts of information. The validity of this assumption, at least as far as this study is concerned, in turn rests upon the method by which the treatment effects are assessed. Given the condition of *hedonic consistency* between characteristics of the informational inputs and atrributes on which impressions are assessed (i.e. when inputs and impression attributes are either both positive or both negative), differences in concreteness–abstractness on impression formation should be reflected more clearly at low than very high levels of informational input. Under the conditions of hedonic inconsistency between inputs and impression characteristics (i.e. when input characteristics are positive and the response categories are negative or vice versa), however, differences between the impressions of more concrete and more abstract individuals should be greater at the high than at the low level of information.

Postulation of these method effects stems from differences between concrete and abstract individuals previously noted.[2] The greater need of the more concrete individuals for structure, consistency and avoidance of dissonance should result in a greater tendency on their part than on the part of the more

1. See Reading 17 for a summary presentation [*Ed.*].
2. See Reading 17 [*Ed.*].

abstract individuals to attribute only positive characteristics to 'good' people and only negative characteristics to 'bad' people. Applied here, this means that more concrete individuals should generalize more than more abstract persons when the input-response characteristics are of the same hedonic quality but that the reverse picture should obtain when the input-impression attributes are of opposite affective qualities.

Because of the preceding considerations and the desire to maximize representativeness of the informational inputs, subjects varying in concreteness–abstractness were exposed, in three steps, to two, four and six pieces each of positive and negative information about a hypothetical person and tested after each step on their impression of the person and the certainty of their impressions. Impressions were assessed through a kind of generalization measure based on subjects' ratings of the plausibility or likelihood that, given the positive or negative input characteristics of him, the object person would possess or manifest certain other, both positive and negative, attributes as well. A certainty rating was made of each plausibility response.

Hypotheses

Under the testing condition of hedonic consistency between input and response characteristics:

1. More concrete subjects will generalize more and be more certain of their impressions than the more abstract subjects, at least under the condition of least information.

Similar differences at the other two, more compelling levels of information would not negate our hypotheses, but would simply indicate that the influence of concreteness–abstractness on impression formation is stronger than we had any bases for hypothesizing.

Under the testing condition of hedonic inconsistency between input and response attributes:

2. More concrete subjects will generalize less but be more certain of their impressions than the more abstract subjects, at least under the condition of greatest information.

Similar differences at the lower levels of information would simply indicate a stronger than anticipated effect of concreteness–abstractness.

No further hypotheses were made about the main or inter-actional effects of quality and frequency of inputs, although effects in addition to those hypothesized were statistically ana-lysed and will be reported.

Method

Subjects

Eighteen concrete and eighteen abstract subjects participated in the experiment. As students in introductory psychology at the University of Colorado during the fall of 1964, they received either course credit or cash payment for serving as subjects.

Measurement of concreteness–abstractness

This was accomplished by the This I Believe Test, an instrument that requires the respondent to complete in two or three sentences the phrase, 'This I believe about — ', the blank being filled suc-cessively by concept referents such as 'the American way of life', 'religion', 'marriage', 'friendship', 'people' and 'guilt' (Harvey, 1964, 1965; White and Harvey, 1965). From the normativeness, absolutism, evaluativeness and simplicity–complexity of the com-pletions, together with criteria suggested in the characterizations noted earlier, respondents may be classified into one of the four principal systems and levels of abstractness posited by Harvey, Hunt and Schroder (1961) or into some admixture of two or more systems. Since the concern of this study was with the effects of concreteness–abstractness, without regard to content differences of the different conceptual systems, only subjects who were classi-fied as representing predominantly System 1, the more concrete mode of conceptual functioning, and System 4, the more abstract way of functioning, were included in the experimental sample.

Stimulus materials

Input stimuli. Impressions of the object person were elicited by brief descriptions of twelve behavioral acts to which all subjects were exposed. As determined by pretesting of a larger number of behavioral descriptions, six of the statements connoted socially desirable behavior (positive inputs), while the other six described socially undesirable behavior (negative inputs). The statements, in typewritten form, were enclosed in glass slides, two desirable or two undesirable acts described in each of the six slides.

Output dimensions. Behavioral output, or the extent to which impressions elicited by the input stimuli were generalized to other aspects of the object person, was assessed from responses to six descriptive statements, three of which had been shown by pretesting to connote socially desirable acts or attributes (*positive outputs*) and three of which had been shown to imply negative attributes (*negative outputs*). After the presentation of each slide, subjects responded to each of the six randomly ordered output descriptions in two ways: by indicating how plausible the attribute was, and by expressing their feeling of certainty about each plausibility response. Both plausibility and certainty responses were in the form of ratings made on graphic rating scales on which only the opposite poles were indicated for each behavioral dimension. 'Extremely likely' and 'extremely unlikely' defined the poles for each plausibility rating, while certainty ratings were made between the poles of 'very certain' and 'very uncertain'.

Procedure

Subjects were instructed:

This is an experiment in judging behavior on the basis of knowledge about some past behavior of an individual. We want to know how likely or plausible you think it is that a person who has shown certain behaviors in the past would also show certain other behavior or characteristics. Information pertaining to some behaviors of an individual will be projected upon the screen. You are to make judgements about the likelihood or plausibility that this individual would evidence other behavior or attributes indicated on your response sheet. Also, you are to indicate how strongly you feel that the plausibility judgements you make are in fact correct. Work as rapidly as possible without too much deliberation, giving only your first impressions.

Following instructions on the use of the scales, half of the subjects in each personality classification were exposed to negative inputs and then to positive inputs, making plausibility and certainty ratings after each slide; the other half of the subjects were presented the positive and negative inputs in the reverse order. Table 1 presents the input statements and the sequence of their presentation and Table 2 contains the six output dimensions.

Table 1

Input Descriptions of Object Persons

Slide no.	Negative inputs	Slide no.	Positive inputs
1	Had high job absenteeism	1	Frequently sent flowers and get-well wishes to hospitalized friends
	Ran over his neighbor's dog with his car		Worked his way through college by part-time employment as a laborer
2	Picked up tips left for the waitress by other patrons	2	Spearheaded a fund-raising campaign for homes for unwed mothers
	Court-martialed while serving in the U.S. Army		Became a vice-president of a large company at an unusually young age
3	Arrested for failure to support his child	3	On several occasions voluntarily assumed the work responsibilities of an ill colleague
	Convicted for pushing dope to high school students		Decorated for gallantry in action while serving in the U.S. Marine Corps

Table 2

Output Dimensions

Positive outputs	Negative outputs
1. Have a strong and physically attractive body	1. Read friends' private letters without their permission
2. Suppress the urge to speak hastily in anger	2. Treat all religious matters as primitive and trivial
3. Help other people feel more secure even if he does not like them	3. Break promises without justification

Results

The assumption that variation in concreteness–abstractness would dispose toward opposite generalization effects depending on whether the input and output dimensions were hedonically consistent or inconsistent necessitated the separate treatment of plausibility ratings of the three positive and the three negative output dimensions. Two generalization scores represented by the respective sums of the plausibility ratings (measured in millimeters) on the three positive and on the three negative output dimensions were consequently computed for each subject for each pair of inputs. For computational ease, all sums were divided by ten and rounded to the nearest whole number. Certainty scores were computed and rounded in similar ways.

Hedonic quality and frequency of inputs

The anticipated effects of variation in concreteness–abstractness rest upon the assumption that manipulation of the stimulus variables would produce certain effects independently of personality: namely, the positive inputs would generate impressions that were more positive than negative; negative inputs would elicit impressions more negative than positive; the tendency of inputs to produce images consistent with their hedonic quality would increase with increased amounts of information.

That these necessary stimulus effects were achieved can be inferred from Table 3.

Subjects clearly considered it more plausible that a person described in positive terms should display positive rather than

Table 3

Mean Plausibility Ratings of Positive and Negative Output Dimensions for Each Pair of Positive and Negative Inputs

No. of inputs	Positive inputs		Negative inputs	
	Positive outputs	Negative outputs	Negative outputs	Positive outputs
2	27·64	9·64	25·25	15·20
4	28·84	9·22	30·05	13·39
6	31·00	5·89	34·25	10·11

negative attributes and that a negatively depicted person should behave more undesirably than positively characterized individuals. As would have to be the case if the stimulus manipulations were effective as desired, these differences were accentuated with increased frequency of informational inputs.

While the preceding results simply show effectiveness of the stimulus variations, other comparisons of the effects of the quality (i.e. positive or negative) of the inputs under the different conditions of input–output consistency and inconsistency generate more interesting results. No significant difference was found by t-tests between the positive generalization (i.e. the plausibility ratings of positive output dimensions) produced by positive inputs with the negative generalization (i.e. the plausibility ratings of the negative output attributes) produced by the negative inputs, for the total generalization or the generalization at each input frequency. This means that the tendency to generalize from positive information about a person to other positive characteristics of him is comparable in strength to the tendency to attribute negative characteristics to another following a negative description of him.

The picture is different, however, when comparisons are made between extent of generalization under the input–output inconsistency conditions. Subjects were less willing at all levels of information to attribute negative characteristics to a person following positive depiction of him than they were to attribute positive attributes to him following a negative description, implying a kind of tendency to see the good in another person rather than the bad. This difference, of similar direction for both the concrete and abstract subjects, was significant for total generalization ($t = 5.60$, $p < 0.001$) and for each of the three levels of information, the smallest t (for two inputs) being 5.04 ($p < 0.001$).

As with extent of generalization or extent of perceived plausibility, Table 4 shows that certainty of ratings became greater as the frequency of inputs increased and that there was no difference between the certainty of the ratings of the positive output attributes following positive information and the certainty of the ratings of the negative output dimensions following negative inputs ($t = 0.33$). Also as with generalization but in the opposite direction, there was a significant difference between the certainty of the ratings under the different conditions of input–output inconsistency. While subjects considered positive behavior following negative inputs to be more plausible than negative behavior following positive representations, they were less certain

Table 4

Mean Certainty of Impression for Each Pair of Inputs under the Conditions of Input–Output Consistency and Inconsistency

No. of inputs	Positive inputs		Negative inputs	
	Positive outputs	Negative outputs	Negative outputs	Positive outputs
2	27·33	28·48	25·34	24·03
4	31·05	31·84	31·25	27·98
6	33·08	34·69	35·56	32·70

of the latter ratings; that is, they felt more certain that a person described as having positive characteristics would be less likely to manifest undesirable behavior than a negatively depicted person would be to display positive characteristics.

Concreteness–abstractness

Given most of the preceding results, a presentation of the effects of concreteness–abstractness becomes appropriate.

Results in Table 5 indicate that when input and output characteristics are hedonically consistent, the extent of generalization or willingness to go beyond the information given in the inferences drawn about another person is greater for the concrete than for the abstract individuals. While our hypothesis stipulated that this difference should be significant at least for the lowest level of information, t-tests showed the difference to be significant at all three levels of information (smallest t, for two inputs $= 1·69$, $p < 0·05$) as well as for the levels combined ($t = 2·95$, $p < 0·005$). Thus concreteness–abstractness exercised significant effects even under the more highly structured conditions represented by the greater frequencies of inputs.

In fact, the difference between the amounts of generalization of the concrete and abstract subjects was greater at the highest than at the lowest level of information. This is accounted for by the fact that while the concrete and abstract subjects both increased in generalization with increased inputs, as should be expected, the rate of increase, as measured by the difference in generalization between two and six inputs, was significantly greater for the concrete than for the abstract individuals ($t = 1.70$, $p < 0.05$). Moreover, it may be noted, as a fact of further interest, that the concrete subjects generalized as much from only four inputs as the abstract subjects did from six.

Table 5

Mean Generalization of Concrete and Abstract Subjects for Three Levels of Information under Each of the Conditions of Input–Output Consistency and Inconsistency

S group	Input–output hedonically consistent			Input–output hedonically inconsistent		
	No. of inputs			No. of inputs		
	2	4	6	2	4	6
Concrete	54·56	61·94	69·22	22·06	19·89	14·06
Abstract	51·22	55·83	61·28	27·61	25·33	17·94

Results in Table 5 also show that under input–output inconsistency both concrete and abstract subjects decreased in generalization with increased inputs, meaning simply that the greater the frequency of positive inputs the less the willingness or tendency to attribute negative characteristics to the object person, and the greater the frequency of negative inputs the greater the unwillingness to attribute positive features to him. This fact is of little theoretical import, but of theoretical interest is the finding that the concrete and abstract subjects differed significantly in this effect at all but the highest level of information. After each of the first and second pair of inputs ($ts = 2.33$, 2.06, $ps < 0.03$) as well as when the combined effects of all six inputs were considered ($t = 2.20$, $p < 0.03$), the concrete subjects considered it less plausible than the abstract individuals that a person who had earlier manifested either socially desirable or undesirable behavior subsequently would evidence behavior of the opposite quality.

In addition to the predicted influence of concreteness–abstractness on generalization, this variable also exercised a significant effect on certainty of the elicited impressions. Results in Table 6

Table 6

Mean Certainty of the Concrete and Abstract Subjects under Input–Output Consistency and Inconsistency

S group	Input–output hedonically consistent	Input–output hedonically inconsistent
Concrete	188·78	189·44
Abstract	178·56	169·89

show that whether the input and output attributes were consistent or inconsistent, a contingency that had no effects on degree of certainty, the concrete individuals were more certain of their impressions than were the abstract subjects (t for combined conditions $= 2·04$, $p < 0·02$).

Discussion

The fact that under the condition of input–output consistency greater concreteness accompanied greater impression generalization at the highest as well as at the two lower levels of information indicates that the variable of concreteness–abstractness exercises considerable influence on the inferences people make of others even in the presence of fairly highly structured stimulus cues. For a more thorough assessment of the effects of this cognitive factor, it is clear that it must be studied under a wider range of stimulus or cue structure than was investigated here, from less information and greater ambiguity through more frequent and more determinate informational inputs. [. . .]

In addition to indicating that concrete individuals make up their minds more completely than abstract persons on little information, the present results also point clearly to a greater need for cognitive consistency on the part of the concrete than on the part of the abstract person. The fact that the concrete subjects generalized more than the abstract individuals under conditions of hedonic consistency between input and output dimensions, but generalized less than the abstract subjects when the inputs were hedonically inconsistent, may be interpreted as supporting the notion that concrete persons, more than abstract individuals, are disposed toward seeing the 'good' person as all good and the 'bad' person as all bad, minimizing the plausibility that the same person could simultaneously possess both good and bad characteristics. This interpretation would be in line with one of our earlier findings (Harvey, 1965) that concrete individuals were less able than abstract subjects to generate superordinate constructs of persons that would be consistent with their possessing simultaneously positive and negative characteristics.

References

HARVEY, O. J. (1964), 'Some cognitive determinants of influencibility', *Sociometry*, vol. 27, pp. 208–21.

HARVEY, O. J. (1965), 'Some situational and cognitive determinants of dissonance resolution', *J. Personal. soc. Psychol.*, vol. 1, pp. 349–55.

HARVEY, O. J., HUNT, D. E., and SCHRODER, H. M. (1961), *Conceptual Systems and Personality Organization*, Wiley.

SHRAUGER, S., and ALTROCCHI, J. (1964), 'The personality of the perceiver as a factor in person perception', *Psychol. Bull.*, vol. 5, pp. 289–308.

WHITE, B. J., and HARVEY, O. J. (1965), 'Effects of personality and own stand on judgement and production of statements about a central issue', *J. exp. soc. Psychol.*, vol. 1, pp. 334–47.

21 Leonard A. LoSciuto and Eugene L. Hartley

Religious Affiliation and Open-Mindedness in Binocular Resolution

Leonard A. LoSciuto and Eugene L. Hartley, 'Religious affiliation and open-mindedness in binocular resolution', *Perceptual and Motor Skills*, vol. 17, 1963, pp. 427–30.

The phenomenon of binocular rivalry has long been familiar in the psychological literature (e.g. Galton, 1883; Meenes, 1930). Recently, however, the work of some of the transactional psychologists has brought it to the fore as a means of exploring the dynamics of human perception (e.g. Kilpatrick, 1961). Engel (1956) studied stimulus characteristics using upright and inverted faces; Bagby (1957) examined the role of cultural content; Davis (1959) used words as stimuli and analysed familiarity and personal perceptual defense mechanisms; Pettigrew, Allport and Barnett (1958) used the approach in a study of racial cleavages. In Beloff and Beloff (1959) and Kaufer and Riess (1960) are found applications to the study of personality, and Toch and associates have used the readiness to perceive violence as a means of evaluating offenders, and of studying the effect of law enforcement training (Toch, 1961; Toch and Schulte, 1961). The present study was designed to evaluate the integration of social and personal variables in the determination of the emergent perceptions of the individual when confronted with complex stimulus patterns. More specifically, the study investigated the responses of Jewish and Catholic students, whose open-mindedness was assessed in accordance with Rokeach's definition (1960),[1] when presented stereoscopically with conflicting Jewish and Christian symbols.

1. See Reading 2 [*Ed.*].

Method

Subjects

The final group of *S*s included twenty male undergraduate students at The City College of New York; ten had Jewish religious affiliations and ten had Catholic.

Procedure

Binocular resolution was investigated, using a fixed focus form of Brewster stereoscope with a manually operated cover card to reveal and conceal the stereograms. Two series of stereograms were prepared, one involving word pairs and one using pictorial symbols.

The first (verbal) series numbered sixteen stereograms of eight word pairs. Each word pair was presented twice to permit reversal of the right-left position. The word pairs employed were:

Kaddish	Convent	Rosh Hashana	Holy Communion
Torah	Saint	Rabbi	Cross
Menorah	Trinity	Synagogue	Monastery
Talmud	Novena	Cantor	Rosary

The sixteen stereograms were presented in random order with approximately one-second exposure.

The second (pictorial) series was a set of six stereograms pairing symbols: Engraved Cross and Menorah; Symbol of Passover and Rosary Beads; Cross and Star of David; Scroll and Chalice; Latin Symbol for Christ and Hebrew Symbol for the Lord; Tablet with Ten Commandments and Bible with Cross on Cover. Three of the stereograms presented the Christian symbol on the left, three on the right. The six stereograms were presented for about thirty seconds each, with full recording of *S*s' reports during that time. Analysis, however, relied primarily on the responses during the first fifteen seconds of exposure.

The first five stereograms of the first series were used as an index of eye dominance. If *S* reported only the words on either the right or the left side of the stereogram for all five, it was assumed that the disparity between his eyes was such as to disqualify him as an *S*. No data from such *S*s were included in the analysis.

Open-mindedness was measured by the use of Rokeach's forty-item Dogmatism Scale Form E (1960, pp. 72 ff.).

Scoring

Responses to the stereograms seemed to fall into four major categories. (a) Only one word or picture was seen and described by S. For this response, 1 point was assigned to the religion represented. (b) Both words were seen with equal clarity; or both symbols were seen with approximately equal time devoted to the descriptions of each. Also, at times a composite symbol was described which included details from both stimuli. For such responses, 0·5 point was assigned to each religion. (c) Again the reports included both stimuli, but with unequivocal evidence of the dominance of one over the other. With the words, only one might be seen clearly or completely, though the other entered awareness. With the pictured symbols, there would be a significant dispro-portion in the times during which each appeared. With such responses, 0·75 point was assigned to the religion whose symbol dominated and 0·25 point was assigned to the other. (d) This form of response appeared only in the verbal series; no word could be detected, only an indecipherable jumble of letters being reported. For such responses, no score was assigned.

From the stereograms, therefore, each S received two scores, one for each of the two religions represented. These two scores (plus the number of 0 ratings) summated to a total of twenty-two for each respondent.

The Dogmatism Scale was scored in accordance with the general plan described by Rokeach.

Results

Table 1 presents the frequency distributions of the scores on the stereoscope task by content for the two religious groups. The general mean point-score for content reported of one's own religion was 14·3 ($\sigma = 1·26$), for content of the 'other' religion the mean was 6·6 ($\sigma = 1·68$); this difference was significant ($p < 0·001$). Failure of the two means, 14·3 and 6·6, to add up to 22 was caused by the zero score described above. The Jewish and Catholic groups both had an equal tendency to see their own reli-gious content in preference to the other. The difference in the strength of this tendency to see 'own' religious content was not significant ($p < 0.1$). The relationship between religious affiliation and the tendency to see content identified with that religion, in this experimental situation, may be expressed by the point-biserial correlation coefficient of 0.95.

Table 1

Stereoscope Scores for Catholic and Jewish Content by Religion of Observers

Scores	C Content		J Content	
	Catholic	Jewish	Catholic	Jewish
0–4	0	0	1	0
5–8	0	7	8	0
9–12	0	3	1	0
13–16	8	0	0	9
17–20	2	0	0	1
21+	0	0	0	0

The difference in mean Dogmatism scores for the Jewish and Catholic Ss was not significant ($p < 0.1$). When the two groups were combined and the open-mindedness score from this scale was correlated with the tendency of the individual to see content of the 'other' religion in the stereoscope task, $r = 0.40$ ($p < 0.025$). The evidence supports the anticipated association between open-mindedness (in the Rokeach sense) and the sensitivity and readiness to respond to unfavored stimuli in a perceptual conflict situation.

Discussion

Despite the limitations of the present study, its findings seem highly interesting. The variable studied, religious affiliation, represents a complex which confounds social and affective involvement with the religious identification, as well as unknown extents of differential familiarity with the competing stimuli used. Significant social variables, however, commonly involve such contamination. Here, however, we were more interested in relating gross social differences to a psychological variable, than we were in isolating the psychological components of the social variable.

The association between open-mindedness and the tendency to see stimuli of the 'other' religion, cutting across both groups, seems illustrative of the way in which the psychodynamics of the individual may achieve form and content through integration with socially presented material. It is through such integrations that there are established the unique environments within which each individual functions, despite the apparent participation of groups of people in a common milieu.

References

BAGBY, J. (1957), 'A cross-cultural study of perceptual predominance in binocular rivalry', *J. abnorm. soc. Psychol.*, vol. 54, pp. 331–4.

BELOFF, H., and BELOFF, J. (1959), 'Unconscious self-evaluation using a stereoscope', *J. abnorm. soc. Psychol.*, vol. 59, pp. 275–8.

DAVIS, J. M. (1959), 'Personality, perceptual defense, and stereoscopic perception', *J. abnorm. soc. Psychol.*, vol. 58, pp. 398–402.

ENGEL, E. (1956), 'The role of content in binocular resolution', *Amer. J. Psychol.*, vol. 69, pp. 87–91.

GALTON, F. (1883), *Inquiries into Human Faculty*, Macmillan.

KAUFER, G., and RIESS, B. F. (1960), 'Stereoscopic perception as a tool in psychotherapeutic research', *Percept. mot. Skills*, vol. 10, pp. 241–2.

KILPATRICK, F. P. (ed.) (1961), *Explorations in Transactional Psychology*, New York University Press.

MEENES, M. (1930), 'A phenomenological description of retinal rivalry', *Amer. J. Psychol.*, vol. 42, pp. 260–69.

PETTIGREW, T., ALLPORT, G., and BARNETT, E. (1958), 'Binocular resolution and perception of race in South Africa', *Brit. J. Psychol.*, vol. 49, pp. 265–78.

ROKEACH, M. (1960), *The Open and Closed Mind*, Basic Books.

TOCH, H. H. (1961), 'The stereoscope: a new frontier in psychological research', *Res. Newslett. Calif. Dept. Correct.*, vol. 3, nos. 3–4.

TOCH, H. H., and SCHULTE, R. (1961), 'Readiness to perceive violence as a result of police training', *Brit. J. Psychol.*, vol. 52, pp. 389–93.

22 Samuel Messick and Fred Damarin

Cognitive Styles and Memory for Faces

Samuel Messick and Fred Damarin, 'Cognitive styles and memory for faces', *Journal of Abnormal and Social Psychology*, vol. 69, 1964, pp. 313–18.

A theory for relating a cognitive style to accuracy in the recall of faces has been given by Witkin *et al.* (1962, pp. 147–8). They suggested that field-dependent persons,[1] being in need of support and guidance from others, are particularly attentive to the facial characteristics and expressions which provide ready clues to other people's moods and attitudes. As a consequence, field-dependent subjects 'tend to be better than relatively field-independent persons at recognizing people they have seen only briefly before' (p. 3). In support of this contention, these authors cited an unpublished study by De Varis in which field-dependent boys were significantly more accurate in selecting cutout photographs of their own noses, eyes, ears, etc., from among a set of similar photographs of the features of others. The results were interpreted as another example of the tendency of field-dependent persons to characterize themselves and others in terms of 'external' attributes (Witkin *et al.*, 1962, p. 148). Crutchfield, Woodworth and Albrecht (1958) tested Air Force captains, who had previously stayed at an assessment center, for the accuracy of their recall of other center residents. The number of correct identifications of photographs of fellow residents was significantly related to field dependence as measured by the Rod-and-Frame Test.

The present study attempted to ascertain whether field-dependent individuals would demonstrate better incidental recall of photographs when they have never interacted socially with the individuals portrayed. In addition, since this research problem was part of a larger study, it was feasible to explore the relationship between accuracy in recall and other cognitive styles and

1. See Reading 10 [*Ed.*].

biases, even though specific theories had not been previously formulated to predict what the relationships ought to be. Pertinent data were gathered from Pettigrew's (1958) Category-Width Scale and from judgements made by each subject of the ages of the photographed faces.

Method

Subjects

The subjects of the present investigation were forty male and ten female volunteers from summer psychology classes at a large metropolitan university. Their average age was 21·7 years.

Procedure

A measure of memory for faces was developed in which the memory requirement was incidental to another task, since it was felt that the active analytical approach of field-independent subjects might enable them to learn the faces rapidly if the true nature of the task were apparent. A Photo Judging Test was devised for administration in two parts. In Part I the subjects were asked to estimate the age of each of seventy-nine persons portrayed in photographs and to check those that seemed to resemble some individual who had been encountered previously in the subjects' everyday lives. Part II was administered without prior warning two hours later at the end of the testing session. The subjects were again asked to estimate the ages of forty persons from photographs. Twenty of the pictures had been shown previously in Part I of the test, and the subjects were asked to identify these without knowing their total number.

The photographs themselves were taken from Burwen and Campbell's (1957) study of the generality of attitudes to authority figures. They represented ten types of persons; teenaged, youthful, middle-aged and elderly men and four similar classes of women, along with two additional groups of middle-aged men selected to typify strength and weakness. Each of these ten types appeared approximately eight times in Part I and twice in Part II of the Photo Judging Test. To focus attention on facial characteristics, all the sitters had worn a black cape while being photographed. Various poses were represented, some smiling and some serious. None of the persons portrayed was likely to have been known to the experimental subjects. Part I of the Photo Judging Test provided a measure of one of the three independent variables, the tendency to estimate all of the faces as relatively old or young.

A group Embedded-Figures Test (EFT) was administered to the sample of fifty college students as a measure of field dependence. To minimize common variance in the embedded-figures and recall procedures due to general memory facility, a group administered EFT was employed which, unlike Witkin's procedure, did not have a memory format (Jackson, Messick and Myers, 1964).

The third independent variable, category-width (C-W) preferences, was assessed by Pettigrew's (1958) test.

Test scores

Six scores were obtained from the Photo Judging Test; they are listed as rows in Table 1. The first measure, correct recall, represents the major dependent variable in the study. It was scored as the number of photographs correctly checked or correctly left unchecked in Part II as having been previously seen in Part I.

Variable 2, correlation between age estimates in Parts I and II, was a correlation coefficient (transformed to Fisher's z) for each person to express the consistency with which his age judgements in Part I of the test were repeated in Part II. It was computed over the twenty items common to both parts of the test. As shown in Table 1, the average individual correlation was 0·84. Individual differences in such consistency, however, were not significantly related to the kind of accuracy measured by Variable 1 or to the other scores discussed below.

Variables 3 and 4 were designed to measure a bias toward belief that 'the face is familiar'. Variable 3, number of faces judged familiar in Part I, was the number of pictures checked as resembling persons encountered outside the experimental situation. Variable 4, number of faces checked as shown before: Part II, was the number of pictures the subject believed to be common to Parts I and II of the test. These two 'bias' scores intercorrelated 0·274 ($0·10 > p > 0·05$). The accuracy score (Variable 1), however, correlated $-0·342$ ($p < 0·05$) with Variable 3 and $-0·541$

Table 1

Scores from the Photo Judgement Test and their Correlations with Cognitive Style Measures

Photo-judgement score	M	Sigma	Reliability[1]	EFT correlation	Factor 1, C-W correlation	Age assigned
1. Correct recall	29·020	3·947	0·708**	−0·291*	−0·361**	−0·373**
2. Correlation between age estimates in Parts I and II	0·840	0·180	—	−0·051	0·030	0·096
3. Number of faces judged familiar in Part I	26·260	15·286	0·936**	0·014	−0·095	0·222
4. Number of faces checked as shown before: Part II	25·980	5·113	0·741**	0·121	0·352*	0·357*
5. Age assigned: Part I	46·180	2·289	0·926***	−0·010	0·117	1·000
6. Variance in age estimates: Part I	301·460	68·476	0·938**	−0·039	−0·138	0·404**

1. Reliabilities are corrected split-half coefficients, odd versus even.

* $p < 0.05$. ** $p < 0.01$.

($p < 0.01$) with Variable 4, suggesting that accuracy may require the subjects to overcome a bias toward judging that faces are familiar. This conclusion is strengthened when we examine the items in Part II. Faces which were common to Parts I and II were correctly identified by an average of 87·5 per cent of the subjects. Faces which were new in Part II were correctly identified by only 57·6 per cent of the subjects, on the average. The t-value for a difference of this magnitude is 26·85. There appears to be a 'constant error' in this experiment that leads subjects to see new faces as more familiar than they really are.

Variables 5 and 6 were taken from the subjects' age judgements in Part I. Variable 5, age assigned: Part I, represents one of the independent variables under consideration. It measures the subjects' tendency to see the faces as elderly rather than as youthful. The average age assigned to the photographs was 46·2 years; unfortunately the average of the sitters' true ages was not available for comparison. Variable 6, variance in age estimates: Part I, has a large average value, reflecting the great heterogeneity present in this sample of faces. Scores 5 and 6 intercorrelated 0·404 ($p < 0.01$).

The EFT was scored in the field-independent direction as the number correct. Two scores were taken from the C-W test to represent the first two factors that Pettigrew (1958) found among the items; high scores for both factors indicate preference for broad categories.

Results

The major findings of the study are presented in row 1 of Table 1. The correct recall score had a reliability of 0·71, and it correlated significantly with field independence (-0.291, $p < 0.05$), with the Factor 1 items in Pettigrew's C-W Scale (-0.361, $p < 0.01$),[2] and with the tendency to see faces as old (-0.373, $p < 0.01$). Thus, accuracy in recall of faces was associated with field dependence,

2. The correlation between the Factor 2 C-W score and accuracy of recall is -0.264 ($p = 0.067$). The correlation between these Factor 2 items and Variable 4 is 0·084. Although the Factor 1 and Factor 2 C-W items typically intercorrelate in the low sixties, the Factor 2 items apparently also reflect quantitative aptitude to some extent (Messick and Kogan, 1964).

with narrow category widths, and with a tendency to judge faces as relatively youthful.

These three relationships appear to be independent of each other – the correlation between EFT and C-W was −0·014, and the correlations of these two cognitive style measures with the age-assigned score were only −0·010 and 0·117, respectively. The multiple correlation for predicting accuracy in recall from the EFT, C-W, and age-assigned scores was 0·57, which indicates that a substantial amount of the variance of the recall score has been accounted for, relative to its reliability of 0·71.

Discussion

The significant negative correlation between accuracy in recall and the EFT supports the Witkin *et al.* (1962) contention that field-dependent persons are more accurate in the recall of faces. This finding is something of an anomaly in the literature on field dependence–independence – usually when differences occur, it is the field-*in*dependent subjects who are superior on perceptual and cognitive tasks. For example, in the larger study of which this experiment was a part, all subjects took an undisguised memory test calling for close attention to designs composed of forms, elements, and patterned backgrounds (Messick and Fritzky, 1963). Correlations between scores from this test and EFT were non-significant except for the tendency of field-*in*dependent subjects to excel in recalling the formal properties of the designs. Witkin *et al.* (1962, pp. 61–71, 99–103, 141–2) found that field-*in*dependent boys were better at the incidental recall of words and TAT cards. There is, therefore, no evidence that the present results can be explained by a superior general aptitude for directed or incidental recall on the part of the more field-dependent subjects.

We are obliged to suppose that the field-dependent subjects did better in the present experiment because they were asked to remember socially relevant stimuli, such as faces, rather than abstract designs or other impersonal material. The conditions of the study rule out prior social or emotional investment in the sitters as a cause of differential memory achievement. We therefore suggest the hypothesis that a continuing need to satisfy strong social drives, such as dependence, may create a fund of information and interpretive skills that enables the field-dependent person to distinguish among faces, just as prolonged study enables the art critic to distinguish among the styles of different painters.

Because women have usually been found more field dependent than men (Witkin *et al.*, 1962, 1954) and because they may also be more socially attentive (Exline, 1963; Witryol and Kaess, 1957), we examined correlations among the cognitive style measures, the two bias scores, correctness of recall and a dichotomously scored sex variable. None of the coefficients was significant, although the correlation of -0.223 between EFT and female sex was in the appropriate direction. Excessive weight should not be placed on this finding, however, since the present sample of subjects consisted of forty males and only ten females. The hypothesized relationships might well emerge from a more balanced group.

Future research might also determine whether field-dependent memory abilities are limited to the human face or whether they extend to other sorts of spatial configurations that are important for interpersonal relationships. For example, photographs of a sample of private homes might be shown to subjects to be judged for some general feature, such as neatness. At a later time one might test for the incidental recall of details which betray the personalities and interests of the occupants. If social relations are important to the field-dependent person, he might distinguish himself here as well as in the task of recalling faces.

In order to explain why narrow categorizers were relatively better than broad categorizers in recalling faces, it will be necessary to discuss the probable source of the 'constant errors' present in this experiment. None of the subjects could have known any of the sitters, yet in the first part of the experiment the subjects marked the faces as familiar quite frequently. In the second part, the subjects were more likely to err by supposing a new face to be an old one than by forgetting a face they had already seen. This constant error may have arisen because the faces that were new in Part II were similar in type to faces that had gone before. Age and sex categories had been used in recruiting all the sitters, but there were additional factors that made each age–sex category look homogeneous. The teenaged boys and girls, for example, were selected from a single high school class and did not span the full age range from thirteen to nineteen. The weak-looking middle-aged men were alcoholics from Skid Row; the strong-looking middle-aged men were Air Force colonels. Persons within a given type tended therefore to be similar in age, in standards of facial grooming, and perhaps also in features impressed upon their faces by a common lot in life. When the twenty old and twenty new pictures were shown in Part II, the old pictures of course looked familiar because they had been seen before in Part I; the new pictures may also have looked somewhat familiar, however, because they represented the same *types* of people that had been seen before in Part I. There was probably no sharp separation between the familiarity feelings aroused by the old and new photographs, but rather a single class with more or less indefinite boundaries consisting of 'somewhat familiar faces'.

Broad categorizers appear to believe that any category with indefinite boundaries, such as whales in the North Atlantic, is capable of including a large variety of specimens, for example, very large whales and very small ones. Narrow categorizers are more conservative (Wallach and Caron, 1959). They put the boundaries of the class closer together, and they appear to believe that all whales are more nearly of an average size (Pettigrew, 1958). Since the category of 'faces seen before' had indefinite boundaries, the broad categorizers should have made over-inclusive errors in reporting that this category contained many of the faces they saw in Part II. Narrow categorizers should have used stricter standards for deciding when familiarity implied identity, and they should have reported fewer faces common to Parts I and II. The correlation between broad category width and Variable 4, number of faces checked as shown before: Part II, is 0·352. Broad category width correlates −0·361 with Variable 1, correct recall, and this correlation reduces to −0·217 when Variable 4 is partialed out. We subdivided Variable 1 into two scores reflecting, respectively, correct identification of the old faces as old and correct identification of the new faces as new. Broad categorizing (on Factor 1, C-W items) correlated 0·084 with the first of these scores and −0·404 ($p < 0·01$) with the second.

Narrow categorizers appear, therefore, to have better recall because they overcome the 'constant error' of judging that 'the face is familiar'. Their superiority may reflect better registration of the stimulus, a finer sensitivity to small differences, or consistent differences in the preferred betting strategy used to resolve uncertainty. Whichever is correct, the superiority of the narrow categorizer is unlikely to be restricted to facial stimuli. These subjects also did better in the Memory for Design Test mentioned above (Messick and Fritzky, 1963) when they were asked to recall the details of abstract designs and use these as cues to identify novel variations of the designs.

Accuracy in recall of faces was correlated with a tendency to judge the sitters as relatively youthful. An overinclusive bias seems to be at work here also, for those who gave older judgements in Part I tended to think that many pictures in Part II were shown before. A cognitively based broad category width would not account for this bias because the correlation between the C-W test and the age assigned to the faces was only 0·117. Age judgements may, however, also reflect the subject's *affective* response to the faces (cf. Kogan, 1960). Younger estimates seem to signify the more favorable attitude. Subjects who can view even old and weather-beaten faces sympathetically may attend more closely to the features and expressions that individualize each face. Those who find many of the faces distasteful, because they look 'lower class', for example, may avoid examining the features just as they would prefer to avoid the person himself, were the subject and the sitter to meet in everyday life. It seems desirable to include measures of affective reaction in future studies of the judgement of faces in order to learn more about the effects of such incipient approach and avoidance responses on perception and memory.

Some abilities and some cognitive styles, such as narrow category width, may facilitate the recall of all sorts of spatial patterns. They may correlate with memory for faces because faces are merely one type of spatial pattern. Other abilities and cognitive styles may be more closely bound up with the perception of the human face as such. Field dependence and biases resulting from affective reactions to the faces may have this sort of specificity. While the first type of ability or style can be studied with many different sorts of visual material, the second type probably requires reactions to human faces. Here photographs can be of particular value. They might, for example, be used to determine whether or not field-dependent persons use more cues in the discrimination and recall of faces than do field-independent persons, and they might be useful in determining whether different cues are used in the recall of liked and disliked faces.

The isolation of the cues themselves, however, may present a thorny research problem. A direct approach, for example, might lead us to suppose that some particular facial cues are used by field-dependent persons and ignored by field-independent persons and then to design a test that would make success contingent on the utilization of these cues. Higher scores for field-*dependent* persons would then be predicted. Unfortunately, the cues in question are details of physiognomy that are firmly embedded in the context of the 'total portrait', and when task success is thus made contingent on the isolation of some part of a stimulus configuration from its context, the field-*independent* person may tend to earn the higher score. Such an approach runs the risk of finding no differences – or differences in the wrong direction – even when true differences in favor of the field-dependent person may exist. A similar problem has plagued research on social intelligence for years.

Multidimensional scaling (Jackson and Messick, 1963; Torgerson, 1958; Tucker and Messick, 1963) might be used advantageously on such problems. Subjects who are high and low on field dependence or affective preference might be asked to judge the similarities and differences among faces which have been exposed for brief periods. One might expect field-dependent subjects to use more (or different) dimensions in judging similarity of faces than the field-independent, and people who liked the face to use more dimensions than people who did not. Even if this were not the case, if the dimensions used by these different kinds of subjects were the same, one might investigate differences in stimulus clustering in the perceptual spaces to see if persons with different cognitive styles use these dimensions for making finer discriminations.

References

BURWEN, L. S., and CAMPBELL, D. T. (1957), 'The generality of attitudes toward authority and nonauthority figures', *J. abnorm. soc. Psychol.*, vol. 54, pp. 24–51.

CRUTCHFIELD, R. S., WOODWORTH, D. G., and ALBRECHT, R. E. (1958), 'Perceptual performance and the effective person', *USAF WADC Technical Note*, no. 58–60.

EXLINE, R. V. (1963), 'Explorations in the process of person perception: visual interaction in relation to competition, sex, and need for affiliation', *J. Personal.*, vol. 31, pp. 1–20.

JACKSON, D. N., and MESSICK, S. (1963), 'Individual differences in social perception', *Brit. J. soc. clin. Psychol.*, vol. 2, pp. 1–10.

JACKSON, D. N., MESSICK, S., and MYERS, C. T. (1964), 'Evaluation of group and individual forms of embedded-figures measures of field independence', *Educ. psychol. Meas.*, vol. 24, pp. 177–92.

KOGAN, N. (1960), 'Age differences in judgments of chronological age', *Amer. Psychol.*, vol. 15, p. 407 (abstract).

MESSICK, S., and FRITZKY, F. J. (1963), 'Dimensions of analytic attitude in cognition and personality', *J. Personal.*, vol. 31, pp. 346–70.

MESSICK, S., and KOGAN, N. (1964), *Category Width and Quantitative Aptitude*, Educational Testing Service, Princeton.

PETTIGREW, T. F. (1958), 'The measurement and correlates of category width as a cognitive variable', *J. Personal.*, vol. 26, pp. 532–44. [See Reading 6.]

TORGERSON, W. S. (1958), *Theory and Methods of Scaling*, Wiley.

TUCKER, L., and MESSICK, S. (1963), 'An individual differences model for multidimensional scaling', *Psychometrika*, vol. 28, pp. 333–67.

WALLACH, M. A., and CARON, A. J. (1959), 'Attribute criteriality and sex-linked conservatism as determinants of psychological similarity', *J. abnorm. soc. Psychol.*, vol. 59, pp. 43–50.

WITKIN, H. A., DYK, R. B., FATERSON, H. F., GOODENOUGH, D. R., and KARP, S. A. (1962), *Psychological Differentiation*, Wiley.

WITKIN, H. A., LEWIS, H. B., HERTZMAN, M., MACHOVER, K., MEISSNER, P. B., and WAPNER, S. (1954), *Personality through Perception*, Harper.

WITRYOL, S. L., and KAESS, W. A. (1957), 'Sex differences in social memory tasks', *J. abnorm. soc. Psychol.*, vol. 54, pp. 343–6.

Part Nine **Studies of Psychopathology**

It is obvious that pathological states often involve changes in thought processes, and on this basis it might be anticipated that research into cognitive style and structure would have an important place in clinical psychology. Three Readings are presented here which bear out this expectation.

Witkin (in what is in fact the original continuation of Reading 10) deals with a variety of pathological conditions and therapeutic problems from the standpoint of a student of psychological differentiation. The other two papers are more specifically concerned with aspects of thought disorder in schizophrenia. Payne, Caird and Laverty (Reading 24) examine schizophrenic delusions in terms of 'overinclusiveness' of thinking. Although their measure (in terms of how patients interpret proverbs) is very different, this notion's affinity with that of 'conceptual differentiation' (used by Gardner and others – see Part Two) is clear. Reading 25 is by Bannister and Salmon, and follows up earlier work deriving from Kelly's (1955) theory of personal constructs. Bannister and Salmon are here interested in the specificity of those changes in construct systems which have previously been shown to occur in some types of schizophrenia.

Other approaches to thought processes in clinical patients are of course possible. Readers might refer to an interesting paper by Silverman (1964), for example. This shows how the cognitive controls of wide or narrow scanning and of field articulation can distinguish between process and reactive schizophrenics.

References

KELLY, G. A. (1955), *The Psychology of Personal Constructs*, Norton, 1955.

SILVERMAN, J. (1964), 'The problem of attention in research and theory in schizophrenia', *Psychol. Rev.*, vol. 71, pp. 352–79.

23 Herman A. Witkin

Differentiation and Forms of Pathology

Excerpt from Herman A. Witkin, 'Psychological differentiation and forms of pathology', *Journal of Abnormal Psychology*, vol. 70, 1965, pp. 324–36.

The concept of differentiation and the techniques devised to evaluate level of differentiation[1] appear useful in both the conceptualization and the assessment of normal personality functioning. They have relevance to pathological functioning as well.

To make this clear, we need to consider the relation between differentiation and integration. Differentiation refers to the complexity of structure of a psychological system. One of the main characteristics of greater differentiation is specialization of function; another is clear separation of self from nonself. Integration refers particularly to the form of the functional relations among parts of a psychological system and between the system and its surroundings. At any level of differentiation varied modes of integration are possible, although more complex integrations may be expected with more developed differentiation. Adjustment is mainly a function of effectiveness of integration – that is, a more or less harmonious working together of parts of the system with each other and of the system as a whole with its environment. Adequate adjustment is to be found at any level of differentiation, resulting from integrations effective for that level, although the nature of adjustment that may be considered adequate varies from level to level. Moreover, impaired integration, with resulting pathology, may also occur at all levels of differentiation. However, and this is of particular importance, impairment is likely to take different forms in relatively more differentiated and less differentiated personalities.

The evidence now clearly indicates that pathology occurs at both extremes of the differentiation dimension. In fact, there is some suggestion of greater frequency of pathology at the extremes

1. See Reading 10 [*Ed.*].

than in the middle of the range. Further, pathology takes quite different forms at the two extremes. And the kinds of pathology that have been found at each extreme may be conceived as having the form which impaired integration is likely to take when more differentiated or less differentiated personalities break down. Let me illustrate this.

When personality disturbances occur among persons with a global cognitive style, and with other characteristics of limited differentiation associated with it, we are likely to find severe identity problems, with little struggle for maintenance of identity; symptoms often considered suggestive of deep-seated problems of dependence; inadequately developed controls, resulting in chaotic functioning; and passivity and helplessness. Several studies have demonstrated marked field dependence in clinical groups with symptoms commonly regarded as rooted in severe dependency problems, or in what we earlier called a lack of developed sense of separate identity. Alcoholics have been found to present a consistent picture of marked field dependence (Bailey, Hustmeyer and Kristofferson, 1961; Karp and Konstadt, 1965; Karp, Poster and Goodman, 1963; Karp, Witkin and Goodenough, 1965; Witkin, Karp and Goodenough, 1959). This picture has been found among alcoholic men and alcoholic women; among current drinkers and among abstaining former drinkers; among alcoholics who are under the influence of alcohol and among alcoholics who are sober; among long-term drinkers and among relatively new drinkers. As another indicator of their limited differentiation, alcoholics also show a relatively global body concept in their figure drawings.

In addition to alcoholics, other clinical groups commonly conceived to suffer severe dependency problems, which also show marked field dependence, are ulcer patients (Gordon, 1953), obese people (Pardes and Karp, 1965) and asthmatic children (Fishbein, 1963).

Other kinds of clinical groups observed to show a global cognitive style have included patients with an hysterical character structure (Zukmann, 1957); patients with character disorders – that is, generally inadequate personalities unable to manage the ordinary problems of living; patients who somatize their complaints and deny any psychological problems; patients whose primary symptom is affective discharge, rather than defensive symptom organization (Korchin[2]); patients with functional cardiac disorders (Soll, 1963); and catatonics (Janucci, 1964).

Taylor (1956) has shown that psychotics who hallucinate are more likely to be field dependent, as compared to delusional psychotics, who tend to be field independent. He predicted this outcome on the ground that hallucinatory states imply dissolution of ego boundaries, whereas delusional states represent attempts to maintain separate identity and ego integrity. Compared to hallucinations, delusions have a more logical structure and they do not represent as gross a fusion between self and nonself. In hallucinations, inner states often become indistinguishable from reality, reflecting reduction of ego-integrity and of sense of individuality to an infantile stage. Taylor's finding has recently been confirmed by Powell (1964).

A recent experimental study (Bertini, Lewis and Witkin, 1964) in which we sought to induce a hypnagogic reverie state in normal subjects yielded results consistent with Taylor's. White noise was fed into the subject's ears and halves of ping-pong balls were placed over his eyes creating a homogeneous visual field. Under these circumstances the subject was asked, while lying down, to keep on talking continuously, describing any thoughts, feelings or images he might have. White noise, which creates a continuous monotonous sound, has been generally known to facilitate drowsiness. It also reduces feedback from the subject's own voice and distorts the quality of the voice. A homogeneous field facilitates imagery and makes the images more plausible. Our subjects were college students, selected as being extremely field dependent or extremely field independent. Each subject was tested first under the conditions described and on another occasion immediately after viewing an exciting film. Preliminary observations suggest, as predicted, that field-dependent and field-independent subjects react quite differently to this experimental-hypnagogic procedure. Particularly relevant to the Taylor finding is the observation that field-dependent subjects more often reported vivid imagery. However bizarre the imagery, it had the quality of 'actually being there', rather than of 'being imagined'. The reports of these field-dependent subjects suggest that the

2. Personal communication from Sheldon Korchin.

experience was one of being caught up in an ongoing scene. Of course, in contrast to Taylor's hallucinating patients, our subjects who had this imagery experience were able to tell it was not 'real' even when it appeared very vivid to them. Another observation was that the hypnagogic reverie of field-dependent subjects, after viewing the exciting film, tended to be flooded with symbolic references to the film. The field-dependent subjects were also made more uneasy and even frightened by the experimental situation. Silverman *et al.* (1961) have also reported greater 'ego weakening' in field-dependent subjects under conditions of sensory isolation; and they report, as do Holt and Goldberger (1959), that field-dependent subjects more often experience imagery which appears to have an 'outside' source. The indication that hallucinatory-like experiences are more readily induced in field-dependent persons, with accompanying feelings of severe discomfort, reflects on their weak ego boundaries.

Turning to the kinds of pathology encountered among differentiated persons, when they break down, we find that they tend to show delusions, expansive and euphoric ideas of grandeur, outward direction of aggression, overideation and continuing struggle for the maintenance of identity, however bizarre the attempt. An articulated cognitive style has been found among paranoids (Janucci, 1964; Powell, 1964; Witkin *et al.*, 1954), obsessive-compulsive characters (Zukmann, 1957), neurotics with organized symptom pictures and those ambulatory schizophrenics who have a well-developed defensive structure (Korchin[3]).

It is not easy to work out precisely the linkages between extent of differentiation and forms of pathology. For one thing, the pathways by which particular kinds of pathology may emerge in a given personality setting are inordinately complex and difficult to trace; for another, level of differentiation is only one determinant, though an important one, of the course that pathological development may take. Moreover, present knowledge of the dynamics of various kinds of pathology is uncertain. Even with these difficulties, it seems possible to see, for at least some of the pathological states listed, why they may be expected in a setting of relatively developed differentiation, on the one hand, or limited differentiation, on the other.

3. Personal communication from Sheldon Korchin.

As one illustration, we may speculate about some of the ways in which the characteristics of limitedly differentiated persons may make the development of obesity more likely among them. Their inadequately developed sense of separate identity makes it plausible that under stress they would seek comfort in oral activities that had been an important source of satisfaction in the period of close unity with mother. As a technique of defense for dealing with anxiety, eating is a non-specialized defense. It is applied indiscriminately in a wide range of stressful situations, and it does not act in a specific, directed fashion upon the source of stress. In particular kinds of persons, it may suffuse the organism with an animal pleasure which blurs anxiety.

We may think along similar lines about alcoholism, a condition which, in its dynamic aspects, is often considered equivalent to obesity. The non-specialized character of the defense which the use of alcohol represents is particularly clear. Alcohol is resorted to when stress becomes too great, regardless of the source of the stress, and it seems to affect experience in general, not only the part responsible for the anxiety. If the drinking is carried far enough, the self, which to begin with is limitedly differentiated, may be temporarily obliterated.

Obviously, a symptom like alcoholism is only one of many possible 'choices' of pathology open to the relatively undifferentiated person when integration is impaired. Reflecting the possibility that the same symptom may be achieved by different dynamic routes, we must note that alcoholism may also sometimes, though rarely, be the choice of relatively differentiated persons. Although we have found that alcoholics who perform in a field-independent fashion are quite uncommon, their very existence points to the need for seeking other routes to the development of alcoholism than the one considered. Cognitive style may be a means of differential diagnosis of these different kinds of alcoholics. And it is possible that through the cognitive style approach other presumably homogeneous diagnostic categories may be broken down and diagnostic classification thereby refined.

A final illustration may be found in patients in whom paranoid reactions are central in the symptom picture. In this patient group, an articulated cognitive style is frequently found. Projection, a characteristic defense of the paranoid, is quite specialized, in comparison to such generalized tension-reducing techniques as eating and drinking. The paranoid projects his own system of ideas upon the world, and does so in a highly selective fashion – particular people, particular situations may be especially implicated. Such selectivity requires that experience of the world be articulated. In this connexion, the paranoid is noted for his detailed, articulated system of ideas. As an attempt at preservation of the self, projection contrasts with the alcoholic's preferred way of dealing with stress, which in extreme cases results in the dissolution of the self in drink. The use of projection as a device for self-preservation, however bizarre, presupposes a self that has achieved some degree of differentiation.

These illustrations, though sketchy, suggest some of the ways in which level of differentiation may help determine form of pathology.

Although cognitive style, and associated characteristics of more developed and less developed differentiation, relate to particular symptoms and symptom pictures, they do not relate to major conventional nosological categories, as neuroses and schizophrenia (Bound, 1951; Franks, 1956). Among hospitalized psychiatric patients we found cases diagnosed 'schizophrenic' scattered throughout the distribution of measures of perceptual field dependence (Witkin *et al.*, 1954). Bailey, Hustmeyer and Kristofferson (1961) and Bennett (1956) have reported similar results.[4] There is no contradiction in the finding that cognitive style relates to symptoms but not to conventional nosological categories. Nosological categories, are, in varying degree, based on symptoms, dynamics, and etiology. There is further a lack of consistency with which nosological categories are applied in assessment. On the other hand, to the extent that a given symptom is the end-product of particular dynamic processes, it may serve to identify these processes. Classification in terms of particular symptom pictures is therefore likely to bring together persons

4. Cognitive style does, however, seem to relate to kind of schizophrenia. As noted, paranoids tend to be field independent (Janucci, 1964; Witkin *et al.*, 1954). On the other hand, catatonics tend to be field dependent (Janucci, 1964). Bryant (1961) has found process schizophrenics to be significantly more field dependent than reactive schizophrenics, although this finding was not confirmed by Cancro (1962). [See also the article by Silverman referred to on p. 389 – *Ed.*]

with common underlying dynamic processes. Although symptoms are the main basis of classification in some diagnostic categories, in many instances classification on the basis of symptoms may transcend common diagnostic categories. For example, depression may be a major symptom regardless of whether the over-all diagnosis is neurosis, schizophrenia, reactive depression, etc.

The finding that cognitive style, which mirrors a deep aspect of psychological make-up, cuts across some of the conventional nosological categories is consistent with the growing shift in clinical classification from an emphasis on behavior to an emphasis on dynamic characterization. Cognitive style may thus offer one potentially useful basis for clarifying nosological problems.

That cognitive style may relate to deeper levels of functioning, and so go beyond manifest behavior, is indicated in an interesting way in a study by Gordon (1953). Gordon found ulcer patients to be markedly field dependent; and he also found significant agreement between their field-dependence scores and ratings made of them by their physicians on a specially devised dependency scale. However, ratings of dependence by the patients themselves, using the same scale, did *not* relate to their field-dependence scores. (Let me interpolate here that, for a comparison group of neurotics, field-dependence measures, physician's ratings of dependence and self-ratings of dependence were all significantly interrelated.)

In interpreting these findings for the ulcer patients, it is of special interest that on the dependency scale they rated themselves as more independent than did their physicians. The direction of the discrepancy between self-ratings of dependency, on the one hand, and physician's ratings and field-dependence measures, on the other hand, seems to suggest that, although tending to be very dependent, these patients viewed themselves as relatively independent. A common clinical view of the ulcer patient is of an overstriving person who, through his striving, is seeking to compensate for deep-seated passivity and persistent dependency needs (see for example, Alexander, 1950). He seeks to make himself appear, both to himself and to others, as more active than he is, and as capable of functioning independently of external support. Such an interpretation would be consistent with Gordon's results. It is thus possible that an individual's cognitive style may 'penetrate' his apparent assertiveness and reflect the strong underlying passivity and need for external support.

Findings such as these suggest again that assessment of cognitive style may, in particular instances, be of aid in differential diagnosis.

The differentiation concept seems to provide a useful approach to the study of differences among people in directions of pathological development and in choice of symptoms. At the present time, however, it is more useful in understanding the basis of differences in general classes of pathology and symptom formation than in understanding of 'choices' within a general class. For example, as we saw, both alcoholics and obese people tend to be extremely field dependent. The question remains as to why some limitedly differentiated people choose drinking as their main symptom while others choose overeating. To answer this question, intensive study of individual cases showing such symptoms is required, with attention given to specific patterns of integration, to particular content aspects of personality and to nature of life circumstances. As an illustration of how these may be important, the suggestion has been made that an individual's personal values, derived from his cultural group, may place a taboo on drinking and so make overeating a more likely symptom choice.

I have tried in this discussion of pathology to suggest that the characteristics of relatively greater or more limited differentiation may play a role in channeling pathological development. It follows from this view that the techniques devised to evaluate level of differentiation in various areas – and particularly in the area of cognitive functioning – may contribute to a more discriminating assessment of psychopathology.

The cognitive style approach has promise for the study of another kind of pathology – mental retardation. Its value is demonstrated by the results of a study we recently completed with two groups of high grade retarded boys (Witkin *et al.*, 1966). One group consisted of 'teachable' institutionalized retarded boys in the 60–80 I.Q. range; the other group consisted of boys in the same I.Q. range but living at home and attending public-school classes for the mentally retarded. All the boys were given the Wechsler tests of perceptual field dependence and the figure-drawing test. We found, first of all, that the pattern of relation among test measures in both retarded groups was similar to that previously observed in normals. Thus, measures of perceptual field dependence for the retarded boys were related to pro-rated 'analytical I.Q.s' (based, it will be recalled, on the Wechsler block design, picture completion, and object assembly subtests); they did not relate to pro-rated 'verbal-comprehension I.Q.s' (based on the vocabulary, information and comprehension subtests). Again paralleling previous findings for normals, measures of analytical competence both from tests of field dependence and from the Wechsler scales were related to figure-drawing measures of articulation of body concept.

A second finding of interest was a marked and pervasive discrepancy in level of functioning between the analytical and verbal-comprehension clusters. Thus, on the Wechsler scales, almost all the retarded boys showed a pattern of extremely poor performance on the triumvirate of verbal-comprehension subtests and relatively much better performance on the triumvirate of analytical subtests. The discrepancy in cognitive functioning that seems to exist in these retarded boys is much sharper when the verbal-comprehension and analytical pro-rated I.Q.s are compared than when the usual Verbal and Performance I.Q.s are compared. Thus, in the group of institutionalized retarded boys the pro-rated verbal-comprehension and analytical I.Q.s were 61·2 and 80·8, respectively, whereas the Verbal and Performance I.Q.s were 71·1 and 76·3.

The frequency of occurrence of cases with relatively high analytical ability and relatively low verbal-comprehension ability in groups now identified as retarded may be the result of 'routing' of children on the basis of particular emphasis upon verbal skills. If we consider children as nature made them, rather than as they are defined by Wechsler performance, we may expect to find a great many different kinds of cognitive patterns among them, with the possibility as well of deficits in one or more cognitive areas. Children with a deficit in verbal skills, whatever other cognitive strengths they may have, are especially likely to come to attention in the family, in society and in school; and on standard intelligence tests they are likely to earn a low I.Q. because of the emphasis on subtests involving verbal skills in the total I.Q. On the other hand, we may speculate, children with other kinds of cognitive deficit than a verbal one, and who function at an overall level similar to those now commonly classified as retarded, do not come to attention as readily. Though not classified as retarded by the standards currently used in our society, such children may be as handicapped in their cognitive and personality functioning as those now labeled 'retarded', but in different ways.

A cognitive-style approach to the understanding and assessment of the retarded has clear advantages over an I.Q. approach. In particular the cognitive-style approach offers a more comprehensive and complex view of cognitive functioning than does the I.Q. It has a more developed conceptual rationale, it encompasses broader segments of cognitive functioning and it recognizes the rooting of intellectual characteristics in personality.

Differentiation and Problems of Therapy

Problems of assessment arise in a particularly complex and interesting way in the area of therapy. Persons functioning at a more differentiated or less differentiated level may be expected to differ predictably with regard to their attitudes toward psychotherapy and their performance in the psychotherapy situation, in ways that are likely to affect the course of therapy. I would like to consider several of the specific areas in which differences may be anticipated. In some of these areas, studies are under way that I can tell you about; for other areas I can only specify the issues involved.

One important area is the nature of presenting symptoms. Our earlier discussion of forms of pathology in relation to extent of differentiation is of course relevant here.

A second area is suitability for psychological forms of therapy. Several studies have shown that therapists are not likely to accept field-dependent patients for psychotherapy; they are more apt to recommend them for somatic forms of therapy. There thus seems to be considerable agreement between the performance of a particular patient on the Rod-and-Frame Test and the judgement independently made by the therapist about that patient. The significance of this finding needs to be explored further; its pursuit may help us in identifying more precisely the criteria used in decisions about suitability for therapy and in determining the validity of these criteria.

A judgement that needs to be made as a prelude to deciding whether a given patient is suitable for psychotherapy is the nature of the problems he is likely to present in the course of therapy. There can be little doubt, from the characterizations given earlier, that more differentiated and less differentiated patients are likely to differ in the difficulties encountered with them. But it is hard to accept the idea that the one kind of patient is amenable to psychotherapy and the other not. Even if there is some difference between them in this respect, it may very well be that each will benefit from quite different treatment procedures. Perhaps the core issue is not suitability for psychotherapy, but which form of psychotherapy for which kind of patient. Focusing on the kinds of therapy that may help persons who show the characteristics associated with field dependence may aid us in finding ways of treating at least some of the field-dependent patients who now seem to be rejected *en masse*.

As a related point, we have the impression – and it is only an impression at this point – that field-dependent persons are less likely to present themselves as candidates for psychotherapy. I am sure that this relation, if substantiated, will turn out to have quite a complex basis. One factor that may be involved is the tendency of field-dependent persons to somatize their difficulties. On this basis, we would be more likely to pick up psychologically disturbed field-dependent patients at medical than at psychiatric clinics. Another factor may be that relatively undifferentiated persons are not as active in seeking help of an out-patient kind.

A third aspect of psychotherapy in which more differentiated and less differentiated patients may differ is in the nature of their relation to the therapist – that is, in the transference. Freedman (1962) has observed that field-dependent patients are likely to 'feel better' earlier than field-independent patients, although the improvement is not maintained. We are now doing a study to check the idea that this difference is a function of differences in manner of relating to the therapist. We may speculate that the easier 'fusion' of the less differentiated patient with another person, dictated by his limited sense of separate identity, manifests itself in his relation to the therapist as we know it does in his everyday relations with people. This fusion represents, in salient ways, a return to an earlier state – that of unity with mother – which, as our studies of family background suggest, such persons may not have outgrown. The re-establishment of this state may itself make such persons feel better without any real problems having been worked through. In addition to this transference effect, it may be expected that less differentiated patients are likely to be more accepting of the therapist's suggestions and interpretations, again with the consequence that they would feel better. On the other side, relatively differentiated patients are apt to be more cautious in the development of their relation to the therapist, and to filter the therapist's suggestions through their own structured systems of feelings and values.

In a study Helen Lewis, Edmund Weil and I are now doing we are examining the development of the patient–therapist relation, in a small group of patients, in the course of the first twenty sessions of therapy. Our patients were at the extremes of the differentiation dimension, selected from a large out-patient clinic population who received our tests as part of the initial clinic screening. Each participating therapist was assigned one highly differentiated and one relatively undifferentiated patient. The therapist knew nothing of our findings on his patients. All therapy sessions were tape-recorded.

The data-gathering phase of this study has been completed, but the microscopic analysis of the records, required to check out hypotheses about differences in patient–therapist relations at the two extremes, is still under way.[5] The kinds of specific issues we are examining in our study of the transcripts of the therapy sessions, bearing on these hypotheses, include the patient's expectations of the therapist – for example, 'you will make me better' versus 'you will help me figure things out so I can think straight'; the patient's reaction to the therapist's suggestions – for example, whether readily accepting or circumspect; the speed with which

---

5. A report of this investigation has subsequently been published. See H. A. Witkin, H. B. Lewis and E. Weil, 'Affective reactions and patient–therapist interactions among more differentiated and less differentiated patients early in therapy', *J. nerv. ment. Dis.*, vol. 146, 1968, pp. 193–208 [*Ed.*].

the patient establishes an overt bond with the therapist; the patient's ability to keep separate the transference and the reality of the doctor–patient relationship.

Though the focus in this study is on the patient's contribution to the patient–therapist relation, inevitably we are dealing with an interaction to which both participants contribute. That characteristics of the therapist himself are important and need to be considered is demonstrated in an interesting way in a study by Pollack and Kiev (1963). This study showed that psychiatrists who tested extremely field independent on our perceptual tests tended to favor either a directive and instructional or a passive observational approach to their patients in therapy, whereas relatively more (though not extremely) field-dependent therapists favored personal and mutual relations with their patients. The importance of considering the patient–therapist relation in inter-action terms is indicated by an observation we made of frequency of comments by the therapist in the course of a therapy session. Therapists made strikingly more comments with limitedly differ-entiated patients than with highly differentiated patients (in the first session, for example, about three times as many); but at the same time therapists seemed to differ among themselves in fre-quency of making comments, whatever kind of patient they were treating.

Obviously, for each comment by the therapist, made at his initiative, there is a patient comment in reaction, and vice-versa. Accordingly, another way of stating the finding on frequency of comments is that there are many more patient–therapist inter-actions per session on the side of relatively undifferentiated patients than on the side of differentiated patients. An analysis we made of transcripts of the first therapy session indicates a variety of reasons for this difference, reflecting differences in interaction that might be expected from already known differences between more differentiated and less differentiated persons. Thus, among undifferentiated patients we find some of whom the therapist had to ask many specific questions in order to obtain the information he wanted, and the patient's responses were typically very brief. The outcome, of course, was a large number of interactions per session. Other undifferentiated patients showed a state of diffuse excitement, spurting out in a pressured way accounts of their pervasive difficulties, troubled feelings and inadequacies.[6] Though in contrast to the first kind of undifferentiated patients these patients 'pour out' a great deal, what they tell often comes in eruptive spurts, involves a great deal of repetition, and requires 'containment' by the therapist. To obtain the information he wants, the therapist may still need to ask many questions, again making for many interactions.

Obviously, with both the 'teeth-pulling' behavior and the 'spilling' behavior observed on the undifferentiated side, considerable participation by the therapist is required for the therapist to obtain the information he wants about the patient's difficulties. In contrast, differentiated patients typically came to the first session with an articulated account of their problems and their ideas about the sources of these problems, whether dynamically correct or not. Sometimes their 'opening presentation' gave the impression of a prepared statement. One of these patients actually brought with him a letter he had written to his wife about himself, which he proceeded to read to the therapist. Because such presentations may go on at great length, sometimes even bypassing the therapist's occasional attempts at intervention, the result is a small number of total interactions per session.

Another characteristic of some undifferentiated patients which contributes to a large frequency of interactions is their ready acceptance of the therapist's suggestions, sometimes in a single phrase of agreement ('You're right, doctor.') or a repetition of part of the therapist's statement. The tendency among more differentiated patients to qualify their agreements with the therapist's proposals or to disagree with them, sometimes at great length, of course makes for a smaller total number of interactions in the session. Another feature of the behavior of some undifferentiated patients contributing to a greater frequency of interactions is their attempt to prolong the hour out of feelings of separation anxiety; this has even been observed in the very first hour. An occasional differentiated patient may also resist the

6. This behavior reflects strong open feelings of shame; such feelings seem prevalent among undifferentiated patients and less common (at least in open form) among differentiated ones. It may very well be that the 'teeth pulling' in the first kind of undifferentiated patient may also have strong feelings of shame as one of its bases.

ending of the session, but where this has been found it was because the patient was interrupted in the midst of a developed account he was presenting and which he was intent on completing. Still another phenomenon observed in some undifferentiated patients, which again increases number of interactions, is their repeated solicitation of support from the therapist. ['Do you think I'm mentally ill, doctor, from the way I'm talking?' 'Is this normal with a person?' 'Did you come across anybody who had this, doctor? (Yes.) Have you helped them?'] Such solicitation was not evident in the first-session transcripts of differentiated patients.

We are now devising ways of pursuing these observations systematically. First, we are attempting to establish criteria for identifying meaningful units of patient–therapist interactions. Second, we are working out methods of evaluating such units with regard to the variables I outlined.

A final aspect of psychotherapy we may consider is the achievement of change. The issue of change in therapy arises in two ways. First, will the characteristics of more developed or less developed differentiation themselves change in the course of therapy? Second, is the potential for change related to initial level of differentiation?

As for the first question, we are inclined to expect that the cluster of characteristics subsumed under differentiation, and the cognitive-style component in particular, are not likely to change with therapy. We expect this mainly because formal features of an individual's psychological make-up, of the kind represented by differentiation, are likely to show considerable stability as compared to content features.

There are already several lines of evidence from areas other than therapy, which support the expectation of marked relative stability of level of differentiation. Stability has been found even over long periods of time and in the face of strenuous attempts to bring about change.

First, longitudinal studies we have done demonstrate considerable relative stability during the growth years in the characteristics of differentiation we have thus far examined. In one study we followed a group of boys for fourteen years, testing them at ages ten, fourteen, seventeen and twenty-four. Of the thirty boys first seen at age ten, we were still able to obtain twenty-eight for testing at age twenty-four. Considering group means, there was a change in the group as a whole, over the fourteen-year span, toward greater field independence and a more articulated body concept. At the same time, test–retest correlations were high, indicating that children who show more developed differentiation in the areas considered at one age, compared to their group, tend to have the same relative standing at other ages as well. Test–retest correlations for the Rod-and-Frame Test for various age combinations were: ten versus fourteen, 0·75; ten versus seventeen, 0·80; ten versus twenty-four, 0·66; fourteen versus seventeen, 0·93; fourteen versus twenty-four, 0·86; and seventeen versus twenty-four, 0·93 (all significant). Test–retest correlations for figure-drawing sophistication-of-body-concept scores were equally high: ten versus fourteen, 0·84; ten versus seventeen, 0·79; ten versus twenty-four, 0·64; fourteen versus seventeen, 0·67; fourteen versus twenty-four, 0·67; seventeen versus twenty-four, 0·68 (all significant). This evidence of stability is particularly impressive since a fourteen-year period was covered, and, moreover, a period when the child enters many new areas of life, when important new needs within himself are emerging, and when ways of coping with these new life circumstances and needs are being developed.

Comparable longitudinal data for adults (Bauman, 1951) again show striking stability in characteristics of differentiation over time. The test–retest correlations after a three-year interval, for Bauman's group of young men, were 0·84 for Rod-and-Frame Test scores and 0·86 for figure-drawing sophistication-of-body-concept scores (both significant).

Another kind of evidence of stability comes from studies which showed that the articulated-global cognitive style could not be changed by experimental intervention. The methods used in an attempt to bring about change have included drug administration (Karp, Witkin and Goodenough, 1965; Pollack *et al.*, 1960), electroconvulsive shock (Pollack *et al.*, 1960), stress due to anticipated heart surgery (Kraidman, 1959), special training (Gruen, 1955; Witkin, 1948), hypnosis.[7] Consistent with these results, Bauman (1951) found no difference in test–retest stability, over a three-year period, between subjects who underwent

7. Personal communication from Rochelle M. Wexler.

important changes in life circumstances (as marriage, divorce, psychotherapy) and subjects who did not.

The nature of differentiation as a structural aspect of personality, and the stability of relative level of differentiation over time and with experimental intervention, leads us to think that the characteristics of differentiation may not change with psychotherapy. A check on this expectation remains to be carried out. It would be of particular interest to examine change with the most probing form of therapy now in use – psychoanalysis.

Let me turn now to the second question I raised about change in therapy – namely, whether more differentiated and less differentiated patients may differ in their potential for change. Even if it turns out that cognitive style and associated characteristics of differentiation themselves remain more or less stable during therapy, we may of course expect other important features of personality to change. A variety of modes of integration is possible at any level of differentiation. Reintegrations, leading to salient alterations in personality, may take place with a given level of differentiation fundamentally maintained. In this connexion the children in our longitudinal studies, though presenting a stable picture with regard to relative level of differentiation, showed many important personality changes during the time we studied them. To answer the question of whether potential for change during therapy, of whatever kind, is at all a function of level of differentiation we must consider the dimension of 'fixity–mobility' which relates to differentiation in a very complex way, and may actually cut across the differentiation dimension.

Our clinical observations strongly suggest that some persons who are field independent and show other characteristics of developed differentiation function consistently at a highly differentiated level, whereas others vary more according to circumstances and inner state. The first kind of subject shows 'fixity' of functioning, the second shows 'mobility'. The perceptual tasks we devised to assess cognitive style, by design, press the subject to perform analytically if he possibly can.[8] They therefore do not

8. For example, in the Embedded-Figures Test the subject, on each trial, is told if his choice of the simple figure is incorrect, and he is required to continue his search for five minutes if he does not find it before then.

permit us to distinguish between these two kinds of subjects. Cognitive tests may of course be devised which leave it to the option of the subject to function at his maximum analytical capacity or not. Results of a study by Perez (1955), using a brightness constancy situation, suggest that with instructions which pushed them toward an analytical attitude subjects identified as field independent tended to perform in a consistently field-independent fashion; with instructions which encouraged a global attitude they varied more with respect to extent of field independence.

We may venture the prediction that patients who are relatively differentiated (and in this sense have developed resources available to them) and who at the same time show 'mobility', would be the best candidates for change. On the other hand, undifferentiated personalities, whose resources are limited and who patently cannot have great 'mobility', would be the least likely candidates for change. It is also possible that patients who are intermediate in the range of measures of differentiation are in general more amenable to change than highly differentiated patients. This view, which remains to be checked, is based on the clinical impression that the latter group is likely to include relatively more patients with limited 'mobility'.[9]

Obviously, differentiation is only part of what must be considered in evaluating change in therapy. Should it turn out that cognitive style, for example, does not change, it would be of considerable interest. For a comprehensive view of the accomplishments of therapy we need to know what changes as well as what does not change. Changes in given characteristics may have a different meaning when occurring in the context of presence or absence of change in other characteristics.

I hope this account has helped suggest some of the ways in which the concepts of differentiation, and the technique we have

9. Numerous studies have shown that greater authoritarianism (as measured by the F-scale) goes with greater field dependence (see, for example, Jackson, 1955; Linton, 1952; Pollack et al., 1960; Rudin and Stagner, 1958). An unpublished study by Mednick suggests, however, that the relation may be nonlinear; both field-dependent and field-independent persons seem to score higher for authoritarianism than intermediates. In view of the personal characteristics associated with F-scale scores, it seems reasonable to consider these scores as rough indicators of 'fixity' or 'mobility'.

devised for the assessment of differentiation, may prove useful to the clinician in the problems he faces in his work in diagnosis and therapy.

References

BAILEY, W., HUSTMEYER, F. E., and KRISTOFFERSON, A. (1961), 'Alcoholism, brain damage and perceptual dependence', *Quart. J. Stud. Alcoh.*, vol. 22, pp. 387–93.

BAUMAN, G. (1951), The stability of the individual's mode of perception, and of perception–personality relationships, *Unpublished Doctoral Dissertation, New York University.*

BENNETT, D. H. (1956), 'Perception of the upright in relation to body image', *J. ment. Health*, vol. 102, pp. 487–506.

BERTINI, M., LEWIS, H. B., and WITKIN, H. A. (1964), 'Some preliminary observations with an experimental procedure for the study of hynagogic and related phenomena', *Archivio di Psicologia, Neurologia e Psichiatria*, vol. 25, pp. 495–534.

BOUND, M. M. (1951), A study of the relationship between Witkin's indices of field dependency and Eysenck's indices of neuroticism, *Unpublished Doctoral Dissertation, Purdue University.*

BRYANT, A. R. (1961), An investigation of process-reactive schizophrenia with relation to perception of visual space, *Unpublished Doctoral Dissertation, University of Utah.*

CANCRO, R. (1962), A comparison of process and reactive schizophrenia, *Unpublished Doctoral Dissertation, State University of New York Downstate Medical Center.*

FRANKS, C. M. (1956), 'Différences déterminées par la personalité dans la perception visuelle de la verticalité', *Rev. Psychol. appl.*, vol. 6, pp. 235–46.

FREEDMAN, N. (1962), The process of symptom modification in psychopharmological therapy, *Paper Presented at a Department of Psychiatry Meeting, State University of New York Downstate Medical Center.*

GORDON, B. (1953), An experimental study of dependence– independence in a social and a laboratory setting, *Unpublished Doctoral Dissertation, University of Southern California.*

GRUEN, A. (1955), 'The relation of dancing experience and personality to perception', *Psychol. Monogr.*, vol. 64, no. 14, whole no. 399.

HOLT, R. R., and GOLDBERGER, L. (1959), 'Personological correlates of reactions to perceptual isolation', *WADC Technical Report*, no. 59–735.

JACKSON, D. N. (1955), Stability in resistance to field forces, *Unpublished Doctoral Dissertation, Purdue University.*

JANUCCI, G. I. (1964), Size constancy in schizophrenia: a study of subgroup differences, *Unpublished Doctoral Dissertation, Rutgers State University.*

KARP, S. A., and KONSTADT, N. L. (1965), 'Alcoholism and psychological differentiation: long-range effects of heavy drinking on field dependence', *J. nerv. ment. Dis.*, vol. 140, pp. 412–16.

KARP, S. A., POSTER, D., and GOODMAN, A. (1963), 'Differentiation in alcoholic women', *J. Personal.*, vol. 31, pp. 386–93.

KARP, S. A., WITKIN, H. A., and GOODENOUGH, D. R. (1965), 'Alcoholism and psychological differentiation: the effect of alcohol on field dependence', *J. abnorm. Psychol.*, vol. 70, pp. 262–5.

KRAIDMAN, E. (1959), Developmental analysis of developmental and perceptual functioning under stress and non-stress conditions, *Unpublished Doctoral Dissertation, Clark University.*

LINTON, H. B. (1952), Relations between mode of perception and tendency to conform, *Unpublished Doctoral Dissertation, Yale University.*

PARDES, H., and KARP, S. A. (1965), 'Field dependence in obese women', *Psychosom. Med.*, vol. 27, pp. 238–44.

PEREZ, P. (1955), Experimental instructions and stimulus content as variables in the size constancy perception of schizophrenics and normals, *Unpublished Doctoral Dissertation, New York University.*

POLLACK, I. W., and KIEV, A. (1963), 'Spatial orientation and psychotherapy: an experimental study of perception', *J. nerv. ment. Dis.*, vol. 137, pp. 93–7.

POLLACK, M., KAHN, R. L., KARP, E., and FINE, M. (1960), Individual differences in the perception of the upright in hospitalized psychiatric patients, *Paper Read at the Eastern Psychological Association, New York.*

POWELL, B. J. (1964), A study of the perceptual field approach of normal subjects and schizophrenic patients under conditions of an oversize stimulus, *Unpublished Doctoral Dissertation, Washington University.*

RUDIN, S. A., and STAGNER, R. (1958), 'Figure-ground phenomena in the perception of physical and social stimuli', *J. Psychol.*, vol. 45, pp. 213–25.

SILVERMAN, A. J., COHEN, S. I., SHMAVONIAN, B. M., and GREENBERG, G. (1961), 'Psychophysical investigations in sensory deprivation: the body-field dimension', *Psychosom. Med.*, vol. 23, pp. 48–61.

SOLL, J. (1963), The effect of frustration on functional cardiac disorder as related to field orientation, *Unpublished Doctoral Dissertation, Adelphi University.*

TAYLOR, J. M. (1956), A comparison of delusional and hallucinatory individuals using field dependency as a measure, *Unpublished Doctoral Dissertation, Purdue University.*

WITKIN, H. A. (1948), 'The effect of training of structural aids on performance of three tests of space orientation', *CAA Div. Res. Rep.*, no. 80.

WITKIN, H. A., KARP, S. A., and GOODENOUGH, D. R. (1959), 'Dependence in alcoholics', *Quart. J. Stud. Alcoh.*, vol. 20, pp. 493–504.

WITKIN, H. A., FATERSON, H. F., GOODENOUGH, D. R., and
BIRNBAUM, J. (1966), 'Cognitive patterning in mildly retarded boys',
Child Devel., vol. 31, pp. 301–16.

WITKIN, H. A., LEWIS, H. B., HERTZMAN, M., MACHOVER, K.,
MEISSNER, P. B., and WAPNER, S. (1954), *Personality through
Perception*, Harper.

ZUKMANN, L. (1957), Hysteric compulsive factors in perceptual
organization, *Unpublished Doctoral Dissertation, New School for Social
Research*.

24 R. W. Payne, W. K. Caird and S. G. Laverty

Overinclusive Thinking and Delusions in Schizophrenic Patients

Excerpts from R. W. Payne, W. K. Caird and S. G. Laverty, 'Overinclusive thinking and delusions in schizophrenic patients', *Journal of Abnormal and Social Psychology*, vol. 68, 1964, pp. 562–6.

The cause of delusional thinking has always been of interest to psychiatrists, who have elaborated a number of explanations. This work has been well reviewed by Cameron (1959). All these theories have in common the assumption that delusions are not basically due to a cognitive defect, but rather are symptomatic of an emotional disturbance. Most psychiatric explanations follow Freud's initial hypothesis that, at basis, a delusion is the result of the mechanism of 'denial', and is associated with a strong but repressed emotional drive. Thus, for example, a paranoid delusion (by far the most frequently occurring type of delusion) occurs in a patient who has a strong, but mainly unconscious and unwanted homosexual love for a member of his own sex. This love is denied, successfully, by feeling the opposite emotion, *hate*, towards the individual concerned. However, this emotion is also unwanted and is thus 'projected' onto the other person. In this way the patient is able to hate back and successfully denies his homosexuality. This explanation leads to the prediction that deluded patients should show other signs of repressed homosexuality. However, it is not entirely successful in explaining how it is that paranoid delusions become so general, and usually involve a large and more or less organized group of people, all of whom hate and persecute the patient.

It is curious that, although paranoid delusions are frequently found in association with thought disorder in schizophrenic patients, no causal link is usually postulated. Thus, although Norman Cameron was one of the first to describe 'overinclusive thinking', one of the cardinal features of thought disorder in schizophrenics, he did not directly relate this to delusion formation, and appears to accept (Cameron, 1959) that delusions are essentially affectively determined.

Norman Cameron (1938a and b, 1939a and b) defined over-inclusive thinking as the inability to preserve conceptual boundaries, so that irrelevant or distantly associated elements become incorporated into concepts, making thought less accurate, more vague, and more abstract. More recently, Payne, Matussek and George (1959) have suggested that overinclusive thinking might be one aspect of a more general disability, consisting essentially of an attention defect. They have suggested that overinclusive patients suffer from some defect of a hypothetical central 'screening' mechanism whereby irrelevant stimuli, both internal (for example, irrelevant thoughts) and external (for example, irrelevant perceptions) are excluded, in order to allow the most efficient processing of incoming information.

Since Cameron's early work, a number of experiments have been performed, and a number of measures of overinclusive thinking have been developed. This work has been summarized recently by Payne (1961). It suggests that:

1. Overinclusive thinking is confined to patients diagnosed as schizophrenic. It has not been found in normals, depressed patients or in neurotics.

2. Different measures of overinclusive thinking correlate significantly, yielding a common factor when the correlations are analysed.

3. Overinclusive thinking is relatively independent of the general retardation which characterizes many psychotic patients.

4. Only about half those patients who are diagnosed as schizophrenics suffer from overinclusive thinking. The remainder, unlike those who are overinclusive, tend to be abnormally retarded in a wide range of psychological tests of speed of mental and motor functioning.

In addition to these findings, it has since been reported (Payne, 1962) that chronic schizophrenics as contrasted to acute schizophrenics are not especially overinclusive.

Payne (1961) has speculated that overinclusive thinking should be specifically related to the presence of delusions in schizophrenic patients. It is reasonable to suppose that delusions have a number of causes, not necessarily mutually exclusive. A small minority of patients seem to have hallucinations which are so detailed and compelling, that the only reasonable way for them to account for their perceptions is by developing an explanation which normal people, not sharing these perceptions, must inevitably regard as a delusion. No doubt emotional factors also play a role in the formation of delusions in many patients. In addition, however, overinclusive thinking could easily help to lead to the induction of unwarranted generalizations. The overinclusive patient, in addition to perceiving the essential features of any problem or situation, is also apparently unable to screen out irrelevant perceptions and these become incorporated into the data of the problem. This is likely to delay solution, but it may also lead to an overgeneral conclusion which is unwarranted. Thus, for example, a patient may genuinely (and normally) believe that a certain individual dislikes him. However, his overinclusive 'concept' (cerebral representation) of this individual may extend to other similar people (for example, all foreigners, all dark men) so that he may develop the same negative emotional reactions to this entire category of people, being incapable of the necessary discrimination which normally circumscribes fairly precisely the stimuli which will evoke the particular response. This could partly explain how it is that delusions so frequently come to include a broad category of people as they develop.

This theory is consistent with one other clinical observation, to which attention is seldom drawn. Many paranoid patients appear to perceive an unusually wide range of stimuli. Thus, for example, a patient may note that one of the two men across the street in shabby raincoats has a folded copy of *The Times* in his pocket, and that he periodically touches this in an unusual way. This the patient may interpret as a signal with some special significance. The delusion is of course abnormal, but what may also be abnormal is the amount of detailed perception on which the delusion is based. In normal people the range of perceptions around whatever engages the attention is very limited, such details go unnoticed, and could thus not form the basis of delusional ideas. The sort of perceptual overinclusion which Payne

(1961) believes forms the basis of overinclusive sorting behavior may thus help to develop delusional thinking.

So far no studies appear to have been carried out to test this hypothesis. The present investigation was designed to do so.

Method

Tests used

The measure of overinclusive thinking used in the present study is derived from Benjamin's (1944) Proverbs Test. Subjects were asked to interpret this list of fourteen proverbs, using the standardized instructions developed by Payne and Hewlett (1960). The main departure from the usual procedure is that the subjects are asked to give a positive indication that they have completed their explanation. (The next proverb is not read until this has been done, although subjects may be reminded to say when they have finished.) The answers were recorded on tape and later transcribed. This was shown to be necessary in earlier studies, where it was found nearly impossible to avoid paraphrasing and condensing answers when they were copied down by hand.

The overinclusion score used is merely the average number of words required to explain each proverb. (Proverbs which the subject says he does not know are excluded.) The rationale is that an overinclusive individual should be unable to exclude from his answer associations to the proverb which are irrelevant to its explanation. These associations may include concrete examples. In addition, the proverb itself should illustrate a more complex and extensive concept for such subjects, and thus require a more extensive explanation. Both factors should increase the number of words needed. Payne and Hewlett found that this score was among the best of a number of measures of overinclusive thinking used in a recent study, as judged by its efficiency in discriminating schizophrenic patients from all others. It also had a relatively high factor saturation on their overinclusion factor (0·58), suggesting that it was reasonably representative of a group of overinclusion measures. It has the additional advantage of being independent of intelligence. Payne and Hewlett found a saturation of 0·00 on their factor of general intelligence, and

415

report similarly insignificant correlations with specific intelligence tests.

Two other scores were derived from this test: the average reaction time and the total time. The average reaction time is the number of seconds elapsing between the time the examiner finishes reading the proverb, and the time the subject begins his answer. Overinclusive subjects should have slower reaction times, since they have more complicated answers to consider before they begin to speak. The total time is the number of seconds required to complete the answer from the time the examiner finishes reading the proverb. Again overinclusive subjects should be slower. Unfortunately, neither time score is a pure measure of overinclusive thinking as subjects who are merely retarded will also be slow. Note that these times were taken later from the recorded tapes and were not measured during the interview. [. . .]

In addition, the subjects were given the Mill Hill Vocabulary Scale (Raven, 1958), to provide a measure of their pre-illness general intellectual level.

Patients tested

In order to determine whether there is, within a schizophrenic group, a tendency for delusions to be associated with overinclusive thinking, a group of fifteen schizophrenic patients with delusions was selected and compared with another group of fifteen schizophrenic patients without delusions. In addition, a third group of fifteen nonschizophrenic patients was tested as a control. All the subjects were recent admissions to the Ontario Hospital, Kingston, and an attempt was made to test each one before treatment was started. This was not always possible, but in all cases (with the exception of three disturbed schizophrenics) the patients were tested not later than forty-eight hours after treatment had started. In addition to the psychological tests, the subjects were given, at the same time, a prolonged interview to appraise their symptoms at the time of testing. The interviewer had no knowledge of the test results, nor had the staff psychiatrists who made the initial diagnoses.

The fifteen non-deluded schizophrenics consisted of ten males and five females. All were regarded as typical schizophrenics, excepting that none were judged to have either ideas of reference or delusions of any sort at the time of testing.

The fifteen deluded schizophrenics included six males and nine females. All were judged to have paranoid delusions at the time of testing. Some had other delusions in addition (for example, somatic), and most had ideas of reference.

Table 1

Age and Intellectual Status of the Three Groups

	Deluded schizophrenics	Non-deluded schizophrenics	Controls
Age			
M	30·87	33·13	36·60
SD	13·10	9·72	6·22
Range	16–56	21–56	25–47
F		1·23	
Mill Hill Vocabulary I.Q. equivalents[1]			
M	93·87	89·53	90·80
SD	5·72	4·61	5·39
Range	86–105	81–97	84–102
F		2·67	

Note: For each group $N = 15$.
1. Computed from Raven's (1958) percentile tables, and based on an M of 100 and an SD of 15 for Raven's normal standardization group.

The fifteen nonschizophrenic patients were intended to be a random sample of the nonschizophrenic intake of the Ontario Hospital. It consisted of eight males and seven females. Seven were diagnosed as depressive, four were regarded as personality disorders, three were alcoholics and one was diagnosed as an obsessional neurotic with marked depressive features. None of the patients in this group had received any treatment prior to testing. None of these patients was deluded.

It had initially been hoped to match the groups for sex. This did not prove feasible. Indeed it required five months to secure the samples obtained, due to the relatively slow rate of admission of suitable schizophrenic patients. The age and vocabulary of the groups are shown in Table 1. It can be seen that the groups are reasonably well matched in both respects.

Results

Overinclusion measures

The results from the Proverb Test are shown in Table 2. As can be seen, all three scores yielded significant differences and all are

Table 2

Overinclusion Scores Derived from the Proverbs Test

	Deluded schizophrenics	Non-deluded schizophrenics	Controls
Average number of words per proverb			
M	33·42	23·44	14·48
SD	15·42	22·82	9·49
Range	10·4–67·2	6·1–101·3	2·5–43·6
F		4·76*	
Average reaction time (seconds)			
M	12·43	11·02	7·70
SD	4·89	6·34	3·83
Range	4·9–22·1	3·6–24·3	3·5–16·8
F		3·37*	
Average total time (seconds)			
M	30·89	24·91	14·43
SD	11·04	18·34	6·59
Range	10·3–51·0	7·2–81·9	6·7–27·7
F		3·28*	

For each group $N = 15$.   * $p < 0.05$

in the expected direction, the largest differences being produced by the purest overinclusion measure. On each score, the non-deluded schizophrenic group has an intermediary position, being more overinclusive than the controls, but not as overinclusive as the deluded schizophrenic group. This is not surprising, as it is very difficult in an interview to be certain that a schizophrenic patient is *not* deluded, since many are defensive about their beliefs. Some of the non-deluded schizophrenics may in fact have been deluded at the time of testing. It is worth commenting that the most verbose of the nonschizophrenic subjects was the single obsessional neurotic.

Table 3

Relationship between Overinclusion and Delusions (number of cases)

	Overinclusive	Non-overinclusive	Total
Deluded	10	5	15
Nondeluded	6	24	30
Total	16	29	45

Note: After Yates' correction, $\chi^2 = 7.56$, $p < 0.01$.

As a further test of the predicted relationship, all the patients, regardless of diagnosis, were divided into two groups on the basis of the average number of words per proverb. Those who used over twenty-five words were labeled 'overinclusive', the remainder 'non-overinclusive'. This score was chosen because previous results suggest (Payne and Hewlett, 1960) that this is for all practical purposes the limit of the normal range. Table 3 shows the relationship between this dichotomy, and the presence or absence of delusions. As can be seen, the relationship is very marked, achieving significance at beyond the 0.01 level. This table yields a contingency coefficient of 0.380, where the maximum upper limit is 0.707.

References

BENJAMIN, J. D. (1944), 'A method for distinguishing and evaluating formal thinking disorders in schizophrenia', in J. S. Kasanin (ed.), *Language and Thought in Schizophrenia*, University of California Press, pp. 65–90.

CAMERON, N. (1938a), 'Reasoning, regression and communication in schizophrenics', *Psychol. Monogr.*, vol. 50, no. 1, whole no. 221.

CAMERON, N. (1938b), 'A study of thinking in senile deterioration and schizophrenic disorganization', *Amer. J. Psychol.*, vol. 51, pp. 650–64.

CAMERON, N. (1939a), 'Deterioration and regression in schizophrenic thinking', *J. abnorm. soc. Psychol.*, vol. 34, pp. 265–70.

CAMERON, N. (1939b), 'Schizophrenic thinking in a problem-solving situation', *J. ment. Sci.*, vol. 95, pp. 1012–25.

CAMERON, N. (1959), 'Paranoid conditions and paranoia', in S. Arieti (ed.), *American Handbook of Psychiatry*, vol. 1, Basic Books, pp. 508–39.

PAYNE, R. W. (1961), 'Cognitive abnormalities', in H. J. Eysenck (ed.), *Handbook of Abnormal Psychology*, Basic Books, pp. 193–261.

PAYNE, R. W. (1962), 'An object classification test as a measure of overinclusive thinking in schizophrenic patients', *Brit. J. soc. clin. Psychol.*, vol. 1, pp. 213–21.

PAYNE, R. W., and HEWLETT, J. H. G. (1960), 'Thought disorder in psychotic patients', in H. J. Eysenck (ed.), *Experiments in Personality*, vol. 2, Routledge & Kegan Paul, pp. 3–104.

PAYNE, R. W., MATUSSEK, P., and GEORGE, E. I. (1959), 'An experimental study of schizophrenic thought disorder', *J. ment. Sci.*, vol. 105, pp. 627–52.

RAVEN, J. C. (1958), *Guide to Using the Mill Hill Vocabulary Scale with the Progressive Matrices Scale*, Lewis.

25 D. Bannister and Phillida Salmon

Schizophrenic Thought Disorder: Specific or Diffuse?

D. Bannister and Phillida Salmon, 'Schizophrenic thought disorder: specific or diffuse?', *British Journal of Medical Psychology*, vol. 39, 1966, pp. 215–19.

Introduction

Work on the psychology of thinking in terms of Personal Construct Theory (Kelly, 1955) confronts us with the idea of construct subsystems. A central argument in the theory is that all constructs have limited and often different ranges of convenience. Thus the construct *two stroke–four stroke* discriminates and predicts for the element 'motor cycle' but is largely unusable with elements such as oysters, people or paintings. Granted there are some types of superordinate construct which have very wide ranges of convenience (e.g. *good–bad*), nevertheless it is anticipated that any examination of a person's total construct system would reveal a number of subsystems characterized by the presence of high relationships between the constructs within each subsystem and relatively weak relationships between constructs from different subsystems. Relationships between constructs can be operationally defined by grid tests and express the lay idea that words can be seen as related or unrelated in meaning.

Thus applying personal construct theory to the problem of schizophrenic thought disorder faces us with the question of whether the thinking of schizophrenics is generally disordered across all subsystems (i.e. are they equally confused whatever topic they think about) or whether it is more specifically disordered in thinking about some areas than others.

The Traditional Concept of Thought Disorder

Historically 'thought disorder' originated as a psychiatric concept. As such it was used at a level of abstraction which made no reference to areas, topics or subsystems of thought. Concepts like concretism, dissociation, derailment, irrelevance and poverty of content occur frequently in psychiatric texts on thought disorder but no suggestion is made that they apply differentially to different areas of thinking. The unstated implication is that thought disorder is a diffuse malaise which affects all areas and aspects of thinking and in this respect it seems a concept somewhat analogous to the notion of general dementia due to a diffuse process such as arteriosclerosis.

Psychologists, in experimentally investigating schizophrenic thought disorder, seem largely to accept the psychiatric notion that it is essentially a defect of style or method unrelated to content. Payne, Matussek and George (1959) provide as test materials variously shaped and coloured blocks, Zaslow (1950) provides geometric figures, Epstein (1953) provides words related to such varied topics as houses, cars and marriage, Gorham (1956) provides proverbs related to manifold aspects of life. All fail to discuss whether schizophrenic thought disorder is more likely to manifest itself with one kind of material rather than another and thereby imply that whatever the thought-disordered schizophrenic thinks about and whatever problem he is faced with, he will be equally likely to manifest his confusion.

Even when psychologists make an attempt to specify the notion of thought disorder more precisely, they tend to resort to concepts which make no reference to content, as for example, the work of Von Domarus (1954) and Gottesman and Chapman (1960) on syllogistic reasoning errors in schizophrenics and the study by Harrington and Ehrmann (1954) in which the complexity of the required responses is argued to be the major variable eliciting thought disorder. When psychologists turn to the question of content differences they are likely to produce something like the work of Binder (1956), who specifically looked for area differences in degree of schizophrenic thought disorder but restricted his areas entirely to what could be tested by the Science Research Associates' tests of primary mental abilities. This presupposes that cognition in the intelligence test or problem-solving sense sets the limits within which we should search for area differences. Alternatively, some studies follow the line of Johnson (1960) in his work on the moral judgement of schizophrenics which looks for specific failures in social comprehension, but implies that this will be merely one more area in which thought disorder might be found rather than seeking to examine whether the manifestation of thought disorder in this area is particularly marked.

Expectations from Personal Construct Theory

Previous studies based on personal construct theory (Bannister, 1960, 1962a) have concentrated entirely on the thought-disordered schizophrenic's construing of people and have indicated that certainly in this area (in terms of repertory grid testing) the constructs of the thought-disordered schizophrenic are remarkably loose and poorly related. Further studies (Bannister, 1963, 1965a) have explored serial invalidation as a hypothetical definition of the causal process underlying schizophrenic thought disorder. This is the notion that the thought-disordered schizophrenic's progressive loss of intercorrelations between his constructs might be an adaptive response to repeated invalidation – he has repeatedly mispredicted the behaviour of elements and therefore loosened the inter-relationships between the constructs that subsume and predict these elements so that his expectations are progressively less clearly formulated and thereby less prone to invalidation. This line of reasoning suggests that thought disorder is unlikely to be diffuse and unlikely to affect all areas of construing equally, since not all aspects of our individual worlds will have equally puzzled us.

If we consider the problem of 'thinking about people' as contrasted with the problem of 'thinking about objects', most of us would confess to holding more loosely formulated expectations about people. Indeed the extreme behaviourist is in one sense a psychologist who seeks to solve the problem by regarding men as 'moving objects'. Clinically, we often observe thought-disordered schizophrenics confidently handling doors, cutlery and shoelaces but failing entirely to distinguish friend from foe. Many of the aetiological studies of workers like Bateson *et al.* (1965), Laing and Esterson (1964) and Lidz (1964) stress interpersonal events as a source of schizophrenic confusion.

In short, a construct theory approach predicts that areas of maximal invalidation will be areas of maximal loosening of construing and we might therefore expect that virtually all of us will be more confident physicists than we are psychologists and thought-disordered schizophrenics may have perforce given up altogether trying to be psychologists.

Experiment

The primary tool used in the experiment to be described is a form of Repertory Grid Test (cf. Bannister, 1962b, 1965b; Bannister and Mair, 1968) and repertory grid tests are essentially instruments which measure the relationships between sorting categories for each individual subject, i.e. they are measures of conceptual structure.

Populations

Eleven thought-disordered schizophrenic subjects (unanimously judged by consultant, registrar and psychologist to manifest in interview the clinical characteristics of thought disorder – blocking, irrelevance, poverty of content, etc.).

Twelve normal subjects (subjects with no history of psychiatric treatment or examination).

Tests

Each subject was individually administered a 'people' grid and an 'object' grid. For the people grid, the subject was faced with photographs of eight people unknown to him and he was told that his judgement of character from faces was under test. He was asked to rank order the eight photographs on six constructs given to him in adjectival form (kind, stupid, selfish, sincere, mean and honest). Immediately on completion he was asked to repeat the task, using the same six constructs but on a *new* set of eight photographs. Eight weeks later subjects were asked to repeat the test on one of the two sets of photographs.

The same subjects individually completed an object-sorting grid. They were faced in the first grid with an array of the names of fifteen objects (e.g. bowler hat, loaf of bread, drawing pin, washing machine, etc.) and asked to rank order these fifteen objects on six constructs (large to small, thin to thick, heavy to light, easy to move about to hard to move about, curved to straight, long to short). They were then asked to repeat the task on a new set of fifteen objects using the same six constructs and eight weeks later they repeated their rank ordering using the same constructs on one of the two original sets of objects.

Scoring

For both object and photo-sorting grids, the rank orders made by the subject were (for each individual) compared by Spearman rho. On each single grid there were six constructs (rank orderings) which yields a matrix of fifteen Spearman rhos representing the relationships between the constructs for each individual for that grid. Thus for each individual the stability of his pattern of construct relationships is measured by rank ordering the derived matrices themselves (from the highest positive correlation through zero to the highest negative correlation) and comparing the two rank-ordered matrices by a further rho. This final rho denotes structural stability (independently of the elements construed) and is roughly equivalent to an index of factorial similarity within one individual's repeated sortings.

It is thus possible to estimate for *each individual subject* the stability of his pattern of construct relationships on immediate retest across two sets of elements. This is a measure of 'equivalent form' reliability. Stability of pattern on the same elements over time represents 'test–retest reliability' for the individual.

Hypothesis

In line with the opening arguments of the study, it was predicted that thought-disordered schizophrenics would not differ significantly from normals in their degree of stability in construing objects (i.e. utilizing constructs about objects) but would manifest significantly less stability in construing photographs of people (i.e. utilizing constructs about people).

Results

A Mann–Whitney U-Test was run on the individual stability correlations across elements and over time for the two groups.

In construing objects, normals had significantly greater stability across elements ($p < 0.02$ two-tail) and over time ($p < 0.002$ two-tail). Thus the first premise of the hypothesis is not supported.

In construing people, normals had significantly greater stability across elements ($p < 0.001$ one-tail) and over time ($p < 0.001$ one-tail). Thus the second premise of the hypothesis is supported.

The results were further analysed to see if within each group object-construing was more stable than people-construing. For normals, object-construing patterns are significantly more stable across elements ($p < 0.003$ two-tail) and across time ($p < 0.02$ two-tail) and for thought-disordered schizophrenics object-construing patterns are similarly more stable across elements ($p < 0.006$ two-tail) and across time ($p < 0.006$ two-tail).

Relative Performance

The generally less stable performance in construing people as compared with objects and the fact that the object-construing of thought-disordered schizophrenics appears to have suffered at least some degree of damage leads us to the question of the *relative* loss of reliable structure as between objects and people as elements for thought-disordered schizophrenics as compared with normals. Does the original hypothesis hold true in relative if not in absolute terms? Stability correlations were converted to standard scores and the percentage loss of stability when changing from objects to people was calculated for each subject. A comparison (by Mann–Whitney) of this percentage loss shows that thought-disordered schizophrenics have lost significantly more stability in construing when shifted from objects to people than have normals, both across elements ($p < 0.05$ one-tail) and over time ($p < 0.001$ one-tail).

A further way of demonstrating and checking this finding is to count the number of individuals who achieve a statistically significant degree of stability in construing objects but produce only a non-significant or negative level of correlation in construing people. One normal and seven thought-disordered schizophrenics fell into this category and Fisher's Exact Method shows this to be a significant difference ($p < 0.001$).

Social Agreement Measure

In addition to measuring the 'across elements' and 'over time reliability' of each individual's pattern of construct relationships, it is possible to examine the degree to which the pattern of construct relationships for each individual agrees with a 'normal' pattern, i.e. the mean pattern for the normal group. This was done and again it was found that thought-disordered schizophrenics were significantly more deviant from the average pattern than normals on both objects ($p < 0.002$ two-tail) and people ($p < 0.002$ two-tail). However, if we again calculate how idiosyncratic each person is in construing people as *compared* with his degree of idiosyncrasy in construing objects, we find that thought-disordered schizophrenics have lost relatively more social agreement in people construing when compared with normals ($p < 0.05$ one-tail) and show more cases of insignificant levels of social agreement ($p < 0.01$ one-tail).

Conclusions

The major flaw in the original hypothesis seems to reside in having stated it in absolute terms and the results do not support it thus stated. However, they are clearly consistent with the view that the area of *maximal* damage for thought-disordered schizophrenics as between object- and people-construing is people-construing. This seems to apply whether we are considering the stability of construct systems over time and across elements or considering the degree to which the pattern of negative and positive relationships between constructs (i.e. the general meaning) approaches an operational norm. This finding is supported by Salmon, Bramley and Presly (1967), who utilized a quite different measure (the Word-in-Context Test).

Personal construct theory might equally account for the spread of damage to areas like object-construing in terms of the linkages between subsystems which are implied in predicating a personal construct *system* for each individual. Core role constructs (constructs which subsume and predict the self) may form the links between our conception of the object-world and the people-world, and damage to these (loss of identity), even though it originated in person-construing, might well affect object-construing.

In so far as this type of finding replicates, it bears in two ways on the study of schizophrenic thought disorder. First, it suggests that tests and measures generally should be designed to investigate the area of interpersonal construing since this seems to be the focus of such disorder. Secondly, it suggests that the explanations of causal process underlying schizophrenic thought disorder (particularly organic explanations) may legitimately be asked to account for a differential degree of thought disorder in different construct subsystems.

References
BANNISTER, D. (1960), 'Conceptual structure in thought-disordered schizophrenics', *J. ment. Sci.*, vol. 106, pp. 1230–49.
BANNISTER, D. (1962a), 'The nature and measurement of schizophrenic thought disorder', *J. ment. Sci.*, vol. 108, pp. 825–42.
BANNISTER, D. (1962b), 'Personal construct theory: a summary and experimental paradigm', *Acta Psychol.*, vol. 20, pp. 104–20.
BANNISTER, D. (1963), 'The genesis of schizophrenic thought disorder: a serial invalidation hypothesis', *Brit. J. Psychiat.*, vol. 109, pp. 680–86.
BANNISTER, D. (1965a), 'The genesis of schizophrenic thought disorder: re-test of the serial invalidation hypothesis', *Brit. J. Psychiatr.*, vol. 474, pp. 377–82.
BANNISTER, D. (1965b), 'The rationale and clinical relevance of repertory grid technique', *Brit. J. Psychiat.*, vol. 479, pp. 977–82.
BANNISTER, D., and MAIR, J. M. M. (1968), *The Evaluation of Personal Constructs*, Academic Press.
BATESON, G., JACKSON, D. D., HALEY, J., and WEAKLAND, J. (1956), 'Towards a communication theory of schizophrenia', *Behav. Sci.*, vol. 1, pp. 251–64.
BINDER, A. (1956), 'Schizophrenic intellectual impairment: uniform or differential', *J. abnorm. soc. Psychol.*, vol. 52, pp. 11–19.
EPSTEIN, S. (1953), 'Over-inclusive thinking in a schizophrenic and a control group', *J. consult. Psychol.*, vol. 17, pp. 384–8.
GORHAM, D. R. (1956), 'Use of the proverbs test for differentiating schizophrenics from normals', *J. consult. Psychol.*, vol. 20, pp. 435–40.
GOTTESMAN, L., and CHAPMAN, L. J. (1960), 'Syllogistic reasoning errors in schizophrenia', *J. consult. Psychol.*, vol. 24, pp. 250–55.
HARRINGTON, R., and EHRMANN, J. C. (1954), 'Complexity of response as a factor in the vocabulary performance of schizophrenics', *J. abnorm. soc. Psychol.*, vol. 49, pp. 362–4.
JOHNSON, D. L. (1960), 'The moral judgment of schizophrenics', *J. nerv. ment. Dis.*, vol. 130, pp. 278–85.

KELLY, G. A. (1955), *The Psychology of Personal Constructs*, vols. 1 and 2, Norton.

LAING, R. D., and ESTERSON, A. (1964), *Sanity, Madness and the Family*, vol. 1, Tavistock.

LIDZ, T. (1964), *The Family and Human Adaptation*, Hogarth.

PAYNE, R. W., MATUSSEK, P., and GEORGE, E. I. (1959), 'An experimental study of schizophrenic thought disorder', *J. ment. Sci.*, vol. 104, pp. 627–52.

SALMON, P., BRAMLEY, J., and PRESLY, A. S. (1967), 'The word-in-context test as a measure of conceptualization in schizophrenics with and without thought disorder', *Brit. J. med. Psychol.*, vol. 40, pp. 253–9.

VON DOMARUS, E. (1954), 'The specific laws of logic in schizophrenia', in S. J. Kasanin (ed.), *Language and Thought in Schizophrenia*, California University Press, pp. 104–13.

ZASLOW, R. W. (1950), 'A new approach to the problem of conceptual thinking in schizophrenia', *J. consult. Psychol.*, vol. 14, pp. 335–9.

Further Reading

Here are several other items laid out in terms of their relevance to each Part of the book. These are *additional to* the references included in the selections printed above. (There is however some overlap between Parts.) Interested readers should examine both the references cited in the main part of the book and those presented below.

Part One Rigidity and Dogmatism

C. C. Anderson, 'A developmental study of dogmatism during adolescence with reference to sex differences', *J. abnorm. soc. Psychol.*, vol. 65, 1962, pp. 132–5.

J. D. Cunningham, 'Einstellung rigidity in children', *J. exp. child Psychol.*, vol. 2, 1965, pp. 237–47.

D. T. Kenny and R. Ginsberg, 'The specificity of intolerance of ambiguity measures', *J. abnorm. soc. Psychol.*, vol. 56, 1958, pp. 300–304.

F. N. Kerlinger and M. Rokeach, 'The factorial nature of the F and D scales', *J. Personal. soc. Psychol.*, vol. 4, 1966, pp. 391–9.

E. E. Levitt, 'The water jar Einstellung test as a measure of rigidity', *Psychol. Bull.*, vol. 53, 1956, pp. 347–70.

M. Rokeach, *The Open and Closed Mind*, Basic Books, 1960.

J. M. Torcivia and P. R. Laughlin, 'Dogmatism and concept-attainment strategies', *J. Personal. soc. Psychol.*, vol. 8, 1968, pp. 397–400.

P. B. Warr, R. E. Lee and K. G. Jöreskog, 'A note on the factorial nature of the F and D scales', *Brit. J. Psychol.*, vol. 60, pp. 119–23.

Part Two Category Usage

G. A. Forehand, 'Relationships among response sets and cognitive behaviors', *Educ. Psychol. Measmt*, vol. 22, 1962, pp. 287–302.

G. F. Mascaro, 'Categorization strategies across different domains', *Percept. mot. Skills*, vol. 26, 1968, pp. 1091–7.

S. Messick and J. R. Hills, 'Objective measurement of personality: cautiousness and tolerance of ambiguity', *Educ. psychol. Measmt*, vol. 20, 1960, pp. 685–99.

E. J. Phares and W. L. Davis, 'Breadth of categorization and the generalization of expectancies', *J. Personal. soc. Psychol.*, vol. 4, 1966, pp. 461–4.

I. Sigel, P. Jarman and H. Hanesian, 'Styles of categorization and their intellectual and personality correlates in young children', *Hum. Devel.*, vol. 10, 1967, pp. 1–17.

H. N. Sloane, L. Gorlow and D. N. Jackson, 'Cognitive styles in equivalence range', *Percept. mot. Skills*, vol. 16, 1963, pp. 389–404.

Further Reading

M. A. Wallach and N. Kogan, *Modes of Thinking in Young Children*, Holt, Rinehart & Winston, 1965.

Part Three   Structural Characteristics

K. Goldstein and M. Sheerer, 'Abstract and concrete behavior: an experimental study with special tests', *Psychol. Monogr.*, vol. 53, 1941, no. 2, pp. 86–94.

O. J. Harvey and H. M. Schroder, 'Cognitive aspects of self and motivation', in O. J. Harvey (ed.), *Motivation and Social Interaction: Cognitive Determinants*, Ronald Press, 1963.

D. E. Hunt and J. Dopyera, 'Personality variation in lower-class children', *J. Psychol.*, vol. 62, 1966, pp. 47–54.

W. A. Scott, 'Measures of cognitive structure', *Multivar. behav. Res.*, vol. 1, 1966, pp. 391–5.

B. Tuckman, 'Integrative complexity: its measurement and relation to creativity', *Educ. Psychol. Meas.*, vol. 26, 1966, pp. 369–82.

Part Four   Psychological Differentiation

R. J. Courter, R. A. Wattenmaker and A. F. Ax, 'Physiological concomitants of psychological differentiation, *Psychophysiol.*, vol. 1, 1965, pp. 282–90.

R. B. Dyk and H. A. Witkin, 'Family experience related to the development of differentiation in children', *Child Devel.*, vol. 30, 1965, pp. 21–55.

F. E. Hustmeyer and E. Karnes, 'Background autonomic activity and "analytic perception"', *J. abnorm. soc. Psychol.*, vol. 68, 1964, pp. 467–8.

H. A. Witkin, 'Origins of cognitive style', in C. Scheerer (ed.), *Cognition: Theory, Research, Promise*, Harper, 1964.

H. A. Witkin, 'A cognitive style approach to cross-cultural research', *Int. J. Psychol.*, vol. 2, 1967, pp. 233–50.

H. A. Witkin, D. R. Goodenough and S. A. Karp, 'Stability of cognitive style from childhood to young adulthood', *J. Personal. soc. Psychol.*, vol. 7, 1967, pp. 291–300.

Part Five   Other Cognitive Styles

D. M. Broverman, 'Dimensions of cognitive style', *J. Personal.*, vol. 28, 1960, pp. 169–85.

D. M. Broverman, 'Cognitive style and intra-individual variation in abilities', *J. Personal.*, vol. 28, 1960, pp. 240–56.

J. Bruner, R. Olver and P. Greenfield, *Studies in Cognitive Growth*, Wiley, 1967.

R. W. Gardner and R. I. Long, 'The stability of cognitive controls', *J. abnorm. soc. Psychol.*, vol. 61, 1960, pp. 485–7.

R. Gordon, *Stereotypy of Imagery and Belief*, Cambridge University Press, 1962 (*British Journal of Psychology*, Monograph Supplement).

R. Holt, 'Imagery: the return of the ostracized', *Amer. Psychol.*, vol. 19, 1964, pp. 254–64.

J. Kagan, 'Individual differences in the resolution of response uncertainty', *J. Personal. soc. Psychol.*, vol. 2, 1965, pp. 154–60.

J. Kagan, 'Reflection–impulsivity and reading ability in primary grade children', *Child Devel.*, vol. 36, 1965, pp. 609–28.

C. L. Lee, J. Kagan and A. Rabson, 'The influence of a preference for analytic categorization upon concept acquisition', *Child Devel.*, vol. 34, 1963, pp. 433–42.

S. W. Lundsteen and W. B. Michael, 'Validation of three tests of cognitive style in verbalization for the third and sixth grades', *Educ. psychol. Measmt*, vol. 26, 1966, pp. 449–61.

S. Messick and F. J. Fritzky, 'Dimensions of analytic attitude in cognition and personality', *J. Personal.*, vol. 31, 1963, pp. 346–370.

E. G. Schachtel, *Metamorphosis*, Basic Books, 1959.

P. L. Wachtel, 'Style and capacity in analytic functioning', *J. Personal.*, vol. 36, 1968, pp. 202–12.

M. A. Wallach, 'Commentary: Active-analytical versus passive global cognitive functioning', in S. Messick and J. Ross (eds.), *Measurement in Personality and Cognition*, Wiley, 1962.

M. A. Wallach and N. Kogan, *Modes of Thinking in Young Children*, Holt, Rinehart & Winston, 1965.

W. C. Ward, 'Reflection-impulsivity in kindergarten children', *Child Devel.*, vol. 39, 1968, pp. 867–74.

R. Wolfe, 'The role of conceptual systems in cognitive functioning at varying levels of age and intelligence', *J. Personal.*, vol. 31, 1963, pp. 103–23.

Part Six   Studies of Interpersonal Behaviour

S. Streufert, 'Conceptual structure, communicator importance and interpersonal attitudes toward conforming and deviant group members', *J. Personal. soc. Psychol.*, vol. 4, 1961, pp. 100–103.

B. W. Tuckman, 'Group composition and group performance of structured and unstructured tasks', *J. exp. soc. Psychol.*, vol. 3, 1967, pp. 25–40.

R. N. Vidulich and I. P. Kaiman, 'The effects of information source status and dogmatism upon conformity behavior', *J. abnorm. soc. Psychol.*, vol. 63, 1961, pp. 639–42.

Part Seven   Studies of Attitude and Belief

W. D. Crano and H. M. Schroder, 'Complexity of attitude structure and processes of conflict resolution', *J. Personal. soc. Psychol.*, vol. 5, 1967, pp. 110–14.

Further Reading

W. D. Crano and J. A. Sigal, 'The effect of dogmatism upon pattern of response to attitudinally discrepant information', *J. soc. Psychol.*, vol. 75, 1968, pp. 241–7.

O. J. Harvey, J. W. Reich and R. S. Wyer, 'Effects of attitude direction, attitude intensity and structure of beliefs upon differentiation', *J. Personal. soc. Psychol.*, vol. 10, 1968, pp. 472–8.

M. F. Hunt and G. R. Miller, 'Open- and closed-mindedness, belief-discrepant communication behavior, and tolerance for cognitive inconsistency', *J. Personal. soc. Psychol.*, vol. 8, 1968, pp. 35–7.

R. E. Kleck and J. Wheaton, 'Dogmatism and responses to opinion-consistent and opinion-inconsistent information', *J. Personal. soc. Psychol.*, vol. 5, 1967, pp. 249–52.

N. Miller, 'Involvement and dogmatism as inhibitors of attitude change', *J. exp. soc. Psychol.*, vol. 1, 1965, pp. 121–32.

P. Suedfeld, 'Attitude manipulation in restricted environments: 1 Conceptual structure and response to propaganda', *J. abnorm. soc. Psychol.*, vol. 68, 1964, pp. 242–7.

B. J. White, R. D. Alter and M. Rardin, 'Authoritarianism, dogmatism and usage of conceptual categories', *J. Personal. soc. Psychol.*, vol. 2, 1965, pp. 293–5.

Part Eight Studies of Perception and Memory

J. R. Adams-Webber, 'Cognitive complexity and sociality', *Brit. J. soc. clin. Psychol.*, vol. 8, 1969, pp. 211–16.

D. Foulkes and S. H. Foulkes, 'Self-concept, dogmatism and tolerance of trait inconsistency', *J. Personal. soc. Psychol.*, vol. 2, 1965, pp. 104–11.

R. W. Gardner, L. J. Lohrenz and R. A. Schoen, 'Cognitive control of differentiation in the perception of persons and objects', *Percept. mot. Skills*, vol. 26, 1968, pp. 311–30.

O. J. Harvey and R. Ware, 'Personality differences in dissonance resolution', *J. Personal. soc. Psychol.*, vol. 7, 1967, pp. 227–30.

M. Karlins and H. Lamm, 'Information search as a function of conceptual structure in a complex problem-solving task', *J. Personal. soc. Psychol.*, vol. 5, 1967, pp. 456–9.

H. Leventhal and D. L. Singer, 'Cognitive complexity, impression formation and impression change', *J. Personal.*, vol. 32, 1964, pp. 210–26.

C. W. Mayo and W. H. Crockett, 'Cognitive complexity and primacy–recency effects in impression formation', *J. abnorm. soc. Psychol.*, vol. 68, 1964, pp. 335–8.

S. Messick and N. Kogan, 'Personality consistencies in judgment: dimensions of role constructs', *Multivar. behav. Res.*, vol. 1, 1966, pp. 165–75.

S. Shrauger, 'Cognitive differentiation and the impression-formation process', *J. Personal.*, vol. 35, 1967, pp. 487–97.

J. E. Sieber and J. T. Lanzetta, 'Conflict and conceptual structure as determinants of decision-making behavior', *J. Personal.*, vol. 32, 1964, pp. 622–41.

J. E. Sieber and J. T. Lanzetta, 'Some determinants of individual differences in predecision information-processing behavior', *J. Personal. soc. Psychol.*, vol. 4, 1966, pp. 561–71.

S. Streufert and M. J. Driver, 'Impression formation as a measure of the complexity of conceptual structure', *Educ. psychol. Meas.*, vol. 27, pp. 1025–39.

S. Streufert, P. Suedfeld and M. J. Driver, 'Conceptual structure, information search and information utilization', *J. Personal. soc. Psychol.*, vol. 2, 1965, pp. 736–40.

F. W. Uhlmann and E. Saltz, 'Retention of anxiety material as a function of cognitive differentiation', *J. Personal. soc. Psychol.*, vol. 1, 1965, pp. 55–62.

P. B. Warr and C. Knapper, *The Perception of People and Events*, Wiley, 1968. (See especially chapter 4.)

Part Nine   Studies of Psychopathology

H. A. Alker, 'Cognitive controls and the Haan–Kroeber model of ego-functioning', *J. abnorm. Psychol.*, vol. 72, 1967, pp. 434–40.

D. Bannister and F. Fransella, 'A grid test of schizophrenic thought disorder', *Brit. J. soc. clin. Psychol.*, vol. 5, 1966, pp. 95–102.

D. V. Hawks, 'The clinical usefulness of some tests of over-inclusive thinking in psychiatric patients', *Brit. J. soc. clin. Psychol.*, vol. 3, 1964, pp. 186–95.

P. Holzman, 'Repression and cognitive style', *Bull. Menninger Clinic*, vol. 26, 1962, pp. 273–82.

D. N. Lloyd, 'Overinclusive thinking and delusions in schizophrenic patients', *J. abnorm. Psychol.*, vol. 72, 1967, pp. 451–3.

B. Maher, *Clinical Psychology and Personality: The Selected Papers of George Kelly*, Wiley, 1969.

R. W. Payne and W. K. Caird, 'Reaction time, distractibility and over-inclusive thinking in psychotics', *J. abnorm. Psychol.*, vol. 72, pp. 112–21.

J. Silverman, 'The problem of attention in research and theory in schizophrenia', *Psychol. Rev.*, vol. 71, 1964, pp. 352–79.

J. Silverman, 'Scanning-control mechanisms and "cognitive filtering", in paranoid and non-paranoid schizophrenia', *J. consult. Psychol.*, vol. 28, 1964, pp. 385–93.

A. J. Yates, 'Data-processing levels and thought disorder in schizophrenia', *Austral. J. Psychol.*, vol. 18, 1966, pp. 103–17.

Acknowledgements

Permission to reproduce the Readings in this volume is acknowledged from the following sources:

Reading 1	British Psychological Society and Penelope Leach
Reading 2	American Psychological Association and Milton Rokeach
Reading 3	American Psychological Association and Riley W. Gardner
Reading 4	American Psychological Association and Alfred F. Glixman
Reading 5	Duke University Press and Henri Tajfel
Reading 6	Duke University Press and Thomas F. Pettigrew
Reading 7	The Ronald Press Co., William A. Scott and O. J. Harvey
Reading 8	John Wiley & Sons, Inc., and J. Bieri
Reading 9	Holt, Rinehart & Winston, Inc., and H. M. Schroder
Reading 10	American Psychological Association and Herman A. Witkin
Reading 11	Duke University Press and Norman L. Corah
Reading 12	International Universities Press, Inc., and Riley W. Gardner
Reading 13	International Universities Press, Inc., and Jerome Kagan
Reading 14	*Educational and Psychological Measurement* and Odin C. Vick
Reading 15	American Psychological Association and Paul Stager
Reading 16	American Psychological Association and Ivan D. Steiner
Reading 17	John Wiley & Sons, Inc., O. J. Harvey and C. W. Sherif
Reading 18	The British Psychological Society
Reading 19	American Psychological Association and David L. Wolitzky
Reading 20	American Psychological Association and O. J. Harvey
Reading 21	*Perceptual and Motor Skills*, Leonard A. Lo Sciuto and Eugene L. Hartley
Reading 22	American Psychological Association and Samuel J. Messick
Reading 23	American Psychological Association and Herman A. Witkin
Reading 24	American Psychological Association and R. W. Payne
Reading 25	British Psychological Society and D. Bannister

Author Index

Subject Index

3918